Best Newspaper Writing

Best Newspaper Writing
2007–2008 Edition

American Society of Newspaper Editors
Award Winners and Finalists

Edited by Aly Colón
and Julie Moos

The Poynter Institute for Media Studies
and

A Division of Congressional Quarterly Inc.
Washington, D.C.

The Poynter Institute for Media Studies
801 Third Street South
St. Petersburg, FL 33701
Phone: 888-769-6837
Web: www.poynter.org

CQ Press
1255 22nd Street, NW, Suite 400
Washington, DC 20037
Phone: 202-729-1900; toll-free, 1-866-4CQ-PRESS (1-866-427-7737)
Web: www.cqpress.com

Copyright © 2008 by The Poynter Institute for Media Studies and CQ Press, a division of Congressional Quarterly Inc.

All rights reserved. No part of this publication may be reproduced or transmitted in any form or by any means, electronic or mechanical, including photocopy, recording or any information storage and retrieval system, without permission in writing from the publisher.

Cover design, interior design and typesetting by Auburn Associates Inc., Baltimore

Cover photos: top—James Estrin/*The New York Times*; bottom—Renée Byer/ *The Sacramento Bee*

Photos in the Community Service Photojournalism section were provided by the photographers. Photos of winners, finalists and other newspaper staff were provided by their news organizations.

Newspaper articles and photos are the exclusive property of the authors and their newspapers and are reprinted with permission.

⊗ The paper used in this publication exceeds the requirements of the American National Standard for Information Sciences—Permanence of Paper for Printed Library Materials, ANSI Z39.48-1992.

Printed and bound in the United States of America

11 10 09 08 07   1 2 3 4 5

ISBN: 978-0-87289-470-9
ISSN: 0195-895X

*This book is dedicated to all who cover
war and its effects, journalists on the home front and
those risking their lives abroad, ensuring that the
free flow of truth remains the cornerstone of
self-government and democracy.*

Contents

Foreword: Beyond Celebrity by Karen Brown Dunlap	xiii
Preface by Aly Colón and Julie Moos	xvii
About The Poynter Institute for Media Studies	xxii
About the Editors and Contributors	xxiii
Introduction: Story As Discovery by Aly Colón	xxvii

PART 1 Breaking News — 1

Industrial Explosion, Staff, *Milwaukee Journal Sentinel*
(winner, team deadline news reporting) — 3
  1. "A Hint Of Trouble, Then Tragedy," Greg J. Borowski — 6
  2. "Gas Leak Suspected As Cause Of Blast," Rick Romell — 12
  3. "Falk Corp. Remains Well Positioned," Rick Barrett — 16
  Conversations with Rick Barrett,
    Greg J. Borowski and Rick Romell — 19
  A conversation about convergence with
    Tom Held and Paul Sevart — 29
  Writers' Workshop — 33

Preakness Stakes, *The* (Baltimore) *Sun*
(finalist, team deadline news reporting) — 34
  4. "Barbaro's Race Ends in Injury," Ken Murray — 34
  Lessons Learned — 38

Amish School Shooting, Staff, *The Philadelphia Inquirer*
(finalist, team deadline news reporting) — 40
  5. "A World Apart, Shattered," Mario F. Cattabiani,
    Jeff Gammage and Keith Herbert — 40
  Lessons Learned — 45

Addiction Admission, *The Providence* (R.I.) *Journal*
(finalist, individual deadline news reporting) — 48
  6. "Kennedy Heads to Rehab," John E. Mulligan — 48
  Lessons Learned — 52

PART 2 Column Writing — 55

Ana Menéndez, *The Miami Herald* (winner, column writing) — 57
  7. "While Shalala Lives in Luxury, Janitors Struggle" — 59
  8. "Nostalgia Is Now For Sale, and It's Costly" — 61

9. "Vigil Of the Elders"	63
10. "We Get What We Deserve If We Stay Silent"	66
11. "Don't Curse Your Fate, Ralph—Just Go Away"	68

X-RAY READING by Roy Peter Clark

"While Shalala Lives in Luxury, Janitors Struggle"	70
A conversation with Ana Menéndez	74
Writers' Workshop	79

**Edward Achorn, *The Providence* (R.I.) *Journal*
(finalist, column writing)** — **81**

12. "Curb Your Environmentalism"	81
Lessons Learned	84

Steve Lopez, *Los Angeles Times* (finalist, Batten Medal) — **86**

13. "As Lovers Of Music, 'We're Brothers'"	86
Lessons Learned	91

**Chris Rose, *The* (New Orleans) *Times-Picayune*
(finalist, Batten Medal)** — **92**

14. "A Night to Remember"	92
Lessons Learned	98

**Mary Sanchez, *The Kansas City* (Mo.) *Star*
(finalist, column writing)** — **100**

15. "Can Any Good Come from His Message Of Hate?"	100
Lessons Learned	102

PART 3 Untold Stories 105

**End Of Life, Barbara Brotman, *Chicago Tribune*
(winner, nondeadline writing)** — **107**

16. "The Final Journey Of Arthur Clifton"	109
17. "Facing the End, with Faith"	121
A conversation with Barbara Brotman	131
Sources say: A conversation with Nita Clifton	137
Writers' Workshop	139

**"An Imam in America," Andrea Elliott, *The New York Times*
(winner, ASNE, diversity writing and winner,
Pulitzer Prize, feature writing)** — **141**

18. "A Muslim Leader in Brooklyn, Reconciling 2 Worlds"	144
19. "To Lead the Faithful in a Faith Under Fire"	156
20. "Tending to Muslim Hearts and Islam's Future"	166

A conversation with Andrea Elliott	176
Sources say: A conversation with Sheik Reda Shata	187
Writers' Workshop	189

**"Land Of Opportunity," Beth Macy, *The Roanoke* (Va.) *Times*
(finalist, diversity writing)** — **191**

21. "Driven to Succeed"	191
Lessons Learned	200

**Film Criticism, Lisa Kennedy, *The Denver Post*
(finalist, diversity writing)** — **202**

22. "A Jack Of All Creative Trades Masters Film Of a Black Icon"	202
Lessons Learned	207

PART 4 Investigative Journalism — 209

**"Your Courts, Their Secrets," *The Seattle Times*
(winner, ASNE, local accountability reporting and finalist,
Pulitzer Prize, investigative reporting)** — **211**

23. "The Cases Your Judges Are Hiding from You," Ken Armstrong, Justin Mayo and Steve Miletich	214
24. "Failures by State, Caregiver Kept Secret in Child-Rape Case," Ken Armstrong, Jonathan Martin and Justin Mayo	225
25. "District Ignored Warnings, Then Silenced Girls Fondled by Teacher," Ken Armstrong and Justin Mayo	234
26. "What the State Didn't Know About Doctor, Malpractice Suit," Ken Armstrong and Justin Mayo	245
27. "Woman's Coma Leads to Secrecy, Silence," Ken Armstrong and Justin Mayo	251
A conversation with Ken Armstrong	259
Writers' Workshop	266

**Ground Rent Lawsuits, *The* (Baltimore) *Sun*
(finalist, ASNE, local accountability reporting and finalist,
Pulitzer Prize, local reporting)** — **268**

28. "On Shaky Ground," Fred Schulte and June Arney	268
Lessons Learned	281

**Child Deaths, *Belleville* (Ill.) *News-Democrat*
(finalist, local accountability reporting)** — **284**

29. "Lethal Lapses," George Pawlaczyk and Beth Hundsdorfer	284
Lessons Learned	291

PART 5 Reporting and Writing Editorials — 295

Jane Healy, *Orlando* **(Fla.)** *Sentinel* **(winner, ASNE, editorial writing and finalist, Pulitzer Prize, editorial writing)** — **297**
   30. "Losing Paradise" — 299
   31. "Failure to Launch" — 302
   32. "Dollars For Dummies" — 305
   33. "The New Villains" — 308
   34. "Eagles For Sale?" — 310

   X-RAY READING by Roy Peter Clark
     "Dollars For Dummies" — 312

   A conversation with Jane Healy — 318
   Writers' Workshop — 325

Lawrence Harmon, *The Boston Globe* **(finalist, editorial writing)** — **326**
   35. "A Child Teaches" — 326
   Lessons Learned — 329

David Barham, (Little Rock) *Arkansas Democrat-Gazette* **(finalist, editorial writing)** — **331**
   36. "Mighty White Of Ya" — 331
   Lessons Learned — 334

PART 6 Covering War At Home and Abroad — 337

The War Back Home, Anne Hull, *The Washington Post* **(winner, Batten Medal)** — **339**
   37. "When Mom Is Over There" — 342
   38. "Call to Duty" — 349
   39. "The Army Vs. Spec. Richmond" — 358

   X-RAY READING by Roy Peter Clark
     "When Mom Is Over There" — 369

   A conversation with Anne Hull — 383
   Writers' Workshop — 389

Fallen Marine, C. J. (Chris) Chivers, *The New York Times* **(winner, individual deadline news reporting)** — **391**
   40. "Medic Tends a Fallen Marine, with Skill, Prayer and Fury" — 393
   A conversation with Chris Chivers — 398
   Conversations about convergence with Chris Chivers,
     Joao Silva and Eric Owles — 403

Writers' Workshop	411
Recovering Soldier, Mark Emmons, *San Jose* (Calif.) *Mercury News*	
(finalist, nondeadline writing)	**412**
41. "Frank's Fight"	412
42. "The Signature Wound"	422
43. "The Home Front"	429
44. "The Turning Point"	436
45. "Coming Home"	442
Lessons Learned	450
Wounded Iraqi, Kevin Cullen, *The Boston Globe*	
(finalist, nondeadline writing)	**452**
46. "Rakan's War"	452
47. "As Healing Begins, a Painful Decision"	461
48. "Restless Patient, Agonizing Choice"	468
49. "At Homecoming, a Gift Elicits Wonder"	476
Lessons Learned	485
Israel-Hezbollah War, Anthony Shadid, *The Washington Post*	
(finalist, ASNE, individual deadline news reporting and	
finalist, Pulitzer Prize, international reporting)	**488**
50. " 'God Stop the Bombs!' "	488
Lessons Learned	494
Narrative Strategies by Thomas French	**497**

PART 7 Community Service Photojournalism 501

Suzanne Kreiter, *The Boston Globe*	
(winner, community service photojournalism)	**503**
51. About "The City Seen"	505
A conversation with Suzanne Kreiter	507
Renée C. Byer, *The Sacramento* (Calif.) *Bee* (finalist, ASNE,	
community service photojournalism and winner,	
Pulitzer Prize, feature photography)	**516**
52. About "A Mother's Journey"	516
Lessons Learned	523
April Saul, *The Philadelphia Inquirer*	
(finalist, community service photojournalism)	**525**
53. About "Kids, Guns and a Deadly Toll"	525
Lessons Learned	531
Suggested Readings	535

Foreword: Beyond Celebrity

BY KAREN BROWN DUNLAP

I remember a cold, rainy weekend in a disappointing hotel right after model Anna Nicole Smith died. Temperatures dropped to the low 30s, rain threatened to ice and the in-room movies were old and dull.

Television didn't help. One station stalled on a scene from "Star Wars." The best reception came from news networks where minute after minute, hour after hour, on channel after channel the focus was Smith's death.

You remember Anna Nicole Smith: *Playboy* Playmate of the Year, wife and later widow of a billionaire who was 63 years her senior, Supreme Court litigant in an inheritance battle with the billionaire's children, mother of a son who died mysteriously and of a daughter whose paternity was hotly contested, model and star of reality TV. She was a celebrity.

The Project for Excellence in Journalism (PEJ) traced coverage of the Smith story during the first 23 days after Smith was found unconscious in a South Florida hotel and subsequently died. During that period about 22 percent of cable news time was devoted to Smith. Newspapers and network news gave much less coverage after an initial burst, as did radio and online outlets. Still, the story ranked number three in coverage for the period.

"Only two other stories during that time—the debate over Iraq and the 2008 Presidential race—generated more attention than Smith's demise—and those only barely," the PEJ report said.

In a world of complex issues, we turn to the news and often find something that is not quite news. We find popular culture, particularly reports on celebrities, the cute and the weird. We find consumer information telling us how to find the best gas price, eat well, learn more about medical conditions and so on.

We also find something academics call cumulation: The same story told over and over and over with little additional information being conveyed. Blame it on cable television, but the repetition appears almost everywhere.

This coverage is light years away from what the Hutchins Commission envisioned in its description of news coverage. In 1947 that distinguished panel, led by scholar Robert Hutchins, produced a report titled "A Free and Responsible Press." The report called on the press to provide "a truthful, comprehensive and intelligent account of the day's events in a context which gives them meaning."

The panel was describing information that fuels a democracy. They were talking about public affairs reporting, news reports that help individuals in their role as citizens.

Fortunately, amidst the din of celebrity coverage and sensationalism, journalists do still report the news, and they're doing it in a number of ways.

The Big Story

In February 2007 *The Washington Post* published a special report on conditions at Walter Reed Army Medical Center. Reporters Dana Priest and Anne Hull (a member of Poynter's Board of Trustees and an award winner featured in this volume) began one story this way:

> Behind the door of Army Spec. Jeremy Duncan's room, part of the wall is torn and hangs in the air, weighted down with black mold. When the wounded combat engineer stands in his shower and looks up, he can see the bathtub on the floor above through a rotted hole. The entire building, constructed between the world wars, often smells like greasy carry-out. Signs of neglect are everywhere: mouse droppings, belly-up cockroaches, stained carpets, cheap mattresses.

In the days that followed, the reporters presented more stories of a deteriorated building, neglected soldiers, discouraged relatives and unresponsive officials. Other media carried reports on the hospital. Less than a month later, hearings were called, senior officials were fired and the president spoke out. Priest and Hull reported in a compelling manner, and change followed.

Public affairs reporting revealed to citizens of King County, Wash., that hundreds of civil suits had been improperly sealed by judges. That meant professional misconduct by doctors, dentists and lawyers, failings by agencies and companies and faults in medical products went unreported until *The Seattle Times* told the stories in its series "Your Courts, Their Secrets," which is showcased in the investigative journalism section of this book. The award-winning series represents the work of multiple reporters and a news organization that invested over a year of digging to provide this important service.

Worth a Thousand Words

A mother's face fills the picture frame; her eyes look into the distance. Fingers cover her lips; they seem oddly small. The frail fingers belong to her unseen child, in her lap, reaching up. Words are unnecessary. Finbarr O'Reilly of Reuters captured the 2005 World Press Photo of the Year award with this image that takes viewers to an emergency feeding center in Tahoua, Niger. Worlds away, in California, a mother's struggle with her son's cancer was captured by photographer Renée C. Byer, whose images are republished here in the photojournalism section.

A Familiar Voice

Howard Troxler's approach in his *St. Petersburg Times* column is to explore Florida's no-fault car insurance law by putting readers in the seat of a driver who has just been in an accident. Does the driver really need no-fault insurance? In fewer than 600 words, Troxler explains changes the state legislature is considering and what the changes might mean to drivers. His column gives a legislative update and civics lesson in a familiar, conversational voice. Jane Healy strikes a similar chord on the subject of Florida's development dilemmas in her editorial series "Florida's Shame," featured in the editorial writing section of this volume.

Sometimes it seems we're frozen in a world of celebrity and the sensational, but there's still plenty of good work being done. That's what you'll find in this book: opportunity to see excellence in daily reporting. Read it and celebrate that which is truthful, comprehensive and intelligent, presented with context. It's also compelling. Read on and see real stories of real people in daily life.

Karen Brown Dunlap is president and managing director of The Poynter Institute as well as a trustee at Poynter and a member of the board of directors of the Times Publishing Company. She is co-author of "The Effective Editor" with Foster Davis and of "The Editorial Eye" with Jane Harrigan.

Links to Material Mentioned Here

- *The Washington Post*'s Walter Reed reporting:
  http://www.washingtonpost.com/wp-srv/nation/walter-reed/index.html
- Finbarr O'Reilly's 2005 World Press Photo of the Year:
  http://www.worldpressphoto.org/index.php?option=com_photogallery&task=view&id=903&Itemid=115&bandwidth=high
- Howard Troxler's *St. Petersburg Times* column, "Are We Sure We Don't Need No-fault?":
  http://www.sptimes.com/2007/05/17/State/Are_we_sure_we_don_t_.shtml
  (Note: The *St. Petersburg Times* is owned by The Poynter Institute.)

Preface

This annual celebration of the best American newspaper writing and photojournalism began as an idea nearly 32 years ago. At the time, Eugene Patterson was president of the American Society of Newspaper Editors (ASNE) and wanted to single out distinguished writing.

Patterson sought to highlight the "lilt and the loveliness" of the language, he told Keith Woods for an essay in "Best Newspaper Writing 2003." Such writing, he said, contained " . . . clarity, grace, brevity. But clarity above all."

To honor exemplary work, ASNE created and still sponsors an annual contest that recognizes and rewards the finest writing in daily newspapers and wire services and the most outstanding community service photojournalism.

To produce "Best Newspaper Writing" ASNE partners with The Poynter Institute, a school for journalists in St. Petersburg, Fla. The book showcases and explores the work of winners and finalists in the annual competition.

This 2007–2008 edition of "Best Newspaper Writing" features the work of winners and finalists in the following categories: the Jesse Laventhol Prizes for Deadline News Reporting by a team and by an individual; the Freedom Forum/ASNE Award for Distinguished Writing on Diversity; Distinguished Writing Awards for nondeadline writing, commentary and column writing, editorial writing and local accountability reporting; and the Community Service Photojournalism Award.

It also includes a new award: the Batten Medal. This new category "honors the memory of revered reporter, editor and newspaper executive James K. Batten. The medal is intended to celebrate the journalistic values Batten stood for: compassion, courage, humanity and a deep concern for the underdog."

In this edition we have created a special war coverage section. It features interviews with journalists who were recognized by ASNE for their work and offers insights into what it takes to cover war abroad and its impact on the home front.

More and more newspapers are working on multiple news platforms, and so we continue to feature "conversations about convergence." In these conversations we ask some of our winners and some of their colleagues about the steps they took to translate their work to the online medium.

We also added a new feature: "Sources Say." We wanted to provide a voice to those who become part of the stories we write. As journalists, we know what we want to achieve. With "Sources Say," we see how subjects experience the process and are affected by its outcome.

How to Use This Book

"Best Newspaper Writing 2007–2008" offers examples of excellent writing and photojournalism. In addition to the exemplary newspaper work produced by the winners and finalists, readers can turn to:

- **Interviews:** conversations with the winning writers and photojournalist about their craft, focusing on news judgment, reporting strategies, developing sources, collaboration, working with editors, writing with context and more
- **Lessons Learned:** essays by the finalists about the trials and tribulations of producing their honored work
- **Writers' Workshop:** discussion questions and assignments that provide opportunities to analyze and emulate winning work
- **X-Ray Readings:** annotated versions of three winning selections in which Roy Peter Clark deconstructs each writer's language and rhetoric and offers a toolbox of techniques for reporting and writing
- **Conversations about Convergence:** interviews with ASNE winners and Web site staff about how their work is presented online
- **War Coverage:** a special section that focuses on the work involved in covering war at home and abroad
- **Sources Say:** a new feature that allows sources to talk about the experience of being part of a story. We hope their feedback offers journalists another frame from which to see how their work affects others.
- **Narrative Strategies:** Pulitzer Prize–winning journalist Thomas French examines the narrative techniques used by some of the reporters featured in "Best Newspaper Writing." He explains how the narrative style captures color and action and advances each story, and he highlights the portions of the writing that show narrative tools at work.

Readers will see that the book has been broken into seven parts that individually represent different types of newspaper writing and photojournalism. The book was organized this way to better follow the structure of classroom teaching and the professional writer's desire to focus on the topics of greatest interest. The seven parts are: Breaking News, Column Writing, Untold Stories, Investigative Journalism, Reporting and Writing Editorials, Covering War At Home and Abroad and Community Service Photojournalism. This structure makes it easier to learn more about a particular form and to compare different forms of journalism.

The foreword, written by Karen Brown Dunlap, president of The Poynter Institute, and the introduction, written by Aly Colón, co-editor of

"Best Newspaper Writing 2007–2008," set the stage for understanding how the ASNE winners and finalists fit into the journalism we practice.

About the Interviews and Other Material

Poynter faculty and fellows interviewed ASNE winners by e-mail and in some cases by phone. The interviews have been edited for clarity, flow and brevity. Faculty, fellows and editors wrote winner and finalist biographies from information provided by the journalists and their news organizations.

News organizations provided Poynter with electronic versions of the winners' and finalists' stories for publication in this book. They may differ slightly from the stories that originally appeared in print. "Best Newspaper Writing" editors made minor changes for spelling and grammar. But wherever possible, the newspapers' original styles remain. Stories were not uniformly edited to conform to AP style or Poynter style, even though other parts of this volume were.

Photos have been reprinted as they originally appeared, with captions edited for length, spelling and grammar.

Reporting and writing can be messy. Once writers know the rules, they sometimes choose to break them for effect. In this book, some writers use the passive voice, and some sentences begin with a conjunction. Some writers use language that may seem offensive. Based on their experience and comfort, writers and editors may make choices that would not be allowed elsewhere. We have preserved those choices so readers can learn the rules and learn from those who know when and how to break them.

About the ASNE Contest

The goal of this book is to help students of the craft become better journalists. We have selected award-winning work honored by ASNE that we believe will help teach craft and values. Unfortunately, we could not reprint all the work by these 2007 ASNE contest winners and finalists:

Batten Medal
- Anne Hull, *The Washington Post* (winner)
- Steve Lopez, *Los Angeles Times* (finalist)
- Chris Rose, *The* (New Orleans) *Times-Picayune* (finalist)

Distinguished Writing Award for Commentary/Column Writing
- Ana Menéndez, *The Miami Herald* (winner)
- Edward Achorn, *The Providence* (R.I.) *Journal* (finalist)
- Mary Sanchez, *The Kansas City* (Mo.) *Star* (finalist)

Community Service Photojournalism Award
- Suzanne Kreiter, *The Boston Globe* (winner)
- Renée C. Byer, *The Sacramento* (Calif.) *Bee* (finalist)

- April Saul, *The Philadelphia Inquirer* (finalist)

Jesse Laventhol Prize for Deadline News Reporting by an Individual
- C. J. (Chris) Chivers, *The New York Times* (winner)
- John E. Mulligan, *The Providence* (R.I.) *Journal* (finalist)
- Anthony Shadid, *The Washington Post* (finalist)

Jesse Laventhol Prize for Deadline News Reporting by a Team
- Staff, *Milwaukee Journal Sentinel* (winner)
- Ken Murray, Doug Donovan, Bradley Olson and Rick Maese, *The* (Baltimore) *Sun* (finalist)
- Staff, *The Philadelphia Inquirer* (finalist)

Freedom Forum/ASNE Award for Outstanding Writing on Diversity
- Andrea Elliott, *The New York Times* (winner)
- Lisa Kennedy, *The Denver Post* (finalist)
- Beth Macy, *The Roanoke* (Va.) *Times* (finalist)

Distinguished Writing Award for Editorial Writing
- Jane Healy, *Orlando* (Fla.) *Sentinel* (winner)
- David Barham, (Little Rock) *Arkansas Democrat-Gazette* (finalist)
- Lawrence Harmon, *The Boston Globe* (finalist)

Distinguished Writing Award for Local Accountability Reporting
- Ken Armstrong, Justin Mayo and Steve Miletich, *The Seattle Times* (winner)
- June Arney and Fred Schulte, *The* (Baltimore) *Sun* (finalist)
- William Glaberson, *The New York Times* (finalist)
- George Pawlaczyk and Beth Hundsdorfer, *Belleville* (Ill.) *News-Democrat* (finalist)

Distinguished Writing Award for Nondeadline Writing
- Barbara Brotman, *Chicago Tribune* (winner)
- Kevin Cullen, *The Boston Globe* (finalist)
- Mark Emmons, *San Jose* (Calif.) *Mercury News* (finalist)

Acknowledgments

We want to thank the many people who helped make this book possible, beginning with the journalists whose work is featured in these pages. Without them, we would know less about reporting and writing.

Many others also helped. We want to thank ASNE, its executive director, Scott Bosley, and his associate Cristal Williams for their work on the contest. We also thank the judges for the 2007 ASNE Awards:

Andrew N. Alexander, Cox Newspapers
Gilbert Bailon, *Al Dia*
Peter K. Bhatia, *The Oregonian*

Susan Bischoff, Houston, Texas
David Boardman, *The Seattle Times*
Jeffrey C. Bruce, Beavercreek, Ohio
James N. Crutchfield, Akron, Ohio
Sonya Doctorian, (Denver, Colo.) *Rocky Mountain News*
Gregory Favre, The Poynter Institute
Carolina Garcia, *Monterey* (Calif.) *County Herald*
Steve Gonzales, *Houston Chronicle*
Karla Garrett Harshaw, Cox Ohio Newspapers
Kenny Irby, The Poynter Institute
Pamela J. Johnson, Missouri School of Journalism
W. Martin Kaiser, *Milwaukee Journal Sentinel*
Bill Keller, *The New York Times*
David A. Laventhol, New York, N.Y.
Carolyn Lee, New York, N.Y.
Rick Rodriguez, *The Sacramento* (Calif.) *Bee*
Sharon Rosenhause, *South Florida Sun-Sentinel*
Mark E. Russell, *Orlando* (Fla.) *Sentinel*
Julia Schmalz, *USA Today*
Melanie A. Sill, *The* (Raleigh, N.C.) *News & Observer*
Mark A. Silverman, *The* (Nashville) *Tennessean*
Michael E. Waller, Hilton Head Island, S.C.
David A. Zeeck, *The* (Tacoma, Wash.) *News Tribune*

We are grateful to the Poynter faculty and fellows who contributed to this volume: Roy Peter Clark, Karen Brown Dunlap, Rick Edmonds, Thomas French, Jill Geisler, Thomas Huang, Kenny Irby, Scott Libin, Bill Mitchell, Christopher Scanlan, Butch Ward and Keith Woods, and to Poynter's staff and administration, especially Howard Finberg, Candace Clarke and David Shedden. Vicki Hyatt coordinated with newsrooms across the country and journalists around the world to collect materials. Katharine Fair, a member of the Poynter family, offered tremendous help on short notice. The following people at CQ Press made this a better book with their creativity, attention to detail and enthusiastic support: Brenda Carter, Charisse Kiino, Dwain Smith, Anna Socrates, Erin Snow, Steve Pazdan, Paul Pressau and Margot Ziperman. Special thanks to Gwenda Larsen, whose tireless patience, endless professionalism and eye for both forest and trees are an inspiration.

—Aly Colón and Julie Moos

About The Poynter Institute for Media Studies

The Poynter Institute is a school dedicated to teaching and inspiring journalists and media leaders. Through its seminars, publications and Web site (www.poynter.org), the Institute promotes excellence and integrity in the craft of journalism and in the practical leadership of successful news businesses. Poynter stands for a journalism that informs citizens, enlightens public discourse and strengthens ties between journalism and democracy.

Each year at its campus in St. Petersburg, Fla., the school offers approximately 40 seminars for professionals, educators and students, including programs for high school students and recent college graduates. Poynter also teaches via the online training portal, News University (www.newsu.org). NewsU, as it is also called, offers interactive e-learning, as well as self-directed and faculty-led online seminars. Poynter faculty and staff also work with journalists at various locations across the nation and around the world.

The Poynter Institute was founded in 1975 by Nelson Poynter, chairman of the *St. Petersburg Times* and its Washington affiliate, Congressional Quarterly. Poynter, who died in 1978, willed the controlling stock in his companies to the school. As a financially independent, nonprofit organization, The Poynter Institute is beholden to no interest except its own mission: to help journalists seek and achieve excellence.

About the Editors and Contributors

About the Editors

In more than a decade with The Poynter Institute, **ALY COLÓN** taught in many areas and over the years led Poynter's reporting, writing and editing program, diversity program and ethics program. As a member of the faculty, he also consulted with news organizations on diversity, ethics, writing and leadership.

Previously, Colón worked at *The Seattle Times* as assistant metro editor, diversity reporter and coach. Prior to that he worked at *The Herald* in Everett, Wash., as an executive editor responsible for business and features, and at *The Oakland Press* in Pontiac, Mich.

Colón is currently the diversity program manager at Safeco in Seattle, Wash.

JULIE MOOS is editor of Poynter Publications and has been the editor of "Best Newspaper Writing" since 2004. She most recently edited "Eyetracking the News," a book about Poynter's research on how people read news in print and online.

Previously, Moos was managing editor for Poynter Online, responsible for the day-to-day operation of the institute's Web site, rated journalists' number one source of industry information. Prior to that, she was managing editor of WRAL.com, the Web site for WRAL-TV in Raleigh, N.C., a locally owned CBS affiliate. Moos also is the founder and editor of DotMoms, a weblog for mothers.

About the Contributors

ROY PETER CLARK is vice president and senior scholar at The Poynter Institute, where he has taught writing since 1979. He founded the Writing Center at Poynter, lending support to the writing coach movement. He is a distinguished service member of ASNE and has recently been inducted by the American Association of Sunday and Feature Editors into its Features Hall of Fame. He is the author of "Writing Tools: 50 Essential Strategies For Every Writer" and is at work on a new book, "The Glamour Of Grammar."

RICK EDMONDS is a researcher and writer at The Poynter Institute. His work centers on the future of the newspaper business and measurement of newsroom capacity. Earlier in his career he was editor and publisher of several magazines for the *St. Petersburg Times* organization and managing editor of the paper's Tampa edition. Before that he worked as a reporter and editor at *The Philadelphia Inquirer* and was a finalist for the Pulitzer Prize for national reporting in 1982.

THOMAS FRENCH, The Poynter Institute's first writing fellow, began work as a *St. Petersburg Times* reporter soon after his graduation from Indiana University. His first newspaper series, "A Cry in the Night," is an account of a murder investigation and trial that French turned into the book "Unanswered Cries." A year spent reporting in a public high school produced the series and book "South Of Heaven." His series "Angels & Demons," about the murder of three women visiting Florida, earned him a Pulitzer Prize for feature writing.

JILL GEISLER heads the leadership and management group at The Poynter Institute. She was the country's first female news director of a major market affiliate, WITI-TV in Milwaukee, where she spent 25 years coaching a team of award-winning, enterprising journalists. She is the editor of Poynter Online's "Leading Lines" column and the author of many articles on journalism and leadership, as well as the book, "News Leadership: At the Head Of the Class."

THOMAS HUANG, an ethics fellow at The Poynter Institute, is features editor of *The Dallas Morning News,* where he has worked since 1993. As a writer, Huang was a two-time finalist for the Livingston Award for Young Journalists and a two-time finalist for the Missouri Lifestyle Journalism Award for feature writing. Before moving to Dallas, Huang worked for five years as a metropolitan reporter for *The Virginian-Pilot* in Norfolk, Va. He contributes to a column on diversity issues for Poynter Online (www.poynter.org/difference).

KENNY IRBY, visual journalism group leader and diversity director at The Poynter Institute, is the founder of Poynter's photojournalism program. Before joining Poynter, Irby worked as a photographer and deputy director of photography at *Newsday* and contributed as a photo editor to three Pulitzer Prize–winning projects there. Irby is the recipient of numerous awards from the National Press Photographers Association, including the 1999 Joseph Costa Award for outstanding initiative, leadership and service in photojournalism and the 2002 President's Award.

SCOTT LIBIN is managing editor of Poynter Online and a faculty member at The Poynter Institute. He specializes in leadership and ethical decision-making. Libin has been a news director at KSTP-TV, the ABC affiliate in Minneapolis-St. Paul, and vice president of news at WGHP-TV in Greensboro/High Point/Winston-Salem, N.C., where he also worked as a reporter, weekend anchor, managing editor and news director.

BILL MITCHELL is editor of Poynter Online (www.poynter.org). Before joining Poynter in 1999, he was editor of Universal New Media (1995–1999) and director of electronic publishing at the *San Jose* (Calif.) *Mercury News* (1992–1995). Mitchell also has worked as a reporter, editor, Washington correspondent and European correspondent for the *Detroit Free Press* and as Detroit bureau chief for *Time* magazine. He served as a juror for the Pulitzer Prizes in 2002 and 2003.

CHRISTOPHER SCANLAN is senior faculty in the reporting, writing and editing group at The Poynter Institute, director of the Poynter-sponsored National Writers Workshops and journalism adviser to NewsU (www.newsu.org), Poynter's e-learning portal. Scanlan joined the Poynter faculty in 1994 from the Knight Ridder Newspapers' Washington bureau, where he was a national correspondent. From 1994 to 2000, he edited the "Best Newspaper Writing" series. Scanlan is the author of "Reporting and Writing: Basics For the 21st Century" and co-editor of "America's Best Newspaper Writing: A Collection Of ASNE Prizewinners."

BUTCH WARD is Distinguished Fellow at The Poynter Institute. He joined the staff of *The Philadelphia Inquirer* after working at *The News American* in Baltimore. At the *Inquirer* he was New Jersey editor, assistant managing editor for the Sunday paper, assistant managing editor in features, metropolitan editor and managing editor. He left the *Inquirer* in 2001 and spent three years as vice president for corporate and public affairs at Independence Blue Cross.

KEITH WOODS is dean of faculty at The Poynter Institute. In 16 years at *The Times-Picayune* in New Orleans, he worked as a sportswriter, news reporter, city editor, editorial writer and columnist. He joined Poynter in 1995 and led the institute's teaching on diversity and coverage of race relations as part of the ethics faculty; he then served as reporting, writing and editing group leader. Woods is a previous editor of the "Best Newspaper Writing" series.

Introduction: Story As Discovery

BY ALY COLÓN

Writing brings new worlds to life. It acts like a special magnet, attracting sights, sounds and smells and attaching them to words, descriptions and stories.

Sometimes we think we know what the story is. Sometimes we don't. Sometimes we're part of the story. Sometimes we're not.

The act of writing helps us capture the obvious and the obscure. It treads familiar ground in hopes of arriving at an unexpected place. When practiced with passion, it becomes an act of discovery.

Henri Nouwen, an internationally known priest, pastor and professor who authored more than 40 books, wrote in "Reflections on Theological Education":

> Most students think that writing means writing down ideas, insights, visions. They feel that they must first have something to say before they can put it down on paper. For them writing is little more than recording a pre-existent thought. But with this approach true writing is impossible. Writing is a process in which we discover what lives in us. The writing itself reveals what is alive ... The deepest satisfaction of writing is precisely that it opens up new spaces within us of which we were not aware before we started to write. To write is to embark on a journey whose final destination we do not know.

Courageous journalists recognize the truth in Nouwen's words. They start with the known. But if they value story over style, they open themselves to the unknown. They allow the story to chart its own journey. They let the story lead. They follow.

This happens whether or not you're part of the story.

When I wanted to know what it felt like to be in the United States and unable to communicate in English, I ended up writing a story for *The Seattle Times* called "Speechless in Seattle." The story chronicled the experiences I had as I moved about the city and spoke only in Spanish. Each of my encounters with other people shed new light for me on the experience of being different.

What happened between the conception of this story and its publication amounted to a personal journey that revealed universal themes. It addressed what it was like to feel alienated and affirmed, to be ignored and invited, to feel human and inhuman.

On another occasion, I followed wheelchair athletes around the city. I watched. I listened. I recorded what they did. My eyes became the eyes for the readers, taking them with the wheelchair athletes as they hurtled down hills, slid around curb cuts and maneuvered through hotels.

Sometimes you get into the story. Sometimes you get out of the way. This year's ASNE winners and finalists did both.

Some of those who personally got into the story included Anne Hull, who won the Batten Medal, Jane Healy, who won the editorial-writing award, and Ana Menéndez, who won the column-writing award.

In "When Mom Is Over There," Hull uses a first-person account of her own journey of discovery about the Iraq War and its impact on the home front. She spent time helping her brother and his children while her sister-in-law served in Iraq. Her eye for detail, her ear for dialogue and her ability to sort out her own feelings draw you into a story that makes you appreciate how the word "extra" can be connected to the word "ordinary."

Healy's editorials on how development and growth threaten Florida's environment resemble the formation of a literary hurricane. Her "Florida's Shame" series builds quickly, picks up speed and smashes through any growth arguments that developers can't nail down. She uses crisp, blunt and powerful language to uproot and blow away the confusing, complicated landscape. Her strong, personal voice speaks directly to the reader.

In her columns, Menéndez uses her passionate and unyielding voice to push the powerful and protect the powerless. In one column, Menéndez vividly conveys the lifestyle difference between a former White House cabinet member and current university president, and a university janitor. Her connection to the theme is personal and powerful.

Some of the other award-winning journalists in this edition focus all their attention on those they're covering. C.J. Chivers, who won the individual deadline award, Andrea Elliot, who won the diversity award, and Barbara Brotman, who won the nondeadline award, are among them.

Chivers transports you to the battlefield in Iraq. He captures the sights, sounds and smells of battle, brothers-in-arms and blood. The reader follows a medic as he cares for a fallen Marine. Chivers offers such vivid descriptions and authentic dialogue that readers feel as if they were looking right over the medic's shoulders.

Elliot takes us into the world of a Muslim imam in New York. She examines the challenges that arise when cultures coexist and collide.

Being different from the dominant culture brings its own pressures. Being different in a country that keeps a spotlight on your activities raises those pressures to another level. Elliot introduces the reader to worlds within worlds and explores what it means to live there.

Brotman brings the reader face to face with the ultimate journey. She follows Arthur Clifton as he prepares for the end of his life. Brotman chronicles each step, each experience, as Clifton, his wife and those who help them try to maneuver their way through the known and the unknown. It makes life, and death, personal.

Readers of this collection will find writing that communicates in a compelling way. The winners and the finalists featured in this volume shed light on, and share lessons about, writing that matters.

Ultimately, it matters less whether the writer is in the story or not. What matters most is whether the reader is.

Aly Colón is co-editor of this edition of "Best Newspaper Writing."

Best Newspaper Writing

Part 1

Breaking News

WINNER

Staff, *Milwaukee Journal Sentinel*
Team Deadline News Reporting

The gas explosion at the Falk Corp. foundry shortly after 8 a.m. the morning of December 6, 2006, literally shook much of Milwaukee.

Reporter and rewrite specialist Greg J. Borowski was sitting at his breakfast table reading the paper when his house, five miles away, began to shake. It sounded as if something had slammed into its side. Thousands of others getting ready for work, or driving there, heard the blast or felt the impact.

The industrial accident killed three and injured 46. But by its nature the blast was also an event many, many more directly experienced.

What's more, it would resonate broadly in Milwaukee, a city with deep working-class roots that retains the sort of heavy manufacturing that has disappeared in many other places in America.

Borowski put it this way later that day in the lead story he wrote for the next day's edition of the *Milwaukee Journal Sentinel*:

> Falk is classic blue-collar Milwaukee. It is a place where life still runs on eight-hour shifts, where co-workers become friends who bowl together, play on the company softball team, trade deer-hunting tales over a post-work beer.

The *Journal Sentinel* had another way to "reflect the communal sense of tragedy the city was experiencing," as editor Thomas Koetting put it.

The first online report was posted 12 minutes after the blast. Throughout the day readers posted accounts and pictures of their experiences. They also were supplying facts and anecdotes that would supplement the information reporters were gathering for the coverage package in the next day's paper.

Editors made a key decision to split the writing. One reporter fed the version on the Web site throughout the day. Borowski and associates focused exclusively on the package of print stories.

The team's execution served as a model for deadline coverage in several respects:

- Two dozen reporters were out gathering relevant facts and anecdotes, allowing Borowski to draw on a rich bank of material for his story.
- The coverage was split in logical fashion: Borowski's narrative lead story, Rick Romell's exploration of the accident's causes and Rick Barrett's takeout on Falk and the metal-casting industry. (There were additional stories and many graphics and photos not considered in the contest judging, or included here.)
- The writing is clean and crisp in all the stories. They avoid clichés of the genre, gushing adjectives like "tragic" and "devastating." The result is writing that is disciplined, direct and vivid.

Borowski is a city hall reporter on most days. He is also one of the newspaper's top rewrite specialists, tapped for that duty when a big story breaks. He has a detailed theory of how to work effectively under deadline pressure. It includes writing a few paragraphs, pausing to self-edit and polish, then doing the same again. That way many blocks of the story are in place near the end of the process.

Borowski and Romell both said that heavy editing, and second drafts, are not part of the equation in this type of deadline story. It's a trapeze act without a net. You need to get it pretty much right the first time through.

The secondary stories by Romell and Barrett illustrate how beat reporting experience, and skill in working sources, can turn up rich insights in a hurry. By the end of the day, for instance, Barrett could report on a likely scenario for Falk's recovery, the unusually deep backlog of orders and how competitors would step up to help.

With this story, the team had the advantage of most of a full working day to develop their stories. They used the time effectively to bring home to *Journal Sentinel* readers a comprehensive and well-written sense of what had happened.

About the *Milwaukee Journal Sentinel* Team

Greg J. Borowski has been a city hall and political reporter for the paper since 1998. He worked previously at the *Lansing State Journal* and the Marion (Ind.) *Chronicle-Tribune*. He is also the author of two books, "The Christmas Heart," a collection of short stories, and "First and Long," a nonfiction narrative about the start-up of a high school football team. Borowski is a native of Milwaukee and a 1989 graduate of Marquette University, where he is a part-time instructor in the journalism program.

Rick Romell is a 30-year veteran of the paper and has spent the last decade as a business reporter. He is a graduate of the University of Wisconsin-Milwaukee and earned a master's degree in journalism at Northwestern University. He was part of the team that was a finalist for the Pulitzer Prize in 2003 for a series on chronic wasting disease. He and *Journal Sentinel* colleagues were also finalists for the ASNE team deadline award last year.

Rick Barrett, a business reporter, has worked for the *Journal Sentinel* since 2000. He worked previously at daily newspapers in Wisconsin, Florida, Michigan, Texas and Arkansas. He has a bachelor's degree in journalism from Central Michigan University.

Many other *Journal Sentinel* reporters contributed to the Falk stories.

—Rick Edmonds, Media Business Analyst, The Poynter Institute

The Jesse Laventhol Prize for Deadline News Reporting by a Team is funded by a gift from David Laventhol, a former Times Mirror *executive, in honor of his father.*

1. A Hint Of Trouble, Then Tragedy

DEC. 7, 2006

By Greg J. Borowski

As the first shift at Falk Corp. cranked along Wednesday morning, the troubling smell of gas drifted through an annex just off the main production building.

Workers called supervisors and began heading for the doors.

Moments later, at 8:07 a.m., a massive and deadly explosion ripped through the Menomonee Valley factory. It killed three, injured 46 and left a swath of one of the city's oldest companies a charred, smoking skeleton.

The three killed were identified as Curtis J. Lane, 38, Oconomowoc; Thomas M. Letendre, 49, Milwaukee; and Daniel T. Kuster, 35, Mayville.

Police Chief Nannette Hegerty said that had employees not discovered the propane leak and begun evacuating, "the death toll would have been much higher."

The death of Kuster, said his uncle, Tim Izydor, "kills my heart."

David Mays, a journeyman machinist, was working inside the annex when the gas smell first became apparent.

"I left," said Mays, 61, who has worked for Falk for 39 years. "But some of them stayed."

The explosion hurled Mays to the ground, reminding him of incoming mortar rounds from his service in Vietnam. It rattled windows and shook houses as far away as Franklin and New Berlin, and filled the gray morning sky near downtown with a chilling spiral of smoke.

The blast shattered the Falk family of workers, and ultimately tested a legion of police, firefighters, emergency personnel and hospital workers.

"We've all been there for over 20 years," said Mays, who later went to the hospital on his own. "We are all like a family."

Journeyman machinist David Sternig, 59, who has worked at Falk for 42 years, was in the southwestern part of the plant when the blast hit. Two of his brothers also work at Falk.

"It was like a bomb went off or a plane crashed," he said.

The light bulbs popped. The room went dark. The whir of machines came to a dead stop.

The room was eerily silent, and the air was filled with gray soot, Sternig said. Huge sections of concrete block were blown out. The annex was leveled.

Milwaukee firefighters remove one of the victims at the scene of an explosion and fire Wednesday at Falk Corp. in Milwaukee. (Photograph courtesy of Jeffrey Phelps/*Milwaukee Journal Sentinel*)

Dean Sternig, 44, was on his way to see his brother when the blast knocked him from his feet like a bowling pin. Looking up from the shaking ground, he saw huge flames fill the sky.

"I didn't know if it was going to start to rain down on me or not, but I wasn't about to lie there and find out," he said.

He scrambled to his feet and ran into a nearby garage, diving on the ground into a pile of glass shards, cutting his arm in three places.

He got up again and worked his way back to his work station. The mood there was calm. No screaming or yelling.

Injured workers were transported in pairs. He was treated at a hospital and released. Neither of his two brothers was seriously injured.

"I feel real lucky," he said.

'There Were People in There'

Falk is classic blue-collar Milwaukee. It is a place where life still runs on eight-hour shifts, where co-workers become friends who bowl together, play on the company softball team, trade deer hunting tales over a post-work beer.

To many people, though, the company passes without notice. Few likely could name its product: giant gears.

From the nearby highway and the viaducts that crisscross the Menomonee Valley, the complex can fade into the mix of brick and smokestacks in the valley.

On Wednesday, Katie Porter was one of those passers-by, following her normal route from Wauwatosa down Canal St. to her job in the Historic Third Ward. Suddenly, her Saturn Ion was shoved off the side of the road.

"There was a truck or a van next to me, and I thought it had slammed into me," Porter said.

But the truck had come to a stop behind her.

"I saw the building explode outward and then just fall in," she said. "The walls were pushed outward, and the whole thing collapsed."

On S. 27th St., car alarms went off. In the nearby Merrill Park neighborhood, windows were broken and garage door bolts were shaken loose. Some thought it was an earthquake—others a sonic boom or an airplane crashing.

Jill Huffer was driving north across the 27th Street Viaduct, taking her two kids—Calvin, 9, and Casey, 5—to Hawley Environmental School. It was not their normal route, but Calvin had an early morning appointment at the orthodontist.

"I saw debris flying way into the sky, and then I saw a flash and then a fire blast down on the ground," she said.

She kept driving, and found herself crying as she drove. Calvin asked what was wrong.

"I just kept thinking," Huffer said, "there were people in there."

In the valley below, forklift driver Otha Beamon, 56, was driving a Jeep about 20 feet outside the building.

"All of a sudden, 'Boom!' That was it," Beamon said.

He got out of the Jeep and was knocked down by falling debris. He got up, was knocked down again. Then, he said, "some guy came out of nowhere" and helped him get to safety.

In a nearby building, 35-year Falk employee Bill Gebhard was working when the blast tossed him into the air.

"Glass was shattering everywhere," he said.

Once he got his bearings, he realized he was looking outside; the building's walls had disappeared.

Sooty Faces, Shock

At the Engine 28 fire station about six blocks north of Falk, the entire building shook and the garage door sucked in, then blew outward—so much that the firefighters could see daylight. Some thought a car struck the station.

It had happened before.

They ran outside. No car. But James Youngblood, a driver for the department, saw smoke rising to the south. An engine and a paramedic

The Falk factory burns shortly after the explosion Wednesday. This picture was taken at 8:09 a.m. from the 27th Street Viaduct by a vendor attending a show at the Mitchell Park Domes. (Photograph by Kris Wiktor)

unit were sent toward the smoke. South of the freeway they could tell the smoke was coming from a large building in the Falk complex.

They arrived about three minutes, 40 seconds after the blast to a scene of devastation about the size of two football fields. Lt. Frank Alioto, a firefighter for 23 years, called in a second alarm and requested extra paramedics and the department's heavy urban rescue team. Ultimately, it was a five-alarm emergency.

"There were people with blackened, sooty faces. Some bloody. They looked in shock. They were kind of wandering aimlessly," Alioto said.

Some workers were carrying out their Falk co-workers.

A triage site was set up to sort through the severity of injuries. Then the effort turned to fighting the fire.

Nearby businesses were pressed into service.

The Palermo's Pizza plant became a gathering place, with Falk workers signing in when they arrived so they could be accounted for.

While they waited for more direction, Palermo's workers served them pizza and coffee.

"It was pretty quiet," said Liz Bentzler, a quality auditor at the Palermo's plant. "Very surreal."

Falk workers were eventually loaded onto a dozen Milwaukee County Transit System buses and taken to nearby Miller Park. As they arrived at the stadium, some still looked shaken, and they walked in with the assistance of co-workers.

Later, worried families streamed into the stadium looking for loved ones, their faces stricken.

Dena Cahala beamed when she saw her husband, Glen, safe and talking on a cell phone. But her elation was tempered by her husband's fears for co-workers.

"I can't tell you how sad this is," said Glen Cahala, who was in the administrative building. "I just hope everyone is OK. I can't think about what this means for some families."

No Foul Play Suspected

The building is part of a complex that covers 61 acres, with 1.5 million square feet of buildings. In all, there were about 600 people working at the complex at the time of the explosion. The building that exploded is actually two structures that are connected, said Evan Zeppos, who was handling public relations for Falk late Wednesday. One, called the annex, was used for storage of component parts used in the manufacturing process. The other, known as the 2-2 building, was used largely as a maintenance facility.

For hours, it was unclear how many people had been in the building when the explosion occurred.

And whether everyone had gotten out.

Law enforcement officials ultimately interviewed some 500 workers and witnesses, trying to sort out the details of what had happened. Hegerty would later say the investigation would take at least a week, but that it "appeared to be a tragic, accidental situation."

No foul play. No crime.

Just tragedy.

Mayor Tom Barrett, who coincidentally had toured the plant the day before, called the blast a "serious tragedy for Falk, for (parent company) Rexnord, for the city of Milwaukee. And I would ask the citizens of Milwaukee to remember the families in their prayers."

Speaking at a news conference at Miller Park, he said investigators did not know how much time had elapsed between the time the propane leak was discovered and the blast.

Barrett said that the city conducted an inspection of the plant on Sept. 14 and found some safety violations.

"They were few and minor, and they were corrected," the mayor said.

Several employees said the plant was very safety conscious. There always seemed to be safety training and drills, they said.

Machinist Robert Long, 46, predicted a quick recovery for Falk, where he has worked for 15 years.

"It will be up and running before you think," Long said.

In briefings through the day, officials laid out what it took to manage the scene. About 125 Milwaukee firefighters were sent to the scene in 34 different vehicles. In addition, 52 Milwaukee police officers arrived, plus 25 detectives. The response also included a host of private ambulances, state and federal officials, and the American Red Cross.

City crews checked nearby bridges for structural damage but did not find any problems. Building inspectors also began visiting homes in nearby neighborhoods, where some windows had been shattered.

By 5 p.m., the search was complete. No one else was missing, although Falk set up a hotline ... for its workers to call to get more information.

Two hours later, Falk employees gathered at Wisconsin State Fair Park. In a brief, emotional meeting, David Doerr, Falk Corp.'s president, assured workers they would be paid while the company regroups.

"They just told us to hang in there," said Michael Kleczka, a third-shift worker.

A day earlier, the meeting would have been a family reunion.

Wednesday night, it was a family in mourning.

Staff of the Milwaukee Journal Sentinel *reporting from Miller Park, surrounding neighborhoods, area hospitals, Oconomowoc and the paper's main office contributed to ... coverage of the Falk Corp. explosion. They include Rick Barrett, Gina Barton, Thomas Content, Joel Dresang, Darryl Enriquez, Tom Held, Annysa Johnson, Mark Johnson, Mike Johnson, Tom Kertscher, Meg Kissinger, Sheila B. Lalwani, Avrum D. Lank, Jacqueline Loohauis, James B. Nelson, Derrick Nunnally, Georgia Pabst, Amy Rinard, Marie Rohde, Susanne Rust, Raquel Rutledge, Steve Schultze, Linda Spice, Felicia Thomas-Lynn, Dave Umhoefer, Don Walker and Ruth Ward. Helicopter photos were taken from WTMJ Chopper 4.*

2. Gas Leak Suspected As Cause Of Blast

DEC. 7, 2006

By Rick Romell

The cause of the deadly blast at the Falk Corp. remained under investigation late Wednesday, but signs point to an explosion of volatile propane gas.

Employees discovered a propane leak shortly before the explosion rocked the Menomonee Valley factory, killing three and injuring 46.

The leak may have allowed the gas to build up inside a warehouse, where enough propane may have accumulated to touch off a blast heard as far away as Franklin and large enough to be detected on the seismometer at the University of Wisconsin-Milwaukee.

Falk stored up to 612,000 gallons of liquefied propane, a report the company filed with Milwaukee County shows. Large storage tanks—which remain intact—stand near the explosion site on the southern edge of the Falk complex.

The company uses propane as a backup power supply for large water pumps in case of an electrical outage.

If propane was indeed involved, it wouldn't be the first such explosion at Falk. In 1976, 12 employees were injured when a blast destroyed most of a small concrete building where liquid propane was vaporized into gas for use in the factory. The explosion occurred as a demonstration involving propane concluded.

A We Energies spokesman, meanwhile, said utility crews responding to the scene found no leak of natural gas, another potential explosion source.

Like any heavy manufacturing operation—Falk's foundry and machine shops turn out large industrial gears—Falk has experienced accidents. But the company appears to have a good safety record, judging by available information from the U.S. Occupational Safety and Health Administration and the City of Milwaukee, comments from workers and observations of outside experts.

"They are always diligent here," said Steve Morrison, a 10-year Falk employee who was one building away from the blast site and escaped injury.

Evacuation Helped

Workers aware of the propane leak had begun evacuating at least some areas of Falk's 61-acre complex—an action Police Chief Nannette Hegerty credited with saving lives.

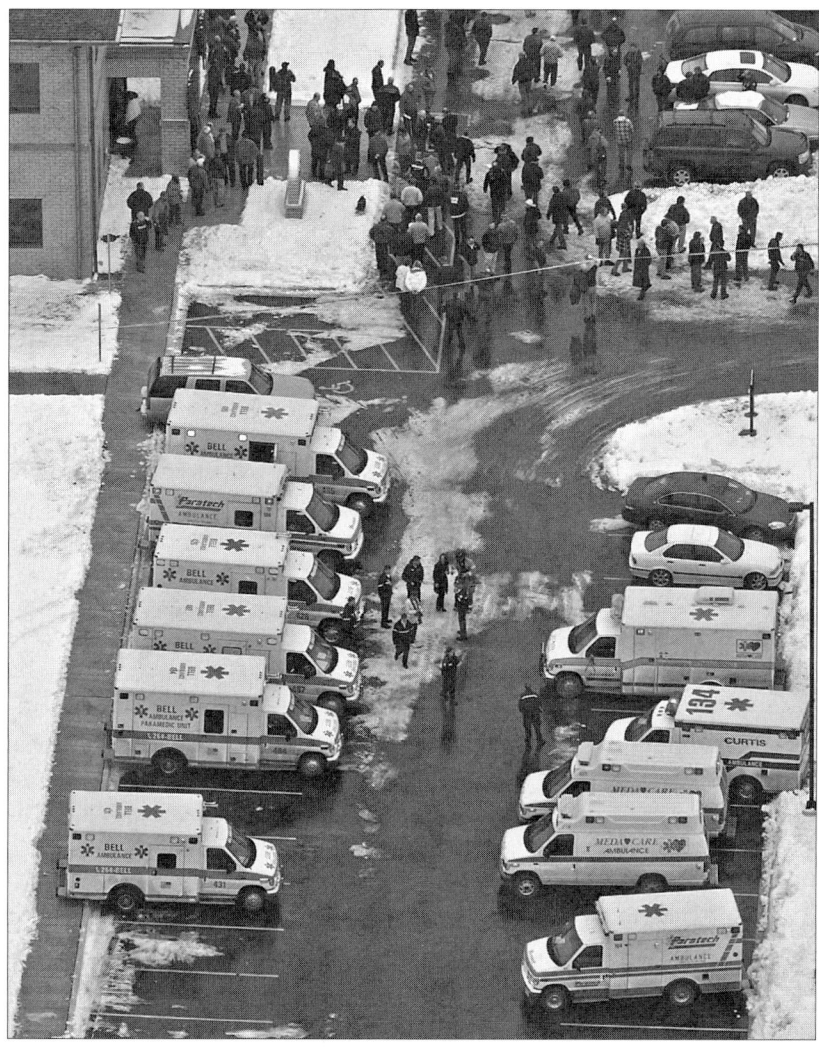

Ambulances and people gather at Palermo's Pizza west of the Falk Corp. Wednesday during a five-alarm fire following an explosion. (Photograph courtesy of Jeffrey Phelps/*Milwaukee Journal Sentinel*)

But one employee said some workers lingered after being told to leave.

David L. Mays, a 61-year-old machinist, said he was working inside the warehouse, known as the annex, when he and his co-workers smelled fumes. They left the building and called a supervisor. A few minutes later, they were told the gas had been shut off and everything would be OK, Mays said.

Exploding with the annex was a connected building used largely for maintenance.

Several government agencies, including the Milwaukee Police Department, OSHA, the Federal Bureau of Alcohol, Tobacco and Firearms, and the Milwaukee County District Attorney's Office, are investigating the explosion.

Hegerty all but ruled out criminal action, saying the blast appears to have been an accident.

Earlier Wednesday, city and state-contracted inspectors said they were mystified as to the cause.

In a September visit to Falk, the city's Department of Neighborhood Services, which conducts annual fire inspections of commercial buildings in Milwaukee, found just two minor fire violations—one related to a door latch, the other to an exit sign, said Todd Weiler, department spokesman. Both were corrected within days, he said.

"When I talked to the inspector and asked, 'How does Falk react to fire code violations and fire safety?' he said, 'Excellent,' " Weiler said. He said the inspector was "mystified" by the explosion, in part because the propane tanks on the site appear to be intact and because no manufacturing occurs in the building that appears to be at the center of the blast.

"It's a storage building with 3-foot aisles, pinions and boxes, and there's rarely anyone in there," Weiler said. "There's no open ignition."

Good Inspection Record

The department doesn't conduct annual inspections on propane tanks, but rather checks installation and repair work, he said. The state contracts with a private company to inspect petroleum tanks, but that company also does not inspect propane tanks. The fuel-tank inspector, from Waukesha-based Independent Inspections, was at the site in February to conduct routine annual inspections of two fuel tanks and found no problems.

"It was absolutely clean," said Jim Hellen, operations manager. Falk has since then installed two more tanks: a 1,500-gallon diesel tank, and a 500-gallon unleaded fuel tank. Hellen's firm was scheduled to return to inspect those in February.

The federal government has fined Falk three times—a total of $5,650—for safety violations in the last five years, OSHA records indicate. Two violations were classified as not serious. The lone serious violation involved powered industrial trucks.

Falk's record indicates "that they are not very careless with their employees," said Michael T. Coleman, co-chair of the manufacturing branch of the American Society of Safety Engineers. "Because I can tell you, OSHA writes everything they see."

James A. Rice, director of graduate studies in mechanical engineering at Marquette University, said Falk has an impressive safety record, especially considering the hazardous nature of its work.

"Any time you have molten material and the processes associated with it, you're going to have dangerous situations," Rice said.

Coleman was impressed by media reports that earlier inspections at Falk had credited the company for keeping aisles 3 feet wide in the warehouse.

Government safety officials ruled two earlier fatalities at Falk as accidents.

They cleared the company in the 1991 death of employee Hugo Schulz, who was killed when a 1,000-pound clutch fell on him. In 1964, investigators blamed a metallurgical fault in a component manufactured by a Falk supplier for an accident in which one worker died and 11 were injured. In that incident, an 1,100-pound fragment of steel broke off a rapidly revolving machine, flew through the roof and soared over the East-West Freeway, landing more than three blocks away.

3. Falk Corp. Remains Well Positioned

DEC. 7, 2006

By Rick Barrett

When the ambulances raced past Maynard Steel Casting Co. on their way to the accident scene at Falk Corp., it was a chilling sight for Bob Thill, Maynard's president.

The companies are competitors, but the employees share a common affinity for the metal-casting industry.

"More than ever, we are concerned about the people involved. They are people like you and I, but they're probably more like us," Thill said.

Falk makes gears, couplings, chains, bearings and other industrial components. Some of the company's gears are among the largest in the world and are used in mining shovels made by P&H Mining Equipment Co., also of Milwaukee.

Falk's business has been robust in recent months as the mining industry, especially, snaps up new equipment to keep pace with the global demand for copper, coal, oil and other mined commodities. Falk also has done well with products used in the agriculture, forest and cement products industries.

Milwaukee-based Rexnord Corp., which acquired Falk in 2005, recently reported a $376.4 million order backlog—up 22% from earlier this year.

Companies such as Falk that make the largest steel gears for mining machines are booked solid with orders for 18 months, said Raymond Monroe, executive vice president of the Steel Founders' Society of America.

"Falk is a leader in technology, and it's a leader in the industry," Monroe said. "How quickly they can come back from something like this will depend on the damages, but there aren't other companies to pick up the slack."

Including Falk, Rexnord currently has 5,800 employees and 33 plants worldwide. The company is not publicly traded. In its second fiscal quarter, which ended Sept. 30, it reported $298 million in sales, up 9% from a year earlier.

"We are well-positioned as we start the second half of fiscal 2007," Bob Hitt, Rexnord's CEO, said in a Nov. 8 statement.

Rexnord executives are confident that they can get beyond the tragedy at Falk, but it's too early to say when production will resume, said Evan Zeppos, a Rexnord spokesman.

"Right now, the company is focused on the employees," Zeppos said. "Until we get through that part, and until we get into the buildings, we are not sure what this will mean in terms of orders and production. We will take care of the payroll, so people don't have to worry about getting paid. But it's quite possible that no one will report to work the next couple of days."

Should Falk's production be stopped for very long, its customers might look elsewhere for large gears and other components made in the foundry and refined in the machine shops. But the large gears are time-intensive projects that take months to complete and are too heavy to be affordably shipped from overseas. So some customers might just have to wait for Falk to reopen.

Falk Corp. History

- Started as a brewery in the 1850s by German immigrant Franz Falk
- Added a machinery repair shop in 1892, eventually developing into a steel foundry
- Built gear drives for U.S. Navy destroyers during World War I
- Acquired by Rexnord Corp. in 2005 for $295 million
- Won a contract to provide gear drives for Miller Park's retractable roof in 2005

The company has a unique niche in the steel-casting industry, said Al Spada, director of marketing for the American Foundry Society, based in Chicago.

"They are one of the large players in the large steel-casting segment," Spada said.

P&H Mining, which makes some of the world's largest mining machines, has bought large gears from Falk for at least 20 years, said Neil Massey, P&H vice president of manufacturing operations. "That's why we are concerned about their people first," Massey said.

P&H has some work in progress at Falk, but it's too early to say how it will be affected. P&H has backup suppliers, should Falk not be able to fill its orders, Massey said.

"They are not our single source on anything," he said. "We don't anticipate being shut down in any way, shape or form" because of the accident at Falk.

Bucyrus International Inc. of South Milwaukee also makes mining shovels. Recently, it has bought gears from Maynard Steel Casting.

"Our industry has been on a pretty big rebound," Thill said. "But it's been a long, tough struggle. A lot of companies have gone out of business, and those still in business are certainly doing much better at this time."

Falk and Rexnord are two of Milwaukee's oldest manufacturers, both more than 110 years old, and they were competitors for decades.

These mammoth gears, shown in 1954, were some of the first completed for ball and rod mills by the Falk Corp. Inspecting the gears are Louis W. Falk (left), manufacturing vice president, and B. C. Bugbee, divisional works manager. (Photograph courtesy of *Milwaukee Journal Sentinel*; file photo)

"In terms of continuous operations on one site, Falk might be in a class by themselves," said John Gurda, a local historian who wrote a book about the company.

Falk was started as a brewery in the 1850s by German immigrant Franz Falk.

"It's a company that has shown remarkable continuity in what it does. They have been making gears since the early 1900s and are still the nation's largest manufacturer of these very large, precision industrial gears," Gurda said.

Over the years, the Falk site has been inundated with floods. There are still places on the walls where you can see the high-water mark.

"They have had catastrophic floods that absolutely shut them down, but they have always bounced back," Gurda said.

"The world needs what they make," he said. "This is a company that has a machine on the shop floor big enough to produce gears that are 40 feet in diameter. That's not something many companies can do."

Conversations with
Rick Barrett, Greg J. Borowski and Rick Romell; and editor Thomas Koetting

The following edited e-mail interviews were conducted by Poynter Institute Media Business Analyst Rick Edmonds with reporters Rick Barrett, Greg J. Borowski and Rick Romell, members of the Milwaukee Journal Sentinel *team that won ASNE's Jesse Laventhol Prize for Deadline News Reporting by a Team, and the team's supervising editor, Thomas Koetting.*

The Reporting and Writing

RICK EDMONDS: How did you get on the story (or your part of it)?

GREG J. BOROWSKI: When the explosion occurred at 8:07 a.m., I was at my breakfast table reading the newspaper. My house, about five miles away, shook. My wife and I thought something had slammed into the side of the house. The radio quickly reported the explosion, and I was on my way to the newsroom downtown. I have handled rewrite on several other major stories, notably the crane/roof collapse at Miller Park that led to the death of three ironworkers. After helping get some information together for online, I was asked to do rewrite on the main bar for the next day's newspaper.

RICK BARRETT: Manufacturing companies, including Falk, and companies that make some of the world's biggest mining equipment, are part of my normal business coverage. It made sense for me to write about Falk's history, and how the century-old company was recovering from the explosion. I also heard that Falk, after the explosion, had outsourced some business to its competitors.

RICK ROMELL: I started out checking OSHA records. If I remember correctly, when I got to the newsroom that morning, I asked Gary Krentz, the day city editor, if I could help in some way. He suggested touching base with OSHA. Things just evolved from there and I ended up being assigned rewrite on the story.

How did you gather the information? What help did you receive from other reporters?

GREG J. BOROWSKI: I spent some time in the morning gathering clips on the Falk Corp., as well as background on other industrial accidents in the area. In addition, as stories were posted online, we discovered that many people were calling or e-mailing the newsroom to describe what they had seen and heard. I spent some time talking with these eyewitnesses—material that went into my story and was fed to others.

However, the bulk of the information came from other reporters, including those on the scene. We had dozens of reporters involved, filing for online usage and for the next day's paper. As the rewrite person, the challenge is to stay on top of all the material that is coming in, quickly assess it to determine where it fits in the "big picture" and whether it is useful to the story (i.e., a great quote, a telling anecdote, a piece that connects to a piece from another reporter). From there, it is writing on the fly, trying to frame out a lead and other key parts of the story.

RICK BARRETT: It was a while before Falk executives agreed to an interview about business conditions. Up to that point, I talked with some of the company's competitors and others in the gear-manufacturing and foundry industries to get an idea of how Falk was doing. Some people would only speak on background, but it helped me prepare for the interview.

RICK ROMELL: We had summaries of Falk's OSHA cases quickly, thanks to the agency's online database. The amount of material that's become available via the Internet over the last 10 years or so is staggering and has significantly affected how reporting gets done. But we got plenty from paper records, too, from the city and county. Other reporters gathered that information. The whole package was a huge team effort. Even the relatively short story I put together used material gathered by several reporters.

How did you decide on the focus of your story and organize it?

GREG J. BOROWSKI: We decided early on that given the timing of the event, the main bar should carry a narrative approach. In one sense, this made organization easier—the story would, at some point early on, shift to a chronological telling of what happened.

While that simplified the organization process, there still was some thinking upfront that helped frame the story. In the lead, I wanted to capture the sudden, shocking nature of what had happened—even after word of a gas leak, and everything seemed fine. From there, we had to cover—briefly—the news. And then get back into narrative mode. In this regard, I thought there were several entry points: the passersby who were shocked by the explosion and worrying about those inside; the workers themselves, inside the plant; the rescue workers who were the first on the scene; the reaction of others, including nearby businesses that pitched in.

RICK BARRETT: The focus of the story quickly developed when I learned that Falk, after the explosion, had turned to some of its competitors for help in filling product orders. That seemed unusual, given the company was in a competitive business. I also thought it was interesting that Falk lost some orders, but not customers, as the result of the explosion and disruption in production. The company is in an old, niche industry where some people have worked together for decades. There's customer loyalty during hard times.

In organizing the story, I tried to capture a little of the mood from the day of the explosion, including a comment from a Falk executive who heard about the explosion on "CNN Headline News" while getting off an airplane in Detroit. Then I quickly got into the business angle, including the challenges that Falk faced in its recovery.

RICK ROMELL: For me, the only major organizational question was how Greg and I would split things. That was easily resolved: Greg was assigned to write a narrative; I was to put together the main news elements. Given that, I just took a straightforward, "here-are-the-facts" approach. It's definitely nothing fancy. In fact, I feel funny being mentioned specifically for something that rests on the work of so many colleagues.

How many drafts did you do, and what revisions did you make before publishing?

GREG J. BOROWSKI: Because the story was written on deadline, there was not time to do a series of formal drafts. One of the hallmarks of a good "rewrite person," I think, is the ability to think clearly about the story from the start, and to develop a general organization plan early on. In this case, we decided to be as narrative as possible, which naturally created a sequential order after the first few paragraphs.

My approach as a writer, whether on deadline or not, is to write a few paragraphs, go back and revise them, then write a few more paragraphs, and go back and revise them all, and so on. I followed this approach throughout the day. This lends itself to a "rewrite" even as it is being written. That is, it is being polished and tightened even as it is being written. I think it also leads to better flow and greater clarity.

In this case, the lead and top of the story were revised many times, to reflect the latest information as it developed. We did not, for instance, learn the names of the three dead workers until early evening.

RICK ROMELL: Drafts? What drafts? I don't think there were any in the ordinary sense of the word. I just collected facts and quotes as they came in and put them together in a way that seemed logical. Going with a probable cause was the obvious lead. We'd also gathered a good deal of safety-related info from records, supplemented by perspective from an employee, an engineering professor and a safety engineer, so we went with that as a subtheme.

RICK BARRETT: The story was written under normal deadlines, along with other articles during the week. There were no special drafts or revisions.

What role did your editor play?

GREG J. BOROWSKI: Within 40 minutes after the explosion, editors had set up two tracks within the newsroom, a different reporter taking the lead in each. Tom Held, a general assignment reporter, would rewrite updates for online.[1] I would do rewrite for the next day's newspaper, as well as contribute where possible to the online coverage.

Executive Editor Marty Kaiser had one mantra for me throughout the day: "Think narratively." Since the explosion occurred at 8:07 a.m., 20-plus hours before we could land a newspaper on the doorsteps of our readers, this was the right approach. It led to a more comprehensive story, as well as one that could draw in readers who had probably heard the key facts in isolation the day before, whether online or through TV and radio reports.

As a journalism instructor, I tell my students the four most important words they can fall back on, as reporters, are these: "Tell me a story." No

---

[1] Editor's note: You can read an interview with Tom Held on pp. 29–32.

one, as a small child, asks their parents to "Tell me an article." A narrative presentation, while hard to accomplish on deadline, is much more reader-friendly, more compelling and more meaningful. It is a role that in the increasingly competitive media world remains the purview of the daily newspaper.

Once the story was submitted, assistant managing editor Tom Koetting gave it a close read, tightening up language and focusing the lead. He also helped assure there was a consistent voice throughout the story, and that it was streamlined as much as possible.

RICK BARRETT: My editor, Jim Nelson, helped with questions for the interviews and also did the editing. He was very familiar with Falk and the gear-manufacturing industry.

RICK ROMELL: Beyond the initial assignment and giving me direction on how my story should work versus Greg's, editors weren't too involved as I wrote.

Talk a little about the tone you were aiming for in this lead story.

GREG J. BOROWSKI: In a situation like this, I think the role of the newspaper goes beyond providing the details of what happened and an explanation of what went wrong. That is a critical role, of course, especially in a disciplined and sustained follow-up to get at the causes of the accident and who—or what—may be at fault.

However, in a community like Milwaukee, this sort of thing can shake people to their core. While less dependent on heavy manufacturing, the city still has strong blue-collar roots. People tend to stay here. Kids take jobs where their parents worked. And the people they work with, especially in some of the factories, are the people they spend time with after work. Thus, I wanted the story to reflect the shock and compassion of the community.

In achieving such a tone, though, I see my role as getting out of the way of the story. My writing should not call attention to itself, use maudlin phrasing or build any artificial drama. There is enough real drama in the story itself. I also tried to follow the idea that good writing shows, it doesn't tell. There are very few adjectives in the story that would tell of a "devastating" explosion, and little—if any—discussion of an "outpouring" of support. Both, of course, are true. But in providing the specific details of what happened, this is conveyed to the reader.

The story pauses and restarts several times with the three subheads. Was this a writing strategy for a long, complicated story?

GREG J. BOROWSKI: In a long story, the use of subheads, of course, is a graphic necessity (breaking up the type). But I also consider it a tool for advancing and telling the story. In this case, I wanted to put the reader in the shoes of people who experienced the day in different ways: Passersby who witnessed it, workers who lived through it, rescue workers who responded and others who pitched in to help.

Thus, I tried to sort of "restart" the story when each perspective is introduced, concentrating the descriptive passages at those points. That is, what did the passersby see on the way to work? What did the workers see and experience? What scene did the rescue workers encounter?

In a sense, each spot also gives the reader a sort of mental breather. It also serves to make the various "characters" in the story more distinct, in that they each are presented in a particular context and are confined to that section. One way to approach a narrative is to find a single person and follow him or her through. In this case, the scope was so large and there were so many aspects to the story, it had to be told from multiple perspectives. In addition, with so many other reporters contributing to the story, it was difficult to have a "character" or two become a thread through the story.

Why did you decide to include passersby in the story (and fairly high)?

GREG J. BOROWSKI: This is touched on above. In a little more detail: The Falk Corp. plant sits in the city's Menomonee Valley, which is crisscrossed with bridges and has a major Interstate running alongside it. Thousands upon thousands of people pass by every day, seeing it mostly as a blur of smokestacks and faded brick buildings.

The explosion, of course, focused everybody on Falk and what the company does (manufacture giant industrial gears). It brought people closer to the workers, even if only on an emotional level—the sense of, wow, that could happen anywhere.

In the story, I wanted to capture that sense of things and figured people could be introduced to the details of the story in the same way people heard about the explosion: A normal day shattered.

For a tragic story, this seems to have a bit of an upbeat ending. Was that your intention?

GREG J. BOROWSKI: I did not give much thought to the upbeat nature of the ending. Since we were taking a narrative approach, we'd be left with the ending as whatever happened last during the day. For a time, it looked like the ending might be the announcement of the names of those who died, or a more somber conclusion.

When the company met with its workers, gathering them together after they were scattered due to the explosion, this became a natural choice for the ending. It was a point when people who may have lost track of each other during the day would see friends and know they were safe, at the same time they would realize who was missing. There would be sort of a bittersweet quality to this.

Additionally, late in the day, the material coming in from reporters contained a different sense than earlier in the day. Some of the shock had worn off and, while three were killed, people realized the entire plant was not gone, that its business was unlikely to go to competitors and that the company was determined to rebuild. I guess, in a way, this is a Milwaukee sensibility—somewhat stoic, but also optimistic and determined.

I consider the ending of the story as important as the beginning. If anything, it is more powerful and memorable. So it is also trickier.

We played around with the final wording. But I knew it was time to end the story, and to do so in a tight fashion. The temptation of writers sometimes is to not just write one ending, but two or three, and to try to throw in the last details somewhere. The power comes when you end it once, cleanly, and in a way that reflects the tone of the story, as well as a sense of what comes next.

A final note: One critical task, given the volume of information, was to compress it as much as possible. Anecdotes were trimmed, quotes were sharpened and the whole story was streamlined as much as possible. My style is to generally be sparing with words. Less is often more. In this case, that was a particular necessity. There simply wasn't room to be flowery or wordy. I think this helped the story.

Part of this process involved sifting through dozens of anecdotes and stories of people who saw/experienced the explosion. Only the best could be included. What's more, in some cases, an additional push of the reporter was necessary—to sharpen the details. I am always on the lookout to include telling details in the story. Not just any detail, but telling ones. I think narrative stories can often get bogged down in a showy sort of way, as the writer describes things for the sake of describing them. Ultimately, this distracts the reader when it is the job of the writer to keep them focused on the key parts of the story.

Talk some about how you were able to find your way to OSHA records, trade associations, competitors and customers.

RICK BARRETT: From my regular beat reporting, I was already familiar with the trade associations. Also, I read trade publications practically every day to keep up with industry trends and what individual companies are doing. Falk is in a small industry, so it wasn't difficult to find its competitors and customers. Most of them would only talk on background, however, so that made things more difficult.

RICK ROMELL: The OSHA stuff, being online, was a snap. Colleagues who knew their way around city hall and the county courthouse came through with relevant material there. We found people with expertise in industrial safety via basic Internet searching.

I take away from the three stories that even a safety-conscious company is a dangerous place in this kind of heavy manufacturing. Was that a theme you intended?

RICK ROMELL: I guess so. The engineering professor from Marquette pretty much summed up the obvious: Foundries are inherently hazardous. The fact that Falk appeared to have a good safety record overall was relevant in a situation where people inevitably would wonder who was to blame. That question hasn't been answered yet, but for what it's worth, the lawyer representing the families of the three men who were killed is targeting not Falk but a contractor who laid a gas pipe.

Finally, not to belabor the point, but 29 reporters worked on stories for the print edition. I can't emphasize strongly enough how much our coverage was a newsroom-wide effort.

The Editing

RICK EDMONDS: How did you sort out the component parts of the package—the three stories here and other stories and graphics?

THOMAS KOETTING: Shortly after the explosion, senior editor Paul Sevart made the single most important decision of the day: separating the online and print functions. A week earlier, Milwaukee had been hit by a blizzard. We had put one reporter in a rewrite role, charged with updating the story through the day online and then putting together the main story for the next morning's paper. It was an overwhelming task—the reporter struggled to say anything fresh when he started writing for print—and the lesson from that experience was on Sevart's mind. He immediately separated the functions of two of our best rewrite people:

Tom Held would update through the day online with reports from the field, Greg Borowski would sift through everything so we could have an original report in print the next morning. Building on that basic delineation of duties, we developed a structure for processing information.

The other critical step was to have informal, standup meetings at the city desk every couple of hours. Local News, Photo, Business, Design, Graphics ... everyone was pulled in. We kept asking: Where are the reporters stationed? What are we hearing from readers? Are there questions we haven't answered? What's the best way to tell that story or convey that information? What don't we know?

What evolved from those meetings—fueled by the online input we were getting from readers—was the sense that our coverage had to reflect the communal sense of tragedy the city was experiencing. That might seem pretty basic, but it helped us in everything from selecting photos to crafting stories.

One example: We made a decision to go with a full-page photo on 1A (see next page) because it brought home the magnitude of the event and gave readers a detailed image they could spend time poring over. A second example: Most longtime Milwaukeeans knew that Falk Corp. had deep roots in the community, but few had a grasp of the history of the firm and what it actually produced, so we made a point of nailing that down. A third example: The whole package of stories has a strong "in-their-own-words" feel to it, with the voices and anecdotes of Falk survivors, nearby business owners and people from the community coming through.

Did anything new develop late in the day that caused you to change your game plan?

THOMAS KOETTING: There were no curveballs at the end of the day that jarred our coverage plans. But there were some surprises that enriched the overall package. We unearthed records that helped us understand how the buildings were constructed and what was stored in them. We found out about a 1964 explosion at the company, which gave us an interesting slice of history. And we picked up some strong anecdotes, like a surgeon who was eager to help care for victims because his father had worked at Falk.

Finally, we have often said that in covering breaking news events such as the Falk explosion, the second day is often harder than the first day. With that in mind, we were well into planning our day two coverage before we finished up day one.

Switch from combat to training urged for Iraq
COMMISSION'S REPORT EMPHASIZES 'DIPLOMATIC OFFENSIVE'; COMPLETE COVERAGE BEGINS ON 8A

MILWAUKEE JOURNAL SENTINEL

WEST FINAL EDITION ★ THURSDAY, DECEMBER 7, 2006 ★ WWW.JSONLINE.COM ★ 50¢ CITY & SUBURBS 75¢ ELSEWHERE

'ALL OF A SUDDEN, BOOM! THAT WAS IT.'

SHATTERED

Three die, dozens are injured as an explosion at Falk Corp. ruptures the December morning.

How did it happen? And how do we pick up the pieces? Coverage begins on Page 2A

Milwaukee firefighters struggle against a five-alarm fire Wednesday morning at Falk Corp. in the Menomonee Valley.

This is how the *Milwaukee Journal Sentinel* front page appeared on Thursday, Dec. 7, 2006.

A conversation about
CONVERGENCE with Tom Held
and Paul Sevart

This edited e-mail interview was conducted by Poynter Online Editor Bill Mitchell with Tom Held and Paul Sevart of the Milwaukee Journal Sentinel. *Held is a general assignment reporter and Sevart is Senior Editor, Local Enterprise and Administration.*

BILL MITCHELL: Greg Borowski told Rick Edmonds that *Journal Sentinel* **Executive Editor Marty Kaiser "had one mantra (for him) throughout the day: 'Think narratively.' " Was there an explicit mantra for what you did online that day? If not, looking back on what you did, how would you conceptualize the online portion of the coverage that day?**

Tom Held

TOM HELD and PAUL SEVART: We posted developments as quickly as we could, piece by piece, on our NewsWatch blog. A blog format is perfect for a developing story, because readers know instantly what's new since they last checked in. For readers who want a traditional story structure, Tom was assigned to online rewrite, and he did four complete write-throughs of the main story. His goal was to give readers a compelling story that included the basics of journalism—the who, what, when, where, how and why— and to deliver some context that can get lost in blog dispatches.

Please give us a snapshot of the logistics. How many people worked on the coverage overall? How did you organize the online coverage, and roughly how many people were involved? Where, physically, is the online operation vis-à-vis the print newsroom? Do people in the print newsroom post directly to the site?

Paul Sevart

We had about 25 reporters and a half-dozen photographers assigned within the first hour after the 8:07 a.m. explosion. About 10 more reporters were assigned during the day. The reporters filed via e-mail or by dictating to an editorial assistant or editor. Print editors handled the blog items and online write-throughs and posted them directly to JSOnline. Our online staff is a separate business unit from the newspaper, but the producers and editors sit in the middle of the newsroom with the print staff. Tom sits within a few feet of Greg Borowski, who wrote the lead story for print. They talked all day about how to best use the information being delivered from the field.

What lessons for online coverage did you draw from the blizzard that hit the area a few days before the explosion?

The blizzard hit on the previous Friday. We had a great day on JSOnline, posting blog items, reader photos and e-mails. But as the snow tapered off and our attention turned toward the next morning's paper, we realized we had been so busy reporting the day's events online that we hadn't done the necessary reporting to spin the story forward, toward a Saturday of digging out, sledding and skiing. We were determined not to make a similar mistake on Wednesday.

Could you address ways in which your body of online work served (and serves) readers in various ways: as developments unfolded that day, as an ongoing resource, other ways?

Our online work reported the news that day to nearly 268,000 unique users. We invited online readers to become a part of the story by sharing their photos, accounts of the explosion and condolences to the families. We also used JSOnline as a reporting tool, to find workers who had been at the plant that morning. And we used online to convey information from police and the company to Falk workers. We maintain the Falk coverage as an ongoing resource on JSOnline so readers can quickly get context and background anytime we publish a follow-up story.

What do traffic figures for that day (and subsequently) suggest about what areas of your online coverage resonated most (and less so) with readers?

Total pageviews for Dec. 6 were 2,887,183, about double a normal weekday. Pageviews on NewsWatch, at 193,248, were three to four times the normal. So the immediate piece-by-piece reporting on NewsWatch kept people coming back. The write-throughs of the main story had 88,925 pageviews, which shows the traditional story structure was still necessary.

The photo gallery had 850,000 pageviews on Dec. 6 and more than 2 million within a couple of days. (One viewer clicking on one thumbnail creates one pageview.) Those numbers clearly show the power of images.

On the NewsWatch blog, you invited reader involvement first by e-mail, then by e-mail and telephone, and then by postings. Please discuss how that process evolved during the day, along with the results of various requests for reader help.

First we invited online readers who had seen the explosion to e-mail us. That brought us dozens of contacts. A couple hours later, we invited Falk workers and their families to contact us. That brought us witnesses who had been at the plant that morning. Around 2 p.m., we invited readers who had seen or heard the explosion to post their thoughts in a moderated forum. That drew more than 90 responses. A separate page for reader photos had 11 snapshots.

How did you process the reader comments to the forum? Did the comments go live as soon as users clicked "submit"? Anybody later ask that their comments be removed? Overall lessons about user-generated content (including the user-submitted photos)?

The moderator approved comments before they appeared on the forum but could not edit their content. There were no requests that a comment be removed. Overall lessons? For the next big story, we might be quicker to set up a reader forum.

More generally, what standards do you follow in posting material online as a story is unfolding? How do those standards differ from those applied for print content (thinking of content across the board here—text, cutlines, images, etc., both by staff and users)? When the package shifts from unfolding coverage to ongoing resource, do you go back and do additional copy editing?

We edit online content to accurately reflect what we know at the moment. We expect print content to provide more completeness and context. We are far more selective in choosing stories and photos for the print edition, where space is limited. We tried to write the online stories to the same standard that applies to stories in print, particularly for accuracy. Whether print or online, the goal is trusted content. Readers today have so many options that it's imperative we stand out for accuracy, clear writing and context. We do not go back and do additional copy editing after content is published online except when we become aware of an error.

Could you address how you approached the writing differently for online as opposed to print? Any lessons learned on this front going forward for writing for the Web?

For online, we wanted to give readers something tight and compelling, following the basics: Tell the story and make sure to cover the who, what, when, where, how and why. We certainly do that for print, as well, but the pacing of a narrative provides that information in a less direct fashion. We also worked on the assumption that people were checking back on our coverage as they went about their day: working, childcare, etc. In that sense, we wanted to make sure we had something new and valuable to offer as often as possible. We didn't want readers to click back and say, "Well, I read that two hours ago."

What lessons have you drawn for future online coverage from the Falk story? Do you have a plan that reflects some of these lessons for use in future breaking news situations?

While we do not have a written plan, the Falk online coverage became our template for covering the big story. The key elements are:
- Get as many reporters and photographers into the field as you possibly can.
- Assign rewrite reporters and editors for parallel, coordinated online and print efforts.
- Use the breaking news blog to report the story piece by piece as it unfolds.
- Use online write-throughs to tell the story in conventional form.
- Invite readers to get involved early and often.

Writers' Workshop

Talking Points

1. Greg Borowski says he believes that less is more in this kind of story—keeping adjectives to a bare minimum and choosing only a few of the best details and anecdotes. Can you find places in his story and the two others where that practice works to good effect? What makes these choices effective?

2. Borowski's story pauses and switches topic or perspective several times (basically where the subheads fall). Why might Borowski have used that technique? Compare its effectiveness to conventional transition phrases.

3. How does the work of the print reporters change when the main part of the story has already been told by local television and the newspaper's own Web site?

Assignment Desk

1. How can you prepare in advance for coverage of a big, complicated and unexpected event? For example: A train hits a schoolbus filled with students, killing several and injuring a dozen more. As editor in charge, list your objectives for coverage. How would you assign your team?

2. As a reporter, describe the three strategies you would use to get telling details and anecdotes. Address any special challenges that talking with accident victims or eyewitnesses might present, especially in the immediate aftermath of a traumatic event.

3. As a writer, identify what strategies you would employ to get a complicated story told in an orderly and polished fashion when there is little time for second drafts and extensive editing. Use the train-schoolbus accident described in the first assignment as an example.

■ FINALIST

Ken Murray, Doug Donovan, Bradley Olson and Rick Maese
Team Deadline News Reporting

4. Barbaro's Race Ends in Injury

MAY 21, 2006

By Ken Murray

A spectacular day of racing turned catastrophic when Barbaro, a 3-year-old colt with a seemingly clear path to the Triple Crown, broke down in the first furlong of the 131st Preakness Stakes yesterday and was fighting for his life last night.

Instead of preparing for the Belmont Stakes and immortality in three weeks, Barbaro left Pimlico Race Course about 7:30 p.m. in an equine ambulance, headed for surgery today at the University of Pennsylvania's George D. Widener Hospital for Large Animals at the New Bolton Center in Kennett Square, Pa.

Barbaro suffered fractures above and below his right hind ankle, an injury that at the least ended his racing career and, according to attending veterinarian Dr. Larry Bramlage, was life-threatening.

While trainer Michael Matz and jockey Edgar Prado attended to Barbaro, Bernardini, a lightly raced bay with royal bloodlines, stormed to a 5¼-length victory ahead of Sweetnorthernsaint.

As the horrified crowd—some crying, others screaming—saw Matz run to Barbaro, one spectator yelled out to Matz, "Don't you dare kill that horse."

Meanwhile, other parts of the record crowd of 118,402, those on the west end of the track, had not seen what happened to Barbaro, and they cheered Bernardini's victory.

Last night at New Bolton, Matz said that doctors had adjusted the splint placed on the horse's leg at Pimlico and that he was "resting comfortably."

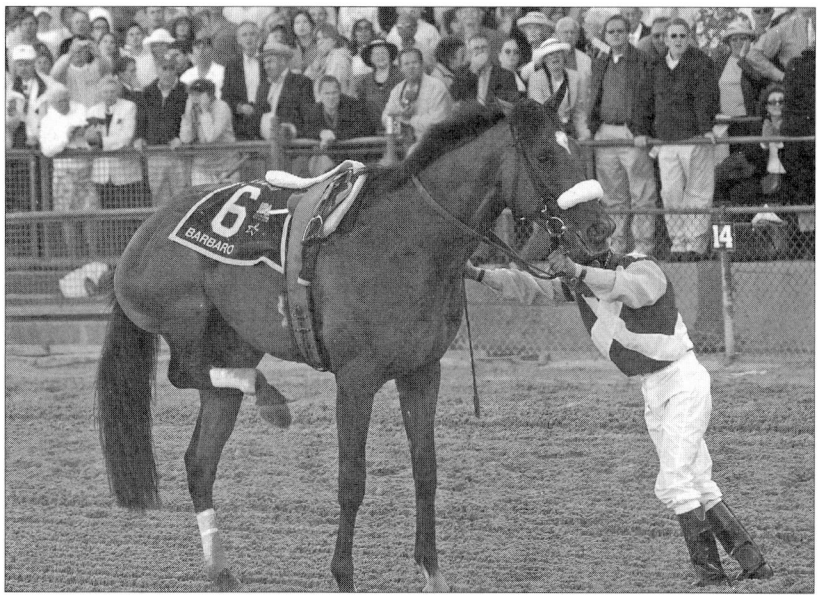

Jockey Edgar Prado tries to settle down Barbaro as the horse nurses his injured right hind leg. (Photograph courtesy of Gene Sweeney Jr./*The Sun*)

"Hopefully, [Sunday] we'll have surgery on his right leg," Matz said.

Bramlage said the injury would require extensive surgery and posed significant risk to the colt's recovery because of blood circulation issues.

"His career is over. This is it for him as a racehorse," Bramlage said shortly before Barbaro left Pimlico. "We're trying to save him as a stallion [for breeding].

"There's some major hurdles here. He has to be stabilized. We're looking at a long surgery that will take hours."

Matz said two surgeons would be performing the surgery: Dr. Dean Richardson, chief of surgery at the New Bolton Center, and Dr. David Nunamaker, chair of the Department of Clinical Studies at New Bolton.

Matz said the injury remains life-threatening because recovery is dangerous.

Bramlage said: "That's an injury you or I would be put in bed for six weeks before we were allowed to walk on it, and that's impossible to do with a horse."

The race got off to an ominous start when Barbaro broke through the starting gate prematurely. Prado slowed him down and circled around to re-enter the gate.

When the race actually started, Barbaro broke slowly from the gate and quickly got into traffic and trouble. When it became apparent to Prado that the horse was injured, he pulled up and jumped off.

Matz rushed to the horse. Prado was on the verge of tears as he told the trainer, "When he broke, he was fine, and then I hear a pop.... I'm so sorry."

Soon after, the horse's owners, Roy and Gretchen Jackson, arrived on the track while the race was in progress. Gretchen Jackson tried to comfort the crestfallen Prado.

"We didn't expect this," she said later. "You can expect being beaten. You didn't think about this."

Barbaro's injury, just two weeks after he won the Kentucky Derby in dominating fashion, left virtually everyone in shock.

"The whole story is this: Let's just hope Barbaro lives," said Nick Zito, the trainer of third-place finisher Hemingway's Key.

"These things happen that no one can dream of. I had the favorite in the Derby Trial for the [George] Steinbrenner family, Protagonist. He was perfectly sound, and he broke a sesamoid leaving the gate. That's why I say you have to cherish the moment in racing, because here's a star. Let's just hope everything is OK."

Jeremy Rose, the jockey on Hemingway's Key, found no satisfaction in his third-place finish.

"It is hard to celebrate with what happened to Barbaro when he gets vanned off and it does not look good," he said. "From my vantage point [breaking from the third post], he broke down right next to me, and I saw Edgar pull him up. I thought maybe someone came over [on] him ... but it looked bad."

Mike Trombetta, trainer of Sweetnorthernsaint, said he didn't see Barbaro break down, but he knew instantly something was wrong.

"I knew it was something terrible because Michael Matz came running past me as if the world had ended," he said.

Prado at first declined to talk about the incident but later offered this account:

"When he went to the gate, he was feeling super, and I felt like he was in the best condition for this race. He actually tried to buck me off a couple of times. He was feeling that good. He just touched the front of the doors of the gate and went right through it.

"During the race, he took a bad step, and I can't really tell you what happened. I heard a noise about 100 yards into the race and pulled him right up."

Prado's quick response might well have prevented further damage to Barbaro.

By about 9 p.m., when a caravan of cars with the ambulance arrived at the New Bolton Center, it was met by 15 people who had gathered at the hospital, displaying a sign that said: "Barbaro, we love you" and "good luck wonder horse."

The ambulance pulled around to the back of the hospital to unload Barbaro.

Sean Keeley, 10, who was holding the latter sign, said he came to New Bolton because "when I saw it happen, I felt like I knew what Michael Matz was going through. Something like that happened to one of my horses. I was just so sad that I made this sign and got here as quick as I could."

Sara Richardson, 28, who also was at New Bolton holding a sign, said she was stunned when Barbaro pulled up.

"It was almost like the world stopped," Richardson said. "Our hearts go out to the people close to the horse."

The last horse who had to be destroyed after breaking down in the Preakness was Union City in 1993. Prairie Bayou won the Preakness that year but broke down in the Belmont, in his next race, and had to be put down.

In 1999, after winning both the Kentucky Derby and the Preakness, Charismatic pulled up lame in the Belmont. He currently stands at stud.

Deaths resulting from catastrophic, fatal injuries suffered at the start of a race are uncommon, according to track statistics that say such deaths occur less than twice per 1,000 starts.

Dr. James M. Casey, a Laurel veterinarian, said the statistic is accurate: "It doesn't happen often, but it does happen. If it happened all the time, who would want to ride?"

It was uncertain whether Bernardini would continue on to the Belmont in three weeks.

Sun *reporters Doug Donovan, Sandra McKee and Bradley Olson contributed to this article.*

Lessons Learned

BY KEN MURRAY

Barbaro's leg dangled like a broken branch.

In a dozen Preaknesses, I had never seen a horse survive the day when a broken limb dangled like that. It was horrifying and gruesome, disturbing at a level you don't expect to find in sports.

When Barbaro broke down in the first furlong at Pimlico, his right hind leg shattered, the 131st Preakness was an afterthought. I had been assigned to write a page one story on the race, capturing the flavor of the day.

Instead, I was writing what seemed certain to be an obituary for a Kentucky Derby winner, two weeks after the coronation. I was numb as veteran jockey Edgar Prado reined in Barbaro, hopped off his back and tried to save the horse. I tried to force my eyes to follow the race as it careened down the backstretch. I couldn't.

What do you learn when you're front row for one of the worst sporting disasters you can imagine?

You learn to trust your instincts. You learn to listen with your eyes. You learn the value of teamwork.

My instincts carried me through the evening. It was as if I was on autopilot. The deflated, even sad, atmosphere enveloping Pimlico struck me as I headed for the Stakes barn. This story didn't require interviews with the winners. It involved observations of the survivors.

Toward that end, I was assisted greatly by our team of *Sun* reporters. Everyone got a glimpse of something important. Sandy McKee heard a fan scream, "Don't you dare kill that horse," as trainer Michael Matz raced to help Prado.

I saw the heartbreak on faces. I heard the anguish in voices. You didn't have to hear what Prado was saying as he comforted Barbaro on the track. You knew. You didn't have to wonder how bad the injury was. The expression on Matz' face told you it was extreme.

It was dark in Pimlico by the time the ambulance rolled out with a sedated Barbaro aboard. We had a reporter drive to the New Bolton Center in Kennett Square, Pa., to follow the story. There were more snapshots of disbelief and grief. More good reporting.

Few expected Barbaro to make it through surgery the next day. That's another thing I learned. I learned a dangling leg doesn't always mean death at the racetrack. Barbaro got another eight months.

Ken Murray has covered the NFL for The *(Baltimore)* Sun *and* The Evening Sun *since 1983 but has been a general assignment reporter for the past two years. He came to Baltimore in 1983 after working as a columnist for the* Austin *(Texas)* American-Statesman.

The Philadelphia Inquirer

■ Finalist

Staff, *The Philadelphia Inquirer*
Team Deadline News Reporting

5. A World Apart, Shattered

OCT. 3, 2006

By Mario F. Cattabiani, Jeff Gammage and Keith Herbert

PARADISE, PA.—The first thing Charles Carl Roberts IV did when he walked into the one-room Amish schoolhouse, police said, was to show the children his semiautomatic pistol.

He was talking, but he didn't make sense.

"Have you seen anything like this?" police say he asked. "Can you help me find it?"

Roberts let all 15 boys leave. A pregnant woman, too. Three adults were allowed to escape with their infant children.

He bound the girls with wire and plastic ties and lined them up at the blackboard. He called his wife to say that he wouldn't be coming home, that he loved her.

And then he began to shoot the girls.

A scene of carnage erupted in pastoral Lancaster County about 11 a.m. yesterday as a lone gunman with a 20-year-old grievance took his revenge on a room full of pupils at the West Nickel Mines Amish School, then turned the pistol on himself.

State police officers stormed the building at the sound of shots—some of the bullets were aimed at them—to discover the doors barricaded by desks and lumber. They broke windows and climbed inside to find Roberts and three girls dead, and eight children badly wounded.

It was the nation's third fatal school shooting in a week.

The murdered children were shot in the head, execution-style, police said. The survivors, many critically injured after being hit at close range, were taken to Children's Hospital of Philadelphia and other medical facilities in the region.

A clutch of Old Order Amish men gather near the schoolhouse. (Photograph courtesy of Ed Hille/The Philadelphia Inquirer)

Authorities have not released the names of the dead or wounded. A group of Amish families, the women in dark dresses and the men in straw hats, declined to comment as they entered the Philadelphia hospital last night. Their children, aged 8, 10 and 12, were listed in critical condition last night, following surgery.

"Clearly, he wanted to attack young female victims," said Col. Jeffrey Miller, commissioner of the Pennsylvania State Police, who briefed reporters at a makeshift press center at the Nickelmines Auction House.

The father of three—who was not Amish—came prepared for a siege, Miller said. Found with Roberts' body were a 9mm pistol, purchased three years ago in a local gunshop; a shotgun; a rifle; a stun gun; two knives; smokeless powder, and 600 rounds of ammunition. He brought a five-gallon bucket filled with tools that included a hammer, a hacksaw, pliers and rolls of clear tape. He also brought a change of clothes.

"It is clear to us that he did a great deal of planning," Miller said last night.

Roberts' wife, Marie Roberts, issued a statement that described him as a loving spouse and caring father, not a homicidal killer. She asked people to pray for the families of the dead—and for her own family.

"Our hearts are broken, our lives are shattered, and we grieve for the innocence and lives that were lost today," she said.

The West Nickel Mines school is located on East White Oak Road near Paradise, 12 miles southeast of Lancaster. It is a simple, cream-colored building, with two large doors at the front entrance, set back about 150 feet from the country road and surrounded by a white pasture fence.

The school, attended by 25 to 30 students, isn't far from the outlet malls that draw thousands of visitors. Tourists come from across the country to see the Amish farmers work their spreads with horse-drawn equipment. The county had only four murders in all of 2005.

Yesterday, horse-drawn buggies parked not far from giant TV satellite trucks, their dishes pointed at the stars. The sky above buzzed with the drone of news helicopters, replacing the roar of emergency medical choppers that had descended hours earlier.

"It's very sad," said Randy Gockley, emergency management coordinator for Lancaster County. "You don't find a more peace-loving people than the Amish."

Police said that Roberts, of nearby Bart, worked as a truck driver, collecting milk overnight from local farms and delivering it to his employer, Northwest Foods. Before proceeding to the Amish school, authorities said, he dropped his children at the school-bus stop.

Roberts left suicide-type notes for his children and his wife, police said. They described the contents as rambling and disjointed. "They don't make a lot of sense," Miller said.

Roberts indicated he was "angry at life and angry at God."

Police believe he made the decision to attack the school several days ago, based on interviews conducted with coworkers. Colleagues said Roberts had been withdrawn, but during the last couple of days he seemed more relaxed.

Miller would not say what may have motivated Roberts, but said it was something that occurred about 20 years ago. That would have been when Roberts was about 12.

Roberts, who had no criminal record, did not appear to be seeking revenge on the Amish specifically, Miller said. They were "a target of opportunity," likely chosen because the school was close to his home and had no security—and because he knew there were girls inside.

Once Roberts arrived at the schoolhouse, events moved with deadly speed. He is believed to have entered shortly before 10 and spent about 45 minutes inside before a call for help reached police. It was placed at 10:36 from a nearby farmhouse where a teacher escaped after Roberts ordered the adults to leave.

The male pupils, ages 6 to 13, were freed. Eleven girls, roughly the same age, were lined up at the blackboard. Among them were three teenage teacher's aides. Some had their feet bound together, others were bound to each other.

Neighbors gather near the school to discuss the tragedy. The school enrolls about 25 to 30 Amish children. (Photograph courtesy of Ed Hille/*The Philadelphia Inquirer*)

State police arrived on the scene at 10:45 and troopers set up a perimeter. They held ballistic shields in preparation to rush the building.

Shortly before 11, Roberts' wife tried to call him on his cell phone. She had found at least one of his notes. He returned the call and reported that police were outside the schoolhouse.

Roberts hung up, then called Lancaster County emergency services. If the police didn't back away in 10 seconds, he warned, he would begin to shoot the children. Authorities quickly relayed Roberts' cell number to a police hostage-negotiator at the scene.

Troopers had already attempted to engage Roberts by calling out on the public-address systems in their police cruisers. There is no phone in the school.

The police negotiator frantically dialed the cell number, but could not get through.

Within seconds, police heard several shots in rapid succession. The 10-trooper assault team stormed the school as Roberts fired at them.

At some point in the morning, Roberts had barricaded the school's doors with lumber he brought in a relative's borrowed pickup truck. Police said he fired three shots from the shotgun and at least 13 rounds from the handgun, the last into his own skull.

When police entered through a window they found two students and a teacher's aide mortally wounded. One of the girls died in the arms of a state trooper, who Miller said is "having a tough time with it."

Late yesterday afternoon, Dwight Lefever, a friend of the Roberts family, read Marie Roberts' statement to reporters: "The man who did this today is not the Charlie that I've been married to for almost 10 years. My husband is loving, supportive, thoughtful, all the things you'd always want and more.

"He was an exceptional father. He took the kids to soccer practice. He played ball in the backyard and took our 7-year-old daughter shopping. He never said no when I'd ask him to change a diaper. . . . Please pray, especially for the families who lost children. And please pray, too, for our family and children."

Staff writers Kera Ritter and John Sullivan contributed to this story.

Lessons Learned

BY JEFF GAMMAGE

It was near the end of that first day, as the afternoon sky faded to dusk, that police finally allowed reporters to approach the shattered Amish schoolhouse.

By then the dead and wounded, 10 little girls in all, had been taken away.

Inquirer reporter Mario Cattabiani walked up the road, to an Amish man who stood near the one-room school, which was bathed in the eerie glow of police floodlights.

"One of my nieces is in [a] Philadelphia hospital," the man said. "One went to heaven today."

That comment, spoken almost off-handedly, remains Cattabiani's most vivid memory of a day in which journalistic lessons were learned and relearned. One was evident in the man's quiet comment: The art of listening is perhaps the most underrated skill in journalism. We want to rush in with our questions. We want to get answers to the things we want to know. But sometimes it's best to say almost nothing, to let people—especially those caught in the midst of unfolding tragedy—tell their own story in their own time.

Another lesson, not learned but reinforced for me: You work with what you have, under the conditions you face, and do the best you can given those two realities.

It would have been better, more humane, more illuminating, to try to speak with members of the Amish community in their homes, or their driveways, or at least away from the crush of the news pack. But that was largely impossible in the midst of a huge, breaking story.

That morning, as word spread that a gunman had invaded the school, reporters representing news outlets from as far away as Korea arrived in Lancaster County. Local authorities restricted reporters' movements, sequestering them at an auction house down the road from the school in tiny West Nickel Mines.

Keith Herbert was the first *Inquirer* reporter at the scene. He was quickly corralled with other early arrivals. Herbert was struck by how the news "kept getting worse and worse"—two children shot, then five, then 10.

He and other *Inquirer* staffers found that when approached with respect and openness, some of the Amish would speak with them. Some were willing to be quoted by name. In Pennsylvania, the Amish have built a world apart from the world. Yet on this day they recognized that their tragedy had drawn the attention of that larger, outside world, and many were willing to try to help reporters tell the story accurately.

"It's news, and that's what you do," one Amish man said, shrugging off a question about the onslaught of camera-carrying reporters and satellite trucks.

One television reporter, near tears, found herself telling an Amish man how sorry she was, how terrible she felt for the people of his community. It was almost as if she was speaking for the entire world of the "English," or at least for the reporters on hand—and that was fine. Empathy is important. It's OK to let it show.

Ours were not the only names on this story—or on others written that day. Two other reporters, Kera Ritter and John Sullivan, contributed. Other *Inquirer* reporters, far from the shooting, showed how not all news is developed at the scene of an event. In culling public records, they learned that Charles Carl Roberts IV had lost a baby years earlier, a fact that eventually would emerge as a crucial, twisted motivation in his attack.

The writing of this story offered both opportunity and risk.

With a story of such inherent drama, and having at our disposal such a rich amount of detail, we felt we could take our time in telling the tale. We didn't lead with the shooting. We led with the killer walking into the schoolhouse. We told readers what he said and how he moved. It was six paragraphs before we said he shot anyone—and we used only eight words to say it.

The biggest challenge in the writing was to get ourselves out of the way, to let the power of the material speak for itself. It was needless to try to amplify the events of the day with words like "heartbreaking."

Anyone who was there, or heard about it, already knew that.

Jeff Gammage is a staff writer on the metro desk at The Philadelphia Inquirer, *where he often writes about race and adoption.*

Mario F. Cattabiani has worked full time as a newspaper reporter since graduating from college in 1987, first for chains of weeklies on Long Island, then with the Wilkes-Barre (Pa.) Times-Leader, The Morning Call *and* The Philadelphia Inquirer.

 *Keith Herbert has been a court reporter at* The Philadelphia Inquirer *since 2002. He came to the* Inquirer *after working for six years at* The Morning Call *in Allentown, Pa., where he was a general assignment reporter and covered criminal justice.*

The Providence Journal

Finalist

John E. Mulligan
Individual Deadline News Reporting

6. Kennedy Heads to Rehab

MAY 6, 2006

WASHINGTON—U.S. Rep. Patrick J. Kennedy has been a pain-pill abuser and a binge drinker for much of his adult life, he said yesterday as he sought treatment for addiction on the heels of a predawn car crash Thursday that he cannot recollect.

"I've got to do total abstinence, period," Kennedy, 38, said in an interview, referring to drugs and alcohol. "From now on, obviously, I'm a very public face with addiction and alcoholism written on my head."

The six-term Rhode Island Democrat spoke at length about his addiction and his manic-depressive illness after telling a news conference yesterday that—for the second time in five months—he was flying to Minnesota for a stay at the Mayo Clinic's rehabilitation center.

Kennedy made the dramatic announcement at the House Radio and Television Gallery just after 3 p.m.—roughly 36 hours after he crashed his speeding Mustang convertible into a security barrier, leading police at the scene to report that he may have been drinking.

Kennedy has denied drinking any alcohol Wednesday but acknowledged being on several medications, including the sleep-inducing drug Ambien.

The congressman said he has felt a responsibility during his public career "to speak honestly and openly about my challenges with addiction and depression." But he took no questions yesterday from the congressional press corps, leaving the Capitol quickly after he read his statement in a loud voice.

During his drive from the Capitol to Washington Reagan National Airport, Kennedy granted an interview to *The Journal* that was marked by the same struggle with denial and candor.

The U.S. Capitol Police cited Kennedy Thursday for "unreasonable speed" and other infractions but did not test him for alcohol impairment before driving him from the accident scene near the Capitol to his home a few blocks away.

Kennedy said he sought no preferential treatment, but the episode has generated an internal investigation of police procedure, amid lurid headlines and TV news bulletins nationwide.

Kennedy said he took two doses of Phenergan for a bad stomach ache Wednesday evening as he participated in House votes that ended just after 9 p.m. (He has produced a letter, dated May 5, in which the attending physician of the Congress, Dr. John F. Eisold, says the drug, prescribed May 2 for gastroenteritis, can cause "drowsiness and sedation.")

Kennedy said he then drove the few blocks from the Capitol area to his townhouse, where he and a female friend kept company until they went to bed. Kennedy said he believes he took Ambien but does not remember doing so.

Nor, said Kennedy, does he remember rising at about 2:45 a.m. to tell his friend that he had to go to the Capitol to cast a vote—nearly six hours after Wednesday's last call of the roll. Kennedy said he does not remember getting dressed, driving his car into the barrier, speaking with police, or being driven home.

He said his friend—whom he would not name—has since told him that "she tried to dissuade me" from leaving the house "and she wishes she had done a better job dissuading me." Kennedy said his friend also "validated" that he did not drink alcohol Wednesday.

The congressman refused to say, however, when he last had a drink—even as he admitted that he can often be seen at Capitol Hill saloons and publicly acknowledged for the first time that his tendency to alcoholic binges has landed him in trouble over the years.

For example, Kennedy owned up to something friend and foe alike have long surmised: many of his public pratfalls over the years have been related to drinking, drugs or manic depression.

During a Democratic fundraising trip in March 2000, Kennedy pushed a security guard at Los Angeles International Airport after she tried to get him to check his luggage through a security X-ray machine.

Kennedy flew back to Los Angeles two months later to apologize during a closed courthouse hearing.

These incidents and other misadventures have "definitely been a result of my mental illness" or of drinking or of drug abuse, Kennedy acknowledged yesterday after years of denial.

Kennedy also revealed for the first time that he checked into the Mayo Clinic's addiction facility for about three weeks over last Christmas vacation. He said he had known for months that he was unable to stop using "a narcotic painkiller" that he declined to name.

It is well known that Kennedy entered drug rehabilitation years ago as a prep-school student. But yesterday, he reported that he had "never gotten over" the chronic back pain and chronic abuse of pain medication that stemmed from an operation to remove a growth near his spine when he was a junior at Providence College.

Kennedy said he started with Tylenol 3, a codeine-fortified version of the pain medicine, and later moved to harder stuff.

But Kennedy declined to name the other drugs he has come to depend on sporadically over the years.

Kennedy said he realized a year or more ago that he had to get off the pain pills. But he made no progress on his own because "when I tried to cut down, I would get sick" from withdrawal.

The final nudge came during the Christmas holiday when he was visiting a cousin. As Kennedy explained it, somewhat haltingly, the cousin saw something ominous in his appearance and demeanor that told him "I was in trouble."

The cousin also took suspicious note of the fact that Kennedy wouldn't stay at his house, checking instead into a hotel.

Kennedy said the cousin persuaded him to seek help, whereupon Kennedy called on a longtime member of the family brain trust, Larry Horowitz, a former chief of staff to Sen. Edward M. Kennedy and a physician. Kennedy accepted his recommendation of the Mayo Clinic and spent three weeks there over the holidays.

Since then, Kennedy declared, "I've been clean, thoroughly," meaning he has been free of the narcotic painkiller that landed him in treatment. But after further prodding, Kennedy conceded that his dalliance with Ambien dates back about two years.

He started taking it, he said, "because I had trouble winding down at the end of the day." But Kennedy avoided being pinned down on whether he took any of the drug between his last return from rehab and April 25, when he got a prescription for Ambien from the attending physician's office.

Kennedy spoke with some emotion about his drinking—and its echoes in the travails of his mother, Joan B. Kennedy, a long-recovering alcoholic who has relapsed seriously in recent times.

Kennedy also said he has abandoned his longtime romance with the notion that it's OK for him to have a drink now and then.

Speaking of his mother and himself, Kennedy said he has "a lot of denial because the manifestation of our illness is different, but just because it's different doesn't mean mine isn't as bad as hers."

"The fact that I was binging and she was maintenance"—drinking daily to maintain a level of alcohol in her body—"is irrelevant," said Kennedy.

"When you've grown up around it, you get a distorted view" of alcoholism, Kennedy said. "Denial creeps in and you think, 'Well, so long as I'm not doing *that*, I must be alright,' " he said, apparently referring to some of his mother's well-publicized drinking misadventures.

Patrick Kennedy's springtime drive to the airport for a second go at rehab was punctuated by a farewell stop at the large, columned house where his father lives, not far from the vice presidential residence at the U.S. Naval Observatory.

It was a reminder of the strangeness of life on the public stage as Senator Kennedy emerged from the house with his son and felt obliged to clear his throat and tell the reporter standing there how proud he is of his son and how his son puts service to Rhode Islanders above personal concerns.

Then the white-haired Massachusetts Democrat hugged his son and saw him off with the words, "Love you."

Somewhere along the way, the elder Kennedy slipped the younger a worn, pale-blue volume for reading on the next leg of his journey.

It was "Honey Fitz," a biography of the long-ago Boston mayor, maternal great-grandfather and namesake to Patrick Kennedy.

With reports from Providence Journal *staff writers Amanda Milkovits and Steve Peoples, and Michelle Mittelstadt and Alan Pusey of* The Dallas Morning News.

Lessons Learned

BY JOHN E. MULLIGAN

Nothing concentrates the mind more powerfully than the prospect of getting scooped on home ground.

So I was reminded when I joined the pursuit of another Kennedy family misadventure—this one unfolding right on my beat, with the media pack in full cry.

For reporting and writing alike, this was no time for experiments. I fell back instinctively on the oldest and simplest tools: "Go with what you've got" and trust the "five Ws."

I got a tip that bad news about Rep. Patrick J. Kennedy was going to be leaked to the cable news network. The tip came about 12 hours after the Rhode Island Democrat's car crashed during the pre-dawn hours near Capitol Hill.

There was nothing I could do about the storm of lurid Web and TV bulletins that was about to break. As a one-man Washington bureau, I didn't have the horsepower to compete on an equal footing. So—go with what you've got.

What I had, at least in theory, was access to the local congressman that only the hometown paper can command. I went immediately for confirmation from Kennedy's office of the essentials of the story that the Capitol Hill police had leaked to the bigger media outlets. I stuck to the modest assets of years of tending the beat: phone numbers of key sources (office, home and cell!); a solid relationship—arm's length but mutually respectful—with Kennedy; a sense of where things are—or where they can be found.

The "location" of this story was Patrick Kennedy and his world. So that's where I went.

I had to entrust to others a lot of spadework (police reports, political reaction, drug research, etc.). I staked out Kennedy's office the evening after his accident. The immediate news payoff was stingy: a terse printed statement. But when Kennedy emerged, I planted the next day's scoop: I asked the congressman for an interview. Kennedy agreed to talk to me the next day.

After Kennedy left his office that night, I spent an hour or two collecting concrete details for the eventual story: appearance of his car; location of the security barrier it had struck; a timeline of the previous day's House proceedings.

Kennedy kept his word to me. But I didn't get the head's-up on the interview until shortly before his hastily scheduled, brief news conference. I was to ride with him afterward to an unspecified destination. (It turned out to be Reagan National Airport, where he would catch a flight for his stay at a distant hospital.)

A few minutes of mental preparation for the interview was essential. I had an idea that Kennedy's announcement would involve alcohol, drugs or mental illness. I resolved to ask him bluntly whether any of these had been involved in several unpleasant episodes during his career, and to pin him down on the particulars.

The wealth of detail in the interview told me that the classic news pyramid was the only way to get this story out. The straight lead brought discipline—forcing me to pick out the good stuff and put it way up high where the reader could see it. Within the harness of the formula, there was still freedom to paint scenes and moods.

Before I wrote the top, I crafted the tagline to my satisfaction—featuring the emotional material on Kennedy's mother and father. It always helps me on deadline to write toward a completed ending.

Then I returned to the top, aiming to load on the biggest foundation stones I had. I worked hard to use the blunt Anglo-Saxon terms ("pain pill," "binge," "car crash") and avoid the softer jargon of addiction recovery ("chemical dependency," "substance abuse").

As I revised, I recited the story back to myself to get the sound right. It seemed that a lot of hard consonants would drive some percussion into the beat of the top of the story. The ending called for gentler, more sinuous lines.

Final note: Yes, I was spurred here by the fear of getting beat. But I also answered an impulse that drives a lot of us to our best work: Maybe this story would do some small bit of good in the world. I strove for a tone that would work at both levels: tough and unflinching, but as free of unnecessary harshness as I could make it.

As I proofed my copy I tried to imagine the lonely addict or alcoholic reader who might benefit from the painful experience of Patrick Kennedy.

John E. Mulligan, the Washington Bureau chief of The Providence Journal *since 1980, has been a newspaperman since his graduation from Columbia University in 1972. He started at weeklies in suburban New York, joined the* Journal's *staff in 1974 and moved to its Washington Bureau in 1978.*

Part 2

Column Writing

WINNER
Ana Menéndez
Column Writing

Her friends call her the accidental columnist, and that might describe the start of Ana Menéndez' rise to prominence as a metro columnist at *The Miami Herald.* But the barbs and razor-sharp commentary she aims at the inane politics of South Florida these days? Well, that's on purpose.

Menéndez, born in Los Angeles and raised in central and south Florida, all but stumbled into journalism after finding herself facing graduation with an English degree but no career path. She joined the *Herald* for the first of two stints in 1991. She later worked at *The Orange County Register* until 1997, and then spent eight years freelancing in South Asia. She returned to Miami in 2005 and proposed writing a food column for the *Herald.* But she was persuaded instead to lend her opinions to the complex and never-dull world that is South Florida.

Being a columnist, she says, "gives me a sense of pleasure" far beyond the name-recognition that comes with her twice-weekly appearances in the *Herald.* Still, the recognition comes. In her first year, she won the Florida Sunshine State Award for Serious and Humorous Column Writing, second place in the Society of Professional Journalists' Green Eyeshades competition and first prize in national commentary from the National Association of Hispanic

Journalists. She won a first-place prize for commentary in the 2007 National Headliners competition.

Her columns, which deliver fierce directness, biting sarcasm, compelling characters and imagery befitting a novelist, are heavily reported. "I prefer to do reporting in the age of blogging," she says. "Opinions are a dime a dozen and now everybody has one. It's incumbent upon me to give readers more. I want them to see that I'm out there trying to understand things just like they are. I try to be, as much as I can, on the side of readers."

Menéndez is the author of two works of fiction, "In Cuba I Was a German Shepherd," which earned her a Pushcart Prize, and "Loving Che." She holds an undergraduate degree from Florida International University and a Master of Fine Arts from New York University.

—Keith Woods, Dean of Faculty, The Poynter Institute

7. While Shalala Lives in Luxury, Janitors Struggle

MARCH 1, 2006

By Ana Menéndez

Zoila Garcia has the toughest job at the University of Miami.

From 10 p.m. to 6 a.m., five nights a week, she washes windows, cleans desks and picks up the potato chip bags and used condoms that students leave behind in the library.

"Ay mamita! And when they decide to draw on those tables, it's scrub scrub scrub," Garcia said.

When she returns to her mobile home off Southwest Eighth Street just after dawn, she takes the pills she gets through a Jackson clinic. Some are for high blood pressure. One is for the pain in her arms.

For now, there's nothing to be done about a blood clot that formed on her calf and blackened the leg from knee to ankle. She needs an operation. But when the doctor told her it would cost $4,000, she laughed. "Where do you get that kind of money?"

Garcia, who makes $6.70 an hour, has no health insurance.

Sunday, janitors voted to strike for better pay and insurance from the company that hires them to clean at UM. They began walking out overnight.

"I have worked hard all my life, but the situation in this country has changed," Zoila said. "The cost of living is so high and no one can live with these salaries. These millionaires just don't understand the struggles of working people."

Always Working

Zoila, 51, arrived from Cuba in 1983. She has never stopped working, first picking peppers, then cleaning hotel rooms. She shares her 24- by 57-foot trailer with her dog Tribilin and her son. She helps a grown daughter with bills. But $6.70 an hour makes for a thin security blanket, and she now faces bankruptcy.

Any way you put it, Zoila Garcia is no Donna Shalala.

Two weeks ago, *The New York Times Magazine* printed an interview with Shalala, who was photographed amid the splendor of her 9,000-square-foot presidential residence, where she lives with her dog, Sweetie.

In the interview, Shalala describes, among other things: "Her perfect day" (which begins with someone giving the university a $10 million donation and ends with her playing three sets of tennis), "What she drives" (a Lexus hybrid SUV), "Favorite vacation spot" (the kingdom of Bhutan), "Her best recent purchase" (a 1790 French country cabinet) and "Possession that best defines her" (a personal drawing by Susan Kapilow).

Here are Zoila's answers to some of the same questions.

Her perfect day: "Friday, when I get my check and know that I'll be OK for a few days."

What she drives: "A 1995 Ford Aerostar. When it rains outside, it rains inside."

Her best recent purchase: "Oh, dear. I can't buy anything . . . Well, yes, some chicken breasts. I have them in the refrigerator."

What she's reading: "My English study books. I just can't retain anything!"

Favorite vacation spot: "I'd like to take my grandchildren to Parrot Jungle, but we can't afford it."

Possession that best defines her: "My smile. I always have a smile for everyone."

Committee Formed

Shalala, who as UM president makes more than $500,000 a year, has the power to make Zoila's life and the lives of 400 other janitors better. Shalala declined to comment beyond an earlier statement noting the formation of a group to look into compensation for contract workers.

Forget study groups. Shalala can begin by promising, as other university presidents have done, to hire only contractors who provide a living wage and health insurance to their workers.

What an irony that this is even an issue for Shalala, the former Clinton cabinet secretary who told the *Times* that what she's reading now is "about healthcare, because I am teaching a class in it."

Ms. Shalala: No one is going to begrudge you your 29-foot motorboat or Sweetie's four beds. But for God's sake, get these people health insurance and a dignified wage. The bare minimum, that's all they're asking.

8. Nostalgia Is Now For Sale, and It's Costly

MAY 24, 2006

By Ana Menéndez

Cuba Nostalgia drew thousands to the fairgrounds last weekend, a three-day extravaganza that proves there is no story so worn or threadbare that it can't be repackaged and sold at a profit.

There was old art, there was sad art and somewhere amid the hackneyed paintings of mulatas and their roosters there must have been some authentic sentiment. It was just hard to spot past the shameless shilling.

Well represented in this paean to sentimentality were: Bacardi Mojito, La Bodeguita Goya, Navarro Pharmacy and Southern Chevy Dealers, this last one honoring the heart-warming Cuban tradition of driving.

Yes, the Cuban American National Foundation was there, featuring a video installation that would have been right at home in an edgy Wynwood gallery. The CANF information booth ("Adopt a Dissident") stood in solidarity alongside Costco Wholesalers, Comcast and Miami-Dade Transit, which was ready to fill the gap for all those not lucky enough to win the 2007 Chevy Cobalt in the drawing next door.

Not to be outdone, *The Miami Herald* was also there, chasing after the lucrative target audience of octogenarians who consider this paper the mouthpiece of Satan.

The Poster

The official posters near the entrance set the cartoon tone for the whole spectacle: Curvaceous Cubanas in frilly cuffs waved maracas while cigar-chomping, congenial-looking fellows strummed guitars. *"Bienvenido a Cuba Nostalgia,"* it said above a prominently displayed logo for Merrill Lynch.

It was downhill from there. After several hours of wandering the space, I was forced to face a series of painful existential questions such as: How many $3.50 magnets of the Virgin of Charity does the average family need? Who buys pillows that say La Habana? Isn't there a better venue for selling boxes of desiccated Gallo Pinto? Is that really a painting of Burt Reynolds with a hat of roosters?

By the time I got to the booth for Memorial Plan cemeteries, I thought I was prepared for anything. But my heart nearly stopped at the sight of dozens of people lined up for some promotional give-away that featured a spinning wheel. Fortunately, this one turned out to be not the Wheel of Fate but the Wheel of Umbrellas and Visors. At that point, I was just relieved that no one was raffling off a free plot.

Cuban Americans have come a long way in this town. Out of the sorrow of leaving family and lives behind, they rebuilt what they could in a new place and struggled through the bad and lean years only to arrive near the end of their story and find it written as farce.

From the sublime to the Bacardi Mojito lounge.

People strolling through the Expo Center Sunday sometimes seemed delighted and sometimes just plain stunned as they gamely powered through the commercial pitches.

"Your roots are your roots," said Stella Menéndez (no relation to me). "Still, it's a shame. It used to be more historical."

'I Feel Good'

Her brother-in-law, Martin Menéndez, 67, had a simple reason to be there. "I come because I feel good here," he said, browsing through the $59.95 guayaberas.

By a certain age, men like Menéndez have earned the right to their nostalgia. The sad thing is that there's so much money to be made from it.

Saturday marked the 104th anniversary of Cuban independence, a struggle that killed thousands, including Cmdr. Antonio Maceo, who survived 24 battle wounds in his career before dying at the battle of Punta Brava.

That was fortitude in the service of an ideal. Today anyone can sell a T-shirt of Ché Guevara with a bullet hole in his head and call it courage.

As rip-offs go, the $12 entrance to Cuba Nostalgia wasn't nearly as offensive as this notion of an Exile's Bazaar: a place where history is a marketing concept and memory is always priced for a quick sale.

9. Vigil Of the Elders

AUG. 6, 2006

By Ana Menéndez

Cuban history weighs heavily on Miami, but in few places does it figure more poignantly than at the Casa Linda Apartments on U.S. 1, a squat building of subsidized homes where Fidel Castro's contemporaries count their nemesis' final days, and their own.

Portraits of dead heroes line the lobby of the gently-worn building: José Martí, Máximo Gómez. Upstairs, Millo Ochoa, last surviving signer to the Cuban constitution of 1940 and the building's most illustrious resident, sits by his television set in a corner apartment on the fifth floor.

Ochoa, who just celebrated his 99th birthday on July 4, finds himself suddenly making plans for Castro's demise.

"I'm on the first plane back," he said, emphatically reiterating what he'd told me a few months ago. "I have a farm near Holguin, and I'm going to go plant yuca and boniato."

Ochoa's neighbors at Casa Linda are almost all elderly Cubans in their 80s and beyond. In many ways, they represent Cuba's lost generation—those men and women who were middle-aged when Castro came to power, too old to start over fully and too young to retire on memories.

Today, they sit in their small apartments and wait.

This is the generation most likely to be derided as "dinosaurs." But there's been no celebrating at Casa Linda, no aping for the cameras, no calls for blood, just wary expectation.

"I knew he'd have to die eventually," said Ochoa, matter-of-factly. "And I knew I'd live to see the day."

Regarded as Cuba's most honest politician, Ochoa remains a life-long defender of the rights of the disenfranchised. He's a fierce foe of Fidel's, but is also just as likely to blame his rise on Batista's illegal grab for power.

Today, his mind occasionally drifts into blank spaces, but he's firm on the need for forgiveness. "The past is past," he said. "What we need to work for is the unity of all people."

Next door lives Yolanda Viera, 69, who shares her apartment with the saints, including a life-sized statue of Santa Barbara with long, black curly hair.

When I visited, the saints stared passively ahead as Viera fidgeted in front of the television set, nervously parsing the meaning of the broadcast.

Cuban-born artist Santiago Llobet, 81, stands before one of his paintings in the lobby of Casa Linda Apartments, where a number of aging exiles await word on Fidel Castro's health. (Photograph courtesy of Donna E. Natale Planas/*The Miami Herald*)

"It's all theater, all lies. In Cuba, there's been 47 years of terror," she shouted, growing more and more frustrated with the lack of news coming out of the country. "There is no reality!"

But during a commercial break she relaxed and said that the future of Cuba should be left entirely to "the people of Cuba."

"The embargo has to go," she said. "What has the embargo done? Nothing except give Fidel excuses."

A while later, the artist behind the lobby paintings drifted in. Santiago Llobet, also Cuban-born, turned out to be more militant a vegetarian than he was anti-Castro. He, too, wished for change in Cuba but was circumspect about Castro's death.

"I don't wish anyone's death. Death is just a passage."

Llobet, at 81, is just one year older than Fidel. When I suggest he looks far healthier, he waves me away: "Some days I wake up with my blood pressure at 200."

Many of their friends have died waiting for Fidel to die, and today the question that hangs over Casa Linda is: Who will survive whom? Everyone may wish for Fidel's passing.

But with death so near, there seems to be a reluctance to make a spectacle of it.

Viera herself is prepared to celebrate the end of Fidel's rule.

But for now, too much uncertainty remains. On Monday night, Viera called her relatives in Cuba. After countless rings, they finally picked up.

"Just to give you my condolences on Luis' passing," Viera said, using improvised code. There was a pause on the other end. Then the brief response: "We'll have to see. We'll have to see."

10. We Get What We Deserve If We Stay Silent

SEPT. 17, 2006

By Ana Menéndez

Here we go again.

One crisis and we Cubans set upon each other like a pack of rabid dogs, scratching and snarling to the amusement of the few outsiders who still give a damn about Cuba.

Forty-seven years and what have we learned? Our history demanded the difficult work of self-reflection. Instead, we've poured our many talents into the business of self-destruction.

Three journalists were fired from *El Nuevo Herald*. It was sad. They were fired too quickly and their bosses were left unscathed. Fine. Anywhere else it might have been just a controversial personnel issue. But no, here in Miami it becomes part of a worldwide communist conspiracy, complete with Castro agents, dark plots and wild accusations. Anyone who dares agree with the dismissals is not just wrong: He's a degenerate, communist puppet of the evil and malevolent prince of darkness.

When faced with a mildly complicated issue, the loudest segment of exiles too often passes reason and heads straight to histrionic conspiracy. On Spanish-language radio, attacks on some *Herald* reporters—who are of Cuban background themselves—has been unrelenting. What is wrong with us?

Central Issue

Meanwhile, the details of why the journalists were fired—taking money from the government to appear on a propaganda station—somehow has become a side issue. It is the central issue. The idea that journalists shouldn't also dabble in government propaganda may be a subtle one for lay people still unclear on the demands of a free press. It should be absolutely obvious to a working journalist.

Those are the facts. But facts often get in the way of a good drama. And drama is what we do best. For almost half a century we've convinced ourselves of our exceptionalism, grown drunk on a heroic narrative of suffering and victimhood.

It's time to grow up.

If Cuba is ever to be a place where pluralism works in anything other than theory, we need to stop acting stupid.

It's fine to disagree with the firings. It's not fine to become a raving lunatic over them. In the week since *The Miami Herald*'s staff writer Oscar Corral printed the story that started it all, the discussion has become less and less about ethics and more about "hidden motives," personal attacks, and paranoid suggestions that Castro pulls the strings at this paper.

The blah-blah-blah crowd is so obsessed with being victims that they've turned a run-of-the-mill *caudillo* into an all-powerful being able to leap walls of logic in a single bound.

Fidel Castro, now playing dominos in his pajamas, will go to hell cackling.

Exile-Bashing

"What is the nationality of Corral," demanded one e-mail. "You are a f—— bitch," said another. Left clapping and cheering on the sidelines are all the people for whom *Herald*- and exile-bashing—no matter the issue—has become a vocation.

The embittered really must have more energy than the rest of us. That's the twisted optimism I cling to. The loudest and angriest voices are also the smallest. I've heard from many nuts. But I've also heard from many Cuban Americans who disagree with the extremist minority that for too long has dominated the conversation.

Unfortunately, too many in my generation fear that to dissent from the prevailing noise is somehow to dishonor our parents. The opposite is true.

If our parents were drawn to this country for its ideals, it's up to us to make sure those ideals are not drowned in a sea of self-pity and pathological self-wounding.

Convictions need to be held in a space apart from ideology and nationality. And the sane, silent majority needs to develop the courage to speak up.

Until then, we will continue to have the leaders—and enemies—we deserve.

11. Don't Curse Your Fate, Ralph— Just Go Away

NOV. 1, 2006

By Ana Menéndez

Halloween is over, but the Monster from Outer Space refuses to go quietly. What part of "be gone, evil scourge" does state Rep. Ralph Arza not understand?

In the week since his crazy phone calls to colleague Gus Barreiro were disclosed, Republicans in Arza's party have been begging him to step down.

Now, even Arza's buddy, Gov. Jeb Bush, wants him out of the solar system. "I think he should resign," Bush told reporters, adding, with admirable ethical reasoning: "because he's going to be expelled, for starters.

"You might as well do it graciously."

Graciously? Ralph Arza? Clearly, Jeb is also from another planet.

Not Known For Tact

Arza so far has shown all the grace of a water ox in a tutu. This is the guy whose idea of a Christian sign-off is "God bless you, bitch." Whose "apology" letters pointed out that he had not called Miami-Dade schools Superintendent Rudy Crew a "racially insensitive word," he had used that word only to describe Barreiro who, in Arza's words, "is white." Big difference, see, because Barreiro is, therefore, not an actual "racially insensitive word" but a fellow "other racially insensitive word." Got it?

What kind of sick, unmoored fanatic picks up the phone on a Saturday night to insult a colleague, anyway?

In the tape, recently available on *The Miami Herald*'s website, Arza calls up Barreiro to regale him with some variations on Arza's second-favorite word: "Hey, bitch. You're nothing but a bitch. You're a bitch. You're nothing but a bitch." He calls back a while later to add: "You ain't nothing but a bitch, brother, my n——."

Then for an encore, someone else, reportedly a cousin, gets ahold of a cell phone and adds his own bilingual serenade: "You're going to see what's coming for you, you punk-a-mother—— n——. F—— bitch.

N——, I'll crack your face open. I'm going to f—— you up, you piece of s——. F—— you. Hey f——, you have a busted a——!"

That fun-loving Arza clan. Nothing like a family reunion to bring out the best in everyone.

There have been far more disgusting political performances—the rush to war comes to mind—but this is the only one for which *The Miami Herald* had to print a box warning sheltered readers that the recording "contains objectionable language that some may find offensive."

What's offensive—not to mention unseemly—is Arza's refusal to go away. The letters Arza sent out Monday are not apologies; they're studies in narcissism.

"It is with sincere contriteness that I write this letter to you today," Arza begins well enough in his letter to J. Dudley Goodlette, the chairman of the House Rules and Calendar Committee.

But then he can't help adding: "Mr. Barreiro's refusal to put this incident in the past and to further levy false accusations against my character caused me a great deal of pain and frustration."

Takes No Responsibility

Poor, misunderstood Ralph Arza. "Two days after putting my only son on a Christian mission to Uganda," he learns Barreiro has filed a complaint. What's a God-fearing bully to do? Call up Barriero and say "God bless you, bitch." Sounds totally reasonable.

Then, taking a page from fellow disgraced Republican Mark Foley, he blames it on alcohol. Whatever happened to the GOP being the party of personal accountability?

More important, when are all the gentle, peace-loving alcoholics of the world going to rise up and protest this defamation?

Lots of families are full of great drinkers and the only reason they've ever picked up the phone during a party is to order more pizza.

Ralph Arza needs to go. Back to Alcoholics Anonymous, Hialeah, Planet X or wherever.

Anyone can get scary now and then. But Arza's behavior suggests a man who cannot learn from his mistakes and is too willing to blame others. And, God bless us, we already have enough politicians like that on this planet.

X-RAY READING   By Roy Peter Clark

I remember my frustration as a college student—and then as a teacher—of working with the "compare-contrast" essay. The topics we came up with (breastfeeding versus bottle feeding; Republican versus Democrat) always seemed obvious or contrived. But as I matured as a writer and a critical thinker, no form of writing became more useful to me or more formative to the way I view the world. Simply put, the ability to compare and contrast is a sign of a disciplined mind.

Less obvious is the way this form of writing can move from straight analysis to powerful persuasion in the public interest, as it does in the skilled hands of Ana Menéndez. The topic of this essay is a labor dispute at a university. But that's just a topic. Moving up the ladder of abstraction, she reveals the great disparities between the highest and lowest paid workers within an important American institution. But that's just an abstraction. What makes it real—and persuasive—is the choice to focus on two workers, two women, two dog-lovers, who share a workspace, but in other respects, might as well occupy different universes.

After you read Menéndez's work, my notations will call your attention to:
1. The several ways in which Menéndez establishes comparison and contrast
2. The use of comparative details that define status and character
3. The editorial content of simple details—such as the name of a dog
4. The value of comparative lists and inventories
5. How the words of a source can be used to express editorial opinion
6. How specific examples can reveal deeper and wider cultural issues and themes

Learn and enjoy.

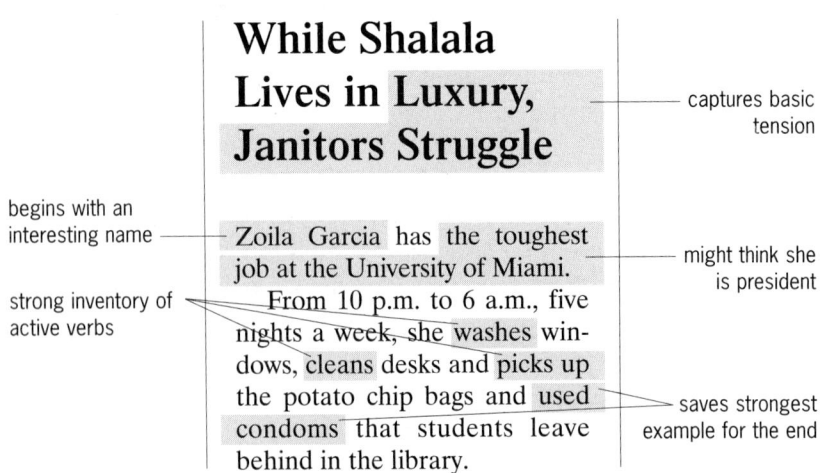

While Shalala Lives in Luxury, Janitors Struggle

— captures basic tension

begins with an interesting name

strong inventory of active verbs

Zoila Garcia has the toughest job at the University of Miami. From 10 p.m. to 6 a.m., five nights a week, she washes windows, cleans desks and picks up the potato chip bags and used condoms that students leave behind in the library.

— might think she is president

— saves strongest example for the end

"Ay mamita! And when they decide to draw on those tables, it's scrub scrub scrub," Garcia said. *(captures her real speech)*

When she returns to her mobile home off Southwest Eighth Street just after dawn, she takes the pills she gets through a Jackson clinic. Some are for high blood pressure. One is for the pain in her arms. *(her problems build our sympathy)*

For now, there's nothing to be done about a blood clot that formed on her calf and blackened the leg from knee to ankle. *(more problems)* She needs an operation. But when the doctor told her it would cost $4,000, she laughed. "Where do you get that kind of money?" *(varies sentence length / varies paragraph length / tension between dollar amounts)*

Garcia, who makes $6.70 an hour, has no health insurance.

Sunday, janitors voted to strike for better pay and insurance from the company that hires them to clean at UM. They began walking out overnight. *(this serves as a nut paragraph, a hook to the news)*

"I have worked hard all my life, but the situation in this country has changed," Zoila said. "The cost of living is so high and no one can live with these salaries. These millionaires just don't understand the struggles of working people." *(Zoila offers her own editorial)*

Always Working

Zoila, 51, arrived from Cuba in 1983. She has never stopped working, first picking peppers, then cleaning hotel rooms. She shares her 24- by 57-foot trailer with her dog Tribilin and her son. She helps a grown daughter with bills. But $6.70 an hour makes *(this embedded narrative makes her more sympathetic / always get the name of the dog!)*

for a thin security blanket, and she now faces bankruptcy.

Any way you put it, Zoila Garcia is no Donna Shalala. *— clever and effective transition; two examples always makes the reader compare and contrast*

Two weeks ago, *The New York Times Magazine* printed an interview with Shalala, who was photographed amid the splendor of her 9,000-square-foot presidential residence, where she lives with her dog, Sweetie. *— always get the name of the dog!*

excellent use of a secondary source

In the interview, Shalala describes, among other things: "Her perfect day" (which begins with someone giving the university a $10 million donation and ends with her playing three sets of tennis), "What she drives" (a Lexus hybrid SUV), "Favorite vacation spot" (the kingdom of Bhutan), "Her best recent purchase" (a 1790 French country cabinet) and "Possession that best defines her" (a personal drawing by Susan Kapilow).

an inventory of the rich and famous—status details

Here are Zoila's answers to some of the same questions. *— a brilliant inversion to establish contrast*

Her perfect day: "Friday, when I get my check and know that I'll be OK for a few days."

status details help define difference—including social class

What she drives: "A 1995 Ford Aerostar. When it rains outside, it rains inside."

Her best recent purchase: "Oh, dear. I can't buy anything ... Well, yes, some chicken breasts. I have them in the refrigerator."

What she's reading: "My English study books. I just can't retain anything!"

Favorite vacation spot: "I'd like to take my grandchildren

to Parrot Jungle, but we can't afford it."

Possession that best defines her: "My smile. I always have a smile for everyone."

Committee Formed

Shalala, who as UM president makes more than $500,000 a year, has the power to make Zoila's life and the lives of 400 other janitors better. Shalala declined to comment beyond an earlier statement noting the formation of a group to look into compensation for contract workers.

Forget study groups. Shalala can begin by promising, as other university presidents have done, to hire only contractors who provide a living wage and health insurance to their workers.

What an irony that this is even an issue for Shalala, the former Clinton cabinet secretary who told the *Times* that what she's reading now is "about healthcare, because I am teaching a class in it."

Ms. Shalala: No one is going to begrudge you your 29-foot motorboat or Sweetie's four beds. But for God's sake, get these people health insurance and a dignified wage. The bare minimum, that's all they're asking.

as we get to the end, the two women come together

make your most forceful argument in the shortest possible sentence

the power of direct address

an appeal to a higher power

it's a dog's life

Roy Peter Clark is senior scholar and vice president of The Poynter Institute.

A conversation with
Ana Menéndez

This edited e-mail interview was conducted by Poynter Institute Dean of Faculty Keith Woods with Ana Menéndez, winner of the ASNE Distinguished Writing Award for Commentary/Column Writing.

KEITH WOODS: Where do you find your column ideas?

ANA MENÉNDEZ: Everywhere. The paper, sources, friends. My sister reads the paper cover to cover, something that I confess I don't always do. And more than once, she's steered me to a good story. Colleagues also will alert me to interesting developments.

I have long conversations with my editor that help me get a sense of what's important, what's worth doing. In all cases, though, I let my own sense of outrage/humor/sadness guide me. If I'm still thinking about something after a few hours then I know it's worth exploring it through the writing.

There's a fair amount of reporting in these columns. How much original reporting do you do for a typical piece?

I do a lot of reporting. And I try to report each column, though that isn't always possible. Sometimes something is so outrageous, or so hilarious, that I don't need to go and do more reporting—it's all been done. In those cases, my job is to cut to the chase and say what the reporter can't say.

Judging from the columns in your winning entry, you're partial to sarcasm as a rhetorical tool. You follow up the fact that Ralph Arza responded to a complaint by hurling an obscenity with this sentence: "Sounds totally reasonable." (p. 69) How do you decide when to hurl a zinger like that?

It's really less a conscious decision than a sense of timing. Writing columns involves a lot of improv ... The goal is to be thoughtful without being stuffy. And the best compliment I can get from a friend is that they could "hear" me as they read a particular column.

How do you know what's enough sarcasm and what's too much?

You can never have too much sarcasm in South Florida, believe me. Frankly, I worry about being too circumspect.

You've also been fairly blunt in some pieces. You call the commercialism in "Nostalgia Is Now For Sale ..." (p. 61) "shameless shilling," and in

"We Get What We Deserve ..." (p. 66) you say, "It's time to grow up." Have there been times when an editor or friend has had to rein you in from strong opinions like that?

Since when are strong opinions something to be feared? That's the whole point of a column. For balance, see the rest of the paper. Fortunately, *The Miami Herald* has a long history of very strong, very sharp columnists (I don't think anyone will ever be able to touch Carl Hiaasen for pointed, acid commentary, for example). And I am lucky to have a supportive editor, Manny Garcia, whom I trust.

Once or twice, he's suggested I tone something down and I've usually taken his advice. But he always stands behind what I do. I think there's a temptation to disapprove of "girls" with strong opinions. Many times you see a woman taken to task for saying something that a man would be praised for. And while I sometimes see that bias in the comments of older male readers, I've never gotten the sense that my own editor holds me back because of some antiquated notion of what it means to be a lady.

Do you read your writing aloud before sending your columns to the editor?

Yes. Not all of them. But if it's a funny column, especially, I'll call up my sister and read her a few graphs. Hearing things aloud helps me decide if a sentence is too long, or not funny, or if the timing is off. Now and then I'll also share a column with my friend Jeff Kramer, a humor columnist in Syracuse, New York. He's brilliant and one of the funniest writers I know. If I can get his respect, my day is made.

How much rewriting/revising do you do once you've drafted a column?

It depends. I never have enough time to do all the rewriting and revising that I want. That was one of the biggest challenges in moving from writing books to writing a twice-weekly column. To keep them fresh, I often don't start them until the night before they're due. And that means working very quickly and writing things that sometimes I wish I could go back and change. And of course, I do. Ask the poor, long-suffering copy desk how often I've called up at 10 p.m. to ask if I can change a word.

Describe your writing process for a typical piece. How long does it usually take?

Sometimes, I'll be writing on deadline off a court hearing or public event. But if I have time, I will start the reporting a day or two before. During that time, I'll jot down ideas or phrases that come to mind. Then, assuming the subject is still relevant, I'll start writing the night before.

I hate going to bed on the night before deadline without at least a lead. If I can get a lead that works for me (and I'll send it to a few people first), then I can sleep well and be fresh first thing in the morning. Then I'll go for an early walk, or run, and start writing at about 8 a.m.

Sometimes, I'll be done in a matter of hours—and then I will spend the rest of the day checking my facts, going over interviews. Sometimes, the writing will take me all day. But I always try to file early—by 5 p.m. or so.

In the Ralph Arza column, you don't flinch in your writing when using the word "bitch," but you use a euphemism and dashes when you get to the word "nigger." Why the difference?

If it were up to me, we would have used the words just as he said them—without dashes or euphemisms. And in fact, that's the way I sent it in. But gentler sensitivities prevailed. At one point, someone wanted to do away with all the references to vulgarities, saying "We've already reported them." Then there was another move to replace the offending words with the word "bleep." You can imagine how I felt about that.

So the compromise was dashes, though I still think it weakened the piece. Newspapers are very eager to join the hip revolution, but they still have a "Leave It to Beaver" relationship with their readers.

It seemed you were setting up a comparison between the spoiled rich and the working poor in the piece about Donna Shalala (p. 59). Then there's a twist in tone in the last paragraph. What were you trying to do there?

Is there? I wasn't trying for a twist in tone. I guess I was just trying to wrap it up in 600 words! I was trying to be as fair as I could to Shalala and in fact, after showing the column to a friend, I softened up the rhetoric a bit. So maybe that's what you're seeing. Again, bear in mind, this was a story I reported on Monday—I spent the afternoon with Zoila—and then wrote it up on Tuesday for the Wednesday paper. I didn't just have to worry about the facts as Zoila gave them to me, but I also had to understand labor law in this case and what was within Shalala's power to do.

Then I had to make sure that Zoila was who she was, that she did work at UM, all those little details that only another journalist realizes needs to go into a piece. All of that checking and verifying (and trying to get Shalala to talk to me) took much longer than the actual writing. And that's the thing with reported columns—the writing sometimes becomes an afterthought.

Given the perpetual time crunch you're in, how much attention do you give to things like sentence length, word choice or the "rhythm" of your writing?

As I said, the writing is probably the most important thing to me, and I dedicate inordinate amounts of time to making sure it meets my standards.

In "We Get What We Deserve . . . ," you turn a wonderful phrase: "Convictions need to be held in a space apart from ideology and nationality." There's another in the "Vigil of the Elders" piece: "Today, his mind occasionally drifts into blank spaces, but he's firm on the need for forgiveness." How did those sentences come to be?

Wow. I don't know. They just came to me in the course of the writing. I've been a writer long enough (my first journalism job was in 1991, and I was writing short stories before that) that I know that writing is a very active game. You can't sit and "think" up lines. They come from putting your fingers to the keyboard and writing.

In two columns—"Don't Curse Your Fate . . ." and "We Get What We Deserve . . ."—you criticize the *Herald* organization. What kind of vetting, if any, must such a column go through?

There have been others before and since. These columns get a lot of vetting, which I understand and accept—they are paying my salary after all. But it also makes me a little uncomfortable. No one else gets to see critical columns about themselves before they run.

I just wrote a column on the newspaper industry and I began it by tweaking the *Herald* over a silly headline. It was the mildest of criticisms, but it made some people nervous. There was a lot of back and forth and at the end of it, the editor on duty said, "Maybe it's because you're sick, but this is not one of your best columns." I thought that was really funny. I'm sure others have their own candidates for worst column, and chances are the reasons are just as personal.

Your pieces on Cuba nostalgia, the *El Nuevo Herald* reporters, and the elder exiles of the Casa Linda Apartments all resonate with the voice of familiarity. What benefits and drawbacks do you find in being a Cuban American writing about people who share your heritage?

All the benefits and drawbacks you might imagine. At a very personal level, I know that I'm probably irritating members of my own family, and that's tough. At the same time, I'm writing from experience, as a member in equal standing, and I think it's important to do that, to be able to register a dissident voice from within the same shared history.

And then, of course, I have a certain authority. I know what I'm talking about—I've lived it. People might not agree with it, and often they don't. But I also hear from Cuban Americans who tell me that one of my columns has given voice to their own hopes and frustrations.

In the column "We Get What We Deserve . . . ," you use the phrase "we Cubans" while describing extremist posturing that you clearly disown. Why use an inclusive pronoun like "we"? Are you really intending to include yourself? If so, why?

Again, it's my attempt to talk about issues as a member, and not as someone dictating from above, or from outside. In the case of that column, and that particular story (the *El Nuevo* firings), it was a deeply personal issue that my own father and I had exchanged words over. So, when I said "we," I really meant "we" in every sense of the word—we Cubans and we, family.

You use a softer tone with the Shalala piece and the "Vigil of the Elders" column. How does your writing voice vary from story to story?

It's not something I consciously think about. I try to write as if I were talking with friends. Different issues demand different story-telling techniques—different voices. I try, as much as I can, to let the subject be my guide. I don't want to get to the point where I'm so predictable that every column starts sounding like every other column.

What else would you like to add about your writing style or writing process?

I came to this job after seven years spent working almost exclusively as a writer of fiction. It was a very contemplative life, experienced on a very intellectual plane. When I took over the column, I knew I would have to deal with completely different challenges. But I wanted to retain my love and respect of writing. That has meant I probably work much harder on the columns than I should.

I will often be up very late the night before trying to get a lead just right. And I'll continue tweaking the writing right up until deadline. It's wasteful and frustrating, and sometimes, honestly, there's little to show for it. Not every column is great. Not every column works. And not everyone appreciates the labor that goes into it, even when a column is successful. But writing is inefficient and heartbreaking. That's just the way it is for all of us. I can't think of doing my job any differently.

Writers' Workshop

Talking Points

1. Sometimes, the way to underscore the ridiculous is to treat it as deadpan serious. Note the way Ana Menéndez does this in a passage from "Nostalgia Is Now For Sale . . . ": "After several hours of wandering the space, I was forced to face a series of painful existential questions such as: How many $3.50 magnets of the Virgin of Charity does the average family need?" What other examples of this technique can you find in her columns?

2. Menéndez has to handle profanity or racial slurs in two columns, "We Get What We Deserve . . ." and "Don't Curse Your Fate . . . ". What do you think of the way she and the *Herald* handled the more explosive words? What guidelines and considerations might affect your handling of such language? To what extent should changing sensibilities affect how news media handle such words?

3. In Keith Woods' interview with Menéndez, she talks about the opportunities and challenges of having a shared heritage with some of the people about whom she writes. How is her heritage reflected in her columns and how does her heritage shape her columns? How does her experience translate to your life? How might your history influence your journalism?

Assignment Desk

1. In her interview, Menéndez says she lets her sense of humor, outrage or sadness guide her to ideas for the column. Spend a week studying the news from as many sources as possible. Keep a running list of the things that ignite some of those emotions in you. Use those ideas to tackle the next two assignments.

2. A reader of these columns will find both blunt, forceful opinion and biting sarcasm. Find an issue about which you have a strong opinion and tackle it from each angle. Is the voice comfortable for you? Write about when it's best to use those tools in your writing.

3. Were you to compare Menéndez' use of details in "Nostalgia Is Now for Sale . . ." and "Vigil of the Elders," you'd find that the tone of

each column is guided by which details she delivers. The former is a sharp criticism of commercialism, the latter a study in how age softens perspective. What details inform each perspective? Write a column in which you set the tone by the details you choose. Highlight those details that you think best set the tone.

The Providence Journal

Finalist

Edward Achorn
Column Writing

12. Curb Your Environmentalism

JAN. 3, 2006

The critically acclaimed HBO show "Curb Your Enthusiasm," based on the life of "Seinfeld" co-creator Larry David, tells the tale of a fabulously rich, petty and self-absorbed Hollywood writer who blunders into various disasters. It's often hilarious, the best thing on TV. But nothing this season was as deliciously funny as the script that real life has been writing for him.

Laurie David, the wife of the real Larry David, is a global-warming crusader who rails against SUVs and preaches the virtues of energy-saving light bulbs. Meanwhile, she lives in multiple houses and flies around in private jets that burn more fuel than the average person could save in a lifetime of switching off lights.

The Davids own a summer home on Martha's Vineyard, where they heard from authorities for building a 21-by-16-foot stage and a large stone-and-concrete barbecue pit near protected wetlands, while ripping up native vegetation and planting sodded grass. A neighbor reportedly asserted that the Davids went ahead on their construction without the proper permits to be ready for a visit by Robert F. Kennedy Jr., of the Natural Resources Defense Council. He had inspired Mrs. David to become an environmental "activist."

It's human nature: The powerful, from Hollywood to Washington to Paris, love to posture as the moral superiors of others, but often do what they darn well please in their own lives.

The Davids' story is sit-com stuff. Far more damaging to the public is the seeming hypocrisy of their hero Mr. Kennedy and his wealthy allies in the quest to kill the proposed Cape Wind project.

Cape Wind Associates Inc. wants to build one of the world's largest wind projects in Nantucket Sound. Nearly five miles away from the nearest shore, but close enough to be economically feasible, making use of the stiff breezes that blow through the sound, it would produce enough clean, renewable energy to meet 70 percent of the Cape and Islands' electrical-energy needs year round.

That's energy that would not need to be produced by the polluting oil-burning Mirant Plant, on the Cape Cod Canal, or at the polluting coal-fired Brayton Point, in Somerset, or other power plants in New England fired by very expensive natural gas.

If you think that sounds like exactly the kind of project the global-warming doomsayers have been advocating for years, you're right. But the Beautiful People's environmentalism often stops, it seems, at their own backyards.

The Kennedys' ancestral estate is in Hyannisport, on Cape Cod, and were the turbines installed, Uncle Teddy and company might be able—on very clear days—to detect bumps on the horizon. This, they apparently believe, would spoil their water view. They also fear that the turbines might make their sailing less pleasant. And so, because of the political clout of the Kennedys and fellow owners of one of the world's priciest stretches of real estate, all sorts of political maneuvers have been undertaken to stop Cape Wind cold.

It is Robert Kennedy's job, it seems, to couch such striking selfishness in the language of compassionate environmentalism. He did so in *The New York Times* on Dec. 16 ("An Ill Wind Off Cape Cod"), making wind power sound like one of the seven signs of the Apocalypse. Wind turbines, he warned, would: slice and dice "migrating song birds and sea ducks"; be too noisy; generate electricity at too high a price; waste taxpayers' money; drain $1 billion worth of tourism from Cape Cod and cost 2,533 jobs; have to be equipped with flashing warning lights that would "steal the stars and nighttime views"; gravely endanger boats in fog and storms; and so on.

But he's not against wind power, mind you! It just can't be introduced into the Nantucket Sound "wilderness," which Americans (especially, one presumes, members of the yachting class) need, to "renew our spirits and reconnect ourselves to the common history of our nation, humanity and to God."

In his piece, Mr. Kennedy advanced the rather novel theory that "our most important wildernesses are those that are closest to our densest population centers, like Nantucket Sound." But if pristine areas and populated regions are both off-limits to energy development, someone afflicted with a logical mind might ask, What's left?

Some environmentalists aren't buying Mr. Kennedy's pitch.

"Nantucket Sound is not a pristine wilderness. It is among the busiest shipping channels on the East Coast and is surrounded by heavily populated communities. Cape Wind, at worst, constitutes a relatively minor intrusion upon this already developed landscape," wrote Ted Norhaus and Michael Shellenberger, in the *San Francisco Chronicle* ("Arctic Battle Should Move to Hyannis Port," Dec. 21).

Worried about global warming, the authors urged "the national environmental community to condemn Kennedy's anti-wind crusade and make the development of Cape Wind one of its highest political priorities." And they urged Mr. Kennedy to resign as senior attorney with the Natural Resources Defense Council.

That seems unlikely. In the real world, money and power speak with great authority. The rich want their water views and sailing vistas unimpeded, and someone else, somewhere else, can pay the price for protecting the environment.

Lessons Learned

BY EDWARD ACHORN

I write my once-a-week column very quickly, in a couple of hours wrested from editing letters and columns and writing daily editorials.

That means, essentially, that I'm always on the alert—at home or at work or somewhere in between—for material that can be turned into columns. Some comes from published sources; often a peculiar fact lodged far down in a story sets me to thinking. Sometimes, I hit on an idea and make phone calls during the week to explore it further. I keep in touch with local political sources, who tip me off to interesting ideas.

"Curb Your Environmentalism" reflects many of my approaches to column writing, lessons learned from doing this for more than 20 years:

Take a line, as H. L. Mencken said. Have a point of view and state it clearly. In this case, I had some fun with the very human hypocrisy of environmentalists who support wind power and wetlands protections—but only in someone else's backyard. Make sure your details contribute to making the main point.

Write as clearly as you can. I always try to put clarity first. I go back over what I have written, paragraph by paragraph, asking myself: Is this easy for the reader to understand? Am I bringing the reader into a complex story as painlessly as possible? Can I lighten the burden of details without sacrificing the point? Do I have to do a better job in grabbing the reader at the beginning, making it clear the column is worth his or her time? In this case, I led with TV star Larry David. He's interesting.

Look for local issues. Those resonate with readers. This column touches on the Cape Wind project, a proposal to place gigantic turbines five miles and more off Cape Cod, in a stretch of shallow water between the Cape and the islands of Nantucket and Martha's Vineyard. That site is the very best in New England for windmills. And it could produce 70 percent of the region's electricity needs, reducing the necessity for coal-burning plants that pump out pollution. Big story.

Look for the bigger story in the local details. Cape Wind is about a regional issue, but it is also about the way the political system is manipulated by powerful people to serve their interests, regardless of their public posturing. Ultimately, it is about hypocrisy and human nature. In this case, the Kennedy family—some of whose members preen as environmentalists, all in favor of "renewable" energy—has used both the megaphone of their celebrity (op-eds) and underhanded tricks (secretive legislative skullduggery) to try to kill off the Cape Wind proposal. The reason? On very clear days, turbines might be seen from the Kennedy compound, at Hyannisport, as tiny projections on the distant horizon.

Employ some healthy skepticism. Often, there's a great story beneath the stereotypes that politicians, and those of us in the media, create and project. Excellent columns come out of challenging illusions.

Take on sacred cows. I think Larry David is a genius, and I love his show, "Curb Your Enthusiasm." Bobby Kennedy is a sainted figure of the environmental movement. But they're both human.

Look for something different. Too much column writing seems like retyping, endless reworkings of the issue of the day (usually out of Washington). Readers appreciate some different topics.

Have some fun. The idea of Larry David's running into environmental trouble preparing a party to honor Bobby Kennedy for his environmentalism is deliciously funny enough to be worthy of his show. Humor can make a column—even about a serious topic—memorable and powerful.

Edward Achorn has been deputy editorial page editor of The Providence Journal *since 1999. Before joining the* Journal, *Achorn was executive editor of* The Eagle-Tribune *of Lawrence, Mass.*

Los Angeles Times

Finalist

Steve Lopez
Batten Medal

13. As Lovers Of Music, 'We're Brothers'

OCT. 29, 2006

All last week, Nathaniel Anthony Ayers wore a T-shirt with Yo-Yo Ma's name scrawled on it, along with the date and location of the concert: October 27, Disney Hall.

We had tickets for that concert, and he couldn't wait. Los Angeles Philharmonic publicist Adam Crane had put in a request for Ma, the world-renowned cellist, to meet with Ayers after the performance. No guarantees, but maybe.

Either way, just watching Ma play would make for a special night for Ayers. Thirty-five years ago, he and Ma were young talents whose paths crossed briefly, when neither could have imagined the life that awaited.

The story begins Feb. 4, 1970, when Ayers, a restless 19-year-old, filled out and sent an application to the Juilliard School. As a freshman, he was doing very well in the music program at Ohio University, but he wanted a stiffer challenge.

The application, which I recently pulled from the school's archives on a trip to New York, asked Ayers to list his father's address.

"Unknown," he answered in black pen. His father had been out of the picture for nearly a decade, and Ayers had been raised by his mother, who ran a Cleveland beauty salon.

Asked about his sources of financial support, he answered: "Small portion from the Cleveland Scholarship Program Inc."

"Please list below the music you plan to play at your entrance exam audition," the application instructed. "Dragonetti Concerto in A," the young Mr. Ayers wrote, along with the first movement of the "Eccles Bass Sonata," unaccompanied.

To his surprise, Juilliard called almost instantly, and he flew "student standby" to New York. There, he stood before three professors with his string bass, reached inside for all he had and nailed the audition.

Ayers was offered a full scholarship and was told to finish up his freshman year of college and then catch a plane to the Aspen Music Festival, a sort of summer school for music students.

Aspen was a success, but also a little intimidating. The talent started at great and went up from there. Still, Ayers proved he could play, and it was a confident young man who settled into New York in the autumn of 1970 to study under Homer Mensch, a longtime bassist with the New York Philharmonic.

"This was Homer's room right here," Joe Russo, a former classmate, told me as he led me on a tour of Juilliard. Russo and Ayers were both in awe of the rich sound Mensch could coax out of the bass and overwhelmed by the intense pressure and competition at Juilliard.

"You were constantly comparing yourself to other musicians," Russo, now a conductor and composer in Connecticut, told me as we walked past the dozens of practice rooms on the fourth floor.

I looked into one, a windowless space the size of a prison cell, a place to test your limits in airless solitude. Russo said that when students walked down the dim, stifling hall, they could faintly hear classmates practicing in the bunkers. If someone was better than you on the same instrument, it could be a motivator or it could break you.

Once, Russo said, he was walking to class on the third floor when he heard a bassist practicing in an audition room. That had to be Mr. Mensch, he thought. What a gorgeous sound.

"But when I opened the door, it was Nathaniel." Ayers wowed teachers, as well. "A very musical performance and a most promising talent," one jury member wrote of Ayers' final exam audition at the end of the first year at Juilliard, giving him an A+.

The following year, Ayers often bumped into a fellow student with a strange name who was thought to be from another universe.

Yo-Yo Ma. For a brief time, they played in the same Juilliard orchestra, although Ayers didn't think of Ma as a peer. Ma, though four years younger, was way out there on his own, a jaw-dropping talent. He was even a notch above another superstar cellist: Ayers' roommate Eugene Moye.

Moye would go on to great success as a soloist and orchestral performer in New York. Ma would become an icon. And Ayers? Even before he left Juilliard, his future was disintegrating. Classmates began to notice increasingly hostile and strange behavior from him, and some grew tired of his tirades about racist white America. Russo thought it must be Ayers' way of dealing with the pressure, which he assumed was even greater for Nathaniel, as one of the only African American students at Juilliard.

In reality, it was the beginning of a breakdown. In his third year at Juilliard, just a few months after more raves from teachers at his year-end audition, Ayers began hearing voices and getting wildly confused, suspicious and frightened. One night, he started speaking incoherently and took off his clothes in the apartment of a classmate. The friend called the police, and Ayers was taken by ambulance to Bellevue Hospital. Soon after, he left Juilliard for good.

In the 33 years since then, many of them spent living on the streets of Cleveland and Los Angeles, Ayers has often wondered about his former classmates, holding onto a connection to them through the music he continued playing. When I met him early in 2005, he played with purpose and joy each day near the Beethoven statue in Pershing Square, even though his violin was missing two strings.

Those of you who read those early columns may recall that for many months he resisted my efforts to talk him indoors. Then, early this year, he finally agreed to take an apartment, and he's been there ever since.

On Easter, he came to my house for brunch and played the violin, cello and piano, recited Shakespeare and Herman Hesse, sang in Italian, spoke French and had a grand time. When we went to a Dodgers game over the summer, he was out of his seat cheering half the time, having abandoned his hometown Indians.

Other days a chemical change comes over him and the darkness never lifts. He can be verbally abusive and menacing, he doesn't care to see a doctor, let alone consider medication, he objects to being called schizophrenic and it seems as though the roller coaster ride will never end.

Our relationship is deeper than ever, more demanding, more exasperating and more rewarding. When it gets exhausting, I remind myself that he's come a long way from two violin strings and a shopping cart, thanks in great part to the staff at Lamp, the mental health agency that has made a life and a home for him.

On Friday, Mr. Ayers—we've agreed to call each other mister, since he refuses to call me by my first name—was playing "Joy to the World" on his new trumpet at Lamp Safe Haven, which is near his apartment. Not everyone at Lamp is thrilled that Mr. Ayers has taken up a brass instrument, especially since the bugling is not always quite on key.

"Joy to the World" didn't sound half bad, though. I waited for it to end before reminding Ayers that I'd be by in a few hours to pick him up for Disney Hall. I also told him the good news. Yo-Yo Ma had sent word that he'd gladly receive Mr. Ayers after the concert.

When I arrived, he had cleaned up well and was wearing a Rite Aid polo shirt on which he had written my name and "Mr. Ma" with a black pen. He wore a red and blue necktie and leather jacket, and his hair was parted in the middle.

Before going to Disney Hall, I drove him over to Lamp Village to check out something that's been in the works for months. Lamp is clearing space for a music studio, and the artist in residence will be Mr. Ayers.

He's going to teach, take lessons, rhapsodize about the Beethoven statue in Pershing Square and, if I had to guess, recite Shakespeare there on occasion.

"This is really going to be something," Mr. Ayers said as he checked out the space and told me he couldn't wait to set up shop.

He talked about it all the way to Disney Hall, where we were greeted by Ben Hong, first assistant principal cellist with the L.A. Philharmonic and another former Juilliard student. Mr. Ayers had met Hong before, at one of several concerts he has now attended, so they spoke of music like old pals.

The concert featured just two musicians, Ma and pianist Emanuel Ax. "There he is," Ayers said when they took the stage to warm applause. "Mr. Yo-Yo Ma." The program was all Beethoven, except for a Mendelssohn encore, and Ayers followed along in a book of Beethoven compositions he had brought with him, running his finger over the notes. He also nudged me several times and whispered for me to take notice of Ma's bowing technique.

"Bravo," he called after each piece.

He laughed with delight at times, and by concert's end, he was of the opinion that it had all come off brilliantly.

Hong led us backstage, and as we waited for Ma, Mr. Ayers was nervous, giddy and chattering like a kid. But not for long.

Suddenly, Ma was in the room, grabbing Mr. Ayers' hand. "You're an amazing player," Mr. Ayers said bashfully.

"Did you like it?" Ma said. "I know you like Beethoven." Ma heard Ayers call him "Mr. Ma" and saw the name printed on the Rite Aid shirt. "First of all," he said, "I'm Yo-Yo. Not Mr. Ma." I could have told him to forget it, but I didn't want to intrude.

"I remember your hands from Juilliard," Ayers said, examining them again as if trying to decode the magic.

It wasn't clear whether Ma remembered his old classmate, but that wasn't important to Mr. Ayers. He told Ma of several specific Ma performances he recalled from their youth, and of bumping into him around school.

Ma reached around Mr. Ayers and pulled him close. "I just want to tell you," Ma said through a bear hug, "what it means to meet you. To meet somebody who really, really loves music. We're brothers."

In a rare moment, Mr. Ayers was practically speechless. Especially after Ma had one of his cellos brought in and told Mr. Ayers to go ahead and play it while he went off to greet some other fans.

Mr. Ayers held the cello in position but was frozen.

"This," he said, awed and bewildered, "is Yo-Yo Ma's cello." He stood there a few moments before fiddling just a bit and brightening at the deep and beautiful tone.

It was not easy to get him out of Disney Hall after that. He talked music with Hong, lingered in the hall, struck up a conversation with pianist Ax and admired photos of L.A. Philharmonic members, specifically the mug of his teacher, cellist Peter Snyder. He would have used his Beethoven sheet music as a pillow and slept on stage if I had let him.

Thinking back on his trajectory 35 years ago, before the fall, it's hard not to wonder what might have been for Mr. Ayers. But he has little time for self-pity or regret.

With several good instruments to play and a studio about to open, he's got work ahead of him. Whatever's been lost, and however isolating his long struggle has been, the music never left him.

Lessons Learned

BY STEVE LOPEZ

Movement, suspense, conflict. All these things can keep a reader engaged, and all of them figure prominently in this story.

We know from the outset that we're going somewhere. In this case, we're going to travel from one of the worst Skid Rows in the United States to one of the great music halls in the world, where Mr. Nathaniel Anthony Ayers, whose dreams died 35 years ago when he suffered a breakdown while at The Juilliard School, will be reunited with his old classmate, Yo-Yo Ma.

My thinking was to let the story unfold without much intrusion by me. It's powerful enough on its own that it didn't need me to dress it up. Understatement is always more powerful than the alternative.

I have the advantage here of a great deal of reporting—more than 18 months worth of research for columns and a book about my two-year attempt to navigate the mental health system and help a brilliant musician and charming but tragically ill man who had spent roughly 30 years on the streets.

In the back of my mind is the belief that it's hard to sell a story about a schizophrenic homeless guy, but not nearly as hard to sell a story that's about a man who, struck down through no fault of his own, has gotten a second chance through a serendipitous encounter with a newspaper columnist who one day crossed his path.

So the story is infused with hope. Hope that we'll quickly get from Skid Row to Disney Hall. Hope that the concert will be as terrific as we expect. Hope that Mr. Ayers will get his chance to meet with Ma afterwards. Hope that there will be something poignant and profound in the much-anticipated moment when two men, on opposite trajectories, meet again.

Ma comes through.

Mr. Ayers comes through.

My role is neither conductor nor cheerleader, but witness.

Steve Lopez is a columnist for the Los Angeles Times. *In his "Points West" columns, he writes about a wide range of topics including politics, immigration and homelessness. Lopez has published three novels set in and around the Philadelphia area. He is also the author of "Land Of Giants, Where No Good Deed Goes Unpunished," a collection of 100 columns published by* The Philadelphia Inquirer, *including wartime dispatches from abroad.*

The Times-Picayune

Finalist

Chris Rose
Batten Medal

14. A Night to Remember

SEPT. 27, 2006

How do you dress your kids for school on the day the Saints play "Monday Night Football" if you don't have any Reggie Bush jerseys in their size?

It was a dilemma that none of my self-help parenting books addressed Monday morning as the ritualistic battle over what my kids would wear took on a different tenor than usual.

To send them to school in anything but black and gold—as the administration had urged parents to do in a show of school spirit and city unity—would have been akin to sending my children out trick-or-treating on Halloween without a costume.

Basic black we've got plenty of in my house but here's the rub: Who, besides Paris Hilton and Elton John, actually owns gold clothes?

There was much give and take and I finally convinced my kids—by heavily referencing Mardi Gras—that yellow actually *is* gold, at least in New Orleans.

"Yellow," I told my daughter, "is the color of kings and Saints." This seemed to satisfy her.

At the parent/teacher/student assembly at my kids' school Monday morning, the only "educational" item on the agenda was whether face-painting would be allowed that day.

This had actually been discussed in administrative meetings that morning.

Alas, it would not be allowed. There were groans. Principals can be so exasperating at times. The many children who had arrived with fleurs-de-lis already in place on cheeks and noses would have to turn themselves in for a scrubbing before reporting to class.

Then the music teacher stepped forward and began pounding out a melody on his chest with his hand, and he asked the parents to follow his lead and chant, over and over, "Saints go marching in, Saints go marching in . . ." which we did, maybe 200 of us, in group baritone.

Then he led the children into a high-pitched and squealy version of the song over our jungle beat and it was beautiful, poetic and touching.

And very strange, really, when you think about it. I looked around and thought: What the hell is going on around here?

Funny: As the meeting broke up and the kids went off to classes, many parents and teachers and kids all hugged each other before parting like it was the last day of school, like there would be some sort of transformation and personal growth before we all saw each other again—the next morning. You knew then that, well . . . Monday would be a day like no other.

And you keep telling yourself: It's only a game.

Who Dat?

I had instructed my children that they were to respond to any questions asked by their teachers Monday with one answer: "The Deuce is loose!" and I was kind of kidding but kind of not and when my son Jack greeted his kindergarten teacher with this as he entered the classroom, she looked at me like I was crazy and maybe I am but it's nothing a little tweaking of my medication can't cure.

What happened after that, I don't know, but I do admit—now that I've had time to consider the implications of the matter—to a little apprehension about all this.

I have witnessed, firsthand, the long-term health effects of being a Saints fan. It's not pretty. It's a meat grinder, truth be told.

You have to ask yourself, after all our children have been through around here—you know, that death and destruction thing—do you really want them to enter a culture that leaves scars worse than fire?

Ah, why not?

As I got to the Superdome about 2 p.m., I could see that what I had witnessed in a microcosm Uptown had layered itself over the city.

Through the fog of a thousand kettle drum grills and Webers smoldering under the interstate overpasses, in the cacophony of hundreds of minivans and pickups with their doors flung open, blasting "Hey Pocky A-Way" and "Yellow Moon," and under portable tents set up in parking lots and on neutral grounds, jammed full of rebels-without-a-care, it smelled, sounded and felt like a new day, a beautiful day.

And a choir of angels did sing from on high, "Who dat? Who dat?"
Or did I just imagine that part?

Clearly, no one went to work; either that, or the term "business casual" has taken on new meaning around here.

It seems like all the adults in town just dropped the kids off at school and hoped some teenager to whom we paid nine bucks an hour would pick them up after school and would feed and bathe them because we had more important matters to attend to: rebirthing a city. Or at least a step in the right direction.

We're Family

Now of course, there were naysayers out there in the Great Elsewhere. All that money, they said, that could have been used to fix people's houses. All that effort that could have gone somewhere else. All this fuss—about a *game*?

The simple answer is that, for the city's economy to survive, the Convention Center and the Dome had to be fixed—first and fast— because they are the bread and the butter.

A more nuanced answer is this: Better a Saints game to rechristen the building than a boat show or a gun show, for the irony of that would have been simply too much, even here in the city whose chief export in the post-Katrina age is, in fact, irony. By the ton.

Bobby, my best friend from first grade, called me from Kansas City on Monday afternoon to say everyone in his office was watching the pregame stuff on ESPN and some were grumbling about our misplaced priorities but I asked him: "Then why is everyone watching TV at your office when they're supposed to be working?"

Obviously, people care about this.

And what can you tell them? The Saints are family around here and you're stuck with that just like you're stuck with, well . . . family.

The Saints are our crazy uncle Frank, prone to off-color remarks and broken promises and *he's* certainly not the guy you send to carpool to pick up your kids when you're stuck at the doctor's office, but you have to admit: Holiday gatherings just aren't as much fun without him.

And every now and then he delivers a nice present when you least expect it.

Outside the Dome before the game, the "family" swelled into the tens of thousands and the crunch of bodies on the concourses around the building was, in fact, chaotic and probably dangerous.

Crowd control was an oxymoron. I wound up pinned in, unable to move in any direction while the Goo Goo Dolls were playing and I was smooshed up against a sweaty, shirtless, moose-jawed guy whose face paint was melting in the sun and we looked at each other and we found the same spiritual impulse overcome us at the same time.

We hugged.

I hugged a sweaty, moose-faced guy and it just felt right, dammit. So go ahead, judge me.

The Goo Goo Dolls' lead singer—he of the famously pasted hair and impossibly east European name—yelled to the crowd: "Thank you for letting us be a part of this. You're amazing."

And yes, we are.

Exhausting, Exhilarating

All the stages fell silent in the minutes preceding the opening of the Superdome doors, silent in that kind of "Star-Spangled Banner" way, and a guy onstage counted backward from 10 like it was New Year's and the crowd joined in and confetti cannons blasted a storm into the air as the doors swung open and little bits of colored paper—and you know what colors—floated across the expanse and people just stood there—tens of thousands of them—silent with their arms raised in the air like it was the Rapture.

And it was.

This building, this monument to our shame, our disgrace and our sorrow, will always be so, but it always has been and always will be more than that. Neither Katrina nor Tom Benson have been able to make the Superdome go away.

Its durability is our durability.

Untold hundreds, maybe thousands, of people were re-entering the building Monday night for the first time since they walked out of it last September—as evacuees, employees, police and rescuers.

They will never forget. *We* will never forget. But we will also never surrender.

There was a game to play but, before that, rock stars and ex-presidents, Hall of Famers and celebrities, cheerleaders and first responders and pomp, circumstance and glory and it was too much, really—all for a game—but then again everything around here is too much, all day, every day, so why not too much here and now?

All the meanderers in the hallways and bathrooms were running into old friends, hugging the ticket takers just because, tipping like madmen, yelling incoherent cries of pride and defiance.

And the drunkest of them yelling: "Super Bowl!"

Funny, just about everyone in the visiting media made Super Bowl references—that was what it felt like—but they failed to realize that Super Bowls have no home teams. There is no sense of desire, longing and need at a Super Bowl.

Irma sang the national anthem. Jesus wept and I died. Then and there. Died over and over. Live, die, rise up. Live, die, rise up. Over and over.

I was exhausted. I was ready to go home. And the game hadn't even started.

Love Potion No. 9

The game. When they blocked the punt and scored the first touchdown, something inside of me that I didn't know was there broke loose. I let out a yell so loud that my throat still hurts today.

I fell into a human scrum that consisted of a tall skinny guy, a short woman, a cop and a beer vendor. Every layer of authority and sociology was stripped away. We literally fell on top of each other. I have never experienced a flashpoint of sudden emotion unloosed so fast.

No drug, religion or meditation has ever brought me there. And, I don't know: Maybe people in cities with great teams do that all the time but this was a crazy good thing. Love Potion No. 9. I started hugging everyone in sight.

And, well, you know what happened after that. After the game, I thought about going to the Quarter or finding all my friends and waking the dead but, in the end, I turned to my wife and said: "I've given everything I've got."

I remember being all worked up in the daze leading up to the game, worried about the message we were sending America and I was all worried about what the guys in the broadcast booth were going to say but the fact is, I don't know what they said or how it all looked because I was acting a fool and hugging strangers and too busy making 70,000 new friends to give a hoot what everybody else thinks.

It is superficial and meaningless and a sign of total loss of perspective but I stand before you and I declare: It is good to feel like a winner.

And out my window today as I write this—my open window, oh, glorious day—I hear the same sounds I hear every day: chain saws and hammers and drills, and it would be foolish to suggest that the workers have more pep in their step today and that everything is going to be easier now because, well . . . because it's not.

It's a long road home no matter what colored glasses you're wearing today but there is something about waking up in a community that is thinking the same thing, that is feeling—if only for a moment—like we all just accomplished something together—when actually it was a bunch of millionaires whose names we hardly know.

Ah, but let us live it, just for today, because who around here hasn't felt like we've had a big L stamped on our foreheads for the past year and I, for one, am ready to wipe it off, like all those silly kids had to do at Lusher Elementary the other day when the principal brought the hammer down.

Only a game, you say?

Like hell it was.

Lessons Learned

BY CHRIS ROSE

The biggest lesson I learned writing this story trumps any notions of journalism and speaks more to the power of community.

It was a life lesson I learned as I spent an afternoon and evening milling aimlessly through the masses gathered for the homecoming of the New Orleans Saints.

The story consumed me, emotionally and artistically, because I let it. Therein was my only strategic maneuver: Be a part of it. All the ingredients for a great story were there; all I needed to do was stir them.

To stand back as an objective chronicler of events that night would not only have diminished the power of the storytelling, but it also wouldn't have been as much fun.

It had been a grueling summer. After the early months of shock and awe, the very telegenic story of wind, water, fire and ruin—the storyline in New Orleans—became less visible to the eye and the camera.

The pace of life and recovery slowed to a crawl. Bankruptcy, suicide, divorce, disillusionment and surrender became the dominant storylines. And the city was consumed in a collective despair that threatened our survival every bit as much as the floodwaters did.

And then, of all things, the arrival of the football season turned the mood. For one, it gave us something—anything!—to talk about besides getting screwed by contractors, insurance companies and FEMA.

And the Saints came home to—of all places—the Superdome, the very image of our national disgrace.

Such a melodious crashing of storylines, themes and symbols (and cymbals!). Such an overwhelming display of the uncompromising determination of a region not only to survive, but to thrive. To restake its claim as America's most celebratory, eccentric and tolerant culture.

Your writing is only as good as your material and when your material is the triumph of the human spirit, then you can write crystal daggers. I let it sweep me up. All I had to do was write it down—and meet an unforgiving post-game deadline.

So I joined the party, walked around and greeted my fellow revelers. It was a chance to make myself feel good and in turn make the readers feel good. In a city that waits for the slow news day that never comes, it was a bracing turn of the tide to have something positive to report.

It's like being a surfer who waits days, weeks, maybe months, for that one perfect wave. That's what I got that night. I caught the wave.

There were, inside and outside the Dome that night, 70,000 different stories of sorrow and joy. And then the hundreds of thousands connected to it by TV—at "home" in their FEMA trailers and spread across the country, bound for one moment in a common celebration. Bound together in a moment of hope. A dream that we can be whole again.

It was hard to exaggerate the power of the moment. (Though surely I tried.) All I had to do was write it down. It was a softball, really; participatory journalism broken from its predictable routine into a story greater than the sum of its parts.

All I had to do was (try) to keep in perspective that this was only one night and only one game and that there was so much more on our road to recovery—most of it devoid of the feel-good nature of the day.

That the starring role of the evening—the heroes of the story—turned out to be the lowly Saints, professional sports' sorriest franchise, was almost too perfect. It was a metaphor lost on no one.

It was a historic event in New Orleans history and to be a part of it was an honor and a joy.

It was more than just a game and more than just a story. It was a collective cry of defiance, a night in which the city proclaimed—and I simply transcribed; a mere factotum steno—that we are not dead and even if we are, we're going to pretend like we're not.

I learned that, contrary to the common belief, good news is more rewarding to report than bad. A night to remember; a lesson for the ages.

Chris Rose started out at The Washington Post *in 1983 and moved to* The Times-Picayune *in 1984. He's covered crime, local and national politics, general features, regional culture and economics and New Orleans nightlife, music and personalities. Upon his return to New Orleans on the Monday after Hurricane Katrina, Rose began to cover the early stirrings of life in its streets.*

THE★STAR.

Finalist

Mary Sanchez
Column Writing

15. Can Any Good Come from His Message Of Hate?

JUNE 20, 2006

This "reincarnated witch of Endor" has some advice for President Bush: Don't bother trying to stifle Fred Phelps.

Witch of Endor is my moniker, according to Phelps, the wacko Kansas minister who pickets the funerals of soldiers killed in Iraq and Afghanistan. Phelps contends that the deaths are God's punishment for the sins of the United States. Acceptance of homosexuality usually tops his list.

President Bush recently signed the Respect for America's Fallen Heroes Act, written to restrict how close Phelps can stand at the funerals. Bush shouldn't have bothered. Phelps and his small crew say the law infringes on their rights. And this "blasphemous, sacrilegious witch" is siding with them on this one.

After years of watching Midwest city councils, state legislatures and county officials try to counter Phelps' protests with similar legislation, a few things are clear: Phelps has the right to his beliefs, however demented. And more good than bad always follows his antics.

Initially, Phelps protested places where gay people congregated. Then he moved to the funerals of AIDS victims.

Among the first to gain widespread publicity was the 1993 death of Kevin Oldham, a New York composer from the Kansas City area. Phelps picketed the Kansas City Symphony when it recorded an Oldham piano concerto. He picketed Oldham's memorial service. He sent fliers to the family home, telling Oldham's parents their son was rotting in hell.

In response, nearly 400 people, many complete strangers, sent loving cards and letters to Oldham's parents. Conservative ministers, many with their own strict views on homosexuality, condemned Phelps.

It's not difficult to raise Phelps' ire: fraternal orders of police (for offering security at gay-friendly public events); Canada (for same-sex marriage laws); a U.N. leader from Brazil ("a national sodomite whorehouse"); high schools that perform "The Laramie Project"; Harvard, Yale and Al Sharpton (for being open to gay groups); Bob Dole and Rudolph Giuliani (for being divorced); and Cher (for her openly gay daughter and other offenses).

But everywhere Phelps goes, good people band together. Sunday, a Florida rock band started a concert next door to Phelps' Topeka church to honor the fathers of fallen soldiers. (Police quickly ended the performance after receiving a noise complaint.)

Many anti-Phelps efforts have triggered positive movements. The all-volunteer Patriot Guard Riders form a barrier of U.S. flags and people to shield grieving soldiers' families from Phelps' protests. Less than a year after forming, the Patriot Guard Riders have drawn support from more than 35,500 people and have attended more than 300 funerals.

Guard leaders note that Phelps is present at fewer and fewer burials. And new riders join solely to honor the fallen soldiers. Phelps is hardly given a thought.

Maybe Phelps' role is a conduit to protect free speech. The new federal law was carefully written to only limit protests at national cemeteries, with distance and time restrictions. A Kentucky law written to lasso Phelps is too broadly crafted and is wisely being challenged by the American Civil Liberties Union.

Despite focusing on an issue that is difficult for so many people—homosexuality—Phelps has few followers. His entourage of about 10 to 15 persons is his children and their families.

Even white supremacist groups are able to drum up new members. Why not Phelps?

Maybe Phelps is right. He is doing something for God.

Thanks, Fred. Your vile acts have encouraged thousands of people to showcase U.S. attributes: honor for the dead, respect for free speech, the ability to get beyond personal views and to stand up for another person in need.

Even we witches participate.

Lessons Learned

BY MARY SANCHEZ

"Can Any Good Come from His Message of Hate?" reflects some of the most often-stated lessons of good column writing: Write what you know, anticipate, then deflate disagreement and stick to one point.

Columnists often rail against things they can't change. They tap into the public's collective angst and attempt to capture it in words. But that approach does little to bring any form of understanding to situations that trouble society. Often, it simply inflames passions, missing the columnist's opportunity to educate and offer differing thoughts for contemplation.

My goals as a columnist are different. What is the point of writing a column if you are simply adding your voice as an echo to what others are already saying?

The storyline of Fred Phelps, the Topeka-based preacher who has made a name for himself picketing the funerals of soldiers killed in Iraq and Afghanistan, offered me the perfect subject. I've known the man for years, long before he'd found national media exposure for his antics at soldiers' funerals.

One of the lessons I learned from writing this column is to not be fearful of stepping away from the pack. To say that Fred Phelps draws scorn is an understatement. As he rose to national prominence, I read along as national columnists weighed in. They were understandably repulsed by his actions. But I also knew that I'd been far closer to the situation.

Letting that sort of experience work for me was the basis of this column. I was hesitant at first to argue that Phelps had caused some good. And some readers did disagree. They wanted him as the villain, period. End of commentary. But ultimately, by not allowing myself to get caught up in the fevered pitch of many, I found a unique column.

There was another lesson, actually connected to the first one. It was to remain close enough to the situation that you feel the passion the subject evokes, but not so close that it distorts your ability to put the many pieces together in a new, possibly more engaging, way. I have gay friends with whom I've discussed Phelps on many different occasions. I see how offended they are by his diatribes. My first inclination was to write for them, to put into words what they felt. But they know how they feel. I wanted to offer something new—yet at the same time not trample the very real offense they take to his deeds.

Obviously, not all subjects can offer such a lengthy build-up as I enjoyed with this one. But good reporting can; the kind that listens, repeats questions and looks for nuances.

Seeking out people who had known Phelps for years could have also covered the same ground for another writer. I got lucky. As a reporter in the early 1990s, I co-authored a long feature story on Phelps. I spent two days with Phelps, family members who populate his church and community leaders alarmed at his views against homosexuality.

I recall being perplexed and intrigued by his intellect during the interviews. He'd been honored years prior for legal work done to advance civil rights causes. He knew scripture like a theologian. And he had a witty banter that made tracking his thought process challenging. These realities made me less reactive to his message and instead find a differing point as a column focus.

When he began to picket the funerals of gay people, I wrote a piece. I still have vivid memories of the evening spent with one grieving family, the parents of the composer mentioned in the column who had died of AIDS.

Later, I'd write columns that occasionally mentioned gay people. Somewhere along the way, Phelps christened me the "reincarnated witch of Endor." He even staged a few pickets on the sidewalk outside *The Kansas City Star* building to protest my work. I walked straight through one once, not realizing I was the cause.

Yet through all of these experiences, I'd seen the good will that often followed in the wake of a Phelps' outburst. That fact was as consistent as his extreme actions. I chose to focus the column on this, rather than waste ink being repulsed by his vile views.

I simply laid out the story to reflect this position, offering solid examples culled through the years. The most recent were the Patriot Riders, motorcyclists who act as a barrier between Phelps protesters and the mourners attending funerals.

In other instances, Phelps had incited vibrant debates about free speech and contributed to legal precedents upholding it. Phelps had reminded many people that even socially unacceptable views—like his belief that soldiers are dying in Iraq and burning in hell as God's revenge on a morally corrupt U.S.—are upheld under free speech.

Technically, more than 15 years of research went into the column. Still, I stuck to one point. I urged readers to refocus energy wasted on hating Phelps to honoring the people he had sparked toward good will.

Mary Sanchez is a weekly syndicated columnist with Tribune Media Services. She specializes in Latin American issues, immigration, race, politics and culture. She also is an editorial columnist and a member of the editorial board of The Kansas City Star. *Sanchez also contributes to a column for Poynter Online, a Web site of The Poynter Institute.*

Part 3

Untold Stories

WINNER
Barbara Brotman
Nondeadline Writing

In telling Art Clifton's story, Barbara Brotman found a way to help readers explore what God means to them. It's not an easy story to tell; but Brotman does not shy away from exploring difficult stories.

For nine months in 1989 and 1990, Brotman covered the issue of abortion for the *Chicago Tribune.* Interviewed about her coverage by David Shaw, the late media writer for the *Los Angeles Times,* Brotman said she wanted to work to capture "the fundamental differences between the two sides that go beyond whether they believe life begins at conception.

"I felt there were fundamental differences in how they looked at the world that had to do with how they saw [a] woman's role in the world, how they saw the role of God in their lives."

More than 15 years later, having studied religion during a John S. Knight Fellowship at Stanford, Brotman again set out to help her readers better understand the role that God plays in their lives. And once again, she chose to tell a difficult story—this time, the story of how a life-long churchgoer faces his death.

A member of the newspaper's special projects team, Brotman joined the *Tribune* in 1978 as a features writer. She went on to become an award-winning reporter and columnist. Her "About the Town" column during the 1980s received a UPI International Award for Illinois Newspapers for Column Writing and a Peter Lisagor Award from Sigma Delta Chi, the Society of Professional Journalists.

In 1994, she joined the women's news section as a staff writer and began writing a column that often focused on her two daughters as they journeyed from kindergarten to high school. The column received honorable mention in 2002 from the American Association of Sunday and Feature Editors. In addition to her project work, Brotman also is the paper's "Outdoors Adviser," writing about outdoor pursuits in the At Play section.

Her series on the last months of Art Clifton's life elicited hundreds of comments from readers. Wrote one, "Bravo to Barbara Brotman for a courageous choice of topic. It took an incredible level of trust by the Clifton family to allow her entrance to their own uncharted territory. Brotman clearly deserved it. . . .

"Thank you for educating your readership by shining light on an often uncomfortable and fearful subject and introducing many to the value of hospice. Her storytelling was true, proved by its resonance with so many readers. Amid the daily onslaught of hard news stories chronicling deaths from drive-by shootings, accidents and war, this was a refreshing change of perspective."

—Butch Ward, Distinguished Fellow, The Poynter Institute

16. The Final Journey Of Arthur Clifton

NOV. 19, 2006

By Barbara Brotman

Arthur Clifton lay in bed in a well-appointed nursing home, looking more elegant in striped pajamas than many men do in dress clothes.

It was a tasteful room in which he was dying. The carpeting was patterned in burnt orange; the wood armoire could have been in a nice hotel, except for the nurse's station across the hall.

Clifton, known to everyone as Art, was a pragmatic man. He understood where emphysema, the wages of a smoking habit he kicked too late, was taking him.

Determined to protect his wife and family from any burdens, the retired insurance executive had spent more than a year planning meticulously.

He transferred his finances to a trust. He arranged for a banker to pay the bills, before and after he died. He made to-do lists to be followed posthumously: The alumni association of Mishawaka High School in Indiana was to be notified; his oxygen machine was to be returned; his medications were to be thrown out.

At 81, he had reached a cherished goal—to live long enough to see his wife of 56 years, Nita, surmount her own health problems. Now he had grown too weak to help her, too ill to help himself.

He wanted to be able to get out of bed. He wanted to be able to walk down a hallway. He wanted to be useful. Nita once came to visit and found three words scribbled on a piece of yellow lined paper: "quality of life."

If he couldn't have it, he kept saying, he did not want to live.

Yet Art waited. Death would come on its schedule, not his. He had carefully arranged the move he and Nita had made from the Wilmette home where they raised two sons to Classic Residence by Hyatt, a retirement community in Glenview. But his next move was beyond his control, and his ultimate destination unknowable.

"Something's got to be there," he said. "But what?"

Death is a mystery, not just philosophically but literally. Many Americans have never seen one. Shrouded in medical routine and cultural discomfort, death is universal, but in this country, largely invisible.

And spirituality in the face of death is especially private territory— one's deeply personal reckoning. But it is on the eve of death when people can find themselves confronting the essential questions of life, and their lives in particular.

What has my life meant? What is the purpose of life? What happens after death? For someone who is dying, these questions are not purely theoretical, and the time in which to answer them is short.

The exploration is not necessarily a religious one. Questions about the nature of existence don't require belief in God. They reach into the core of what it means to be human and back to the beginning of thought and reason.

Not every dying person embarks on such a contemplative journey. Some people are not so inclined; some die in too much pain or too abruptly to afford the luxury of introspection.

Sociable and always looking for ways to be of help, Art allowed the curtain to be pulled aside on his own final journey. If this might prove useful to other people facing death, he was willing to share it.

He was known for his optimism; his Boy Scout nickname was Smiley. But although his last months would be warmed by visits with family and friends, the final, slow stages of death would test his upbeat nature and mock his nickname.

He would be tormented by the wall clock in his room that showed as minutes what felt like hours. His Baptist upbringing and his 44 years as a member of Trinity United Methodist Church in Wilmette would not protect him from doubt about his faith.

He would feel abandoned by God. He would pray in vain for a swifter death.

Nita Clifton would pray in the opposite direction—for her husband to live—rejecting reality even as she accepted it. She would castigate herself for her selfishness.

They would not struggle in isolation. Art was receiving hospice care; the services of Midwest Palliative & Hospice CareCenter included regular visits by chaplain Kathleen Foy.

She would be his spiritual companion, a kind of guide into death, a modern echo of the Greek myth that saw Charon ferrying souls into the underworld over the River Styx. But in a larger sense, Art himself would be the guide, leading the way to a death on which he was the only expert.

To the extent that many people think about death, it is often in hopes of experiencing a good one—a death free of pain, eased by acceptance of the inevitable and a deliberate leave-taking of family and friends.

But every death is unique, Foy said. She did not subscribe to the notion of an ideal one.

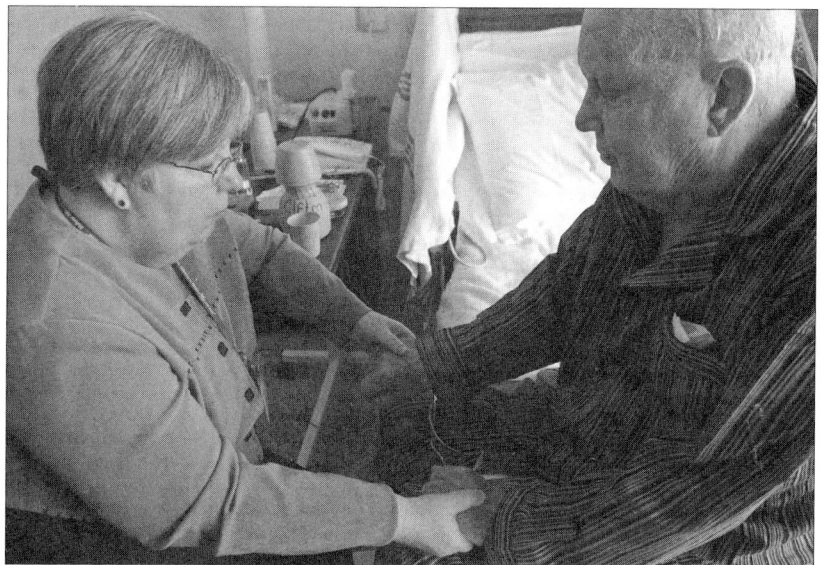

Kathleen Foy, a chaplain with Midwest Palliative & Hospice CareCenter, prays with Art Clifton in the Classic Residence by Hyatt nursing facility in Glenview. (Photograph courtesy of David Trotman-Wilkins/*Chicago Tribune*)

"There's no such thing," she said. "The death you have is the death you have."

This is the death Art Clifton had.

A Wife's Dread

When Foy prayed for God to bring whatever was best for Art, Nita prayed along with her.

But she didn't really mean it, not if what was best meant his dying.

Slight and soft-voiced, with the delicate presence of a fawn, Nita—no one calls her Juanita—sat with Foy in her living room.

Her hair was white; her demeanor fragile. Art had always taken care of everything.

Nita, then 80, didn't think she could manage without him. "Don't you die before me," she had told him, more than once.

Their apartment was in the independent-living building of the Classic Residence complex, the kind of place where people who have lived well can retire well. The dining rooms were chandeliered. The parking was valet.

Nita's color scheme was white and pink. Her husband's retirement from Washington National Insurance Co., where he was executive vice president and a member of the board of directors, had been her invitation to redecorate.

She had let her inner girl fly; there were pink roses on the sofa, red and blue flowers on the pink ceramic lamps and pink sconces on the wall with little floral lampshades.

She had thought hard about the flowers.

"I thought, 'Cripes, what if I die before he does?' " she said, a hint of her native West Virginia playing about the words.

For a time, the sequence had been in doubt. Art was dying slowly, but Nita was hit by several swift crises—gastrointestinal surgery, then while recovering, a near-fatal heart attack.

She had rebounded from that as well, though she had been hospitalized several times for dehydration and continued to battle intestinal woes.

Still, it was fairly clear who would be going first. She would not be leaving her husband marooned in flowered fabric.

The prospect of his dying was appalling, devastating. "I don't want him to go," Nita told Foy.

Nita's eyes reddened and filled; she cried.

Behind her delicate appearance, she was raging. "I just won't accept the end. I just won't accept it," she said. "I won't admit he's leaving me."

She didn't know who she was anymore, she said; neither a wife nor a widow, but in some strange limbo.

The memories, though, were so fine. A smile rising on her lips, she padded through the apartment, showing Foy the mementos—the retirement plaque, the needlework, the photographs.

From a frame in her bedroom, young Art grinned, his hair wavy and his World War II infantry uniform pressed. "He was so handsome," Nita sighed, still smitten.

They met just after the war. Art, born in Fair Oaks, Ind., was a fledgling insurance salesman in Washington. Nita was a medical secretary with an apartment in the same complex as his.

One day he spotted her and a girlfriend leaving a restaurant, hurried into his car and offered them a ride home. Maybe Nita rushed for the middle seat and maybe she didn't, but their life together began. They married, he rose at Washington National and after being transferred to several different cities, he was promoted to the home office, then in Evanston.

They raised their sons in a Wilmette house Nita loved so much she had an artist paint it in watercolor. After Art retired in 1987, they bought a condo in Naples, Fla., where they spent winters. He played golf. They watched sunsets over the Gulf of Mexico, sipping glasses of wine.

But illness came calling on the good life. Art's emphysema was worsening and Nita's run of medical problems began. They sold their Wilmette house in 2001 and moved into the Classic Residence. The next year, with Art too ill to go to Florida, they sold the condo, too.

Art got pneumonia 11 times. After his last bout, he entered the nursing home at the complex. His ravaged lungs could no longer put enough oxygen into his bloodstream.

When he began hospice care, he had been virtually bedridden for five months. Once he had traveled frequently to New York on business; now he could barely shuffle a few feet to the washroom.

Nita was agonizing over a decision she could not make. A friend had told her that before her own husband died, she reassured him that she would be OK after he was gone. It was the hardest thing she had ever done, the friend told Nita, but it seemed to ease her husband's mind.

Nita couldn't do it. Wouldn't that be like encouraging him to die? Or implying that she wouldn't mind if he did? Besides, she wasn't sure it was true; she didn't think she really would be OK.

"He's always taken care of me," she told Foy, the injustice of it nearly palpable. "He ought to be here, holding my hand."

A stalwart at Trinity United Methodist Church like her husband, Nita had been searching for comfort in prayer. But prayer itself had become the nexus of her inner conflict.

She knew her husband was praying to die. But Nita, in the twilight of a harmonious marriage, was praying that her husband not get his wish.

"I feel really guilty sometimes," she said. "He wants to die, and I want him to live. Who is God going to listen to?"

Spiritual Checklist

Foy sat in her car in the parking lot outside the Glenview nursing center, looking through paperwork on the patients she would visit that day.

She was watchful and calm, with a way of filling a hard silence with a soft murmur.

Her black Prius was her mobile ministry office. She drove from the west suburban home she shared with her husband and college-student son to the hospice's office. From there, the car's global-positioning system guided her to patients' homes. The cargo area held her plastic bottles of holy water and anointing oil, a Bible and a pyx, the small round case that holds communion wafers.

Her mobility reflected the nature of her work. Hospice is not a facility, although Glenview-based Midwest Palliative & Hospice CareCenter has an inpatient unit in Skokie. It is an array of services for people at the end of life. Most hospice patients live at home or in a nursing home.

On this morning, shortly after last Thanksgiving, she put away her papers, got out of the car and walked up the wide drive to the entrance of the nursing center. The hallway to Art's ground-floor room was tasteful and serene. A little past it there was a large dining room with expansive windows and china place settings. In his yearlong stay at the nursing home, Art rarely had the strength to make it there.

Foy knocked on the door to Art's room. "Mr. Clifton? It's Kathi, the hospice chaplain," she said.

He was sitting on the edge of the bed, his feet hanging down. His head was round and smooth, his eyes bright and mildly impish. A handkerchief was folded neatly in his pajama pocket. The skin on his shins was mottled; there was so little oxygen in his body that blood was being shunted away from his extremities and toward his vital organs.

Foy chitchatted. Had he eaten lunch yet? Had he been sleeping a lot lately?

It wasn't idle conversation. Foy was building their relationship and also discreetly gauging Art's condition. Sleep is a clue; the more a disease saps a patient's energy and organ function, the more the patient sleeps.

She had dealt with bigger questions on her first visit. Matters of faith and God are vast and profound, but Foy had a down-to-earth tool to establish a patient's beliefs: a spiritual-assessment form. Many hospices use such forms to help chart patients' needs.

The form used by Foy and her colleagues seeks to bring the ineffable down to the specific. There are boxes to be checked off. Does the patient have eternal life beliefs? A sense of peace? Feelings of guilt or loss? Unfinished business? Loss of faith?

The idea, she said, is to see how patients make sense of their lives, the world and whatever may lie beyond it.

At 53, Foy had come to hospice work after her own journey. Raised Roman Catholic, she found herself moving away from a faith centered on scriptures and a concept of God in which she did not literally believe.

Her new spiritual home was in Ethical Culture. Founded in the late 19th Century by Felix Adler, Ethical Culture is a humanistic religious fellowship of people who believe that the highest purpose of life is to create a better society and that the source of ethics is not God, but the human condition.

Foy became an Ethical Culture leader, as the movement's clergy are called, and then a chaplain. Some of her Ethical Culture colleagues have asked how she can in good conscience pray with patients to a God in whom she does not believe. But she sees no conflict. Her agnosticism does not dismiss divine possibilities.

"For me, God is a concept that helps people find meaning out of life, to try to make sense out of the world and our place in it," she said. God is "that essential place you reach when you just don't know.... My leap of faith is mostly into acknowledging that I am comfortable with not knowing."

She saw her chaplain's role as traveling with patients wherever they led her. Some people wanted to pray; some wanted to talk; some were comatose, in which case she simply sat, offering her prayerful presence.

There were those who accepted their approaching death, and those who fiercely rejected it. One young woman vowed to beat cancer, right up to the day she died of it.

"She died in denial," Foy said. But she taught Foy a lesson. Denial was a choice, and a chaplain had to respect it.

Art was looking straight at his death and not blinking. He figured it was up to God.

"I'm willing for him to take me any time he wants to take me," he once told Foy. "I only hope he doesn't wait too long."

Foy's spiritual assessment was that Art was ending his life comforted by significant strengths.

He had accepted that he was going to die soon. He had a sense of his life's meaning and purpose. He had close ties to his church in Wilmette, where he had once served as treasurer; the pastor visited him regularly.

The spiritual-assessment form, though, only hinted at the richness of his life. He and Nita thrilled to their sons' successes. Richard Clifton, 55, is a federal appeals court judge who lives with his wife, son and daughter in Hawaii. Kevin Clifton, 49, is a partner in a commercial real estate firm. He and his wife have raised their three sons—the older two are in college—in Winnetka, where proximity gave the boys a particularly close relationship with their grandparents.

Art adored his grandchildren and was deeply devoted to Nita. They shared a ritual at each parting: "Love you," one of them would say. "Love you best," the other would reply.

His business life had brought accomplishment and pride. He had been "a 100 percent straight shooter" at Washington National, said his closest friend, Kendall Carver, 69, also a longtime executive there. Art spoke frankly at work even when it was impolitic to do so, Carver said, and would not tailor his views to make them more acceptable: "Art wasn't that kind of guy."

He was the kind of guy who called an ailing colleague every day to ask how he was.

He was the kind of guy who did not mention that he was wounded by shrapnel twice while serving in the infantry in Europe during World War II and was awarded the Purple Heart with Oak Leaf Cluster. He did not speak of the time in France when he rescued wounded members of his platoon from an enemy minefield, or the resulting Bronze Star.

For all his strengths, he was not immune to despair. He found waiting to die agonizing. He told a startled friend who was visiting that if he had a gun, he would shoot himself. He was taking antidepressants.

He was not afraid of death, he had told Foy at one of their meetings. He had grown up believing in heaven, although youthful certainty had yielded to some adult skepticism.

As his life waned, however, he found himself wondering if his belief "was as strong as I originally thought it would be."

He would find out the truth, he figured, when he died.

"If there's something after, I'll know about it," he said.

God's Silence

A lifelong churchgoer, Art still wasn't a man for a lot of God-talk. God was a given, a presence, a fundamental fact of his eight-decade life.

Until the facts seemed to shift beneath his feet.

One day Foy encountered Art in uncharacteristic anguish. He told her, she recalls, that waiting for death was unbearable. He had sinned in his life, and God must be punishing him. He was in tears.

While the details of their conversation would remain private, Foy later characterized it not as a confession to a particular sin, but a universally human look back on life with some regret.

They talked about how to ask God for forgiveness. Art was so exhausted that Foy pushed no further. She urged him to get some rest.

She returned the next day, and pulled a chair close to his bed.

"I know yesterday was a rough day for you," she said.

"The last few days," he said quietly.

He was lying in bed, one hand behind his head. He was thinking about God.

"Sometimes I wonder if he's still there," Art said.

He stared at the ceiling.

"I'm there, but where is he?"

The oxygen machine hummed. A life's faith wavered.

"Have you asked him?" Foy said softly.

"I tried to," Art said, still staring up. "I didn't hear him."

"It's a rough, rough place to be," Foy said.

"I know," Art said. "And I've been here a long time. Bobbin' up and down like a bobber."

Foy looked at him, adrift. Then she carefully waded in.

"When you felt him there before, how did you know he was there?" she said.

"Well, that's what I'm wondering," Art said. "I wish I knew."

"It's hard to remember how that felt," Foy said. "It's like, 'Was that real, or was that a fantasy?' That's a hard place to be."

"Nowhere," Art said.

The painful assessment hung in the air.

"When you think about your children, what's that like?" Foy asked.

Art beamed.

"I love them very much," Art said. "When they were little tykes, they were just so loving. And my grandchildren—they were there all the time."

"Was God around those times, when you think of those memories?"

"Oh, yeah," Art said. "We fixed up a bedroom into . . . our make-believe room. We pretended we had canoes and go up and down the sides of the beds. We'd get umbrellas, open them up and jump off the bed like a parachute."

He had conquered the bitter present with the sweet past. Back then, he was not a bedridden patient, but Papaw, the adored grandfather who eagerly took to the floor to play with his grandchildren. He was strong, Nita was healthy and everything felt happy and alive.

Foy asked if Art could try to recreate those moments in his mind, searching for God by summoning times when his presence had been so strong.

"I wish you could, but you can't," he said. "You can't just tap into any moment."

Foy offered him a cup of water. He took it, his hand shaking.

He forced himself back into good humor when Nita peered into the room.

The hospice offered bereavement services, Foy told the Cliftons. "After your death," she said to Art, "we will be following Nita for a year."

It was a matter-of-fact acknowledgement that did not faze Art. Lest it hurt Nita, he protectively batted it away with a quip.

"Well, if you're going to be following me, I hope I'm going up that way," he joked, nodding upwards.

Nita was not laughing.

"I don't know what we're talking about," she said. "Idle chatter."

"Do you have any questions?" Foy asked her. "It's not an easy subject; it's not an easy time."

Nita hesitated. "I guess I don't know the kind of thing you're supposed to talk about," she said.

Foy turned back to Art with a discreet acknowledgement of their earlier conversation.

These were hard times, she said: "Nobody's planned this; nobody asked for it."

"And we don't get too many answers," Art said.

War Stories

Kevin Clifton leaned over from his considerable height to kiss his father. He sat on the window ledge, squeezing into the space between the bed and window.

It was a sunny day, but the blinds were drawn. The room overlooked a patch of grass, a thin tree and a wall. Nita, sitting on a wing chair in the corner, had wanted Art to transfer to a room with a better view, but he was not interested. The time for him to care about views had passed.

Kevin goaded his father to talk about the war. "Didn't the shrapnel hit your Bible?" he prompted.

"Yes; I was carrying a Bible in my shirt pocket and it hit the pocket," Art said. "It was just luck."

"The Bible kind of helped, though," Nita said dryly.

Art had told his sons a few things about the war. He and one of his best friends had been smoking cigarettes when shots rang out. His friend had been shot in the head and killed.

"They were this close," Kevin said outside his father's room, gesturing to his side. The experience, Kevin thought, had helped make his father grateful for life and shaped his thoughts about death: It could come at any time.

Kevin had been measuring his father's decline by his shrinking interest in the things he had always loved. An Indiana University alumnus, Art stopped caring about basketball games. Even news of an upcoming visit by his grandchildren didn't always rally him.

Art's older son, Richard, was visiting every few weeks—a remarkable schedule considering that he was flying in every time from Hawaii.

The sons knew their father was hoping to die.

"The hardest struggle for me is wishing for something different," Kevin said. "I want to be able to call him tomorrow."

In the Wilderness

Something strange often happened to Foy when she was around death or felt an intense connection with a patient at the end of life: The top of her head would start to tingle and itch.

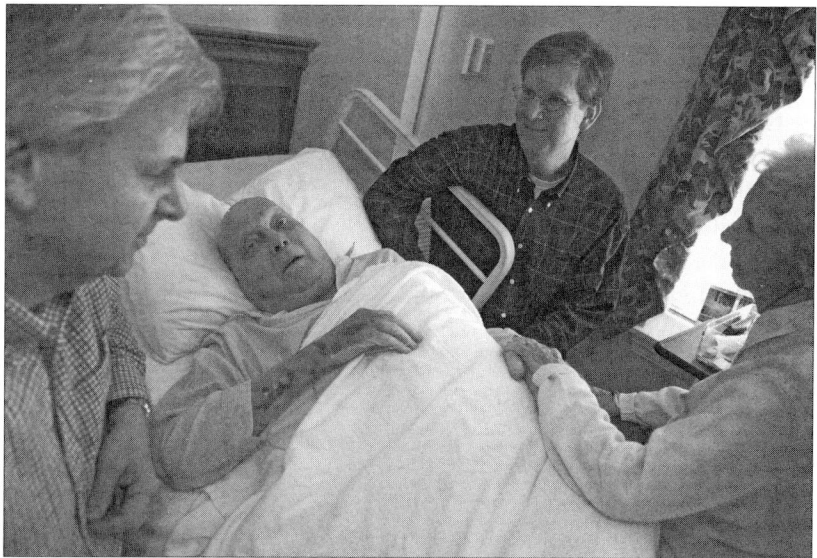

Art Clifton's wife, Nita, and sons Richard (left) and Kevin visit him in his nursing-home room at a Glenview retirement complex. Art accepts that he is dying, but his family is struggling to let go. (Photograph courtesy of Zbigniew Bzdak/*Chicago Tribune*)

"I call it my crown chakra," she said, the center of energy at the top of her head reacting to something spiritually electric.

Art was coming ever closer to the end of his life. He still ate his meals, but did little else. He had stopped reading the newspapers that he once devoured daily from front to back. He no longer read books, though he had previously finished as many as five a week. He was too weak now to hold them up.

Sometimes he was too tired to talk with Foy. But one day she arrived to find him strong enough to confront pain.

He wasn't sure he was doing what God wanted of him, he told her. He wasn't sure what God did want of him. And how could he serve God if he wasn't strong enough to help his wife?

"When you don't feel that you're helping God, you try to proceed and help your fellow man," he said. "But when you get to the point where you don't feel you're helping them, you feel lost."

The clock, his tormenting reminder of the slow crawl of time, ticked.

"You're in unfamiliar territory, aren't you, Art?" Foy said gently.

"Yes," he said. "Still not certain who I am or should be."

He coughed wetly.

"You don't have the energy you had," she said. "And your role is changing. It's like, 'Who is Art now?'"

Art was quiet for a moment.

"To tell you the truth, right now I'm just a little bit lost," he said.

But in Foy's eyes, he was also deeply courageous.

Outside his room, in a quiet corner of the nursing home, she paid tribute.

"He's going out to the absolute edge of not knowing anything," she said. "It's like, 'Who am I now as I'm dying?' . . . He was really crying out in the wilderness."

And the veteran chaplain, professional companion to the dying, cried.

Foy would offer support, but not false comfort. "This is his only death," she said. "You don't jolly him out of it and say, 'Everything's going to be OK.' You say, 'I'm going to go there with you, as much as I can.' "

Before she left his room that day, Foy stood next to Art's bed to pray with him. She looked directly into his eyes; he looked back, just as directly.

Foy's head was tingling.

They grasped hands and bent their heads.

"Even though it's unfamiliar territory and there's none of us who can say how you feel and it's hard for you to say some things, God is with you," Foy said. "He may look different from the God you knew before; it may be changing.

"My prayer is that you have everything you need and that you have no fear and that it's peaceful, even if it's unfamiliar territory. And we call upon the words Jesus taught us: 'Our Father Who art in Heaven . . .' "

Art Clifton joined in, praying to the Father whose presence he no longer sensed, in the heaven he was not certain existed.

17. Facing the End, with Faith

NOV. 20, 2006

By Barbara Brotman

Arthur Clifton was slipping away.

The emphysema that had choked off his life was now poised to end it. One morning last April, his blood pressure plummeted. His breathing turned labored. A hospice nurse advised his wife, Nita, to call their sons.

The nurse told Nita that Art was close to death, but Nita didn't believe it. And to see him that afternoon, neither would most people.

He was a man transformed.

He was wide awake, completely lucid and eager to talk about God, sports and anything else. He was sharp, he was reflective, he was joking, he was serious.

Nita was dumbfounded. But those in hospice care see the phenomenon too often to be surprised.

Just before death, people sometimes rally to a degree that families can mistake for a recovery. A patient who had seemed nearly comatose may sit up in bed, ask for food or hold complex conversations.

In hospice, they call it the "power surge."

It is one of the signposts of dying that are clear to those familiar with the process, and astonishing to those who are not.

Another sign had come four days earlier, when Kathleen Foy, Art's hospice chaplain, arrived for her regular visit. Art had been confused that morning, a nurse told her, and he had said something odd:

My car is waiting.

With that, Foy knew.

It was no random expression of befuddlement to her ear, but a harbinger. When patients start talking about taking a trip, packing their bags or some mode of transportation, she had found, they were close to dying.

When she entered Art's room, the evidence mounted. Art, 81, was agitated and seemed unaware of his surroundings. His schedule was too full for them to talk, he told her. "The time is bad," he said briskly. "I have a lot going on today."

It was a businessman's approach to his final meeting, she thought, in which the language of his life became symbols for his death.

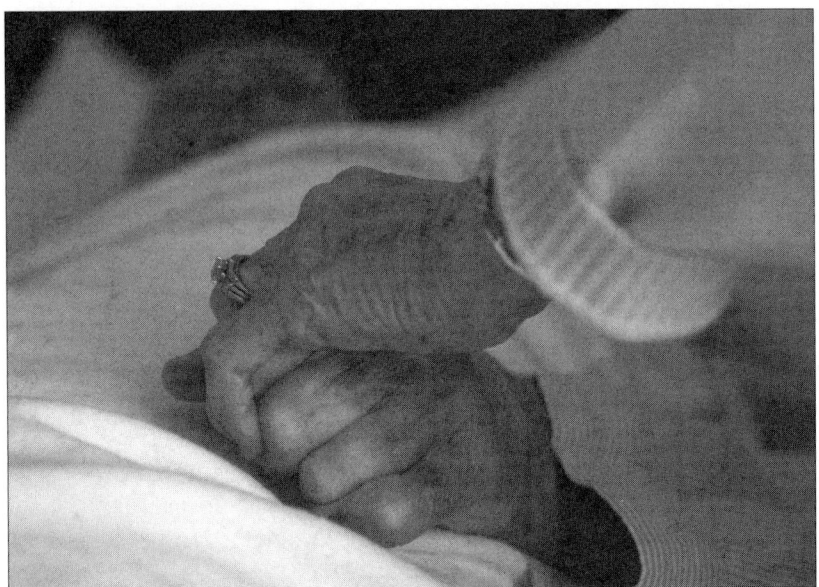

Nita Clifton holds the hand of her husband, Arthur, who was dying of emphysema in a Glenview nursing home. His decline was a test of faith. (Photograph courtesy of Zbigniew Bzdak/*Chicago Tribune*)

"People die the way they live, only more so," said Foy, who worked for Midwest Palliative & Hospice CareCenter. "He lived by the schedule; now he was scheduling himself for death, in a metaphorical way."

Art, a retired insurance executive from Wilmette, had been in hospice care for six months, dying by degrees in the nursing center of the Classic Residence by Hyatt, the Glenview retirement community where he and Nita, 80, lived.

He had struggled with his faith; he had faced his doubts. He had told his friends and family he was ready to die. He despaired that it was taking so long, as he was reminded by every glance at the large clock on the wall, ticking off the passage of time.

That particular anguish, Foy suspected, would end. "There will be a time when he looks at the clock and doesn't know it's a clock," she said.

Now Art would say—and receive—final goodbyes. Now his thoughts about spirituality would become his last. Now would come his last chance to say anything that needed saying.

Dr. Ira Byock in his influential book, "Dying Well: Peace and Possibilities at the End of Life," suggested that people find some way to tell their loved ones five things before they die:

I forgive you. Forgive me. Thank you. I love you. Goodbye.

Last Soliloquy

Science has yet to explain the power surge at the end of life. It could be the result of hormones and adrenaline released by the body, but no one knows whether it is the body's reaction, the mind's or both.

Whatever the cause, the effect on Art was striking.

He was lying in bed, as always. Purple blotches bloomed on his hands, a common marker of impending death.

For months, steroids and morphine had spared him the agonies of emphysema.

Now even that wasn't enough; he was struggling to breathe.

But he was alert, aware of his precarious condition and eager to talk. And for one remarkable hour, with Nita by his side, he did. He wasn't feeling too well, he conceded.

"If I want to go to the men's room, they said I should take one of the nurses with me because I'm losing my balance a bit," he said.

"See, things aren't always as pleasant as we would like," he added, his eyes steady and intent. "You make plans, but you don't know how they're going to turn out."

But he knew now.

"Right now I'm on the loser side," he said. "But I'm still waiting for the Lord to do what he's going to do."

Nita looked at her husband.

"Are you comfortable with that, waiting for the Lord to do what he's going to do?"

"Yes, I am," he said firmly. "Anytime he wants, he can take me, and the sooner he takes me the better it will be. I've done what I can for other people. I've served the life I wanted."

Nita stroked his hand. "You mean you don't want me to keep talking to the Lord?" she said, her voice teasing but her intent serious.

"I don't know what you're saying," Art said. "You can keep talking to him."

"I've been giving him a different message," Nita confessed.

"What message have you been giving him?" Art asked.

"Oh, about being with you," she murmured. "Being selfish."

While Art had been praying to die, his wife had been praying for him to live.

Art understood.

"No, that's OK," he told her.

I forgive you.

"I'd be with you if I could be helpful," he said. "But if there isn't anything you can do for other people, that is just a mere existence. I know it's hard to say, but that's how I feel."

He told Nita he was ready to join the soldiers who died by his side in World War II. "Everything is in fairly proper order...." he said. "I would be happy to go with them down that path."

And the spiritual pain that had sometimes darkened his last months? Did he still feel abandoned by God?

In a sense, he did.

"For some reason, he's not talking to me right now," Art said.

But it was a simple acknowledgment, not a lonely cry. He had circled back to the pragmatism with which he had begun.

"I have faith; I've had faith all my life. But whether my belief is completely and 100 percent true, I can't know," he said. "When I go, if I see Jesus Christ our Lord and Savior, I will know the Book is correct. If not, the Book is incorrect."

"But you don't believe that," Nita said, half statement and half question.

"I believe," Art said.

"You believe in the hereafter?" she pressed.

"I do," he said, and his voice now expressed no doubt. "I'll be there."

"I'll be there too," she said.

"I'll be waiting," he said.

And yet he was not taking entry to heaven for granted. In his last opportunity to look back, he did so soberly, even regretfully.

"Maybe in my life I was not good enough," he said to Nita.

"Oh, you were," she assured him. "You were always a good guy."

"Oh, I've been bad, many times," he said.

Forgive me.

It was Nita's turn to deflect pain with a joke.

"I didn't know you then," she said, fliply.

"No—what's your name?" Art said, equally flip.

They both laughed.

Then they turned serious.

Nita, who had tried so hard to avoid the reality coming at her, addressed it head-on.

"You've been a wonderful husband, father, grandpa," she told Art. "Can't get any better than that."

Art knew how uncertainly he was perched. Twice that day, he said, he had thought death was moments away. The first time, he had felt so ill that he wanted to die.

But the second time, he had felt strong and almost euphoric.

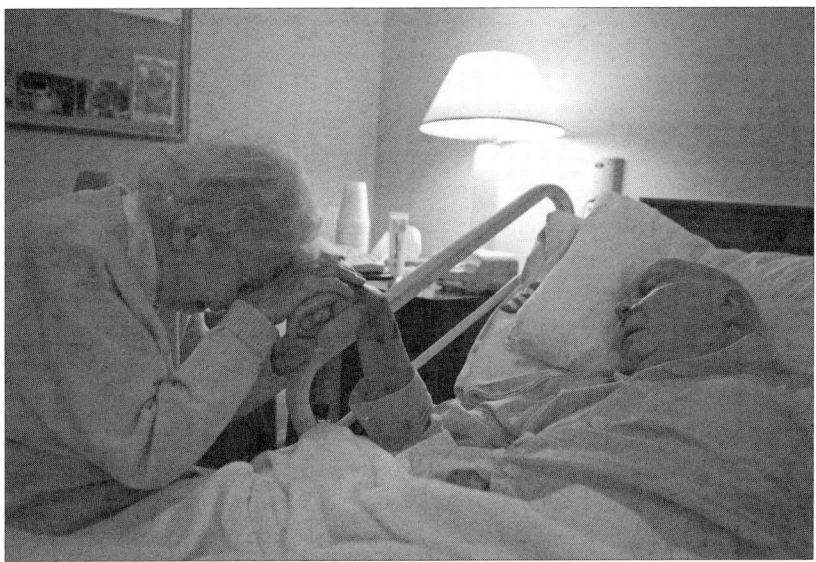

Nita Clifton is overwhelmed by grief as she watches her husband, Art, slip away. "You've been a wonderful husband, father, grandpa," she told her husband just days before he died in April. (Photograph courtesy of Terrence Antonio James/*Chicago Tribune*)

"That's right now," he said. And then the man who for so long had been praying to die said: "I wish I could go on for years."

Suddenly, it was on to the Cubs. "I've been a Cub fan since 1934," he remarked as Nita balanced a stuffed Cubby bear on his chest. "But I don't pray for the Cubs to win. That's not a prayable object for me."

Still, he was happy when the White Sox won the World Series.

"Why root against my sport's enemies? When I can't win, I still root for them," he said. "People say they never root for the Yankees, but they're out there, trying their best."

Nita was goggle-eyed.

"You haven't talked this much for a month," she said.

Art knew. And he knew more.

"Being this spirited, I still may not live through the night," he said, with a laugh. "But I would not object; really, I would not. I think it would be nice not to go out on a sour note, but to go out on a good one."

It was a breathtaking final act, a blazing last soliloquy. In swift succession, he expressed his gratitude for his family, his love for his children and grandchildren, his delight in the world of people and his sadness at how much he would miss that world when he was gone.

Thank you. I love you. Goodbye.

Then he stopped talking.

"I think I'm finished," he said.

And he was.

Heart's Resilience

Two days later, he was barely responsive.

His eyes were unfocused. His body was twitching with an involuntary jerking movement called myoclonus. When he spoke, it was an incomprehensible mumble.

His body was closing down.

"Think of it like a domino effect," said Dr. Jason Sobel, Art's hospice doctor and the CareCenter's associate medical director. "The lungs have the job of getting oxygen into blood circulation and taking away carbon dioxide. When the lungs decline, you lose the ability to give nutrients to the organs."

Art's kidneys were starting to fail. Morphine had been helping him breathe; the drug eases the sensation of breathlessness and lowers the respiratory rate by reducing pain and anxiety.

But now that Art's kidneys were no longer able to process it, the morphine was building up in his body, possibly contributing to the twitching.

The rest of his organs also were shutting down; he would soon be in a coma. The brain, a particularly voracious consumer of oxygen, was being starved. The last to go, Sobel said, was usually the heart.

"The heart is an organ of incredible resilience," he said.

Art's spiritual grappling was over, at least on a conscious level.

He had faced painful doubts and lonely moments. And though the questions he had asked were personal, they also were universal.

His yearning for God reflected millennia of similar human hopes. His wondering why God was making him suffer had echoes reaching back to Job. His concern about the afterlife has been shared by every civilization throughout history.

His acknowledgment that he had sinned in his life reflected a central doctrine of Christianity and Art's spiritual maturity, said his pastor, Rev. Kirk Reed of Trinity United Methodist Church.

"If you are a human being, I would hope that you would be humble enough to realize that all have sinned before God," he said.

And his doubt? It is an inextricable element of most people's spiritual lives.

Art's doubts and suffering spoke to his courage and honesty, Reed said. "If you don't go through some of that," he said, "you've probably got some pseudo, shallow faith that has never been tested."

Art's testing was over; the worst for his family was about to begin.

Journey Completed

Kevin Clifton thought he was prepared. Still, as he sat in a chair next to his father's bed, he was shaken.

Art's power surge had come on a Friday, and he had been lucid Saturday night. When Nita had said the traditional, "Love you" upon leaving for the night, he had replied with the ritual, "Love you best."

Now, on Sunday, Art's eyes fell on the wall where the clock—his nemesis—hung.

He did not seem to know what a clock was.

He pulled at his oxygen tube. He reached his hand into the air. Kevin took it.

Nita sat on the bed. Art thrashed; his arms pulled at his bedclothes. It was agony to watch. Sobel prescribed anti-anxiety medicine, more for the family's benefit than Art's. He didn't think Art was suffering, but he knew Nita was.

Nita, who had worried she was not strong enough to manage without her husband, found it in herself to hold him firmly in her arms as he flailed at the air.

"I love you," she said softly. "I wish I knew what you were trying to tell me."

She leaned her elbow against the bedrail and cried.

Brenda Kitchka, a chaplain from the hospice, arrived.

Kathleen Foy, Art's spiritual companion through his months-long journey toward death, was out of town visiting family.

She had suspected that Art was near the end and had wanted to be there, but professional guidelines discourage hospice workers from rearranging their personal lives in case a patient dies. If a chaplain insisted on being present for every patient's death, she would neither rest nor sleep. The Clifton family understood.

Kitchka sat next to Nita, took her hand and told her she shouldn't be afraid to leave out of fear that Art would die alone.

"Sometimes they wait until you leave, and then they die. They consider that their gift to you," Kitchka said. "So if you leave some time and it should happen, it's nothing you should feel guilty about; it's something he intended."

Nita nodded.

"Hi, Mr. Clifton," Kitchka said.

He mumbled what could have been a reply.

"You hanging in? It's hard work, isn't it?" she said.

"This is one of the hardest things you are ever going to have to do," she said to Nita. "But you are not alone."

Nita wept. "I feel so empty without him," she said.

Kitchka turned again to Art.

"It's OK, Mr. Clifton," she said. "You are safe. . . . And you are dearly loved. We are going to take good care of you. And we are going to sit here and share this journey with you for however long it takes."

Arthur Clifton died shortly after 9:30 p.m. the next day, April 24, drawing his last breath in the presence of two nurse's aides who had come in to make sure his feet were covered.

Kevin Clifton and Nita had left for the night just five minutes earlier.

Parting Words

Nita Clifton sat in the front row of Trinity United Methodist Church, an elegant stone Gothic building in Wilmette, not far from the lake. Her eyes were red-rimmed, but she smiled gamely at a church full of well-dressed friends, Art's legacy of a lifetime.

The family had just buried his ashes in the church's memorial garden, and Nita was numb. Behind eight huge vases of brilliant flowers, Rev. Reed spoke of Art's graciousness and modesty.

"He never told me about his combat medals; instead he told me about trying to enlist in [an Army Air Corps training program] and getting rejected because in his right eye he couldn't tell the difference between green and red," Reed said. "He never talked about how cool he was; he talked about how thankful he was that Nita loved him."

As for Art's despair as he approached death, Reed quoted Rabbi Harold Kushner, pointing out that the 23rd Psalm speaks of going through the valley of the shadow of death, not around it. Only by going through the painful valley of grief at his death, Reed said, could Art emerge from the other side.

"Yes, he did struggle with his faith at times, as all of us do at times if we're honest. I'm grateful to his hospice chaplain, Kathi Foy," he said, nodding to her.

From her seat in a pew, Foy, who had learned of Art's death upon her return from vacation, smiled back.

"But through it all, his faith was strong when it mattered," Reed said.

Art's sons offered eulogies. Kevin's, in the form of a letter to his father, honored his upbeat disposition, his eagerness to help others, his defense of the chair-throwing Bobby Knight on the grounds that the basketball coach was "just having a bad day."

"The characteristic I treasure you most for is your unconditional love," Kevin said. "I am comforted by your faith in the Lord. . . . I will see you soon in heaven. Rest easy, and we will take care of Mom."

Richard Clifton spoke of his father's good cheer despite his awareness of the dark sides of life, the fatherly guidance that never strayed into control and the way he valued fairness, hard work and humility.

"He was an amazing person," he said. ". . . I've lost so much because he gave me so much."

The final hymn was "The Old Rugged Cross," Art's favorite from his Baptist youth. The stone church rang with the organ and voices:

To the old rugged cross I will ever be true/Its shame and reproach gladly bear/Then He'll call me some day to my home far away/Where His glory forever I'll share.

Final Chapter

Nita took her husband's pillow home from the nursing home and put it in her bed. It smelled like him.

At first, she talked to his picture on the wall. She told him what she was going to do that day and who had asked about him. She upbraided him for leaving her. She dreamed about him, so vividly that she would wake up and stare at the ceiling, waiting for him.

She was hospitalized several times, for dehydration and a brain hemorrhage after a fall.

But she recovered. And as time passed, she found herself talking to her husband a little less. She stopped telling him she was angry that he had left her; he deserved, she thought, to rest in peace. He had taken care of her, to the very end. "He even waited until we left to die," said Nita, now 81.

Art had been in good spirits at the end. The antidepressants he was taking, Sobel said, had helped him return to the customary cheeriness that had earned him the childhood nickname Smiley. The drugs had not cut short his spiritual questioning, the doctor said; on the contrary, they had enabled him to pursue it.

"When people feel a sense of despair, they can't communicate with anybody, even themselves," he said. "I think helping the depression helped him to communicate with God."

Shortly after Art died, hospice chaplain Kathleen Foy moved to Albuquerque to be near her daughter and sister, taking a job as bereavement coordinator with a hospice there.

She regretted that circumstances had kept her from being with Art when he died; she felt a certain lack of closure herself. Their conversations remained on her mind.

"In some ways, I was amazed he went so far," she said. "There's a lot of stuff at the end of life that can be very scary for people. It can rattle some people. But it's also very freeing and energizing."

He had died without certainty, but he hadn't needed it.

"That is the essence of the 'leap of faith' that believers take," Foy said. "Art was a man of faith, and doubt was an ingredient of his faith."

Arthur Clifton died looking back on his life with gratitude, and forward with acceptance.

He had arranged for Nita's ease and security. He had accepted Foy's invitation to confront hard questions. He had asked forgiveness; he had expressed love; he had said goodbye.

He had said he would find out the truth about his beliefs when he died.

His waiting was over.

HOW THIS SERIES WAS REPORTED

Tribune staff reporter Barbara Brotman spent five months following Arthur Clifton at the end of his life and documenting his conversations with hospice chaplain Kathleen Foy. Clifton allowed his experience to be described in hopes that doing so might help others. All direct quotes were from conversations heard by Brotman; extended scenes described in the story were witnessed by her. In addition to observing Clifton's conversations with his family and Foy, Brotman interviewed numerous other people for this series, from Clifton's pastor and friends to experts on hospice care and dying.

A conversation with
Barbara Brotman

This edited e-mail interview was conducted by Poynter Institute Distinguished Fellow Butch Ward with Barbara Brotman, winner of ASNE's Distinguished Writing Award for Nondeadline Writing.

BUTCH WARD: Where did the idea for "The Final Journey of Arthur Clifton" come from?

BARBARA BROTMAN: When I returned from a Knight Fellowship at Stanford where my study proposal was about religion, I joined the Projects Team with the idea of doing in-depth stories about religion. The *Tribune* had been doing a yearlong project on the future of Islam, and I did one part of that. Then I did a story on a college seminary, and how men were trying to decide whether to become Catholic priests. So I was chipping away at the subject of how people think about God. But that subject was unworkable—just too broad. I had to narrow the idea.

I realized that the conversations I was having with experts were too academic. They might be interesting to me, but they weren't going to engage readers. It needed to be a story. How could I write about when people think about God? When does it matter the most? What are those pivotal moments in their lives?

I concluded that the most pivotal was when they were facing death.

How did you convince an editor to let you pursue this story?

My role on the Projects Team was specifically to examine this subject. Projects Editor George Papajohn encouraged me to try to find a way to write about how people think about God. I kept talking to him as I was reporting, and we kept working on finding a focus.

Where and how did you collect the information?

First I interviewed experts on the sociology of religion. Then, when I focused on the end of life, I talked to a number of hospices and hospice chaplains. I began accompanying hospice chaplains as they visited patients. The hospices required me to get written permission from the patient, or the family, but a number of people gave that permission. I visited a number of families several times. But as I got to know the Cliftons, I decided to focus on them.

Why? How did you decide what the focus would be?

I changed the focus several times, with George Papajohn's guidance. At one point it was going to be about a chaplain and her visits with various people in different circumstances; then it was going to be about this particular chaplain and her visits with Art Clifton.

Finally, George felt that Art and Nita had such a compelling way of grappling with Art's impending death that the focus should be on them, and that the chaplain should be more peripheral.

Art Clifton had thought about his faith; he talked about it openly; he was completely lucid; and his faith was of a moderate and pragmatic nature that I thought would resonate with many readers. He agreed to participate because the chaplain told him the story could help people face the end of life. He said he wasn't sure how, but if so, he was happy to help.

To this day, I look back and think how scary it is how lucky I was. My visits to other patients did not yield such rich material. If Art Clifton's story had not worked out, I had no equally compelling alternative. I could have ended up with a story that was very different. My editor says it was more than luck—I chose to follow Art. But it was extraordinary luck to encounter him in the first place.

You received remarkable access to the Cliftons. Did you have to make any agreements?

No. The hospice required that I get written permission from the patient or family. Their release form asked for signatures agreeing that a reporter could be in the room, that the patient agreed to be a subject of a newspaper story and that the patient agreed to have photographs taken that would be published. At first, a hospice communications staffer was present during my visits. But in time, the hospice felt comfortable with my going alone with the chaplain.

Did you re-create any of the scenes in your story?

I witnessed and was present for all of them. I was not there at the moment of death. But I had been in the room a day earlier when Art was declining into a coma. The family told me that when they had left Art for the night, they had asked the nurses' aides to make sure his feet were covered. He died in the aides' presence, five minutes after his wife and son had gone.

What about the dialogue involving Art and his faith?

I had intended just to be a fly on the wall. But because the chaplain worked by listening and then reflecting back to Art, I realized that she would not necessarily ask all of the questions I was interested in. So some of his remarks were in response to my questions. But the conversations between Art and the chaplain about his loss of faith were just between them. I was only listening.

Did you use a tape recorder?

No. Art spoke slowly enough, and the conversations were deliberate enough, that I could capture them. I also have a fear of technology, so I knew I would need to use a notebook anyway.

In addition to the conversations, what else did you put in your notebook?

I described the room, the sounds. I have always found it challenging to describe people or places. That was something *Tribune* Editor Ann Marie Lipinski had me work on, and those notes were essential.

All of the action was taking place in one room, so I tried to notice details. Were Art's feet covered? What was he wearing? It struck me as a good detail how nice his pajamas were. He was a well-dressed man when in good health, and his wife had picked these out. It was no accident that he looked good.

How did you organize your story?

I organized it mainly chronologically, with thoughts about how people deal with the end of life interspersed at appropriate moments. I never really thought about ordering it any other way, because the story proceeds naturally toward his death.

The first part opened with some of the major themes, like the urgency that matters of faith can take on when death is near, and the existence of a profession, hospice chaplains, who can counsel and guide us through death. I also wanted to give some hints of what was to come. But that was always a balancing act between how much to offer as an inviting look at what was to come, and how much to hold in reserve to give the reader a sense of wonderment.

Did you write as you went along, or begin after you had finished reporting?

I finished reporting first. It's hard to explain, but I had this feeling of needing to wait to write the story until he died—out of respect, in a way, to wait until he was dead before writing the obituary. But I wish I had transcribed my notebooks as I went along. There were a few points when I was writing when I wanted to clarify something Art had said, but by then it was too late.

How many drafts did you do?

I lost track of how many drafts. Many, many. I wrote and rewrote for several months. The lead stayed fundamentally the same, but we shrank it from three parts to two early on.

What revisions did you make to the story before publishing?

We made countless revisions, right up to hours before publication as we were going through page proofs. It was a humbling experience to see that no matter how many times we had read it, we were still finding ways to make it better.

What role did your editors play?

In addition to helping me identify the focus, both George Papajohn and Assistant Projects Editor Flynn McRoberts were pivotal as I was writing the story. George showed me that each section had to have a narrative purpose, and that I had to ruthlessly prune anything else, no matter how interesting. They both helped shape the sidebars, which started out longer and kept getting tighter under their direction. They line-edited so carefully that at one point we had a lengthy discussion about what word to use to describe the fabric on Nita Clifton's sofa.

Clearly, this story had the potential to elicit emotion from your readers. Did you do anything with your writing to elicit that emotion?

I think I felt the story would do that on its own. I just needed to get out of the way. There was one part, though, where I was very aware of crafting the story; listening to what would turn out to be Art's final conversation with his wife, I realized he was going through the five things that people find a way to tell their loved ones before death. (*I forgive you. Forgive Me. Thank you, I love you. Goodbye.*) When I wrote that part of the story, I very deliberately crafted it around those five things.

This is a story to which all of us would bring personal perspectives—like on religion, for example. You must have formed a bond with the family. How did you manage your personal involvement in the story?

I wrote the first part of this story sitting next to my mother's bed in the intensive care unit of New York-Presbyterian Hospital after she had open-heart surgery. (It actually was a great place to write. There were stretches of time with few interruptions, and the room overlooked the Hudson River.) Part of the reason that I wanted to write the story is that death is a fearful thing for me. That was part of why I wanted to report on it, why

I wanted to see it. The feeling extends to my mom. We're very close; she's in good health now that she's recovered from the surgery, but I dread the thought of losing her. So there were a number of personal reasons why this subject was on my mind—not to mention that everyone my age is going through the same thing. We're all thinking about death.

When my mom got sick, I really didn't think about whether it would affect my ability to write this. But looking back, I know it would have been hard to write if she had died. I definitely formed a bond with the Cliftons. This was a very private thing they were allowing me to share by entering into their lives. I was grateful, and I liked them. Art was a very genial guy. It was a pleasure talking to him.

And Nita was such a gracious person. I found out later that he hadn't told her what kind of story I was doing. He was so afraid that she would be upset that he told the administrator at the nursing home not to tell Nita what the story was about. So the first time I visited the room, Nita arrived and had no idea who I was. But she was so gracious. She just treated me as if I belonged there. Of course, when I found out later she didn't know, I had a very long conversation with her about what I was doing. This was not the kind of thing she ever would have done. But she agreed to it because she was honoring her husband's wish.

Did that cause you any concern?

I worried a lot about how she would react to the story, which of course wouldn't be published until after his death. Art had given me permission, but what if the story in any way harmed her? He had lived his whole life to protect her. Would I be betraying his trust?

What did Nita think of the story?

She was very pleased. She received positive feedback and she felt good. She read the stories every night for two weeks because it brought him back to her. In the end, Art accomplished his goal of helping people, which became clear from the outpouring of letters and e-mails we got, and did something that helped his wife, too—which was what he lived his life to do.

Why do you think readers responded in such large numbers to this story?

Because it's about death. People want to talk about death, and they don't talk about it. People want to see death and they never do. After they've seen it, they want to create a narrative about it. If you go to a wake or funeral, you see that people have this need to tell and retell the story of the person's death. It becomes part of the narrative of their lives. After they read this story, they wrote to us, "So that's what I can expect to happen," or "That's what it was like." We heard, "After reading the story, I knew what to expect when I went through this with my family."

I spoke with Art's son, Kevin, four months after the story ran. He said that even then, the story came up in conversation at least five times a week. People thanked the *Tribune* for giving the topic so much attention and playing it on the front page. It's really humbling to have people say a story "affected my life." I know it's less about my story and more about Art allowing people to become part of a communal experience and talk with each other about life and death.

You set out to do a story about God. Did readers see it more as a story about death?

Maybe a little bit. But a lot of the reaction we received, especially in the chats, involved God and how Art grappled with his faith in God. We received comments about how the chaplain did her job. Many were impressed. One asked for more information about the Ethical Culture movement of which she is part. But one writer said it was wrong for her to just listen to the patient and reflect back; she should have shored up the person's faith.

What did you learn from this experience?

No one has the answers. Even lifelong church-going people do not have certainty, or answers. Even chaplains do not, when it comes to the subject of death. Some people do profess to have the answers. But this story took place in the mainstream world where a lot of people reside—and for them, it remains unknowable.

I also, again, can't get over how much luck was involved. Not only that Art turned out to be as open as he was. I also was lucky that the hospice called me at just the time to get me to the nursing home during the two-hour window when Art had his "power surge" and fulfilled those five things. Any earlier or later, and I would have missed it.

Sometimes it seemed almost too lucky to be luck.

A conversation with
Nita Clifton

This edited interview was conducted by Poynter Distinguished Fellow Butch Ward with Nita Clifton, whose husband, Art, was profiled by Barbara Brotman in two Chicago Tribune *articles.*

Before she met Barbara Brotman in her husband's room at the nursing home, Nita Clifton had never met a newspaper reporter. She is quite sure that she never would have agreed on her own to participate in a story about the end of her husband's life.

It was all Art's idea, she said. He thought that maybe his experience would help someone else. And so, as she often did, she went along with her husband.

Looking back, she credits Brotman with making her experience with journalism, despite the terrible circumstances, a positive one.

"She was so kind," Mrs. Clifton recalled during a telephone conversation two weeks before the first anniversary of her husband's death. "She was so unobtrusive; she was there without me even knowing it. I respected her.

"It was the way Barbara spoke. She was in a corner of the room, and I often forgot she was there. I didn't feel the least bit self-conscious as far as expressing my feelings with my husband."

Mrs. Clifton recalled meeting Barbara for the first time at the nursing home and wondering what the reporter was doing there. Her husband had been afraid of how she would react if she learned he had agreed to a newspaper story about his dying. She said Brotman's "approach, her mannerisms" helped win her confidence.

"I wondered, could I expose myself as much as [Art] was?" Mrs. Clifton said. "If Barbara had not been the kind of person she was, I don't know if I could have done it."

When the story appeared, Mrs. Clifton said, she was relieved. She was also surprised, both by the story's length and by the reaction of people who read it.

"I live in a senior citizen community," she said, "and I became well-known after that."

She also was pleased that reaction to the story was positive.

"I'm glad if it helped people," she said. "That's why Art was willing to do it.

"If he accomplished that, I'm happy for him."

Writers' Workshop

Talking Points

1. Art Clifton's story is, in one sense, the most ordinary of stories: a man facing his death. Within this story, however, are numerous conflicts that give the narrative its tension and propel it forward. What are the conflicts? And how does the writer develop them to give the story its depth and complexity?

2. Barbara Brotman said her goal was to examine how people think about God. She narrowed that idea by identifying the moments in life when God matters most to people. In addition to the time of death, what other moments could a reporter have chosen, and how would you set out to report those stories?

3. In Part 2 of this series ("Facing the End"), Brotman used the five things people tell their loved ones before they die to frame the narrative, giving the reader crucial points of reference during Art's last hours. What did the writer use to frame the action in Part 1 ("Final Journey")? What details, devices or scenes keep you focused on the story's purpose while propelling you forward?

Assignment Desk

1. Barbara Brotman said her editors directed her to work more description into her stories—details like Art's appearance: "looking more elegant in striped pajamas than many men do in dress clothes." Circle 10 other examples of useful description in Brotman's stories; then read your most recent stories and identify examples of scenes that could have come alive with more description. What kinds of descriptions could you add to give more telling details?

2. The writer used extended conversations between Art and the chaplain, and between Art and Nita to convey tension, frustration, fear and love. The writer let the conversations stand on their own without commentary. Often we have those extended conversations in our notebooks, but elect to use single quotes and fragments, embellished by further explanation—which sometimes just repeats the quote. Read through your recent stories for patterns of single quotes; then

see if your narrative might have benefited from letting the conversation continue.

3. "Final Journey" takes place, in Barbara Brotman's words, "in the mainstream world where a lot of people reside." Unlike many stories that are framed by extremes (pro/con, right/left) Brotman's work focused on the ambiguities and uncertainties that fill most people's lives. Review your recent stories about issues that are usually treated by a focus on the extremes and identify "middle ground" where you could instead tackle the issues through stories of people who live—as most do—in the mainstream world.

WINNER

Andrea Elliott
ASNE, Diversity Writing
Pulitzer Prize, Feature Writing

The New York Times

As a small girl, Andrea Elliott listened to her Chilean relatives fill the house with folk songs late at night. Her mother strummed the guitar. Her uncles and aunts sang in an off-key chorus, reviving memories of the country they had left after the 1973 military coup.

Those songs still resonate with Elliott, whose early childhood on a farm in northern Virginia was immersed in the language and culture of her mother's South American homeland.

"I never felt fully Chilean, or fully American," says Elliott, 34, whose father is from upstate New York. "I was always something in between, and I think that gave me a combination of longing and detachment. Anyone who has straddled two cultures knows that feeling. You learn to be more of an observer than a participant. So, naturally, journalism appealed to me."

That combination of longing and detachment now informs her most powerful work. A metropolitan reporter for *The New York Times* since 2003, Elliott brings a detached observer's eye for detail. But she also brings a human, emotional connection to the people she writes about. She covers Islam in America, focusing on the impact of Sept. 11 on American Muslims, a beat she pitched to her editors.

Her approach to telling stories is cinematic. She writes in vivid scenes. She paints multidimensional portraits. She gives careful thought to the dramatic arc of her stories. Before she became a professional journalist, she was drawn to documentary filmmaking as a student at Occidental College in Los Angeles.

During her junior year, while living in Chile, she landed a job as a field producer with "La Tierra en que Vivimos," a natural history television program. She spent months in the Patagonia of Argentina with a small crew, filming the mating rituals of whales.

After graduating from college, she moved to San Francisco to work on "It's All Good," a documentary film about the subculture of aggressive inline skating, an extreme sport that was spreading among American teenagers. She codirected, coproduced and wrote the narration of the film, which tracked skaters from New York and Los Angeles.

"That film taught me that I did two things well—writing the narration and getting people to open up on camera," she said. "In sum, reporting and writing."

One month after finishing the film, she entered the graduate journalism program at Columbia University. She had not written a newspaper story since her college days.

"During my first assignment, I felt this sudden clarity," she said. "I no longer had a film crew—just a notepad—and it felt liberating."

After graduating, Elliott took an internship at *The Miami Herald*, where she was soon hired as a night cops reporter. Her next assignment, in 2001, was to write about immigration trends at a time when thousands of professionals from Venezuela, Argentina and Colombia had landed in Miami, fleeing political or economic turmoil. Doctors and lawyers were parking cars and waiting tables.

"They experienced this striking reversal of fortunes," said Elliott. "They had left countries with a rigid class system only to find themselves living in this strange, new meritocracy. It was a great story."

Two years later, she joined the *Times*. She worked on a range of stories as a general assignment reporter, from a feature about what cab drivers talk about on their cell phones to an investigative piece about the private policing system in Macy's department stores.

Before she began covering Islam in America, Elliott learned from two previous assignments. The first came in the summer of 2004, when Elliott was sent to the *Times*' Washington bureau to help report on the Abu Ghraib prison scandal. She tracked down a unit of military interrogators who had previously been in Iraq and had alerted senior officers to abuse in the prison long before the abuse came to light.

"I came away from that believing that some people will risk a lot to talk to a reporter when they feel that a story needs to be told," she said.

That fall, *Times* editor Joe Sexton—who later edited Elliott's imam series—assigned her to write about the children of the Sept. 11 victims. She had never spent much time reporting on children.

"It was such a sad story," she said. "But I learned that my own emotions could get in the way of the writing. When I stripped the story down, it was more powerful."

Elliott knows that being a journalist does not simply require collecting the facts. It's about capturing moments. She wrote about this in a 2003 essay for the American Society of Newspaper Editors:

"The greatest thing about journalism is how it inserts us—often uncomfortably, sometimes unforgettably—into the world. We look, we listen and we share the story of life. The story is almost always larger than we are, but without us, who would tell it?"

—Thomas Huang, an assistant managing editor, *The Dallas Morning News* and contributor, Poynter Online

18. A Muslim Leader in Brooklyn, Reconciling 2 Worlds

MARCH 5, 2006

By Andrea Elliott

The imam begins his trek before dawn, his long robe billowing like a ghost through empty streets. In this dark, quiet hour, his thoughts sometimes drift back to the Egyptian farming village where he was born.

But as the sun rises over Bay Ridge, Brooklyn, Sheik Reda Shata's new world comes to life. The R train rattles beneath a littered stretch of sidewalk, where Mexican workers huddle in the cold. An electric Santa dances in a doughnut shop window. Neon signs beckon. Gypsy cabs blare their horns.

The imam slips into a plain brick building, nothing like the golden-domed mosque of his youth. He stops to pray, and then climbs the cracked linoleum steps to his cluttered office. The answering machine blinks frantically, a portent of the endless questions to come.

A teenage girl wants to know: Is it halal, or lawful, to eat a Big Mac? Can alcohol be served, a waiter wonders, if it is prohibited by the Koran? Is it wrong to take out a mortgage, young Muslim professionals ask, when Islam frowns upon monetary interest?

The questions are only a piece of the daily puzzle Mr. Shata must solve as the imam of the Islamic Society of Bay Ridge, a thriving New York mosque where several thousand Muslims worship.

To his congregants, Mr. Shata is far more than the leader of daily prayers and giver of the Friday sermon. Many of them now live in a land without their parents, who typically assist with finding a spouse. There are fewer uncles and cousins to help resolve personal disputes. There is no local House of Fatwa to issue rulings on ethical questions.

Sheik Reda, as he is called, arrived in Brooklyn one year after Sept. 11. Virtually overnight, he became an Islamic judge and nursery school principal, a matchmaker and marriage counselor, a 24-hour hotline on all things Islamic.

Day after day, he must find ways to reconcile Muslim tradition with American life. Little in his rural Egyptian upbringing or years of Islamic scholarship prepared him for the challenge of leading a mosque in America.

The job has worn him down and opened his mind. It has landed him, exhausted, in the hospital and earned him a following far beyond Brooklyn.

"Here you don't know what will solve a problem. It's about looking for a key," said Sheik Reda Shata, the imam of a thriving mosque in Bay Ridge, Brooklyn. (Photograph courtesy of James Estrin/The New York Times)

"America transformed me from a person of rigidity to flexibility," said Mr. Shata, speaking through an Arabic translator. "I went from a country where a sheik would speak and the people listened to one where the sheik talks and the people talk back."

This is the story of Mr. Shata's journey west: the making of an American imam.

Over the last half-century, the Muslim population in the United States has risen significantly. Immigrants from the Middle East, South Asia and Africa have settled across the country, establishing mosques from Boston to Los Angeles, and turning Islam into one of the nation's fastest growing religions. By some estimates, as many as six million Muslims now live in America.

Leading this flock calls for improvisation. Imams must unify diverse congregations with often-clashing Islamic traditions. They must grapple with the threat of terrorism, answering to law enforcement agents without losing the trust of their fellow Muslims. Sometimes they must set aside conservative beliefs that prevail in the Middle East, the birthplace of Islam.

Islam is a legalistic faith: Muslims believe in a divine law that guides their daily lives, including what they should eat, drink and wear. In countries where the religion reigns, this is largely the accepted way.

But in the West, what Islamic law prohibits is everywhere. Alcohol fills chocolates. Women jog in sports bras. For many Muslims in America, life is a daily clash between Islamic mores and material temptation. At the center of this clash stands the imam.

In America, imams evoke a simplistic caricature—of robed, bearded clerics issuing fatwas in foreign lands. Hundreds of imams live in the United States, but their portrait remains flatly one-dimensional. Either they are symbols of diversity, breaking the Ramadan fast with smiling politicians, or zealots, hurrying into their storefront mosques.

Mr. Shata, 37, is neither a firebrand nor a ready advocate of progressive Islam. Some of his views would offend conservative Muslims; other beliefs would repel American liberals. He is in many ways a work in progress, mapping his own middle ground between two different worlds.

The imam's cramped, curtained office can hardly contain the dramas that unfold inside. Women cry. Husbands storm off. Friendships end. Every day brings soap opera plots and pitch.

A Moroccan woman falls to her knees near the imam's Hewlett-Packard printer. "Have mercy on me!" she wails to a friend who has accused her of theft. Another day, it is a man whose Lebanese wife has concealed their marriage and newborn son from her strict father. "I will tell him everything!" the husband screams.

Mr. Shata settles dowries, confronts wife abusers, brokers business deals and tries to arrange marriages. He approaches each problem with an almost scientific certainty that it can be solved. "I try to be more of a doctor than a judge," said Mr. Shata. "A judge sentences. A doctor tries to remedy."

Imams in the United States now serve an estimated 1,200 mosques. Some of their congregants have lived here for generations, assimilating socially and succeeding professionally. But others are recent immigrants, still struggling to find their place in America. Demographers expect their numbers to rise in the coming decades, possibly surpassing those of American Jews.

Like many of their faithful, most imams in the United States come from abroad. They are recruited primarily for their knowledge of the Koran and the language in which it was revealed, Arabic.

But few are prepared for the test that awaits. Like the parish priests who came generations before, imams are called on to lead a community on the margins of American civic life. They are conduits to and arbiters of an exhilarating, if sometimes hostile world, filled with promise and peril.

An Invitation to Islam

More than 5,000 miles lie between Brooklyn and Kafr al Battikh, Mr. Shata's birthplace in northeastern Egypt. Situated where the Nile Delta meets the Suez Canal, it was a village of dirt roads and watermelon vines when Mr. Shata was born in 1968.

Egypt was in the throes of change. The country had just suffered a staggering defeat in the Six Day War with Israel, and protests against the government followed. Hoping to counter growing radicalism, a new president, Anwar Sadat, allowed a long-repressed Islamic movement to flourish.

The son of a farmer and fertilizer salesman, Mr. Shata belonged to the lowest rung of Egypt's rural middle class. His house had no electricity. He did not see a television until he was 15.

Islam came to him softly, in the rhythms of his grandmother's voice. At bedtime, she would tell him the story of the Prophet Muhammad, the seventh-century founder of Islam. The boy heard much that was familiar. Like the prophet, he had lost his mother at a young age.

"She told me the same story maybe a thousand times," he said.

At the age of 5, he began memorizing the Koran. Like thousands of children in the Egyptian countryside, he attended a Sunni religious school subsidized by the government and connected to Al Azhar University, a bastion of Islamic scholarship.

Too poor to buy books, the young Mr. Shata hand-copied from hundreds at the town library. The bound volumes now line the shelves of his Bay Ridge apartment. When he graduated, he enrolled at Al Azhar and headed to Cairo by train. There, he sat on a bench for hours, marveling at the sights.

"I was like a lost child," he said. "Cars. We didn't have them. People of different colors. Foreigners. Women almost naked. It was like an imaginary world."

At 18, Mr. Shata thought of becoming a judge. But at his father's urging, he joined the college of imams, the Dawah.

The word means invitation. It refers to the duty of Muslims to invite, or call, others to the faith. Unlike Catholicism or Judaism, Islam has no ordained clergy. The Prophet Muhammad was the religion's first imam, or prayer leader, Islam's closest corollary to a rabbi or priest; schools like the Dawah are its version of a seminary or rabbinate.

After four years, Mr. Shata graduated with honors, seventh in a class of 3,400.

The next decade brought lessons in adaptation. In need of money, Mr. Shata took a job teaching sharia, or Islamic law, to children in Saudi Arabia, a country guided by Wahhabism, a puritan strain of Sunni Islam. He found his Saudi colleagues' interpretation of the Koran overly literal at times, and the treatment of women, who were not allowed to vote or drive, troubling.

Five years later, he returned to a different form of religious control in Egypt, where most imams are appointed by the government and monitored for signs of radicalism or political dissent.

"They are not allowed to deviate from the curriculum that the government sets for them," said Khaled Abou El Fadl, an Egyptian law professor at the University of California, Los Angeles.

Mr. Shata craved greater independence, and opened a furniture business. But he missed the life of dawah and eventually returned to it as the imam of his hometown mosque, which drew 4,000 worshipers on Fridays alone.

His duties were clear: He led the five daily prayers and delivered the khutba, or Friday sermon. His mosque, like most in Egypt, was financed and managed by the government. He spent his free time giving lectures, conducting marriage ceremonies and offering occasional religious guidance.

In 2000, Mr. Shata left to work as an imam in the gritty industrial city of Stuttgart, Germany. Europe brought a fresh new freedom. "I saw a wider world," he said. "Anyone with an opinion could express it."

Then came Sept. 11.

Soon after, Mr. Shata's mosque was defiled with graffiti and smeared with feces.

The next summer, Mr. Shata took a call from an imam in Brooklyn. The man, Mohamed Moussa, was leaving his mosque, exhausted by the troubles of his congregants following the terrorist attacks. The mosque was looking for a replacement, and Mr. Shata had come highly recommended by a professor at Al Azhar.

Most imams are recruited to American mosques on the recommendation of other imams or trusted scholars abroad, and are usually offered an annual contract. Some include health benefits and subsidized housing; others are painfully spare. The pay can range from $20,000 to $50,000.

Mr. Shata had heard stories of Muslim hardship in America. The salary at the Islamic Society of Bay Ridge was less than what he was earning in Germany. But foremost on his mind were his wife and three small daughters, whom he had not seen in months. Germany had refused them entry.

He agreed to take the job if he could bring his family to America. In October 2002, the American Embassy in Cairo granted visas to the Shatas and they boarded a plane for New York.

A Mosque, a Magnet

A facade of plain white brick rises up from Fifth Avenue just south of 68th Street in Bay Ridge. Two sets of words, one in Arabic and another in

Each morning, Mr. Shata accompanies his daughters Esteshhad, 10, left, and Rahma, 6, to the bus stop of their Islamic school. Along the way, he quizzes them on passages from the Koran. (Photograph courtesy of James Estrin/*The New York Times*)

English, announce the mosque's dual identity from a marquee above its gray metal doors.

To the mosque's base—Palestinian, Egyptian, Yemeni, Moroccan and Algerian immigrants—it is known as Masjid Moussab, named after one of the prophet's companions, Moussab Ibn Omair. To the mosque's English-speaking neighbors, descendants of the Italians, Irish and Norwegians who once filled the neighborhood, it is the Islamic Society of Bay Ridge.

Mosques across America are commonly named centers or societies, in part because they provide so many services. Some 140 mosques serve New York City, where an estimated 600,000 Muslims live, roughly 20 percent of them African-American, said Louis Abdellatif Cristillo, an anthropologist at Teachers College who has canvassed the city's mosques.

The Islamic Society of Bay Ridge, like other American mosques, is run by a board of directors, mostly Muslim professionals from the Palestinian territories. What began in 1984 as a small storefront on Bay Ridge Avenue, with no name and no imam, has grown into one of the city's vital Muslim centers, a magnet for new immigrants.

Its four floors pulse with life: a nursery school, an Islamic bookstore, Koran classes and daily lectures. Some 1,500 Muslims worship at the mosque on Fridays, often crouched in prayer on the sidewalk. Albanians,

Pakistanis and others who speak little Arabic listen to live English translations of the sermons through headsets. It is these congregants' crumpled dollar bills, collected in a cardboard box, that enable the mosque to survive.

Among the city's imams, Bay Ridge is seen as a humbling challenge.

"It's the first station for immigrants," said Mr. Moussa, Mr. Shata's predecessor. "And immigrants have a lot of problems."

Skip 911. Call the Imam.

Mr. Shata landed at Kennedy International Airport wearing a crimson felt hat and a long gray jilbab that fell from his neck to his sandaled toes, the proud dress of an Al Azhar scholar. He spoke no English. But already, he carried some of the West inside. He could quote liberally from Voltaire, Shaw and Kant. For an Egyptian, he often jokes, he was inexplicably punctual.

The first thing Mr. Shata loved about America, like Germany, was the order.

"In Egypt, if a person passes through a red light, that means he's smart," he said. "In America, he's very disrespected."

Americans stood in line. They tended their yards. One could call the police and hear a rap at the door minutes later. That fact impressed not only Mr. Shata, but also the women of his new mosque.

They had gained a reputation for odd calls to 911. One woman called because a relative abroad had threatened to take her inheritance. "The officers left and didn't write anything," Mr. Shata said, howling with laughter. "There was nothing for them to write."

Another woman called, angry because her husband had agreed to let a daughter from a previous marriage spend the night.

To Mr. Shata, the calls made sense. The women's parents, uncles and brothers—figures of authority in family conflict—were overseas. Instead, they dialed 911, hoping for a local substitute. Soon they would learn to call the imam.

A bearish man with a soft, bearded face, Mr. Shata struck his congregants as an odd blend of things. He was erudite yet funny; authoritative at the mosque's wooden pulpit and boyishly charming between prayers.

Homemakers, doctors, cabdrivers and sheiks stopped by to assess the new imam. He regaled them with Dunkin' Donuts coffee, fetched by the Algerian keeper of the mosque, and then told long, poetic stories that left his visitors silent, their coffee cold.

"You just absorb every word he says," said Linda Sarsour, 25, a Muslim activist in Brooklyn.

The imam, too, was taking note. Things worked differently in America, where mosques were run as nonprofit organizations and congregants had a decidedly democratic air. Mr. Shata was shocked when a tone-deaf man insisted on giving the call to prayer. Such a man would be ridiculed in Egypt, where the callers, or muezzinin, have voices so beautiful they sometimes record top-selling CD's.

But in the land of equal opportunity, a man with a mediocre voice could claim discrimination. Mr. Shata relented. He shudders when the voice periodically sounds.

No sooner had Mr. Shata started his new job than all manner of problems arrived at his worn wooden desk: rebellious teenagers, marital strife, confessions of philandering, accusations of theft.

The imam responded creatively. Much of the drama involved hot dog vendors. There was the pair who shared a stand, but could not stand each other. They came to the imam, who helped them divide the business.

The most notorious hot dog seller stood accused of stealing thousands of dollars in donations he had raised for the children of his deceased best friend. But there was no proof. The donations had been in cash. The solution, the imam decided, was to have the man swear an oath on the Koran.

"Whoever lies while taking an oath on the Koran goes blind afterward," said Mr. Shata, stating a belief that has proved useful in cases of theft. A group of men lured the vendor to the mosque, where he confessed to stealing $11,400. His admission was recorded in a waraqa, or document, penned in Arabic and signed by four witnesses. He returned the money in full.

Dozens of waraqas sit in the locked bottom drawer of the imam's desk. In one, a Brooklyn man who burned his wife with an iron vows, in nervous Arabic scrawl, never to do it again. If he fails, he will owe her a $10,000 "disciplinary fine." The police had intervened before, but the woman felt that she needed the imam's help.

For hundreds of Muslims, the Bay Ridge mosque has become a courthouse more welcoming than the one downtown, a police precinct more effective than the brick station blocks away. Even the police have used the imam's influence to their advantage, warning disorderly teenagers that they will be taken to the mosque rather than the station.

"They say: 'No, not the imam! He'll tell my parents,'" said Russell Kain, a recently retired officer of the 68th Precinct.

Marriage, Mortgage, McDonald's

Soon after arriving in Brooklyn, Mr. Shata observed a subtle rift among the women of his mosque. Those who were new to America remained quietly grounded in the traditions of their homelands. But some who had assimilated began to question those strictures. Concepts like shame held less weight. Actions like divorce, abhorred by Mr. Shata, were surprisingly popular.

"The woman who comes from overseas, she's like someone who comes from darkness to a very well-lit place," he said.

In early July, an Egyptian karate teacher shuffled into Mr. Shata's office and sank into a donated couch. He smiled meekly and began to talk. His new wife showed him no affection. She complained about his salary and said he lacked ambition.

The imam urged him to be patient.

Two weeks later, in came the wife. She wanted a divorce.

"We don't understand each other," the woman said. She was 32 and had come from Alexandria, Egypt, to work as an Arabic teacher. She had met her husband through a friend in Bay Ridge. Her parents, still in Egypt, had approved cautiously from afar.

"I think you should be patient," said the imam.

"I cannot," she said firmly. "He loves me, but I have to love him, too."

Mr. Shata shifted uncomfortably in his chair. There was nothing he loathed more than granting a divorce.

"It's very hard for me to let him divorce you," he said. "How can I meet God on Judgment Day?"

"It's God's law also to have divorce," she shot back. The debate continued.

Finally, Mr. Shata asked for her parents' phone number in Egypt. Over the speakerphone, they anxiously urged the imam to relent. Their daughter was clearly miserable, and they were too far away to intervene.

With a sigh, Mr. Shata asked his executive secretary, Mohamed, to print a divorce certificate. In the rare instance when the imam agrees to issue one, it is after a couple has filed for divorce with the city.

"Since you're the one demanding divorce, you can never get back together with him," the imam warned. "Ever."

The woman smiled politely.

"What matters for us is the religion," she said later. "Our law is our religion."

The religion's fiqh, or jurisprudence, is built on 14 centuries of scholarship, but imams in Europe and America often find this body of law insufficient to address life in the West. The quandaries of America were foreign to Mr. Shata.

Pornography was rampant, prompting a question Mr. Shata had never heard in Egypt: Is oral sex lawful? Pork and alcohol are forbidden in Islam, raising questions about whether Muslims could sell beer or bacon.

Tired of the menacing stares in the subway, women wanted to know if they could remove their headscarves. Muslims were navigating their way through problems Mr. Shata had never fathomed.

For a while, the imam called his fellow sheiks in Egypt with requests for fatwas, or nonbinding legal rulings. But their views carried little relevance to life in America. Some issues, like oral sex, he dared not raise. Over time, he began to find his own answers and became, as he put it, flexible.

Is a Big Mac permissible? Yes, the imam says, but not a bacon cheeseburger.

It is a woman's right, Mr. Shata believes, to remove her hijab if she feels threatened. Muslims can take jobs serving alcohol and pork, he says, but only if other work cannot be found. Oral sex is acceptable, but only between married couples. Mortgages, he says, are necessary to move forward in America.

"Islam is supposed to make a person's life easier, not harder," Mr. Shata explained.

In some ways, the imam has resisted change. He has learned little English, and interviews with Mr. Shata over the course of six months required the use of a translator.

Some imams in the United States make a point of shaking hands with women, distancing themselves from the view that such contact is improper. Mr. Shata offers women only a nod.

Daily, he passes the cinema next to his mosque but has never seen a movie in a theater. He says music should be forbidden if it "encourages sexual desire." He won't convert a non-Muslim when it seems more a matter of convenience than true belief.

"Religion is not a piece of clothing that you change," he said after turning away an Ecuadorean immigrant who sought to convert for her Syrian husband. "I don't want someone coming to Islam tonight and leaving it in the morning."

Trust in God's Plan

Ten months after he came to America, Mr. Shata collapsed.

It was Friday. The mosque was full. Hundreds of men sat pressed together, their shirts damp with summer. Their wives and daughters huddled in the women's section, one floor below. Word of the imam's sermons had spread, drawing Muslims from Albany and Hartford.

"Praise be to Allah," began Mr. Shata, his voice slowly rising.

Minutes later, the imam recalled, the room began to spin. He fell to the carpet, lost consciousness and spent a week in the hospital, plagued by sev-

Marking the end of Ramadan, Mr. Shata's mosque, the Islamic Society of Bay Ridge, attracted an overflow crowd. Since the mosque was founded a few blocks away in 1984, it has grown into a vital center for new Muslim immigrants. (Photograph courtesy of James Estrin/*The New York Times*)

eral symptoms. A social worker and a counselor who treated the imam both said he suffered from exhaustion. The counselor, Ali Gheith, called it "compassion fatigue," an ailment that commonly affects disaster-relief workers.

It was not just the long hours, the new culture and the ceaseless demands that weighed on the imam. Most troubling were the psychological woes of his congregants, which seemed endless.

Sept. 11 had wrought depression and anxiety among Muslims. But unlike many priests or rabbis, imams lacked pastoral training in mental health and knew little about the social services available.

At heart was another complicated truth: Imams often approach mental illness from a strictly Islamic perspective. Hardship is viewed as a test of faith, and the answer can be found in tawwakul, trusting in God's plan. The remedy typically suggested by imams is a spiritual one, sought through fasting, prayer and reflection.

Muslim immigrants also limit themselves to religious solutions because of the stigma surrounding mental illness, said Hamada Hamid, a resident psychiatrist at New York University who founded "The Journal of Muslim Mental Health." "If somebody says, 'You need this medication,' someone may respond, 'I have tawwakul,' " he said.

Mr. Gheith, a Palestinian immigrant who works in disaster preparedness for the city's health department, began meeting with the imam regularly after his collapse. Mr. Shata needed to learn to disconnect from his congregants, Mr. Gheith said. It was a concept that confounded the imam.

"I did not permit these problems to enter my heart," said Mr. Shata, "nor can I permit them to leave."

The conversations eventually led to a citywide training program for imams, blending Islam with psychology. Mr. Shata learned to identify the symptoms of mental illness and began referring people to treatment.

His congregants often refuse help, blaming black magic or the evil eye for their problems. The evil eye is believed to be a curse driven by envy, confirmed in the bad things that happen to people.

One Palestinian couple in California insisted that their erratic 18-year-old son had the evil eye. He was brought to the imam's attention after winding up on the streets of New York, and eventually received a diagnosis of schizophrenia.

Mr. Shata had less success with a man who worshiped at the mosque. He had become paranoid, certain his wife was cursing him with witchcraft. But he refused treatment, insisting divorce was the only cure.

Time and again, Mr. Shata's new country has called for creativity and patience, for a careful negotiation between tradition and modernity.

"Here you don't know what will solve a problem," he said. "It's about looking for a key."

19. To Lead the Faithful in a Faith Under Fire

MARCH 6, 2006

By Andrea Elliott

The F.B.I. agent and the imam sat across a long wooden table at a Brooklyn youth center last August.

Would the imam, the agent asked, report anyone who seemed prone to terrorism?

Sheik Reda Shata leaned back in his chair and studied the agent. Nearly a year had passed since the authorities had charged two young men, one of whom prayed at Mr. Shata's mosque, with plotting to blow up the Herald Square subway station in Manhattan.

The mosque had come under siege. Television news trucks circled the block. Threats were made. The imam's congregants became angry themselves after learning that a police informer had spent months in their midst.

At the meeting, the imam chose his words carefully. It is not only the F.B.I. that wants to stop terrorism, he answered; Muslims also care about keeping the country safe.

"I would turn him in to you," Mr. Shata finally said, pointing his finger at the agent, Mark J. Mershon, the top F.B.I. official in New York City. "But not because I am afraid of you."

The moment captured one of the enduring challenges for an imam in America: living at the center of a religion under watch.

Mr. Shata is under steady pressure to help the authorities. At the same time, he must keep the trust of his congregants, who feel unfairly singled out by law enforcement.

The balance is delicate. It requires a willingness to cooperate, but not to be trampled on; pride in one's fellow Muslims, yet recognition that threats may lurk among them.

"It's like walking a tightrope," said Mr. Shata, 37, speaking through an Arabic translator. "You have to give Muslims the feeling that the police are not monsters. And you have to give the police the feeling that Muslims are respectful and clean."

Months spent with Mr. Shata, both around the city and in his mosque, the Islamic Society of Bay Ridge, revealed the vastly complex calling of imams in the United States.

In the Islamic world, imams are defined as prayer leaders. But here, they become community leaders, essential intermediaries between their immigrant flocks and a new, Western land. When Islamic traditions clash with American culture, it is imams who step forward with improvised answers. Outside the mosque, many assume the public roles of other clergy, becoming diplomats for their faith.

But in the years since Sept. 11, diplomacy has given way to defensiveness. For American imams, no subject is more charged than terrorism. While under scrutiny themselves, imams are often called upon to usher the authorities past the barriers of fear that surround their communities. Many are reluctant. They worry that their assistance will backfire in unwarranted investigations, or a loss of credibility at the pulpit.

At Mr. Shata's mosque, people can recite a list of dubious cases as easily as popular verses of the Koran: The three Moroccan men in Detroit who were falsely accused of operating a terrorist sleeper cell; the Muslim lawyer Brandon Mayfield, who was mistakenly linked to bombings in Madrid; the two teenage girls from New York City who were held for weeks but never charged after the F.B.I. identified them as potential suicide bombers.

At the same time, imams must contend with their own mixed reputation, which is marked by a few high-profile cases, like that of Sheik Omar Abdel Rahman, the blind Egyptian cleric who was convicted in 1995 of plotting to blow up New York landmarks.

Imams like Mr. Shata—men who embrace American freedom and condemn the radicals they feel have tainted their faith—rarely make the news.

The authorities are well acquainted with Mr. Shata, and speak highly of him. The officers of Mr. Shata's local police precinct often turn to him for help when Muslims in Bay Ridge refuse to be questioned. The senior F.B.I. counterterrorism official in New York, Charles E. Frahm, described his interaction with Mr. Shata as "very positive."

Mr. Frahm was in the room last August when Mr. Mershon challenged the imam. Mr. Shata and other Muslim leaders had agreed to meet the agents at the Muslim Youth Center in Bensonhurst in an effort to improve relations between the two camps.

"I have been impressed with his desire, as he's expressed it to me, to do good and do right," Mr. Frahm said.

Yet for Mr. Shata, cooperation brings conflicting emotions. He can charm a class of rookies at the 68th Precinct in Brooklyn, turning a perfunctory cultural sensitivity seminar into a comedy hour. But he is quietly

"Whoever is afraid of dialogue is hiding something," said Sheik Reda Shata, speaking of the Muslim duty to assist the authorities. (Photograph courtesy of James Estrin/*The New York Times*)

outraged that an unmarked car shadows a respected Palestinian board member of his mosque.

The imam is saddened to see so many Muslims leave America, pushed out by new immigration policies, intimidation or despair. He also fears for those who have remained: for the teenage boy in his mosque who is suddenly praying at dawn, having drifted from a high school that left him alienated.

Still, Mr. Shata said, the anger and fear, no matter how deeply felt, are tempered by something greater: the devastating impact of Sept. 11 on non-Muslim Americans.

"It will take them a while to come to terms with us," he said.

A Necessary Dialogue

The competing demands on Mr. Shata became plain when he arrived in Bay Ridge about a year after Sept. 11.

Crisis gripped the city's Muslim neighborhoods. Law enforcement agents searched businesses and homes, and held hundreds of men for questioning. Women were harassed in the subway. Elementary schools lost Muslim children as their families packed up and left.

Mr. Shata's predecessor, Mohamed Moussa, was drained. "I needed a change or I would destroy myself," said Mr. Moussa, who now works as one of three imams at a well-funded mosque in Union City, N.J.

Like many mosques in struggling immigrant neighborhoods, the Islamic Society of Bay Ridge had little choice but to search abroad for a replacement. America produces few imams with the qualities sought by foreign-born Muslims: fluency in Arabic, and a superior command of the Koran and the laws that codify Islamic life.

Mr. Shata was an enticing candidate. Like Mr. Moussa, he had trained at Al Azhar University in Cairo, a citadel of Islamic scholarship. Through an Azhar professor, Mr. Moussa found Mr. Shata in Germany, where he had been working as an imam.

The men who sit on the mosque's board were pleased to find charisma in their new imam. The white brick mosque on Fifth Avenue in Bay Ridge survives largely on the donations of its congregants. Only a riveting speaker can draw them.

But soon after Mr. Shata arrived, he became aware of another, less visible audience. In mosques around the city, informers were hidden among the praying masses, listening for what officials call "double talk"—one voice of extremism inside the mosque, and another of tolerance outside.

The attention did not worry Mr. Shata, he said, because he had nothing to hide. "My page is clean," he said.

But when the authorities came seeking his help, he faced a choice. He could welcome them and improve the mosque's public standing, or he could rebuff their inquiries at the risk of seeming obstructionist.

"There's a wall of silence around these mosques," said Representative Peter T. King, a Long Island Republican and chairman of the House Homeland Security Committee. "It's not necessarily the imam himself who is actively engaged, but he looks the other way or allows activities in his mosque that could be dangerous."

Mr. Shata viewed cooperation as his Islamic duty. "Whoever is afraid of dialogue is hiding something," he said.

Mosque Under a Microscope

The greatest test of Mr. Shata's relationship with the authorities came with the arrest of a young Muslim congregant who was accused of plotting terrorism.

Shahawar Matin Siraj, 23, was a chatty Pakistani immigrant who worked in the Islamic bookstore next to the mosque. On the job, he was sometimes seen talking to James Elshafay, 21, a soft-spoken Muslim American from

Staten Island. In August 2004, both were charged in Brooklyn federal court with conspiring to blow up the 34th Street subway station at Herald Square.

The men had been videotaped discussing the plot and scouting the subway station with a paid police informer who told them he belonged to an Islamic "brotherhood."

In the days after the arrests, reporters swarmed into Bay Ridge. Anonymous threats were called in to the bookstore, Islamic Books & Tapes. One letter to the store read, "You're all dead meat."

The imam and others at the mosque soon realized they knew the informer: a gray-haired Egyptian who called himself Osama Daoudi and said he lived in Staten Island.

"He used to say, 'My name is Osama, like Osama bin Laden,' " Mr. Shata recalled.

Mr. Daoudi had surfaced at the mosque a year earlier, said Mr. Shata. He tried to interest the imam in a real estate deal, proposing that Mr. Shata use his influence over Muslims to collect money owed to Mr. Daoudi in exchange for a secret cash commission, Mr. Shata recalled.

The imam wanted nothing to do with the scheme, he said, and kept his distance. He found Mr. Daoudi off-putting. He claimed to be the son of a famous Egyptian sheik and was known at the mosque for weeping when he prayed. But he also smoked.

"Piety in Islam forbids smoking," Mr. Shata observed.

Most striking was the anti-American sentiment that Mr. Daoudi espoused, Mr. Shata said. During visits with the imam, Mr. Daoudi complained that Americans might fear him because he had a Ph.D. in nuclear engineering. He also said that the F.B.I. wanted to search his home, the imam recalled.

"I told him, 'As long as you do nothing wrong, open your house and your heart to people,' " said Mr. Shata.

The imam said he believed that after Mr. Daoudi found him uninterested, he turned his focus to Mr. Siraj and Mr. Elshafay.

Starting in September 2003, the informer spent months drawing Mr. Siraj into the plot, teaching him about violent jihad, said Mr. Siraj's lawyer, Martin R. Stolar.

The authorities would say little about the case, which is set for trial next month. Efforts to locate Mr. Daoudi, whose name was provided by Mr. Stolar, were unsuccessful.

The Police Department's chief spokesman, Paul J. Browne, dismissed Mr. Stolar's claim that the police had manufactured the plot. "We didn't propose that," he said. "We took action to stop it and there's a big difference."

Mr. Siraj had an "interest in violence" that was known to the authorities prior to an informer's involvement, Mr. Browne added.

For the imam, the informer's supposed maneuvering was not surprising. Mr. Shata shares a view common among Muslims in Bay Ridge that confidential informers are untrustworthy because some have criminal records or work for pay.

This perception irks Mr. Frahm, the F.B.I. official. Informers' reports are closely vetted, he said, and their motives are irrelevant if they provide correct information.

Mr. Frahm devotes much time to building trust among Muslim leaders. But he also warns them not to turn a blind eye to questionable activity. "You can't play part-time American," he said.

'From the Stones Of Insults'

Anger at the authorities came easily at the mosque. But a quiet, if disturbing, question soon followed: Entrapped or not, what had caused these young men to entertain thoughts of terrorism?

The imam looks for answers on the crowded sidewalk outside the mosque.

The worn cement slabs along Fifth Avenue have long been divided into two social camps. After the Friday prayer, the section in front of the mosque fills with the neighborhood's Arab pioneers, gray-haired and balding Palestinians and Egyptians.

Several feet south, under the marquee of a movie theater, the neighborhood's Arab teenagers gather. Before Sept. 11, the groups rarely mingled. But in the years since, many of the younger set have returned to their faith.

The imam now rises to deliver his Friday khutba, or sermon, before rows of young men, some in low-hanging jeans and baseball caps turned backward. Many have come to learn more about their religion so they can defend it at work or at school. Others no longer feel at home elsewhere. They have been passed over for jobs, or stopped and questioned by the authorities too many times.

It is these men, and their sense of alienation, that most worry Mr. Shata. The mosque is not their only refuge. A new crop of sheesha cafes opened along the avenue after Sept. 11, filling with male chatter and the sweet smoke of water pipes.

"I once read a Spanish proverb," Mr. Shata said one evening. "The wall of hatred was asked, 'How were you built?' And the reply was, 'From the stones of insults.'"

Over the last three decades, the European immigrant enclave of Bay Ridge has given way to Gazan barbers, halal butchers and Egyptian jewelers. But the newest settlers have not always been welcome.

"It became, 'This ain't Bay Ridge anymore, it's Beirut,' " said Russell Kain, a retired community affairs officer from the 68th Precinct.

America has brought the imam his own share of taunts. A woman on a plane once asked him if he was Muslim and then demanded to change seats. Mr. Shata grew up wearing the long robes of his Egyptian homeland. He now travels in a suit.

But in Bay Ridge, he fights alienation with an open heart. He is increasingly a blend of East and West, proudly walking to the mosque in a robe and sandals, while warding off the cold with a wool Yankees hat. "I feel like I'm living in my country," he said.

It is a message he repeats everywhere he goes, one he says is the antidote to hatred. He meets with Muslim youth groups at mosques around the city, telling them not to wait for an invitation to embrace America. Even if Muslims feel singled out, Mr. Shata often says, America is still the freest country in the world.

The imam plans to stay for "as long as God wills it," he said. He got his green card in November.

Mr. Shata knows most of his congregants by face, and the 400 who pray daily by name. If he sees a young person taken by sudden devotion, his impulse is to probe. Is the person driven by faith or isolation? He can't always be sure.

The imam's concerns are shared by the F.B.I. Several officials said the bureau had recently focused its surveillance on the city's Muslim youth after learning that the London bombings last July were mostly carried out by South Asians raised in Britain. Mr. Shata and the authorities agree that young Muslims are most captive to the messages of militant sheiks.

"Islam is a religion based on intellect," he tells his young listeners. "Islam says to you: 'Think. Don't close your eyes and just follow your emotions. Don't follow the sheik. Perhaps you have a better mind than his.' "

"If you do wrong," he says, "you do wrong to the whole Islamic world."

One Imam, Many Audiences

One evening in July, Mr. Shata sat in the neat, air-conditioned living room of a brick row house in Queens. An Egyptian family had invited him over to bless their newest member, a 5-week-old girl.

The infant, swathed in soft pink cotton, slept in a car seat on the floor as her mother and grandmother offered tea and pastries. On a wide-screen television, Al Jazeera flashed news that two Algerian diplomats had been killed in Iraq.

Mr. Shata was bothered by the killers' description of the victims as "infidels." The world, he said, needed to agree on a definition of terrorism. "What I may see as terrorism, you may not see that way," he said.

Few subjects pose a more complicated test of loyalties for Mr. Shata than the struggle between Arabs and Israelis. Many Palestinians attend his mosque. When he discusses the conflict, one gets the sense that he is, again, speaking to several audiences.

Like Arabs around the world, Mr. Shata disagrees profoundly with the United States' steadfast support of Israel, and views the militant group Hamas as a powerful symbol of resistance.

When Sheik Ahmed Yassin, the founder and spiritual leader of Hamas, was killed by Israelis in March 2004, Mr. Shata told hundreds who gathered at a memorial service in Brooklyn that the "lion of Palestine has been martyred."

Mr. Shata is also acutely aware that the United States classifies Hamas as a terrorist group. In the same speech, he condemned all violence. "We don't hate Jews," he recalled saying. "To kill one man is to kill all mankind."

Yet in another sermon, the imam exalted a young Palestinian mother, Reem Al-Reyashi, who blew herself up in 2004 at a crossing point between Gaza and Israel, killing four Israelis. Mr. Shata described the woman as a martyr.

When asked about the speech, Mr. Shata seemed unusually conflicted. He has forged friendships with rabbis in New York—something he never imagined in Egypt. Engaging in a discussion about the Arab-Israeli struggle would invite controversy, he said, both within his mosque and outside it. "I worry this will cause trouble with my Jewish brothers," he said. He rarely broaches the topic in sermons and addressed it only reluctantly in interviews.

"I do not accept suicide operations that target civilians at any time or place," Mr. Shata said. But striking Israeli soldiers "as a means of defense" was justifiable.

The Israelis, he said, have "killed Palestinian women, destroyed their homes, taken their land and materials and made them into refugees," while Palestinians lack the military means to fight back. Islamic law forbids suicide, he said, but the Koran says Muslims can defend themselves if attacked. Ms. Al-Reyashi killed two soldiers, a border police officer and a security guard, though Palestinian and Israeli civilians were hurt.

Mr. Shata, center, joined more than 1,000 Muslims in Manhattan last month to protest cartoons depicting the Prophet Muhammad. Insults, the imam said, can breed alienation and anger among Muslims. (Photograph courtesy of James Estrin/The New York Times)

Mr. Shata acknowledged that his opinion, while common among Arabs, is strongly opposed not only by many non-Muslims, but even by some of his congregants. "Some Muslims, if they hear this, would make me out to be a nonbeliever because they see that all these suicide operations are a must," he said. "And there are other Muslims who feel that all of these operations are forbidden.

"My nature is always to be in the middle," he said. "It's always the person in the middle who ends up being the enemy of the right and the left. I don't want to open up two fronts against me."

Mr. Shata is forceful in his condemnation of terrorism in the West, a message he feels is rarely heard. After the suicide bombings in London last year, he and other Muslims called a news conference in Brooklyn to denounce the violence. Nobody came.

In his sermons, Mr. Shata repeatedly makes the point that terrorism violates the tenets of Islam. "I feel that I breathe underwater, or that I cry in a desert," he said recently. "That nobody responds."

It was part of Mr. Shata's annual Sept. 11 speech, a tradition he began in 2003. Recordings of the sermon, titled "What Muslims Want From America," sold out at the mosque overnight.

The three Sept. 11 speeches echo the imam's journey in America. His first speech was conciliatory in tone; a treatise on the peaceful nature of Islam. In 2004, he urged Muslims to respect the law, and trust that America is not "the enemy." Last September, his message hardened.

"We want the U.S. to be just in dealing with our issues," Mr. Shata declared. A man "should not feel that he is under surveillance for every word he says, every move he makes and every piece of paper he signs."

Muslims feel isolated, yet crave acceptance, he said, likening them to their ancestors 14 centuries ago, who sought refuge from the king of Abyssinia.

"O king, we have come to thy country having chosen thee above all others," he said, reciting the words of the group's leader, Jafar Ibn Abi Talib.

"It is our hope, o king, that here, with thee, we shall not suffer wrong."

20. Tending to Muslim Hearts and Islam's Future

MARCH 7, 2006

By Andrea Elliott

The young Egyptian professional could pass for any New York bachelor.

Dressed in a crisp polo shirt and swathed in cologne, he races his Nissan Maxima through the rain-slicked streets of Manhattan, late for a date with a tall brunette. At red lights, he fusses with his hair.

What sets the bachelor apart from other young men on the make is the chaperone sitting next to him—a tall, bearded man in a white robe and stiff embroidered hat.

"I pray that Allah will bring this couple together," the man, Sheik Reda Shata, says, clutching his seat belt and urging the bachelor to slow down.

Christian singles have coffee hour. Young Jews have JDate. But many Muslims believe that it is forbidden for an unmarried man and woman to meet in private. In predominantly Muslim countries, the job of making introductions and even arranging marriages typically falls to a vast network of family and friends.

In Brooklyn, there is Mr. Shata.

Week after week, Muslims embark on dates with him in tow. Mr. Shata, the imam of a Bay Ridge mosque, juggles some 550 "marriage candidates," from a gold-toothed electrician to a professor at Columbia University. The meetings often unfold on the green velour couch of his office, or over a meal at his favorite Yemeni restaurant on Atlantic Avenue.

The bookish Egyptian came to America in 2002 to lead prayers, not to dabble in matchmaking. He was far more conversant in Islamic jurisprudence than in matters of the heart. But American imams must wear many hats, none of which come tailor-made.

Whether issuing American-inspired fatwas or counseling the homesick, fielding questions from the F.B.I. or mediating neighborhood spats, Mr. Shata walks an endless labyrinth of problems.

If anything seems conquerable, it is the solitude of Muslim singles. Nothing brings the imam more joy than guiding them to marriage. It is his way of fashioning a future for his faith. It is his most heartfelt effort—by turns graceful and comedic, vexing and hopeful—to make Islam work in America.

"Married life in Islam is an act of worship," said Sheik Reda Shata, who promotes marriage and blesses the newborn in his work as an imam. (Photograph courtesy of James Estrin/*The New York Times*)

Word of the imam's talents has traveled far, eliciting lonely calls from Muslims in Chicago and Los Angeles, or from meddlesome parents in Cairo and Damascus.

From an estimated 250 chaperoned dates, Mr. Shata has produced 10 marriages.

"The prophet said whoever brings a man and woman together, it is as if he has worshiped for an entire year," said Mr. Shata, 37, speaking through an Arabic translator.

The task is not easy. In a country of plentiful options, Muslim immigrants can become picky, even rude, the imam complains.

During one date, a woman studied the red-circled eyes of a prospective husband and asked, "Have you brought me an alcoholic?"

On another occasion, an Egyptian man stared at the flat chest of a pleasant young Moroccan woman and announced, "She looks like a log!" the imam recalled.

"This would never happen in Egypt," said Mr. Shata, turning red at the memory. "Never, never. If I knew this boy had no manners I never would have let him into my office."

The Imam's Little Black Book

The concept of proper courtship in Islam, like much about the faith, is open to interpretation.

Islamic law specifies that a man and woman who are unmarried may not be alone in closed quarters. Some Muslims reject any mingling before marriage. Others freely date. Many fall somewhere in between, meeting in groups, getting engaged and spending time alone before the wedding, while their parents look the other way.

For one Syrian in New York, a date at Starbucks is acceptable if it begins and ends on the premises: The public is his chaperone.

Mr. Shata is a traditionalist. There were few strangers in his rural town of birth, Kafr al Battikh, in northeastern Egypt. Men and women often agreed to marry the day they met, and a few made the deal sight unseen. It was rare to meet anyone from a distant province, let alone another country.

New York is not only the capital of the world, imams often joke, but also the crossroads of Islam, a human sampling more diverse than anywhere save Mecca during the annual pilgrimage known as the Hajj. Beyond the city's five boroughs, Muslim immigrants have formed Islamic hubs in California, Illinois, Michigan and Texas.

At the center of these hubs stands a familiar sight in a foreign land, the mosque. What was a place of worship in Pakistan or Algeria becomes, in Houston or Detroit, a social haven. But inside, the sexes remain largely apart.

A growing number of Muslim Web sites advertise marriage candidates, and housewives often double as matchmakers. One mosque in Princeton, N.J., plays host to a closely supervised version of speed dating. And so many singles worship at the Islamic Society of Boston that a committee was formed to match them up.

Fearing a potential surplus of single Muslim women, one Brooklyn imam reportedly urged his wealthier male congregants during a Ramadan sermon last year to take two wives. When a woman complained about the sermon to Mr. Shata, he laughed.

"You know that preacher who said Hugo Chávez should be shot?" he asked. "We have our idiots, too."

More than a matchmaker, Mr. Shata sees himself as a surrogate elder to young Muslims, many of whom live far from their parents. In America, only an imam is thought to have the connections, wisdom and respect to step into the role.

Mr. Shata began the service three months after arriving in Brooklyn in 2002, recruited to lead the Islamic Society of Bay Ridge, a mosque on Fifth Avenue.

Dates chaperoned by Mr. Shata—or "meetings between candidates," as the imam prefers to call them—often take place in his distinctly unromantic office, amid rows of Islamic texts. As a couple get acquainted, the

While drafting a marriage contract, Sheik Reda Shata consults the pocket-size Koran he carries with him at all times. (Photograph courtesy of James Estrin/The New York Times)

imam sits quietly at his desk, writing a sermon or surfing the Arabic Web sites of CNN and the BBC.

If there is an awkward silence, the imam perks up and asks a question ("So tell me, Ilham, how many siblings do you have?") and the conversation is moving again.

Candidates are vetted carefully, and those without personal references need not apply. But instinct is Mr. Shata's best guide. He refused to help a Saudi from California because the man would consider only a teenage wife. Others have shown an all-too-keen interest in a green card.

Those who pass initial inspection are listed in the imam's version of a little black book—their names, phone numbers, specifications and desires. Some prefer "silky hair," others "a virgin." Nearly all candidates, men and women alike, want a mate with devotion to Islam, decent looks and legal immigration status.

Scanning the book, the imam makes his pitch with the precision of a car salesman.

"There is a girl, an American convert, Dominican, looks a little Egyptian. Skin-wise, not white, not dark. Wheat-colored. She's 19, studies accounting," Mr. Shata told a 24-year-old Palestinian man one afternoon.

"This is my only choice?" replied the man, Yamal Othman, who lives in Queens.

Such questions annoy Mr. Shata. An imam, he says, should be trusted to select the best candidate. Often, though, his recommendations are met with skepticism.

"It's harder than choosing a diamond," said Mr. Shata.

Sometimes, on the imam's three-legged dates, no one seems more excited than Mr. Shata himself. He makes hurried, hearty introductions and then steps back to watch, as if mixing chemicals in a lab experiment. Love is rarely ignited, but the imam remains awed by its promise.

Mr. Shata discovered love 15 years ago, when he walked into the living room of the most stately house in Kafr al Battikh.

The imam was tall, 22, a rising star at the local mosque. For months, Omyma Elshabrawy knew only his voice. She would listen to his thunderous sermons from the women's section, out of view. Then, one evening, he appeared at her home, presented as a prospective groom to her father, a distinguished reciter of the Koran.

The young woman, then 20, walked toward Mr. Shata carrying a tray of lemonade.

"She entered my heart," said the imam.

After serving the drinks, she disappeared. Right then, Mr. Shata asked her father for her hand in marriage. The older man paused. His daughter was the town beauty, an English student with marriage offers from doctors. The imam was penniless.

But before Mr. Elshabrawy could respond, a sugary voice interrupted. "I accept," his daughter said from behind a door.

"I loved him from the moment I saw him," Ms. Elshabrawy said.

They now have four children.

The family posed last year for a Sears-style portrait, taken by a woman in Bay Ridge who photographs Muslim families in her basement. A blue sky and white picket fence adorn the background. The imam sits at center, with the baby, Mohammed, in his lap, his three daughters smiling, his wife wrapped in a lime-green hijab.

Mr. Shata carries the picture in the breast pocket of his robe. It is as close as most people get to his family. At the mosque, they are a mystery. His wife has been there twice.

Their years in America have come with great hardship, a subject the imam rarely discusses. The trouble is the illness of his 7-year-old daughter, Rawda, who is severely epileptic. She has dozens of seizures every day and rarely leaves home. No combination of medicine seems to help.

"Rawda is the wound in my heart," the imam said.

Mr. Shata offers long, stubborn theories about the value of marriage, but to observe him at home is to understand the commitment he seeks to foster in other Muslims.

The family lives in a spare, dimly lighted apartment two blocks from the mosque. Headscarves are piled over Pokémon cards. The gold-painted words "Allah is Great" are framed over a threadbare couch. In the next room, an "I ♥ New York" bumper sticker is slapped on the wall.

Mr. Shata spends long hours away from his family, lecturing at mosques, settling disputes, whispering the call to prayer in the ears of newborn babies. On his walk home at night, he shops for groceries, never forgetting the Honey Nut Cheerios, a favorite American discovery of his children.

When he walks in the door, his face softens. Loud kisses are planted on tender cheeks. Mohammed squeals, the girls smile, sweet laughter echoes.

But then there is Rawda.

"My beautiful girl," the imam says softly one evening, holding his limp daughter in his lap after a seizure has passed. He places one pill in Rawda's mouth, then another. She looks at him weakly.

"There we go," he whispers. "Inshallah."

Her lids close with sleep. He lays her in bed and shuts off the light.

Hardship, the imam believes—like marriage, like life—is a test from God.

Foreign and Familiar

It is proof of the imam's uncommon popularity among women that he is trusted with roughly 300 female marriage candidates.

The mosque on Fifth Avenue is a decidedly male place. Men occupy every position on the board of directors. They crowd the sidewalk after prayer. Only they may enter the mosque's central room of worship. Only men, they often point out, are required to attend the Friday prayer.

One floor below is the cramped room where the women worship. On Fridays, they sit pressed together, their headscarves itching with heat. They must watch their imam on a closed-circuit television that no one seems to have adjusted in years.

But they listen devotedly. Teenage girls often roll their eyes at foreign imams, who seem to them like extraterrestrials. Their immigrant mothers often find these clerics too strict, an uncomfortable reminder of their conservative homelands.

Mr. Shata is both foreign and familiar. He presides over a patriarchal world, sometimes upholding it, and other times challenging it. In one sermon, he said that a man was in charge of his home and had the right to "choose his wife's friends."

Another day, to the consternation of his male congregants, he invited a female Arab social worker to lecture on domestic violence. The women were allowed to sit next to the men in the main section of the mosque.

The imam frowns at career women who remain single in their 30's, but boasts of their accomplishments to interest marriage candidates. He employs his own brand of feminism, vetting marriage contracts closely to ensure brides receive a fair dowry and fighting for them when they don't.

Far more than is customary, he spends hours listening to women: to their worries and confessions, their intimate secrets and frank questions about everything from menstruation to infidelity. They line up outside his office and call his home at all hours, often referring to him as "my brother" or "father." He can summon the details of their lives with the same encyclopedic discipline he once used to memorize the Koran.

"Are you separated yet?" Mr. Shata asked a woman he encountered at Lutheran Medical Center one day last July. She nodded. "May God make it easier for you," he said.

A Chaperoned Date

By most standards, the Egyptian bachelor was a catch. He had broad shoulders and a playful smile. He was witty. He earned a comfortable salary as an engineer, and came from what he called "a good family."

But the imam saw him differently, as a young man in danger of losing his faith. The right match might save him.

The bachelor, who is 33, came to Brooklyn from Alexandria, Egypt, six years earlier. He craved a better salary, and freedom from controlling parents. He asked that his name not be printed for fear of causing embarrassment to his family.

America was not like Egypt, where his family's connections could secure a good job. In Brooklyn, he found work as a busboy. He traded the plush comfort of his parents' home for an apartment crowded with other Egyptian immigrants. His nights were lonely. Temptation was abundant.

Women covered far less of their bodies. Bare limbs, it seemed, were everywhere. In Islam, men are instructed to lower their gaze to avoid falling into sin.

"In the summertime, it's a disaster for us," said the bachelor. "Especially a guy like me, who's looking all the time."

Curiosity lured him into bars, clubs and the occasional one-night stand.

But with freedom came guilt, he said. After drifting from his faith, he visited Mr. Shata's mosque during Ramadan in 2004.

The imam struck him as oddly disarming. He made jokes, and explained Islam in simple, passionate paragraphs. The bachelor soon began praying daily, attending weekly lectures and reading the Koran. By then, he had his own apartment and a consulting job.

Now he wanted a Muslim wife.

If the bachelor had been in Egypt, his parents would offer a stream of marriage candidates. The distance had not stopped them entirely. His mother sent him a video of his brother's wedding, directing him to footage of a female guest. He was unimpressed.

"I'm a handsome guy," he explained one evening as he sped toward Manhattan. It was his second date with Mr. Shata in attendance. "I have a standard in beauty."

From the passenger seat, the imam flipped open the glove compartment to find an assortment of pricey colognes. He inspected a bottle of Gio and, with a nod from the bachelor, spritzed it over his robe.

The imam and the bachelor were at odds over the material world, but on one thing they agreed: it is a Muslim duty to smell good. The religion's founder, the Prophet Muhammad, was said to wear musk.

The car slowed before a brick high-rise on Second Avenue. Soon the pair rode up in the elevator. The bachelor took a breath and rang the doorbell. An older woman answered. Behind her stood a slender, fetching woman with a shy smile.

The young woman, Engy Abdelkader, had been presented to the imam by another matchmaker. A woman of striking beauty and poise, Ms. Abdelkader is less timid than she first seems. She works as an immigration and human rights lawyer, and speaks in forceful, eloquent bursts. She is proud of her faith, and lectures publicly on Islam and civil liberties.

She was not always so outspoken. The daughter of Egyptian immigrants, Ms. Abdelkader, 30, was raised in suburban Howell, N.J., where she longed to fit in. Though she grew up praying, in high school she chose not to wear a hijab, the head scarf donned by Muslim girls when they reach puberty.

But Sept. 11 awakened her, Ms. Abdelkader said. For her and other Muslims, the terrorist attacks prompted a return to the faith, driven by what she said was a need to reclaim Islam from terrorists and a vilifying media. Headscarves became a statement, equal parts political and religious.

"There's nothing oppressive about it," said Ms. Abdelkader. "As a Muslim woman I am asking people to pay attention to the content of my character rather than my physical appearance."

Mr. Shata performs marriage ceremonies weekly, encountering a diversity in America that he never imagined in Egypt. Here, he unites an Ecuadorean and a Syrian man, though he would not convert her until she learned more about Islam. (Photograph courtesy of James Estrin/The New York Times)

The pair sat on a couch, awkwardly sipping tea. They began by talking, in English, about their professions. The bachelor was put off by the fact that Ms. Abdelkader had a law degree, yet earned a modest salary.

"Why go to law school and not make money?" he asked later.

Ms. Abdelkader's mother and a female friend who lived in the apartment sat listening nearby until the imam mercifully distracted them. The first hint of trouble came soon after.

It was his dream, the engineer told Ms. Abdelkader, to buy a half-million-dollar house. But he was uncertain that the mortgage he would need is lawful in Islam.

Ms. Abdelkader straightened her back and replied, "I would rather have eternal bliss in the hereafter than live in a house or apartment with a mortgage."

An argument ensued. Voices rose. Ms. Abdelkader's mother took her daughter's side. The friend wavered. The bachelor held his ground. The imam tried to mediate.

Indeed, he was puzzled. Here was a woman who had grown up amid tended lawns and new cars, yet she rejected materialism. And here was a man raised by Muslim hands, yet he was rebelliously moderate.

After the date, the bachelor told the imam, "I want a woman, not a sheik."

Months later, he married another immigrant; she was not especially devoted to Islam but she made him laugh, he said. They met through friends in New York.

Ms. Abdelkader remains single. The imam still believes she was the perfect match.

That evening, the imam stood on the sidewalk outside. Rain fell in stinging drops.

"I never wanted to be a sheik," he said. "I used to think that a religious person is very extreme and never smiles. And I love to smile. I love to laugh. I used to think that religious people were isolated and I love to be among people."

The rain soaked the imam's robe and began to pool in his sandals. A moment later, he ducked inside the building.

"The surprise for me was that the qualities I thought would not make a good sheik—simplicity and humor and being close to people—those are the most important qualities. People love those who smile and laugh. They need someone who lives among them and knows their pain."

"I know them," said Mr. Shata. "Like a brother."

A conversation with
Andrea Elliott

This edited e-mail interview was conducted by Thomas Huang, an assistant managing editor at The Dallas Morning News *and a Poynter Online contributor, with Andrea Elliot, winner of the Freedom Forum/ASNE Award for Distinguished Writing on Diversity.*

THOMAS HUANG: How did you begin to think about creating a beat on Islam in America? And what drew you to covering that community—what are the things that appeal to you about it?

ANDREA ELLIOTT: The idea for my beat grew out of a small assignment I got one month after joining the *Times* as a Metro reporter in May 2003. My task that day was to write a sidebar to accompany a National story about how thousands of Muslim immigrants faced deportation as a result of a federal counterterrorism program.

The *Times* had run no local stories on the subject. I had little to go on, so I headed to Midwood, the Brooklyn neighborhood better known as "Little Pakistan." As I walked along Coney Island Avenue, I was struck by what I found. Shops were boarded up. Attendance at the local mosque had fallen dramatically. Curry packets were gathering dust on the shelves of grocery stores. Thousands of Muslim immigrants had left, fearing deportation.

I filed the story, but it stuck in my mind. The following year, I returned to Midwood and met with an activist. When I asked him to describe how Sept. 11 had changed his neighborhood, he handed me a thick binder. On page after page, a history unfolded. A boy told how he was beaten and called "Osama" at school. An old man reported losing a new job after his employers learned he was Muslim. The accounts were part of a survey that had been commissioned by the city. It captured a major story that we were missing.

That month, I proposed a new beat to my editors: Islam in a post–9/11 America. I saw it not as a religion beat, but as an interdisciplinary one, combining immigration, news, politics and social trends. I wanted to avoid reductionist themes, like the "victimization" or "radicalization" of Muslims. My idea was to explore the gray and complicated narratives of Muslim life, like the struggle to redefine Islam under the gaze of public scrutiny.

Telling the story of an imam is a powerful way of getting at the tensions within a community that is under scrutiny and being challenged to change. Was that an idea you already had as you created the beat, or did it come to you in some other way?

The imam series was, in some ways, born of frustration. I had launched into my beat with dozens of story ideas. But for every person I interviewed, 10 others refused to talk. I began referring to my job as the "no-one-will-talk-to-you" beat. Everywhere I went, it seemed, Muslims had the same complaint: They felt the press had maligned their faith and was largely to blame for their recent problems in the United States. As a result, they put up walls around their community that I, as a non-Muslim outsider, could not seem to get past.

When my first stories began to appear, some doors opened. People began to call with tips. But I realized that unless I spent a lot of time in one neighborhood or mosque, I would never capture a deeper story. So six months in, I pitched the idea of a series on one imam.

It seemed like a promising subject. Imams have access to every facet of Muslim immigrant life. Nobody in the Muslim community is more exposed to the problems of its people. At the same time, imams face their own painful process of adaptation in America, one that says a lot about the experience of Islam in the West.

I got an early clue of this when James Estrin, the photographer of the series, heard about a group of mental health professionals in New York who were teaching imams about psychology. While priests and rabbis are routinely trained in pastoral counseling, most imams come to the United States unprepared for that. In Muslim countries, they simply lead the daily prayers and give the weekly sermon. But the job here is far more complex and after Sept. 11, some imams in New York began suffering from depression and anxiety. Just from hearing that, I sensed there was a great story there.

More generally, how do you generate your story ideas?

I ask a lot of questions that start with, "Forgive my ignorance, but . . ." I have found that the most basic questions elicit fascinating answers. I listen to my gut. If something piques my curiosity, it will probably pique the reader's. I ask people I meet who else I should meet. I carry around a list of story ideas and bounce them off anyone, from hot dog vendors to professors. This beat is so rich, I rarely leave a good conversation without new ideas.

How did you decide what the focus would be for each part of the imam series?

From start to finish, I spent eight months on this series. Not surprisingly, I began with one set of ideas, and came out the other end with a different story. At the outset, I had three themes I wanted to pursue: how immigrant imams change in America, how their mosques work and how American and Islamic law are balanced in the lives of Muslim immigrants.

Many weeks after I found Sheik Reda and began reporting, I stumbled upon two gems. First, I learned that his mosque was at the center of a major terrorism case involving an undercover police informer whom Sheik Reda had gotten to know personally. Then I found out that the imam was acting as a chaperone for single Muslims who were searching for spouses. Those discoveries became the basis for two parts of the series.

My editor and I decided that the first part of the series needed to serve as an introduction to the life of imams and Sheik Reda's passage to America. The second day would explore the imam's dealings with law enforcement officials. The third day would look to the future of young Muslims by exploring their courtships.

How did you organize each part of the series?

When I sat down to write, I had hundreds of pages of transcribed notes and some scenes I had already sketched out, not knowing where they would fit. I printed out all these notes and then sat there staring at the pile. I had no idea where to start, so I just read my notes in order, beginning with my first interview of Sheik Reda.

I wrote down anything that struck me as essential—themes, characters, scenes, ideas—on one giant legal notepad. Then I put away my notes and began a very detailed outline of the series. This proved to be a crucial filter. I honed my outline until I felt it was organized and thorough enough to guide the writing.

Of course, writing has its own way of generating ideas, and sending the narrative off in new directions. So I allowed room for that. And I continued to report while writing for two reasons: New questions constantly emerged, and staying close to the mosque kept the story fresh in my mind.

Sheik Reda Shata seems like a dream of a person to write about—he's charismatic, funny, serious, reflective, honest. He makes things happen. How did you find him? Were there other imams you considered along the way? What was it about Mr. Shata that made you decide to write about him?

I interviewed roughly a dozen imams before I met Sheik Reda. By then, it was clear that imams tended to be as wary of the press as their congregants. One imam in New Jersey sat with me for five minutes and then said, "Well, that should be enough for your story."

I didn't worry much about the fear I encountered because another problem distracted me: I had not found the right subject. I was looking for an imam who had been in the United States long enough to have built a following, but not so long that he had overcome the greatest obstacles. I wanted to find someone who was still changing and adapting.

The first thing I heard about Sheik Reda, from another Egyptian imam, was that he had spent a week in the hospital after collapsing during a sermon. I began calling his mosque and finally got an appointment to see him a few weeks later. I'll never forget the day I arrived at the Islamic Society of Bay Ridge. A man in a suit led me to Sheik Reda's office. When I began talking to the imam, through my translator, the man in the suit pulled out a digital recorder. "We record all interviews," he said. I later learned that Sheik Reda had never been interviewed by a newspaper reporter. They were just nervous.

In spite of that, I knew then that Sheik Reda was the right subject. He was thoughtful and open and curious. He had this urge to explain things. During that first meeting, he described the challenge of assimilation like this: "If you plant foreign organisms in a body, there is a kind of negotiation that takes place. That's why we have to understand, as a human society, that not everything that's different from us is an enemy." And that was just the first interview.

I'm sure that one of the greatest challenges of covering the Muslim community is gaining people's trust and getting access to them. How did you gain Mr. Shata's trust? What are some specific things you needed to do to start gaining the community's trust?

It was a slow and delicate process. The mosque's board of directors had deep reservations about letting us in. Other imams were warning Sheik Reda to steer clear of us. So Jim and I began taking him, and the most influential board members, to dinner. We started a dialogue that never really ended until after the stories ran.

They felt they had everything to lose and little to gain. The argument I made to them was that if nobody lets the media in, the public's understanding of Muslims will remain one-dimensional. Jim and I kept saying, "Help us understand the Muslim community." That resonated with them, because they yearned to be understood.

In the end, though, I think what won their trust was simply our daily presence at the mosque. We kept going back, day after day. Eventually, they stopped seeing us as outsiders. We faded into the background. That's when interesting things started to happen.

Is there any part of Mr. Shata's work or life that he made off-limits to you?

By the third month of reporting, I had a view into every part of his life, including the most private corner of it, his family. There were a few meetings that congregants requested I not attend, involving business disputes that he brokered or counseling sessions. But for the most part, I was given free rein.

You mention that Mr. Shata doesn't speak a lot of English and that you had to use a translator for the series. Sometimes, that can be like trying to talk under water. How did you handle it, and how were you able to get the nuances of what Mr. Shata said?

It would have been far easier to choose an imam who spoke some English. But I think that kind of convenience would have prevented me from observing something important, which is the experience of imams who arrive here with no English and still have to make sense of the world around them.

I certainly feared that things could get lost in translation, and because of that, I spent a lot of time reviewing complicated subjects with Sheik Reda to make sure I had understood him. I also worked with the best Arabic translators I could find.

Of course, some things did not translate culturally. In the beginning, we needed his permission to follow him around for months, so I tried to explain the journalistic process to him. I told him I wanted to be "a fly on the wall." He thought that was bizarre. Then Jim tried the shadow metaphor—"We just want to be your shadow." He looked alarmed.

Finally, I told him to imagine that we were making a film about his life. A film has scenes. And he got it. He said, "A film has a story." I suppose it's ironic that I had to reference a different medium to get him on board with this one.

In a story with cultural and language barriers, a reporter's skills at observation seem key to me. Have you thought about your approach to getting details and witnessing certain moments? What advice would you have for younger reporters?

When I see odd or moving or amazing things happen, I just start scribbling madly, trying to absorb everything. I don't worry about where it fits in the story. Often, with a project, you don't know at the time if something will be useful. It could be the lead. So when interesting moments come, both big and small, I feel like I can't have too many details stored in my notebook, especially with a scene-driven story. I write everything down—how the person sounds, how the room feels, what song is playing in the background.

The other thing that helped me during this project was to transcribe my notes while they were still fresh. Sometimes, I would come home at night and just try to write a scene, not knowing whether I would use it. It's much harder to reconstruct something once the details are stale.

Knowing that all reporters are human beings, what are some things you learned about yourself in reporting the imam series?

I learned that I need to be patient, and trust in the process. It's one of the hardest things to do on a project like this because you're investing so much time, hoping that you will find something novel and great. But there are no guarantees. For the first month or so of my reporting on Sheik Reda, he and others at the mosque would often pull back when we got too close, and that was deeply discouraging. But it takes time to build trust.

What did you bring to the table, and how did your own upbringing and personal experience shape your approach to reporting and telling the imam's story? It seems to me that, in order to write powerful stories from diverse communities, we need to tap into what's different and unique about ourselves.

It's very true. And yet there is often a sense among reporters that in order to protect the integrity of our work, we cannot open up to a source and reveal our own humanity; we see it as a one-way street. I don't think I could have gotten Sheik Reda and others at the mosque to open up to me without doing the same myself.

I sometimes talked with them about my experiences growing up Catholic, and what it was like to be the daughter of a Chilean immigrant. Sheik Reda was very pleased to learn that I was getting married. Whenever we had an awkward moment, he would ask me about my wedding plans. Marriage became a point of connection between us—an institution we shared.

When you mention that you talked with Mr. Shata about growing up Catholic and growing up as the daughter of a Chilean immigrant—can you give me an anecdote on that?

I related to his children a lot. Growing up, I felt much more at home in America than my mother. She was highly educated and spoke fluent

English. But like any immigrant, she struggled to understand this country and I sometimes found myself acting as her cultural interpreter. That happened to a much more extreme degree in Sheik Reda's family, because he spoke no English. But we talked a lot about the weight that children of immigrants carry, because they tend to acclimate to a new country so much more quickly than their parents.

There are moments between Mr. Shata and his children that stir strong emotions in me. There's a photo of him walking two of his daughters to the school bus that reminds me of what it was like to be a child with immigrant parents. Did the experience of Mr. Shata and his family resonate with you because of that?

Yes, my experience growing up in a bicultural, bilingual home enabled me to connect with his family. But I don't think that reporters should let their lack of common ground with a particular source, or community, hold them back. I have heard people say that it would be better to have a reporter with an Arab and/or Muslim identity work on this kind of story. It certainly would have helped me at times. But I don't think my own background hindered me. Outsiders can bring a fresh perspective.

That said, I think most newsrooms have a lamentable shortage of reporters with Arab, and South Asian, backgrounds. That needs to change.

One of the many strengths of the imam series is that you're able to write with authority. Can you tell me a little bit about the research you did on Islam before you embarked on this series?

I had read a lot of books on Islam. I debriefed many professors and other experts. But I think what helped me most, in the early stages of my beat coverage, was simply diving in and doing stories. You learn a lot by doing.

You have the instinct not only for selecting the right details, but also selecting the right stories—the anecdotes that show rather than tell. In the first story, for example, we learn about the U.S.-Muslim cultural differences through a series of anecdotes: women dialing 911 to report inheritance disputes; a tone-deaf man allowed to be a *muezzin* because the mosque doesn't want to discriminate; a creative response to combative hot dog vendors. How do you select these anecdotes? Do you leave a lot on the cutting room floor?

The cutting room floor was about a foot deep in lost anecdotes and scenes. That's always a painful process. But when you are spending this much time on a story, you have to be as ruthless in your editing as you are passionate in your writing. If a certain passage does not fully serve the story, it has to go. A former professor and mentor of mine at Columbia University, Sig Gissler, refers to it as "drowning kittens."

What revisions did you make to the story before publishing?

I revised until the last minute, tweaking and polishing and obsessing. That's the way I am. I wouldn't recommend it.

The most significant change I made was to the top of the first story. Writing that lead was challenging because I had to capture so many things at once about a subject that was little understood—what an imam does, why his job is so different in the United States, what his story reveals about Islam in America.

When I began writing, I had spent months inside the mosque, and knew it intimately. But I was losing sight of the big picture. I think that's a common experience with projects like this. You have to wade in deeply to report it. You have to pull back to write it.

In my very first draft, I tried an anecdotal lead that didn't quite work. My editor, Joe Sexton, urged me to step back and try something more simple. I began thinking about the imam's daily rituals and that's when I got the idea to write about his morning walk. I liked the familiarity of that image. Almost anyone could visualize a robed, Muslim immigrant walking along a city street. But here, the story follows that man into his mosque and his life.

What role did your editor play?

Joe had shepherded many impressive projects into the paper before we began working on this one. He has incredibly good instincts, and a talent for seeing the architecture of a series. He gets involved long before the writing begins. We talked a lot. He was always interested in hearing about my latest triumph or struggle. When I got mired in the minutiae of the story, he steered me back to thinking broadly. I was very lucky to have him.

In the second story, which focuses on the mosque and community being under the FBI's watch, there's a difficult and sensitive passage where Mr. Shata talks about Israel, Hamas and suicide bombing operations. Tell me more about how you got him to open up about that.

With the help of translators, I had gone over dozens of Sheik Reda's sermons and found that in one of them he had exalted a female Palestinian suicide bomber, calling her a martyr.

At first, Sheik Reda didn't want to talk about it. He insisted that no matter what explanation he gave, he would be misunderstood. I said that

I had an obligation to include this in the series, and urged him to explain himself. Readers would draw their own conclusions, I told him. But many of them would never have a window into his thinking unless he opened up. Looking back, I don't believe he would have talked about this had I not spent so much time with him. But he did, and I think the story was better and more nuanced as a result.

In the third story, you describe Mr. Shata's matchmaking as "his way of fashioning a future for his faith. It is his most heartfelt effort—by turns graceful and comedic, vexing and hopeful—to make Islam work in America." That strikes me as the core—the essence—of your series. What do you mean by "make Islam work in America"?

I think a lot of people see Islam and the West as incompatible. Muslim immigrants are often portrayed, especially on television, as inflexible or intolerant. But what I found in Brooklyn is that Muslims tend to be deeply engaged with Western culture and influenced by it, because their survival here depends on it.

The thing I kept hearing from readers after the series ran was, "They're like us." And essentially it's true. They have the same struggles and yearnings of every other immigrant group that has settled in this country. They want to make it here; they want their children to succeed. And they are trying to figure out how to do that without losing their culture and faith.

One memorable scene from the third story is when an Egyptian bachelor heads to a date, with Mr. Shata as his chaperone. Mr. Shata takes some of the bachelor's cologne and spritzes it on his robes. Funny and so human. And then there's the awkward conversation between the bachelor and his date, an opinionated lawyer. So I have to ask: How did you persuade the couple to let you in on their date?

This was an unusual reporting experience, to say the least. The sheik thought the couple would back out if they knew I was coming in advance, so he introduced me to the bachelor on the evening of the date. I made my pitch and the bachelor agreed to allow the translator and me to tag along, provided I did not use his name. So off we went in his car.

The woman he was meeting only knew that the sheik was bringing him and some guests. When we arrived, she hardly noticed the entourage standing behind the bachelor. Later that evening, when she learned that I was a reporter, she was a bit startled. So when the sheik and the bachelor paused for the evening prayer, I pulled her aside and assured her that I would only write about that evening with her permission. She relaxed and agreed to let me keep taking notes, on the condition that we would meet again to talk.

When we later met, I explained the scope of my project. When she realized I was working on a serious story, she decided it was important to contribute. Like so many Muslims I interviewed, she really wanted to be better understood by non-Muslims. She agreed to go on the record and let me freely use the material from the date. I also continued to interview the bachelor. With both of them, I went over the date again and again, to understand what they had been thinking that evening. So I really reported this in reverse, getting to know the subjects after witnessing the scene that came to define them in the story.

In the third story, we get a glimpse of Mr. Shata's family, and we learn about the illness of his 7-year-old daughter. Was it difficult to get him to open up about his family and give you access to them?

It took me several months to meet his family. I felt an immediate bond with his wife, Omyma, and their four children, which helped a lot. Sheik Reda is a complicated, fascinating man. But until I saw him at home, I didn't have a full sense of him as a person.

He has one personality as a preacher and another personality as a father. At the pulpit, he is an erudite, authoritative man. At home, he's a soft, goofy dad. When he laughs, his whole body shakes. He is addicted to his children.

When I finally saw that side of him, I began to feel ready to write.

What kind of reaction did you get when the series was published? Did it achieve what you hoped it would achieve?

The reaction was pretty overwhelming. People began calling the mosque from all over the country. Prison inmates wrote to Sheik Reda. Hundreds of unmarried Muslims sought his help as a matchmaker. Priests and ministers and rabbis reached out to him.

I was relieved that Sheik Reda found the series fair and accurate. At first, he enjoyed the status of a minor celebrity. The stories were reprinted in Arabic all over the Middle East. But the attention turned negative when scholars began to debate his interpretation of Islamic law, which many people found too liberal.

A jihadist Web site in Britain lampooned him. Some members of his mosque began to agitate against him. Flyers appeared on the streets of Bay Ridge, declaring him "a devil." At one point, the articles set off a fist fight outside the mosque. Eventually it all became too much for Sheik Reda, and he found a new job at a mosque in Middletown, N.J., which I reported in a follow-up story.

He says that the move has improved his life. He has a nice house, a better salary and good schools for his children. But I think only time will tell. I have mixed feelings about this outcome. I feel immensely grateful that he allowed us into his life. But, I also feel troubled by the hardship it caused him.

One positive and lasting effect of the series was how much it changed my relationship with the Muslim community. It's as if a giant door has opened. People talk to me now.

A conversation with Sheik Reda Shata

This edited e-mail interview was conducted by Thomas Huang, an assistant managing editor at The Dallas Morning News *and a Poynter Online contributor, with Sheik Reda Shata, with help from* New York Times *reporter Andrea Elliott and Sadek Ahmed, the translator used for the related* Times *stories on the imam.*

THOMAS HUANG: What surprised you about being a part of the story, or the story itself?

SHEIK REDA SHATA: When the astronaut Neil Armstrong landed on the moon he said, "That's one small step for man, one giant leap for mankind." These were the words that moved me in the beginning to get involved with this story. I knew that I was somehow like Armstrong, making a small step on a personal level, yet a giant leap that would benefit the Muslim community and, in turn, humanity. It was a step that I believe was bigger than our differences.

What have you learned from this experience?

It is very difficult to tell all what I have learned from this experience. But I'll tell some of it.

First, the continuous repercussions that I have faced following the publication of the articles, whether on the personal level, the community level or the public level, were like drum beats in the theater of life. I am like a person in the audience who has been watching a live, educational play.

Second, honesty, honesty, honesty. We have to say what we believe. And what we say in secret must not differ from what we say in public.

Third, we are like waves in the ocean. We appear similar but in reality we are all different, and ever-regenerating. The ocean cannot stop moving. Once it gets calm it dies.

Fourth, every so often, a person walks by the ocean and is amazed at its beauty, yet throws a stone at it. We have to be prepared for people's unexpected reactions to our well-intended actions.

What would you like to say to other journalists who cover similar fields?

I want to say that a great writer is not someone who can put together the most beautiful words and sentences. Rather a great writer is someone who can break into your world, and quietly enter your soul, one who possesses the ability to draw your picture with words. Andrea was able to do that, simply because she looked at me through my own eyes, used my own words to question me and measured me according to my own standards. That is the way to do it.

In Shakespeare's "Hamlet" I read something very amazing. There was a man in Hamlet's court who could not play the flute. Hamlet told him, "How do you think that you can find my secrets and play on the strings of my soul when you cannot even play this simple musical instrument?" What I am trying to say is a writer must live the life of the person he or she writes about. They must involve themselves in their lives, experience their experiences and then step aside and simply write.

To journalists, I would like to mention an old proverb I once read that says, "A drop of honey will catch more flies than a barrel of bitter substance." The same applies to people. If you want to describe a certain faith or community, or write about a person, convince him first that you are an honest person. This is the drop of honey that will open the heart and stir the mind and start the cooperation.

Writers' Workshop

Talking Points

1. Andrea Elliott writes, "In America, imams evoke a simplistic caricature—of robed, bearded clerics issuing fatwas in foreign lands. Hundreds of imams live in the United States, but their portrait remains flatly one-dimensional." Discuss the techniques Elliott uses to portray Sheik Reda Shata as a multidimensional person. What do we learn about his past, his family life, his personality?

2. In "A Muslim Leader in Brooklyn, Reconciling 2 Worlds," one challenge Mr. Shata faces is navigating the American culture and adapting Islamic mores to that culture. Give some examples of how he does this. How does he handle couples who wish to divorce? What does he have to say about mortgages, music and attitudes toward sex?

3. In "To Lead the Faithful in a Faith Under Fire," describe how Mr. Shata feels about cooperating with law enforcement officials who monitor the Muslim community post–9/11. What anecdotes does Elliott use to show Mr. Shata's conflicted emotions about this situation?

4. "Tending to Muslim Hearts and Islam's Future" focuses on dating and marriage in the Muslim-American world. Why do you think Elliott chose to take an in-depth look at this topic? Discuss what you learned about young Muslim-Americans in this story.

Assignment Desk

1. Andrea Elliott created a new beat because she recognized that the Muslim-American community was undercovered. Draw up a list of other groups in your community that you think are undercovered. Select one group and write down three steps you would take to start understanding and covering that group.

2. Elliott uses details to show, rather than tell. For example, this is how she describes Mr. Shata's family's apartment: "Headscarves are piled over Pokémon cards. The gold-painted words 'Allah is Great' are framed over a threadbare couch. In the next room, an 'I ♥ New York' bumper sticker is slapped on the wall." These details reinforce a theme Elliot explores in the series. Choose a room in your house

or apartment. Take a minute to fill your notebook with details that you observe in that room. Then sit down and choose the three or four details that can help you tell a story about that room.

3. Identify three experts that Elliott quotes in her stories. Write down what each expert brings to the story. Now consider a story that you would like to report. Who are the expert sources you would need to talk to for the story? What background do you need to understand in order to write the story?

4. Elliott wrote a series about an imam who does not speak much English. How did Elliot get around the language barrier? To gain experience in dealing with the language barrier, identify an interesting person you'd like to profile who does not speak English. Then find someone who can serve as a translator. This might be a friend who knows the language, or someone who works in a school, church or nonprofit agency that serves the immigrant community. Set up a meeting with your profile subject and practice interviewing him or her through the translator. How did working through a translator change the interviewing experience?

THE ROANOKE TIMES

Finalist

Beth Macy

Diversity Writing

21. Driven to Succeed

JULY 24, 2006

Rocio Ortiz has a monster inside her.

It screams at the factory workers she supervises when they slack off or talk too much.

It growls when her teenage son explains why he can come and go as he pleases, and when the high school principal calls—again—to say her son was skipping school.

We could have died just getting here from Mexico, Rocio tells him for the umpteenth time.

And: *Forget about these cushy Roanoke County suburbs. When I was your age, I didn't have a house.*

I didn't even have socks.

There was a time when the monster protected Rocio, when it pushed her as she scrambled across the border and away from a life dependent on cheap shoes sold from the back of her rickety bike.

It helped her shed the shameful "illegal immigrant" label, propelling her from factory worker to plant manager to business entrepreneur.

But sometimes, the monster still keeps her up at night.

A Chicken All to Yourself

To this day, Rocio can barely look at her childhood photos. She's 3 or 4 in one of them, wearing a frayed poncho and clutching an equally sad-looking mutt. By 12, she was a sixth-grade dropout, on the gang-infested streets of Mexico City. When her parents split earlier that year, her mother abandoned the kids, and her father started a second family of his own.

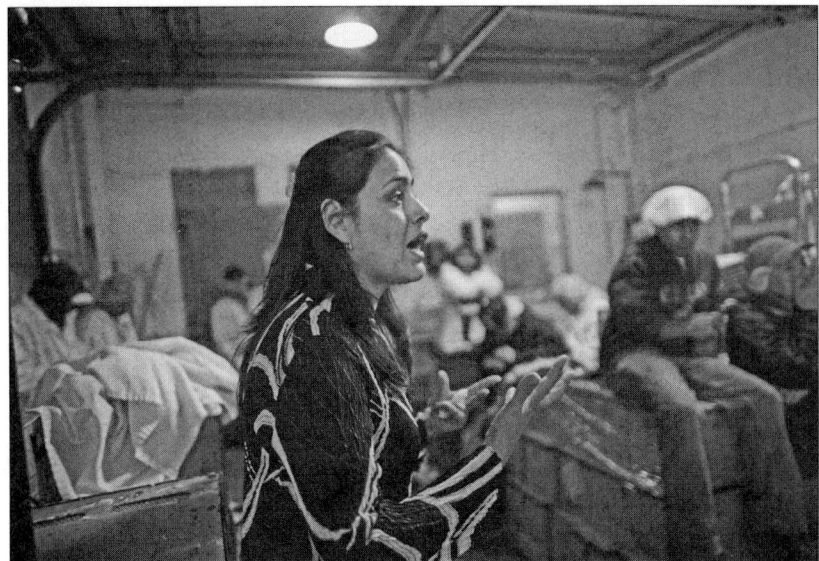

Rocio Ortiz meets with workers at a local factory to discuss whether they will take May 1 off from work to campaign for immigrants' rights. Ortiz still works part time at the factory, which has become a highly successful business, thanks largely to her Type A work ethic. (Photograph courtesy of Josh Meltzer/*The Roanoke Times*)

Ask her to explain what prompted her homelessness—both her parents were alive; her father owned a small chair factory—and she can't. She stares into space, speechless for a minute, then sobs.

"They . . . didn't . . . care about me," she says.

The only person she could rely on was herself. At 13, Rocio mounted a suitcase onto the back of her bicycle and filled it with shoes, which she sold door to door for the equivalent of $3. She collected parental figures the way most little girls collect dolls.

The first one was her mother-in-law. Rocio was 15 when she met Carlos and became pregnant before long. Rather than a "quinceañera"—the elaborate coming-of-age ceremony held on a Hispanic girl's 15th birthday—Rocio had a small wedding.

Carlos' family embraced the newlyweds, giving them a room in their house. The room was tiny but Rocio managed to pack in a bed, table, stove and kitchen sink. When Roberto was born in 1988, the couple made a child's seat out of an old cardboard box.

Rocio painted the walls to give the "apartment" a homey feel and complained when the in-laws in the next room crowded her space. She loved that she had a family now, especially a mother, but she wanted a house of her own and complained loudly to Carlos about it.

"If I hadn't screamed, I'd still be there," she says, looking at photographs. In one, precocious Roberto is sitting on an airplane he'd fashioned out of scrap wood, a rusty table and cinder blocks. "My brother-in-law is still in his room with his family, still living in his mother's house."

Then, as now, jobs were scarce: Carlos was lucky to make the equivalent of $5 a day. Roberto still has scars on his legs—from riding around the city on the back of his mom's bike.

When Rocio dreamed of the United States, it was an unattainable place, somewhere past the end of a gleaming white street and over the top of a hill. In her dreams, she never made it to the other side.

In reality, a friend told her, he knew a way she could. He had made the trip himself with the help of a smuggler, returning home with stories of lip-smacking meals. And cash.

He told the couple, "In America, you can have a whole chicken, and you don't even have to share. In America, you make more in one day than you make here in a week."

Only 'Temporary'

The first time Carlos Ortiz tried to sneak into the country, the plan was to go to Roanoke. He had a sister, already working for the El Rodeo Mexican restaurant chain, who could set him up. Once he saved enough money, he'd hire a coyote—a guide, essentially a human smuggler—to bring Rocio and Roberto to "El Norte," as they called the United States. The North.

Many Hispanic immigrants who migrated in the early and mid-'90s came to work just long enough to save money—for a house, a needed surgery, a daughter's quinceañera—then returned home. More than anything, Rocio wanted her own house in Mexico.

But U.S. immigration officials caught Carlos near Tijuana and sent him back. When Rocio found him on the doorstep—pale, dirty and dehydrated—they both burst into tears.

The second time around, in 1993, the plan worked. Carlos found himself in Virginia, living 10 restaurant workers to a house. He borrowed $2,000 from a co-worker and hired a coyote from Colombia.

To avoid being raped by corrupt Mexican police or gangsters, Rocio wore multiple shirts and dressed like a man, hiding her hair under a cap. The coyote helped her carry 4-year-old Roberto across the desert.

After serving a busy lunch crowd at their El Charly and Family restaurant, Rocio and her husband, Carlos Ortiz, steal a kiss while sitting down for a quick lunch of tacos sprinkled with fresh lime juice. (Photograph courtesy of Josh Meltzer/*The Roanoke Times*)

Eight hours and several prearranged car rides later, she was staring at the strangely clean streets of San Diego and clutching Roberto's hand.

In Roanoke, Rocio bused tables at El Rodeo while Carlos cooked in the back. When a bout of strep throat landed her at an area hospital, it took an hour just to explain, using hand gestures, what was wrong.

Roberto would not feel that shame, she vowed, enrolling him in a free Baptist-run preschool on Elm Avenue. She rode the bus with him from her sister-in-law's house. For three hours every morning, she waited outside while teachers taught him his colors and how to count to 10.

When a teacher spotted Rocio on the porch, she invited her in and gently asked: "Does your boy need socks?"

He had socks, albeit holey ones, and only a single pair. But that was OK, Rocio tried to explain, because she washed them out in the sink every night when he went to bed.

The next day, the teachers gave the boy a bag full of stuffed animals, clothes and several brand-new pairs of socks.

"They even had tennis shoes for me," she recalls. "In Mexico, nobody gave me anything. In Mexico, if you have one pair of socks, even holey ones, you have enough. If you have two, that's plenty."

Rocio was grateful for the gifts. But, she adds, "I was so ashamed."

'Never Seen Someone So Driven'

In two years, the couple saved $23,000—enough to buy a three-room bungalow on the outskirts of Mexico City. They thought they were returning for good.

Rocio fancied the house up, installing kitchen cabinets as she could afford them and nailing boards over cinder block walls.

But like many Mexicans who have tasted America, the lure of El Norte began to tug. Rocio took sewing classes and had hopes of opening a small sewing factory, but she couldn't raise the funds. The chair factory where Carlos worked was constantly laying people off.

"In Mexico, if you are 30, they will fire you to hire somebody younger," she says. "At 35, you're considered old."

In 1994, they had another son, Daniel, and little money for milk, fruit or meat. Carlos pleaded with his wife to quit wasting money on things like kitchen cabinets. "I want big pieces of meat," he said.

Rocio worried about Roberto, now 12, a ripe age for being targeted by gangs. "They will hurt you if you don't join their gangs," explained Carlos' sister, Isabel Booth, who came to Roanoke for the same reason Rocio and Carlos returned in 1999: to educate her kids.

This time, the family crossed the border together. Daniel, 4 at the time, remembers crawling under barbed-wire fences, his elbows rough from burrowing through the sand.

Back in Roanoke, fake documentation was easily acquired. Friends advised the couple to mail away for Social Security and green cards—for $100—and restaurant managers jump-started the process of applying for legitimate documentation, finally acquired in 2003.

Rocio found work at a meat packaging plant and, because they had no car, she bummed rides from a co-worker. She bought her first car, a 1987 Mercury, for $1,700.

Determined this time to learn English, she took night classes at Patrick Henry High School. Before long, when the boss wanted to tell the other Hispanic workers something, he relied on Rocio to translate.

"You have never seen someone so driven," recalls Rocio's English teacher, Shari Conley-Edwards. Out of the hundreds of foreign students she's taught over the years, "I can't think of anyone I'd hold up higher than Rocio. She still comes to my classes every now and then, just to review."

The public library became her refuge. Rocio bought books at yard sales and, at the suggestion of a librarian, checked the same books out on CD so she could follow along.

196 Untold Stories

Exhausted after spending the morning working in a local factory and a lunch hour serving immigrant workers at El Charly and Family, Rocio Ortiz curls up on a recliner with her stuffed animals in the back office to briefly recover. (Photograph courtesy of Josh Meltzer/*The Roanoke Times*)

The first novel she read all the way through was "Before I Say Goodbye," a romantic thriller by Mary Higgins Clark. It took nine months.

In 2001, word came down that the meat plant was closing, but another factory would be taking its place. The new owner needed employees, and it was his opinion, based on experience, that Hispanics worked the hardest.

Of the 24 Mexicans and Hondurans this man currently employs, he said, "They work so hard and so fast, sometimes they run from one workstation to the next. It would take 50 Americans to replace them."

There was just one problem: The man didn't speak Spanish.

Not only was Rocio bilingual, but she also worked harder for him than anyone else—65-hour workweeks were routine during the busy season. When she was promoted to manager, the authority gave her a rush.

Her boss, a father figure right away, encouraged her to set goals. He even let her leave work to take English classes without clocking out.

"He knew right away I had a monster inside me," Rocio says. "He had the experience, but I had the drive."

The Downside Of Driven

The factory owner agreed to be interviewed several times, under the condition that his name and the name of his business not be published. Like many area employers, he fears the attention could prompt an Immigration and Customs Enforcement raid.

But he will say this: Rocio was as instrumental in making his business a success as he was. Promoted to plant manager in 2001, the woman who was once homeless bought her first American house—she now owns two, including one she rents out for extra income—and invested in a 401(k).

"She feels, and I do, too, that we built what we have here together," her boss says. "She's very proud of the company and what it's done, and she blames me for being the way she is."

Still, Rocio found herself wanting more—especially for Carlos, who seemed to have no ambition beyond restaurant cooking and playing in his band. *Why don't you learn English? Why don't you have a monster, too?*

The monster caught up with Rocio last year, when there were one too many production orders at work and one too many arguments with employees. She and her boss were routinely putting in 70-hour weeks.

After Rocio fired a Honduran woman who couldn't get along with another employee, the woman's brother showed up, threatening to beat Rocio. Another time, after a bad storm, Rocio climbed atop the leaking roof, tacked down a tarpaulin and told her workers: *We have a deadline to meet. Get back to work.*

"In retrospect, I probably worked her too hard," the plant owner says.

After not missing a day of work in five years—not even when she had the flu—Rocio finally crashed. She was exhausted, depressed, wracked with back and stomach pains.

Why am I doing this?

And: *How much more do I need?*

Then she remembered Roberto's holey socks and thought: *Maybe Carlos is right. Maybe we have enough.*

'I Am So Scary'

Rocio quit the plant manager job. At 35, she now works 20 hours a week as a consultant, doing inventory spreadsheets and moderating employer-worker disputes.

Though the workers have a love-hate relationship with her, it's Rocio they call when they land in jail or need to borrow money.

In late April, the week before the national Day Without Immigrants protest, she held a staff meeting, asking for input and interpreting for the boss. After intense debate, a consensus was reached:

Though the employees had considered joining a public protest, they changed their minds, fearful of attracting attention, and took the day off to stay at home, without pay. (Plant employees receive free individual health insurance, and the average wage is $10 an hour.)

"They decided that it's better to be 'please' and 'thank you' with the country," Rocio said. "If immigration officials are not bothering us here now, why make protest?"

She tries to funnel most of her energy into the business she and Carlos opened last year, a grocery/restaurant/money-wiring business on Melrose Avenue called El Charly and Family.

When you enter the store, "You are in Mexico," she says. It's an all-Spanish oasis where construction workers come to wire money home, shoot pool and watch soccer and Spanish-language soap operas.

After doing paperwork at the plant and delivering lunch from her restaurant to the plant workers, who preorder and pay for the food, she works most afternoons at El Charly.

She's still hard on people, she admits. She gets mad when the plant workers refuse to stay after work for free English classes. "The boss will even pay them for taking the class!" she rants. "But they complain they are too tired!"

To confirm her suspicion that they were not studying on Saturday mornings as promised, she even drove by one of the worker's houses and, as expected, there were no extra cars there. Thus setting off another rant.

Worst of all: A few weeks before graduation, Rocio was in daily contact with administrators at Hidden Valley High School. Roberto, now 18, still aced his tests, but he was routinely skipping classes, and there was a chance he wouldn't graduate.

Rocio threatened to station herself in a lawn chair outside his classroom door.

It's her goal one day to be buried with a college diploma in her hands, and she can't understand why that's not her son's goal, too.

"He is so brilliant and people love him," she says. "He can be a lawyer if he wants to, but he is too lazy."

In the weeks leading up to graduation, she said repeatedly that she was so "scary" that he wouldn't graduate—one of the few English words she still messes up.

And yet she praised Roberto for avoiding drugs and alcohol, for translating for his dad and other Hispanics at the store.

It's hard to be the son of the woman with the monster, she knows, although she is trying her best now to chill: She put an old recliner in her store office. She tries to nap there every afternoon, with her blanket and a pile of stuffed animals.

Rocio (center) admires Roberto's (left) school diploma after the commencement ceremony. The Ortiz family, in Roanoke since 1999, has had permanent resident status since 2003. (Photograph courtesy of Josh Meltzer/*The Roanoke Times*)

"I try to relax, but I still feel like Rocio the Illegal Immigrant who has to do more, more, more," she says.

"I have too much energy on my soul."

Postscript

June 9 was more than graduation day. It was all the graduations Rocio herself had forgone, the quinceañera, the elaborate wedding, the fancy clothes.

Between her two job shifts, she managed to buy new suits for the sons and husband, decorate the ranch-style house with balloons and streamers, and cook enough Mexican food to feed 30.

In fact, she was so busy playing drill sergeant beforehand—*the snapshot collage goes here, the food table there*—that they were late for the ceremony.

During commencement, Roberto walked to the stage with a Mexican flag tacked to his gown. It was the proudest moment of Rocio's life, she said later, proof that she had "made him to be a nice person and to be a man."

Outside afterwards, Roberto thanked his parents and hugged them.

"This is mine," Rocio said of his diploma, in all seriousness, and yanked it from his hands.

Lessons Learned

BY BETH MACY

First, follow your goose bumps. When you hear about Mexican immigrant Rocio Ortiz—from a trusted source who's helped you with other stories—recognize it as more than the typical "happy immigrant" story.

Remember what novelist Lee Smith said of desire: It's the only thematic quality worth your while. When Rocio tells you she was so determined to learn English that she spent nine months reading her first book, know you're on the right track.

But wonder: Why are people a little afraid of her?

When Rocio looks deep into your eyes during the middle of a long first interview and says, "Will you be my friend?" squirm a little bit because, after all, you're a journalist first.

Mutter something. Then, in all truthfulness, say, "Yes, of course."

Weeks later, ask to see her old photos: of the dirt-floor childhood home, of the first one-room apartment in America, of the dining-room table she made out of a moving box.

Ask to see the marks on her son's legs, scars from riding around Mexico City on the back of her bike.

Watch Rocio threaten to station a lawn chair outside of her son's suburban school—to keep him from skipping classes. Listen to her berate the cook in her restaurant/store for ruining $200 worth of shrimp.

In her ranch house, the second she's managed to buy, eat the slices of lime-marinated cucumber she prepares for you. Cringe when she drinks the salty juice at the bottom of the bowl.

Spend afternoons hanging out in her store, watching her pay bills and wait tables. Watch her steal a nap in a thrift-store recliner, clutching a stuffed animal in her arms.

Realize she may be the most honest subject you've ever profiled—about herself, her family, her monster.

Ask again about her shame.

When she cries, put your notebook down and take her by the hand.

Thank Carole, your editor, for giving you time to see this messy truth. Thank Josh, the photographer, who spends as much time with Rocio as you do—and tells you what he hears, sees, feels.

Worry about themes and narrative threads, and sleep poorly until the first draft is nailed.

Later, after the story runs, go out to lunch at some place non-Mexican. The new Thai place downtown. You practice Spanish, and Rocio speaks English. Correct each other. Make fun of each other.

Later, when her son's heavy-metal band plays the Latino festival, stand next to her in the front row and cheer—even though you have no idea what they're singing.

Later, at your own home, make lime-marinated cucumbers. Watch your family cringe when you drink the salty juice.

Realize that Jimmy Breslin had it right all along: Empathy is the key to human understanding.

To do honest journalism, be a person first.

Beth Macy is the families beat reporter for The Roanoke Times, *where she has worked since 1989. She's won state, regional and national awards for writing, including a Casey Medal for Meritorious Journalism, a first place in the American Association of Sunday and Feature Editors competition and numerous Virginia Press Association honors.*

The Denver Post

Finalist

Lisa Kennedy
Diversity Writing

22. A Jack Of All Creative Trades Masters Film Of a Black Icon

APRIL 23, 2006

He named his company no credits production "because it's about the work. It's not about the credit," says donnie l. betts with the kind of idiosyncratic humility that often belies his résumé.

He's a moviemaker, an actor, an educator, a radio show producer, a writer. He has worked with Morgan Freeman on Broadway. In 1993, Roy Romer awarded him the Governor's Award for Excellence in Arts.

His journey from DeKalb, Texas, to Denver didn't have a map. Yet the points in between (Fresno, New Haven, New York), the people he met, the jobs he worked have readied the 53-year-old for what lies ahead.

Where betts is now has the twin feeling of a culmination and a beginning. First feature films as long in gestation and as accomplished as "Music Is My Life, Politics My Mistress" can do that to a filmmaker.

At his Aurora home, the office walls provide a mini-museum exhibit of black theater in Denver. In the late '70s, betts' story was entwined with the Black Arts Company and the City Stage Ensemble. He also performed at the Denver Center.

The floor was carpeted with vibrant red-washed posters and cardboard cards for "Music Is My Life." On them, Oscar Brown Jr. has his head tilted back in what looks like praise and ecstasy. And, this being the trickster, poet-activist Brown, it may be simply sweet pleasure of rocking the mic better and longer than most.

Since December, betts has been traveling frequently with his Brown documentary.

Filmmaker donnie l. betts' most recent documentary release, "Music Is My Life, Politics My Mistress," has won many awards. (Photograph courtesy of Glenn Asakawa/*The Denver Post*)

Michigan. Portland. Kansas City. Austin. Chicago. On Chicago's Southside—where Brown, the son of a prominent lawyer, grew up—betts attended a week-long run of his movie.

It's an independent filmmaker's itinerary. You take your film on that very long road not simply in hopes of distribution.

"It's exposure for your film with an audience," said betts. "You're not sitting in the editing room, thinking it's great. You get 10 people in the audience, and you got 10 different opinions. That's invaluable input."

One of the first groups betts ever got feedback from was the audience attending the Starz Denver Pan African Film Festival.

Fittingly, the seventh edition of the festival will honor betts on Thursday with its first Oscar Brown Jr. Award and show the completed film.

On May 5, the film, which won the audience award for best documentary at November's Starz Denver International Film Festival, will begin a one-week run at the Starz FilmCenter on the Auraria campus.

"We love that documentary," said festival founder Ashara Ekundayo. "And we loved Oscar."

Now is as good a time as any to address that nagging question: What's with the lowercase name?

"I've always wanted to honor my elders in some kind of way," said betts.

"The short version is that's how I do it. I feel that I'll never be as large as they are. That I stand on their shoulders. For us to be sitting here casually having a conversation instead of working in the fields somewhere.... That's my way of giving back."

Siblings Old As Parents

That's the short version. The longer version has to do with Norris Betts. The way the 12th and youngest child of Norris and Mayme Betts—who died when he was 9—talked about his father, Norris was all uppercase.

Norris, said betts, was a simple man. He was a farmer in DeKalb and also a janitor for years. He was even a bootlegger, given to drink and smoke, activities he quit later in life.

Betts takes out a framed photograph of a handsome couple. Norris stands in a pair of denim overalls. By his side, Mayme smiles into the camera, wearing a print dress.

His siblings are fond of telling him that because he was so much younger, he was raised by a different man. There is an age gap of 23 years between the oldest child and betts. All of his siblings are old enough to be his parents, he joked. So there may be a truth to that different-man theory.

His father's role in the civil life of their small Texas town contributed to betts' pragmatic approach to the arts, he said.

"I'm attracted to activists," he said. "I'm attracted to people who put their words into action. Maybe that is my way of being an activist myself."

Two earlier shorts provide solid evidence of his unapologetic bias.

Denver hip-hop activist and educator Jeff Campbell is the focus of "Common Good: Living in the City," which won a Heartland Emmy last year.

In 1995, working with former Denver news anchor Reynelda Ware Muse, betts made a hybrid drama/documentary called "Dearfield: The Road Less Traveled." It tells the story of a short-lived black settlement near Greeley.

If betts and Muse found an uplift-the-race visionary in entrepreneur-founder O. T. Jackson (betts plays him), they found a winking star in Carrie Wright. Wright, whose parents moved to Dearfield when she was a child, relishes her memories. A favorite tale is about the time a group of people planned to divert water on her mother's property, saying that while she owned the land, no one had rights to the water. The punch line? Her mother rushed to Denver to file a water claim.

'You Captured Me'

Betts met Oscar Brown Jr.—who was also a singer, songwriter and playwright—when he was looking to resurrect an old radio show about the African-American experience called "Destination Freedom." Brown and Studs Terkel had been involved with Richard Durham's original radio pieces in Chicago. And betts invited the two out to perform a re-creation.

He asked Brown about doing a film on him. Betts wasn't the first with that request. But he followed through—for more than five years.

"We would sit around in our underwear, talking baseball, talking women, just kicking back," said betts. "He loved the way I cooked. So I'd cook him some salmon. Otherwise, he didn't eat that good. He was old-school, greasy-spoon style."

They clicked over the work too.

"I dealt in radio. I dealt in theater. I dealt in film. All those things he liked, I'd deal with," betts said.

For many audiences "Music Is My Life" will be like one of those obits that makes you kick yourself for knowing so little about a person when he was alive. Brown died last May.

"That's why it was so important to me that I finished the film before he died," he said.

"You captured me," Brown told betts after a screening at the Los Angeles Pan African Film Festival January 2005.

"Then," adds betts softly with a laugh, "since he always had to come back with some kind of humor, Oscar said it is about my favorite subject, which is me."

Lessons Learned

BY LISA KENNEDY

I walked into donnie l. betts' home in Aurora, Colo., one sunny afternoon and took the stairs down to his office. Although he was battling back from a cold, he was about to begin a phone interview for a Washington, D.C., radio station.

In a couple of weeks his documentary "Music is My Life, Politics My Mistress" would be screened at the D.C. International Film Festival. Like an itinerant preacher, betts was traveling the film-fest circuit, bearing witness to the life of the poet-activist-performer Oscar Brown Jr.

So, as he sat at a desk crowded with papers, and began rapping to the interviewer, I looked around. The walls of the office were covered with posters that provided a trove of information about theater and African-American performance in Denver. His floor was blanketed with postcards and posters for the movie, testaments to the many roles an indie filmmaker must often take on: producer, director, publicist.

Some of these details made it into a profile intended to explore the deep bond between a filmmaker and his first movie.

First features of the independent variety are notoriously difficult to birth. They are labors of love, obsession, desperation. They require begging and borrowing and stealing time away from other endeavors, other relationships. It still surprises me that documentaries can be even more demanding, and revealing of their makers, than narrative features.

A fine documentary tells a rich, unexpected tale. It calls out for a "who knew?" response. But behind the movie is a story, or two, about the makeup of the filmmaker—his fortitude, his bone-headedness, and, yes, his weirdness.

donnie betts' story is one of humility and of necessary hubris.

I got close to one part of that equation. He's a humble and gentle man. But the journey of a young black man from DeKalb, Texas, to points all over our nation's map feels truncated.

Sturdy, secondary quotes would have been a salvation. Sometimes you have to choose between the artist's work and other voices. In betts' case, the film had to bear witness. In a world where space dictates some choices, this is a right one. Still, as a reader, I hanker for the voices of betts' siblings and his mentors.

And the image of betts and Brown sitting in their skivvies talking into the night still tickles. What must Brown's children—who are in the movie—have made of this filmmaker, who grew closer and closer to their father over the five years he documented his gnarly, charismatic life?

One of the fine achievements of "Music is My Life" is that the audience is left satisfied yet craving. That well-calibrated mix of learning about a figure and wanting to know so much more was what interested me in the story in the first place. It was also what I hoped to pull off with the profile. Maybe I came close. Spending time with betts, I learned what it takes to do that well.

Lisa Kennedy has been film critic at The Denver Post *since May 2003. She has also worked for* The Village Voice, Us Magazine *and was editor-at-large for* Out Magazine.

PART 4

Investigative Journalism

WINNER

Ken Armstrong, Justin Mayo and Steve Miletich

ASNE, Local Accountability Reporting
Finalist, Pulitzer Prize, Investigative Reporting

It happened over and over again. And it happened to reporters on all types of beats: religion to politics, schools to sports, business to government. It seemed like whenever *The Seattle Times* beat reporters sought court documents, the courts denied them access. Their litany of complaints reached the ears of *Seattle Times* investigative reporter Ken Armstrong.

Armstrong wanted to know not only why files were being sealed, but how often. So he went to Justin Mayo, a specialist in computer-assisted reporting, to try to figure out what was going on.

"We wanted to know: How many files were sealed, in whole or part; who wanted the files sealed, and why; which judges sealed the files; and were the rules restricting secrecy followed in each case?" Armstrong said in an interview for this book.

Those questions led Armstrong, Mayo, and later Steve Miletich, to embark upon a marathon search through the legal system after sealing orders, court files and those involved. *The Times* filed motions, gathered information and went behind what Armstrong describes as "the courthouse curtains."

The result was a series of stories: "Your Courts, Their Secrets."

It took *The Times* two years, and huge legal fees, to investigate the secrets sequestered in a slew of documents that belonged to a public unable to view them. And because they wanted the public to understand the personal impact it had on them, *The Times* wrote the stories in a very personal way.

"As for the actual writing of the stories, we decided, early on, to speak directly to our readers," Armstrong said. "We used a lot of pronouns—you, us, our, them. We wanted our readers to understand that they had a stake in this; that the principle of open courts is one that matters to the public at large, and not simply to newspapers. We also used a conversational tone, one that didn't push readers away or create distance."

"Your Courts, Their Secrets" was a finalist for the Pulitzer Prize in Investigative Reporting.

About *The Seattle Times* team

Ken Armstrong's interest in legal issues comes naturally. He studied law (although after one year at law school he knew he didn't want to be a lawyer). He previously worked at the *Chicago Tribune,* where he cowrote six series on criminal justice issues, including an investigation of capital cases that helped prompt the Illinois governor to suspend executions and then empty Death Row. Previous honors include the George Polk Award, the Worth Bingham Award, the APME Public Service Award, the Scripps Howard Public Service Award, Sigma Delta Chi awards for public service and investigative reporting, National Headliners Best of Show/Print, the Silver Gavel and others. He is a four-time finalist for the Pulitzer Prize and the Goldsmith Prize.

Justin Mayo has been a reporter with *The Seattle Times* investigative team for more than eight years. He specializes in database and spatial analysis, covering issues such as courts, demographics, elections, education and housing. He contributed to a *Times* series on high school coaches accused of sexual misconduct that won the Heywood Broun and Scripps

Howard awards. That series was a Pulitzer finalist in 2004. Mayo's work on a series about indigent defense in the courts earned him recognition as a finalist for the Goldsmith and Selden Ring awards in 2005. Before joining *The Times,* Mayo was the database administrator at the National Institute for Computer-Assisted Reporting, in Columbia, Mo.

Steve Miletich has been a reporter for 30 years. He has been with *The Seattle Times* since 1999, and a member of the investigative team since 2002. Miletich has specialized over the course of his career in coverage of courts, law enforcement and the federal judiciary. He and two colleagues won a national Sigma Delta Chi award for a 2004 investigative series on problems at the Transportation Security Administration. Miletich was on a team of *Times* reporters who were finalists for the Pulitzer Prize in 2003 for  coverage of the arrests of two men in the Washington, D.C.-area sniper killings. His other major stories include coverage of the January 2000 crash of Alaska Airlines Flight 261 and maintenance problems that contributed to the crash.

—Scott Libin, Managing Editor, Poynter Online, and Leadership and Management faculty member, The Poynter Institute

23. The Cases Your Judges Are Hiding from You

MARCH 5, 2006

By Ken Armstrong, Justin Mayo and Steve Miletich

Four years ago, a lawsuit was filed in King County Superior Court, alleging that a medical device was unsafe. A woman using it wound up in a coma. You'd probably like to know: What's the device? Does anyone in my family use it? Unsafe how?

But you can't know. You're not allowed to know. Medtronic, the multibillion-dollar company that makes the device, asked a judge to conceal the whole file from public view—and the judge said OK.

Twelve years ago, an Eastside family sued KinderCare, one of the country's largest child-care companies, saying it was responsible for the sexual abuse of a child. You'd like to know: *Who* was accused of sexual abuse? How was KinderCare involved? Were police notified?

But you can't know. That file, too, is sealed—hidden away by a court commissioner who has sealed dozens of cases, stamping his name on one secrecy order after another.

Document after document, file after file, has been sealed—and sealed improperly—by the judges and court commissioners of King County Superior Court. A wrongful-death lawsuit against Virginia Mason Medical Center? Sealed. A lawsuit accusing a King County judge of legal malpractice? Sealed. A lawsuit blaming the state's social-services agency for the rape of a 13-year-old girl? Sealed.

Since 1990, at least 420 civil suits have been sealed in their entirety, *The Seattle Times* found. That means everything—from the complaint, which says who's accused of what, to the judgment, which says how the case wound up—has been concealed, locked behind electronic passwords or number-coded keypads that restrict access to computer records and shelved files.

These sealed records hold secrets of potential dangers in our medicine cabinets and refrigerators; of molesters in our day-care centers, schools and churches; of unethical lawyers, negligent doctors, dangerous dentists; of missteps by local and state agencies; of misconduct by publicly traded companies into which people sink their savings.

Files sealed by the King County Superior Court are stored out of public view in a locked room at the King County Courthouse. (Photograph courtesy of Mark Harrison/*The Seattle Times*)

The Washington Constitution says: "Justice in all cases shall be administered openly." To this, many King County judges have effectively added: "unless the parties don't want it to be."

The judges have displayed an ignorance of, or indifference to, the legal requirements for sealing court records. They have routinely sealed files while 1) offering little or no explanation, 2) applying the wrong legal standard, and 3) failing to acknowledge, much less weigh, the public interest in open court proceedings.

At least 97 percent of their sealing orders disregard rules set down by the Washington Supreme Court in the 1980s.

The state's highest court says court records should be sealed only in rare circumstances. Its message is: Your taxes pay for the courts. You're entitled to know what goes on there. You elect the judges. You need to know how they do their job. The public cannot evaluate its court system—nor hold judges accountable—if the courthouse curtains are drawn.

Judges and commissioners have sealed at least 46 cases where a public institution is a party. Is some public agency slipping up? Some public employee? Are taxpayer dollars at risk? Good questions all, but you can't have the answers. Local school districts, the University of Washington, the state Department of Social and Health Services—all have had files sealed.

Judges and commissioners have sealed at least 58 cases where a fellow lawyer is a party, usually as a defendant. Leading firms, prominent lawyers, judges—all have had files about them sealed.

The courts have sealed cases where the person being sued was a licensed professional—for example, a doctor, psychologist or counselor—who was subsequently disciplined by the state. Those lawsuits might have served as a warning, had they not been concealed from the public.

And the courts have sealed one case after another at the request of the rich and influential, including leaders in real estate, advertising, banking, medicine, software development, the Internet, general business and sports.

The 420 cases that we found represent but a sliver of all the sealed records in our courthouses. That number applies only to civil suits in one court: King County Superior. We excluded other types of cases, such as divorce, adoption, paternity or child-custody matters. The 420 also accounts only for cases sealed in their entirety. Many others are sealed in part. We stopped counting those at 1,000.

Two years ago, the Washington Supreme Court wrote: "The open operation of our courts is of utmost public importance. Justice must be conducted openly to foster the public's understanding and trust in our judicial system and to give judges the check of public scrutiny. Secrecy fosters mistrust."

The court wrote that while unanimously reversing a King County judge who had improperly sealed court records in a business lawsuit. And this was a case where the judge sealed *part* of the file, not the whole thing.

The same judge, Sharon Armstrong, has sealed the entire file in at least 11 cases since 1990. A lawsuit involving a pedophile priest? Sealed. A lawsuit against Metro for hitting a pedestrian in a crosswalk? Sealed. She has also sealed two lawsuits against the state Department of Social and Health Services, and three against lawyers or law firms.

In months to come, *The Seattle Times* plans to get files unsealed and questions answered. The court's leadership crafted a plan that would have opened files with minimal delay, but other judges rebelled, saying the newspaper should be required to file a formal motion in each case that was improperly sealed.

We're going to be filing lots of motions.

Hiding Harm

When something goes wrong—a product fails, a doctor is negligent, a company cheats its customers or investors—lawsuits often follow, generating court files crammed with evidence accumulated by each side.

But by sealing records, judges can conceal that evidence. Many also sign sweeping protective orders that allow the parties to dictate which records the public can see. Many permit the parties to settle secretly, even in cases involving public hazards.

Examples abound nationally of dangers hidden by such steps. Tire treads that separate. Car fuel tanks that explode. Priests who molest children. Heart valves, painkillers and birth-control devices linked to dozens or even hundreds of deaths.

Litigation has become a system of secrecy. A defendant, accused of wrongdoing, wants records produced during a lawsuit to stay between the parties. The plaintiff goes along to pave the way for settlement. The judge signs off because it's the easy thing to do. When the case is settled, the parties sign a confidentiality agreement. You ask the plaintiff about the lawsuit, and he says he can't talk.

One result is that patterns—with products and with people—can get obscured.

Take the case of LaVar Riniker, a Bellevue dentist with an unusual practice. He treated some patients' backaches or hip problems by changing the shape of their jaws, state records show.

In 1996, Riniker's lawyer wanted a malpractice lawsuit against his client sealed. The plaintiff joined in, and a judge signed off. Two months later, the lawyer wanted a second lawsuit against Riniker sealed. The plaintiff went along, and so did a court commissioner. In 1998, the lawyer showed up again—with secrecy request No. 3. But this time, a judge said no. Judge LeRoy McCullough knew the law and said sealing the whole file would be improper. He did, however, allow the settlement terms to remain confidential.

In 2000, the state refused to renew Riniker's dental license, finding he was incompetent. By then, Riniker had been sued for malpractice at least 16 times, court records show. Most of those lawsuits involved some level of secrecy—either the whole file was sealed, or the case was resolved confidentially.

Riniker was, of course, an individual dentist. You probably never went to him. But other sealed lawsuits have alleged malpractice at such medical institutions as Group Health, Swedish, Virginia Mason and Harborview.

Lazy sealing practices have allowed some people to play the courts for a fool.

Michael Cassini, a convicted con man, scammed more than $4 million from banks by pretending to be a Microsoft millionaire. One way he covered his tracks was by changing his name—and, with the help of Preston Gates & Ellis, a prestigious law firm, getting a King County judge to seal the court file.

Seth Warshavsky became rich in the 1990s selling pornography on the Internet. He was profiled extensively—the "Bill Gates of Porn," some stories called him—but proved an elusive figure. That's because the courts kept allowing him to erase his history.

Kinds of cases that were sealed

The King County Superior Court assigns each civil suit a case type, using broad categories. These 420 cases, sealed between 1990 and 2005, fell into the following case types:

97 — Tort/personal injury/wrongful death: We combined these categories because they frequently overlap. A tort is a civil wrong or injury. Generally in these cases, someone got hurt, and someone is being blamed.

78 — Domestic violence: You might be tempted to write these off as private matters. But the people accused of violence in these cases include police officers and others in positions of public trust.

54 — Miscellaneous: A catch-all category used by the court. One of these lawsuits involves a pedophile priest. Others involve alleged wrongdoing by lawyers, doctors and businesses.

43 — Commercial: Business disputes, mostly. These cases can reveal financial misconduct by publicly traded companies or alleged wrongdoing by law firms or other businesses.

27 — Unlawful harassment: Harassment includes words or actions that annoy or alarm, causing fear or emotional distress.

24 — Medical malpractice: These cases typically allege negligence by doctors, dentists or other health-care professionals.

21 — Injunction: Someone sues to prevent someone else from doing something wrong.

15 — Change of name: Authorities in Seattle recently accused a con man of covering his tracks by changing his name and getting the file sealed.

13 — Other malpractice: These mostly involve alleged malpractice by lawyers.

48 — All other categories combined: These run the gamut, with lawsuits involving everything from unpaid debts to damage to property to threats to the safety of children or vulnerable adults.

Source: Seattle Times analysis of King County court records
GRAPHICS BY THE SEATTLE TIMES

According to King County court records and newspaper reports, Warshavsky managed to seal: one civil suit in which he was accused of overbilling thousands of customer credit cards; a second civil suit accusing him of choking his former girlfriend; and criminal files in adult and juvenile court listing such priors as theft and trying to sell a stolen laptop.

Warshavsky couldn't be reached for comment. Some reports say he fled to Thailand several years ago.

Secrecy Triumphs

In lawsuits filed in King County, the parties' desire for secrecy has regularly trumped the public good.

Consider case No. 95-2-22817-8. Because a judge sealed the file, all you're supposed to know about this case is the names of the parties and that it involves a tort—a wrongful act that you can sue somebody for.

But someone made a mistake and left this file open. Every document popped up on the courthouse computer. (The file was closed two weeks ago, after we notified the clerk's office.)

The documents told this story:

In 1995, a young man sued Donald Sidwell, an aerospace worker with "top secret" security clearance whose job was so sensitive that he couldn't divulge what projects he worked on.

The plaintiff accused Sidwell of sexually abusing him when the plaintiff was a child. (*The Seattle Times* does not name alleged victims of sexual abuse.)

Sidwell denied the allegations. His attorney called them "totally false" and likened them to an extortion attempt.

Still, Sidwell agreed to settle.

On Jan. 30, 1997, the parties filed a document saying Sidwell would pay the young man $212,000. The same day, Sidwell's lawyers asked Superior Court Judge Harriett Cody to seal the whole file.

Here's the reason they offered:

Sidwell worked in the "high-security aerospace defense industry." His employer was Lockheed Martin, in Southern California. (He previously worked for Boeing in Washington state, which is where the alleged abuse occurred.) His "top secret" security clearance was granted to fewer than one in 20 employees.

Sidwell's work made him subject to close surveillance and record-checking. Discovery of this lawsuit could mean loss of his security clearance and job. Without his job, he couldn't pay the young man.

So, out of concern "for the plaintiff's recovery and the defendant's livelihood," the file should be sealed, Sidwell's lawyers wrote.

Judge Cody sealed the file.

The sealing request and the judge's order make no mention of Lockheed's interest in knowing what Sidwell was accused of. Nor do they mention the interest of the federal government, which issues security clearances—and has the power to take them away. Nor do they mention the potential for blackmail created here. What would happen if the wrong people learned of Sidwell's secret?

Sidwell kept his job. The "defendant's livelihood" was protected. Now 67, Sidwell retired about a year and a half ago.

But as for the "plaintiff's recovery"? That didn't work out so well. Nine years after the case was settled and the file sealed, Sidwell has paid only a fraction of the $212,000, according to the young man's lawyer.

Sidwell told *The Times* that he still owes about $160,000—and hopes to pay that off by selling some land.

He still denies the sexual abuse. He settled, he said, because his attorney fees were getting too steep. And he's convinced that if Lockheed had learned of the lawsuit and settlement, he would have been fired. (Lockheed declined comment for this story.)

So, in the end, the only person that secrecy served was Sidwell—the man who was accused of molesting a child, the man who agreed to pay $212,000 but hasn't.

Unlawful Orders

The Washington Supreme Court says that to seal a file, a judge must: 1) find "compelling circumstances," a demanding legal standard; 2) explain, in an order, why secrecy is needed; and 3) weigh the arguments for privacy against the public's interest in open courts.

We were able to get the sealing orders in 383 of the 420 sealed cases. Here's what they show:

- In 361, or 94 percent, the court failed to find "compelling circumstances." The order used the wrong legal standard—citing "good cause," a much lower threshold—or used no standard at all.

The difference between "good cause" and "compelling circumstances" is the difference between having some reason for secrecy—for example, the defendant doesn't want to be annoyed—and having a superior reason, one so persuasive it outweighs the constitutional presumption of openness.

At right, in Example 1, a judge sealed a file involving a priest accused of molesting children, writing in, by hand, that "good cause" was shown.

Flawed sealing orders

EXAMPLE 1: WRONG STANDARD USED
Sealing requires "compelling circumstances." Here, a judge finds "good cause" instead.

THIS MATTER having come on regularly for hearing before the undersigned judge, who has considered plaintiff's Motion to Seal File and the files and records herein, and being fully advised, now therefore, *for good cause shown* (✓)

EXAMPLE 2: NO EXPLANATION GIVEN
A judge must say why secrecy is needed. Here, the explanation line is left blank.

The Court has reviewed the motion and declaration of the applicant and finds the following good cause for sealing the above-captioned file or the document(s) indicated:

_____

EXAMPLE 3: PUBLIC INTEREST IGNORED
Secrecy must be weighed against the public good. That didn't happen here.

The Court has reviewed the motion and declaration of the applicant and finds the following good cause for sealing the above-captioned file or the document(s) indicated: DENIED RIGHT TO OBTAIN A SECURITY JOB.

THE SEATTLE TIMES

- In 196 cases, or 51 percent, the sealing order offered no explanation for secrecy, much less a detailed one. And we were being generous here, counting such throwaway lines as "nature of allegations" as *some* explanation.

In Example 2, a court commissioner used a fill-in-the-blank form to seal a medical-malpractice lawsuit. The top line is reserved for the court's explanation. She left that line blank.

Note how this form uses the wrong standard—good cause—and leaves little room for explanation. The court is supposed to describe, in detail, the arguments for secrecy and weigh them against the Washington Constitution—but you couldn't even fit this sentence into that space. More than 100 cases have been sealed with this form. Nineteen times, the explanation line was left blank.

- In 373 of the orders, or 97 percent, the judges not only failed to weigh the public interest—they didn't even acknowledge there is such an interest.

This disregard can border on the absurd. In 1998, a King County man asked to have three lawsuits sealed. Two accused him of domestic violence, the other of harassment. A different woman filed each one. Here's why he wanted secrecy: The man wanted to be a security guard—a job that can require background checks—and said these lawsuits were in his way. A commissioner sealed all three.

As you can see, in Example 3, the sealing orders did not take into account the obvious public interest in letting licensing officials and prospective employers view these court files.

Without question, some records can meet these sealing requirements: bank-account numbers; personal information about children; psychiatric records; legitimate trade secrets. But the state Supreme Court has told judges to seal only those documents that need sealing—or, better yet, redact account numbers or use initials for minors.

About half of these 383 cases were sealed by court commissioners, not judges. Commissioners have many of the same powers as judges but are not elected. Commissioners sealed files mostly while in a cattle-call court called the Ex Parte Department, where orders get signed with dizzying speed.

King County judges tend to explain widespread sealing this way: The parties agreed to it—and judges like it when the parties agree. Judges sometimes view their role narrowly: to settle disputes, not start them; to handle issues raised by the parties, not to bring ones up.

Michael Trickey, who became presiding judge of King County Superior Court in January, said: "I think the culture, among the bar and even the bench, used to be that if an agreed order was presented, it was just signed."

Judges' Roadblock

Judge Trickey uses the past tense when he describes such relaxed sealing practices. He says judges have become more attuned to the public's right to open records.

After we showed the judges our findings, they began to fix some problems. The court is throwing out its old sealing forms, providing extensive training to judges and commissioners on sealing restrictions, and taking the power to seal away from substitute commissioners.

Late last year, when we alerted the court's leadership to the hundreds of improperly sealed files, a small group of top judges came up with a plan that would have opened many, if not most, with minimal delay. These judges included Trickey; Richard Eadie, the presiding judge from 2002 until this January; and William Downing, one of the state's leading experts on open court records.

Under their plan, the court would have notified parties that files appeared to have been sealed improperly, and that the court would be opening them unless the parties voiced objection.

But other judges on the court objected. In January they overturned the plan, by a vote of 21–9.

Instead, the court is requiring *The Seattle Times* to file a motion in every case. Feel free to file 400 motions, the court has said, a demand that imposes extraordinary expense and delay.

The judges who voted against the leadership's plan cited General Rule 15, a rule adopted by the Washington Supreme Court in 1989. The rule says that once sealed, records shall be unsealed only upon agreement of the parties, or upon motion and "proof of compelling circumstances."

But this is the same rule that says a file should be *sealed* only for compelling circumstances.

So: The judges ignored General Rule 15 while sealing hundreds of these cases. Now, they are requiring us to follow that rule to undo something that should not have been done in the first place.

And, if they follow the rule to its letter, they will require the newspaper to show compelling circumstances to unseal, while they sealed on far less. That would flip the presumption of open courts on its head.

Not every judge is going along. Judges are elected individually and can handle their cases as they choose. Dean Lum, the court's chief civil judge, unsealed one lawsuit last month without requiring the newspaper to file a motion. Judge Eadie unsealed another. "I see that the judge has an individual responsibility to step forward," Eadie says. "Not everybody agrees with that view."

In 1999, Eadie sealed a medical-malpractice lawsuit. But he recently looked at his sealing order and said: "It doesn't give any description of why, or reflect any weighing of the public interest, or any indication of why the compelling circumstances outweigh the public interest."

So Eadie sent a letter to the attorneys in January, saying: "This should not have been done. It was inconsistent with the rules in effect at the time and is in conflict with recent case law."

His letter said he would open the file in a month. In the meantime, he wrote, the lawyers could ask that individual documents remain sealed, provided they could show compelling circumstances.

The lawyers made no such request—and the whole file was opened.

But hundreds of other files remain under seal.

We start filing motions tomorrow. We'll let you know how it goes.

24. Failures by State, Caregiver Kept Secret in Child-Rape Case

AUG. 27, 2006

By Ken Armstrong, Jonathan Martin and Justin Mayo

Like books on a shelf, every court file tells a story. In King County, file No. 03-2-27609-0 tells how a 13-year-old girl, a slip of a kid with a lost look in her eyes, wound up being raped while in the state's care and protection.

For the state's social-services agency, it's a story of bureaucratic bungling and a lack of backbone. For YouthCare, a high-powered nonprofit that operates several licensed group homes in Seattle, it's a story of unheeded warnings and the consequences of not paying $33 for a criminal-background check. For the state's lawyers, it's a tale of audacity, with attorneys under then-Attorney General Christine Gregoire claiming the teenage victim was partly at fault for being raped by a 29-year-old youth worker.

But important as the story is, this court file has been under seal for more than two years, banned from public viewing. A judge granted a motion by the girl's attorney that said the file "demonstrates unfavorable facts" about both the state of Washington and YouthCare and should be hidden away "to protect all parties from embarrassment."

Nearly all of the file was opened in July after a four-month court battle by *The Seattle Times,* which argued that such sweeping secrecy should never have been granted. When court files are sealed improperly—as this one was—the public suffers, deprived of information on the workings of its government and on the conduct of contractors entrusted with children's care.

The newspaper pursued this case as part of a continuing investigation of sealed court files. At least 420 civil suits have been sealed in their entirety in King County Superior Court since 1990, the newspaper has found. Almost all were sealed in violation of laws that restrict secrecy and recognize the importance of open courts.

The Times has filed motions to open dozens of those cases, to tell their stories of alleged medical negligence, unsafe consumer products, and wrongdoing in schools, churches and corporate boardrooms.

'I Just Did Not Realize It Was So Loosey-Goosey'

For years, Barbara Rosenwald, a licensing inspector for the state Department of Social and Health Services (DSHS), voiced concerns about YouthCare. DSHS ensured that YouthCare met licensing standards and also paid the nonprofit to care for wards of the state.

YouthCare helped troubled adolescents, especially runaways. Its board of directors included powerful business executives, state senators and state Supreme Court Justice Bobbe Bridge. Victoria Wagner, the chief executive officer, was once a runaway herself. She had helped YouthCare grow from an annual budget of $500,000 to $5 million. Pearl Jam and the actor Tom Skerritt pitched in on fundraising.

YouthCare helped more than 1,500 kids a year in its group homes, shelter and street-outreach programs. The group-home residents—maybe three dozen at any given time—had often been victims of abuse. The homes were meant to be safe havens, a place for kids to get direction and supervision from adults they could trust.

But Rosenwald documented chaotic conditions and lax practices that threatened the kids' safety: slipshod record keeping; inadequate staffing levels; assaults among residents not reported to police; and youth workers and supervisors unqualified for their demanding jobs.

The Times obtained Rosenwald's records and thousands of other documents—e-mails, memos, letters, investigative records and deposition transcripts—through the court file and a public-disclosure request to the state.

As early as 1996, Rosenwald expressed alarm that YouthCare allowed some workers who hadn't passed criminal-background checks to be left alone with kids.

In May 2000, Rosenwald was particularly unnerved by a visit to YouthCare's Threshold home, a long-term residential facility. The home's new director was a "novice" in over her head, Rosenwald wrote. Loose supervision allowed one girl to be sexually exploited while away from the home. That incident had not been reported to DSHS.

"I was at YouthCare yesterday—found some really really questionable supervision practices, philosophy, etc.," Rosenwald wrote to her boss. "As I explained to them—they would never pass a [headquarters] review. Like, it would be their programs—gone! zap! poof! I just did not realize it was so loosey-goosey."

In June 2000, DSHS managers met with YouthCare's top leaders, from Wagner on down, and stressed the need for YouthCare to hire qualified staff members.

'All-Around Nice Guy'—with Nine Criminal Convictions

Two weeks after that meeting, James Leonard Gregory Jr. applied to YouthCare for a job. "I would bring professionalism, dedication, creativity and lots of energy to your staff," he wrote.

Gregory's résumé showed he had worked as a corrections officer in South Dakota. His job application said he had no criminal convictions in the past seven years. His employment references described him as honest and trustworthy. One called him an "all-around nice guy."

But unbeknownst to YouthCare, Gregory had been fired from that corrections job for spitting on an inmate. He had been convicted of nine misdemeanors, including reckless endangerment, passing bad checks and making obscene or harassing phone calls. And his three references? Two girlfriends and a brother, Gregory later acknowledged.

YouthCare hired Gregory as a caregiver, at $18,000 a year. He began work in July 2000 at Threshold, the group home that had just caused Rosenwald such anxiety. The two-story brick home, on a dead-end street in Rainier Valley, was home to kids between 12 and 17, nearly all wards of the state.

As required, YouthCare submitted Gregory's name for a criminal-background check. Rosenwald processed the request. Within weeks she learned from the Washington State Patrol of Gregory's reckless-endangerment conviction—a disqualifying offense. (Renton police records say he fired shots while chasing people he suspected of stealing a friend's car.)

Rosenwald asked YouthCare in September for a signed waiver from Gregory, so she could disclose details of his rap sheet. YouthCare sent waivers twice. But Rosenwald, buried in a backlog of hundreds of unfinished background checks, later said she saw neither.

So Gregory kept working.

For 5 ½ months, DSHS failed to let YouthCare know the seriousness of Gregory's record. YouthCare, meanwhile, failed to push DSHS for details, even knowing something had popped up on his background check.

YouthCare could have learned of Gregory's criminal history on its own. The year he was hired, a private company had offered to do background checks for YouthCare with a turnaround time of two or three days. Gregory's would have cost $33. But YouthCare didn't take up the offer.

While Gregory worked at Threshold, his nine convictions became 10.

Four months into his job, Gregory picked up belongings from an apartment he once shared with a girlfriend—one of his sterling job references. After loading his car, he returned to the apartment, locked the door, and said how glad he was they could be so civil about the breakup, a Kent police report says. Then he slapped her across the face, twice.

He knocked her down, kneed her, then turned up the radio to drown out her screams.

Gregory was convicted of assault in January 2001 and sentenced to 365 days in jail, all suspended.

"I feel horrible about this case. I always have," says Victoria Wagner, who left YouthCare in 2004 after 19 years as its chief executive. "The last thing I wanted was to have a child in my care abused. . . . This case has haunted me." (Photograph courtesy of Alan Berner/*The Seattle Times*)

Meanwhile, his criminal-background check was still on a desk at DSHS, lost in a paperwork shuffle.

'If You Ever Looked in Her Eyes, She's Lost'

Three weeks after Gregory's assault conviction, DSHS placed a 13-year-old girl in Threshold, leaving her in Gregory's care. Within days, he began grooming her, offering massages and kisses. He called her "Sexy Mama."

Her middle name was Lynn. *The Seattle Times* does not normally identify rape victims, so we are using only that identifier.

She was a skinny kid, with a background typical of a state ward. Her mother, a housecleaner with 13 kids and a gambling problem, had given Lynn up to DSHS. Lynn, in a court filing, said her mother would force her to stay home from school to care for six younger siblings. The two fought violently, she said.

Lynn's family life was so chaotic that she once ran into a brother but didn't realize they were related until they began talking. She hadn't seen him in about 10 years.

Her mom described Lynn this way: "If you ever looked in her eyes, she's lost."

Lynn filled out papers to move into Threshold on Feb. 8.

Because Gregory's background check hadn't cleared, he wasn't supposed to be alone with Lynn or other residents. But he was. On Feb. 16 he even escorted Lynn and two other girls to a musical performance at Seattle's Benaroya Hall, an evening they called "Girls Night Out."

'Keep It on the Down Low'

Gregory's shift on Feb. 17, 2001, was to begin at 3 p.m. But before work he got into a fight with and beat up another girlfriend—the YouthCare reference who had called him an "all-around nice guy."

She called police and went to a hospital, where she received five stitches for a split lip. Around 4 p.m., she filled out a domestic-violence form, saying Gregory had abused her at least six other times, leaving her with black eyes and bruises.

At about the same time, Gregory was at Threshold, working alone.

Lynn wanted to buy a soda. Gregory agreed to get one from the office. She followed him upstairs, got the drink and started to leave. Hold up, Gregory said. He locked the door and turned up the radio. "Where's my hug?" he asked.

This same afternoon, Rosenwald was scrambling to alert YouthCare administrators that they had uncleared staff members working alone at another group home, where a teenager had alleged being raped by a visitor. This cannot continue, Rosenwald told a YouthCare executive. He replied that "it would be taken care of immediately."

Inside the Threshold office, Gregory kissed Lynn and pulled down her pants. "I just laid there, because I was scared of him," Lynn said later. "I didn't know what to say. I didn't know what to do. I didn't know if he was going to hit me."

Afterward, Gregory told Lynn: "Keep it on the down low."

At 8:40 p.m., Seattle police arrived at Threshold and arrested Gregory for the assault earlier that day, not for the rape. Before taking him away, police let Gregory find someone to cover his shift. He was, after all, working alone.

Later, Lynn let Gregory's replacement know what had happened upstairs. But he didn't call police or DSHS. He decided to let someone else handle it the next morning, he later told a state investigator.

Lynn was a "flirty, showtime girl," this worker later told DSHS, adding: "I think it was consensual even though she is only 13."

According to a roommate, Lynn spent the night crying.

It wasn't until 2:45 p.m. the next day that YouthCare took Lynn to the hospital. Police weren't called until 7 p.m., more than 24 hours after the rape.

'How Do We Justify This?'

Lynn's rape quickly reverberated through state government. The head of DSHS, Dennis Braddock, sent a written alert to then-Gov. Gary Locke's chief of staff—Braddock's third such alert about YouthCare in a week. The two others concerned a group home for young mothers, where one teen had reported being raped by a visitor.

DSHS considered banning admissions to all of YouthCare's programs but instead issued "stop placement" orders on just the two group homes with alleged rapes. These stop placements were the first in YouthCare's 27-year history.

A DSHS spokeswoman let administrators know Feb. 20 that she planned to issue a press release about the YouthCare incidents and the state's response. This news appeared to alarm Nancy Zahn—DSHS's head of group-home licensing statewide—who responded by e-mail:

"Please be aware that Youth Care has a very high powered board in Seattle; it is a long term agency with a ton of community support. Not to say that changes what we do but if we think [a particular boys ranch] had connections; we have seen nothing yet!"

The press release was never issued. What's more, DSHS quickly lifted the stop-placement orders after Wagner, YouthCare's CEO, called Zahn.

The admissions ban triggered by Lynn's rape lasted only four days—even though DSHS initially said the order would be reassessed only after its investigation was completed months later.

Rosenwald, the DSHS inspector, protested in an e-mail to her boss:

"The decision to reverse this action based on a call from a very influential CEO totally undermines our ability to work with this agency and weakens any case for them to actuate any changes. There is no way that they can take [regional DSHS licensers] seriously after this. We have absolutely no clout. How do we justify this when we take more serious action with other agencies for lesser things?"

Zahn declined comment for this story. So did Rosenwald.

Ten days after Lynn's rape, Wagner wrote YouthCare employees a letter, saying there was no single explanation for the series of group-home incidents. "The saying that 'bad things happen to good people' is true, they also happen to good organizations," Wagner wrote. "And sometimes they come in clusters."

DSHS investigators continued to turn up more problems at YouthCare's group homes and shelters. One employee described a graveyard-shift worker who slept so soundly while on duty that kids couldn't even wake her to get medication. Another employee said higher-ups told her to schedule staff members to work alone even if they hadn't cleared background checks—and to "cross our fingers that nothing happens."

DSHS ultimately found fault with individual YouthCare workers—lower-level ones, mostly—but decided that the nonprofit as a whole was not negligent, saying it had "no foreseeability" that Gregory would do what he did.

For YouthCare, a neglect finding could have been a virtual death sentence.

'A Through-the-Looking-Glass Quality'

In August 2001, Rosie Oreskovich, DSHS's chief of child welfare, wrote to Lynn and apologized for her being raped. "I know my apology cannot right this terrible wrong," she wrote.

But when Lynn sued DSHS and YouthCare two years later, the state's lawyers argued that the girl was partly at fault for what happened.

They contended that Lynn consented to sexual relations with Gregory, and they even objected to any description of what happened as "a sexual assault."

Lisa Erwin, a senior counsel with the Attorney General's Office, said in an interview that the state's lawyers never disputed that a statutory rape occurred. But they argued that any money the state might pay Lynn should be reduced because there was "consent to the touching, even though it was a crime."

"What happened to her was horrendous, whether she consented or not," Erwin said. But Lynn would be owed more were this a forcible attack, Erwin said. The state, she said, had evidence indicating it wasn't: a lack of tears or bruises consistent with an attack, and what Erwin referred to as a "relationship" between Lynn and Gregory.

The state's "fault-of-plaintiff" defense infuriated Lynn's lawyer, Jeffrey Herman, who pointed out that under Washington law, a 13-year-old cannot consent.

"This position has a through-the-looking-glass quality," Herman wrote to the court, adding: "If [Lynn] were capable of consenting to sexual relations on the date of the crime, Mr. Gregory might have an excellent civil-rights claim against the State for unlawfully imprisoning him."

Gregory had already pleaded guilty to second-degree rape of a child and been sentenced to 6 ½ years.

The state wanted details of Lynn's sexual history. Herman objected, saying this invaded Lynn's privacy. The judge, Robert Alsdorf, concluded the state's request went too far and restricted Lynn's answers to dates of prior encounters and whether they were consensual.

Jeffrey Herman, Lynn's lawyer, was infuriated by the argument of the state attorney-general's office that the 13-year-old had consented to sexual relations. "It is such an outrageous position," said Herman, a former social worker for street kids. (Photograph courtesy of Alan Berner/The Seattle Times)

Alsdorf also fined the state $1,000, in part for contending in court documents that there was "no basis" for Lynn's claim of sexual assault.

In 2004, the parties settled the lawsuit. Herman said he didn't want to put Lynn through trial: "I thought it would hurt her. She had been through a lot of sorrow and trauma in her life."

At the same time, Herman filed a motion to seal the entire court file. YouthCare had agreed to settle "only upon execution of a confidentiality provision," Herman wrote. The file, he wrote, "demonstrates unfavorable facts about both defendants" and contains material "very troubling" to Lynn.

Alsdorf granted the motion, even though Lynn's identity had been protected from the outset, with only her initials used in all but two court documents.

Now retired from the bench, Alsdorf said recently that he sealed the file to protect a minor's privacy. As a practical matter, closing the whole file was easier than redacting individual documents. "In hindsight, yeah, it would have been better not to seal it," he said.

Last month, the court's presiding judge opened the file, granting a motion filed by *The Times*. The newspaper argued that potential embarrassment to the state and YouthCare was no reason to grant such extraordinary secrecy. YouthCare objected, citing Lynn's interests and its concern that she had not been found and notified of the unsealing request.

The file, when opened, showed that the lawsuit was settled for $290,000, with the state paying $140,000, and YouthCare, $150,000.

After attorney fees and costs, Lynn received $157,000.

"I feel horrible about this case," Wagner said in a recent interview. "I always have. The last thing I wanted was to have a child in my care abused. . . . This case has haunted me."

'I Can Defently Take Care Of Myself'

Since the 2001 rape:

YouthCare hired the private company that had been offering to do criminal-background checks.

Some workers were fired in YouthCare's lower levels, but Wagner and two deputies left for top jobs at other nonprofit agencies.

Six days after Lynn's lawsuit was sealed, Wagner received a lifetime-achievement award for her work at YouthCare.

Rosenwald, the licensing inspector, received a letter from DSHS taking her to task over Gregory's bungled background check. The rebuke came 10 days before she retired from DSHS, after 31 years.

At YouthCare, problems with unscreened workers continued. In 2002, a supervisor was fired for kissing and hitting on a teenager living in a group home. He had been spending time alone with the girl—even though he had yet to clear his criminal-background check.

In 2003, the DSHS inspector who succeeded Rosenwald visited a YouthCare home and documented violations that caused "great concern." One employee had received a badge saying he was cleared to work with children, but in fact he wasn't, she wrote.

"This type of information is rather alarming," the inspector wrote. "No one," she added, "wants to experience" a repeat of what happened to Lynn.

Gregory remains in prison. He could get out as soon as October.

Lynn was emancipated—given the rights of an adult—at age 17. She wrote to the court in 2004: "I can defently take care of myself."

The next year, she burned through nearly $15,000 of her lawsuit settlement to pay for a hit-and-run accident she caused.

Two months ago she was charged with stealing a car. She failed to show up for her arraignment and has a warrant out for her arrest.

A reporter went to Lynn's last five addresses but couldn't find her.

25. District Ignored Warnings, Then Silenced Girls Fondled by Teacher

OCT. 22, 2006

By Ken Armstrong and Justin Mayo

She was 10 years old, a fourth-grader in the Northshore School District, when John Carl Leede began fondling her, according to court records.

He was a teacher, but not hers. He would spy her in the school library, approach, turn her away from him and begin grabbing, rubbing her breasts. She'd try to break away, but he would yank her back and put her in a kind of headlock.

The girl told her mother, and the mother called the principal, Ed Young.

It all could have ended there—in the spring of 1996, years before Leede was finally convicted of assaulting girls. Young, the principal at Kokanee Elementary near Woodinville, could have investigated and found other students with similar stories.

Instead, Young called the girl to his office. When she got there, she found the principal and Leede, and no one else. Not her mother. Not a counselor. Young questioned her—and Leede explained it all away. A "misplaced hug," he called it, saying he was a "touchy-feely" kind of guy.

Young didn't discipline Leede. He didn't report the matter to police or Child Protective Services. He didn't even write the girl's story down and file it, to help spot any pattern. His next evaluation of Leede offered only praise, saying: "I have appreciated his professionalism and efforts in helping us 'move outside the box.' "

The girl's mother was stunned at Young's response. The girl would later tell police: "This was brushed under the table." She would become violent and defiant, say Leede was what she got for being "a good girl," and scratch her wrists with broken glass.

This family and two others filed a claim that accused the school district and four principals of ignoring repeated warnings about Leede. But you haven't read about that claim before, or of how it was quietly settled for $700,000. A confidentiality agreement ordered documents destroyed, computer records purged, and lips and court records sealed.

David Spicer, the families' attorney, said he was "outraged" and "beyond amazed" at the district's failure to protect students from Leede.

But the secrecy agreement, he said, "was a condition the school district had, and we just had to live with it."

Three of Leede's victims—including the girl called into Young's office—cannot say a disparaging word about the teacher who assaulted them or the district that made it possible. Speak ill, and they face a fine of $10,000. The secrecy agreement even restricts what they can tell any therapist.

The Seattle Times unearthed this claim—and the allegations against Young, now principal at Skyline High School in Sammamish—as part of a continuing investigation of sealed court records. A reporter came across a lawsuit against Leede that had been sealed improperly and that referred to a secret settlement involving the Northshore School District.

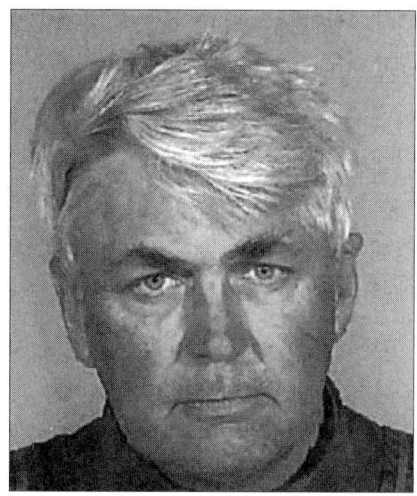

Teacher Carl Leede was sentenced to jail in 2000. (Photograph courtesy of Washington State Patrol/*The Seattle Times*)

The families' claim and thousands of other documents were obtained in the past several months through public-disclosure requests and a motion to unseal. Those records tell the story of how one teacher fondled students day after day, year after year, with principal after principal doing little or nothing to stop him.

A Teacher Pursues His 'Educational Asperarions'

Carl Leede, now 55, taught full time in the Northshore School District for more than 20 years. His personnel file reflects a tumultuous career, making any hands-off treatment all the more baffling.

He applied to the district in 1976, after teaching for two years in Kitsap County. His letter, peppered with typos and misspellings, said he wanted to reduce his "commutation time" and pursue his "educational asperarions." Northshore hired him the following year.

Leede eventually worked at five elementary schools in the district, which straddles King and Snohomish counties and is considered one of the state's best. His students were mostly fifth- and sixth-graders, kids 11 or 12 years old.

His early reviews were mixed. One principal praised Leede's enthusiasm but panned his work ethic and arrogance: "He often assumes he has a better answer than anyone else has ever devised." Leede called the evaluation an "unfortunate and unnecessary slam and assault upon my career" and even filed a grievance.

Another principal attended a math lesson in which Leede let students do whatever they wanted. Some read ski magazines. Some doodled. Others talked. The principal met with Leede and suggested the time be used more productively. Leede stormed out before she could finish, her notes say.

With time, Leede's reviews shined. But other parts of his personnel file reveal a divide among parents, teachers and principals. To some, Leede was lazy, petulant, reckless. To others, he was creative and caring. Some parents called Leede the best teacher their kids ever had. Others pulled their children from his class.

Leede tickled kids and kissed their cheeks. Was this good-natured fun? Or was it creepy? Other times, his conduct left no doubt, veering into cruelty or boorishness, according to personnel records, a district investigative report and, ultimately, police statements.

He used profanity and made sexual remarks in front of kids. He pointed to one girl and said, "This is an example of pretty, but not smart," then to another girl and said, "This is an example of smart, but not pretty." In a teachers' meeting, he went down his class list and categorized each student as "dumber than a stump" or "a little sh— ."

He called boys "jerkballs." One wrote Leede a letter, saying: "Why do you treat the boys like crud?" He hugged the girls, beckoning with "Come here, gorgeous." He'd remark to other adults about the girls' developing bodies and predict who'd get pregnant first.

Once, according to his personnel file, he made students announce their test scores, then he charted them on a board, designating "geniuses" and "idiots." Another time, according to police reports, he had students spell words such as "ejaculation," "pubic" and "tampon," put them in an essay, and read the essay aloud to the class, using a microphone.

Early Warnings: 'Principals Don't Like Problems'

Warnings of Leede's touching go back at least to the 1980s. Cheryl Cone warned two principals herself—and would have warned others, if she'd known Leede was still around.

Now retired in South Dakota, Cone gave this account to *The Seattle Times*:

Cone used to be a teaching assistant at Woodinville Annex, a school that's now closed. She walked into Leede's classroom one day—in 1989, she believes—and saw him tickling a girl lying on a table. When Cone appeared, Leede stopped tickling. But the whole time he talked to Cone, he kept his hands on the girl's breasts.

Cone was dumbfounded. She told Anne Boone, the principal. Boone replied that she would take care of it—but Cone never heard anything back.

A few years later, Cone saw somewhere that Leede was now at Woodmoor Elementary: "I thought, 'Shoot, what's he still doing around?'" She called Woodmoor's principal: "He sounded really kind of ticked off that I'd brought up a problem. Principals don't like problems, because some of these people have tenure and they have the teachers union behind them."

Years later, news reports said an unnamed teacher was accused of fondling girls at a different Northshore school. Cone checked a registry and saw Leede's name: "I couldn't believe that he was still there and in contact with kids. I felt that I'd been betrayed. They were just pushing it aside.

"How many people were damaged along the way? It's just sickening."

At Woodinville Annex, Boone, the principal, received at least three warnings besides Cone's, according to police and school records.

In the late 1980s, a teacher saw Leede holding a girl on his lap, face to face, tight. The teacher "was so shocked that, if it had been her daughter, Carl would have no hair left on his head," she recounted years later. The teacher told Boone, but Boone never got back to her.

Another teaching assistant saw Leede touch a girl's breasts. She told Boone, who replied that she had scheduled a speaker on inappropriate touching. When the assistant checked back, Boone said Leede hadn't shown up for the training.

Leede's personnel file includes four evaluations by Boone, all positive. None mentions inappropriate touching. Boone called Leede a "very creative educator" and said: "The emotional well-being of the students is an important goal for Mr. Leede."

Boone, now retired in Hawaii, said she remembered three complaints from staff members about Leede's touching. She didn't note them in his personnel file but did tell him once to stop putting girls on his lap: "He sort of admitted it wasn't a good idea, but said there was nothing meant by it.

"I really believed that he was stupid, that he wasn't thinking about what he was doing. But I didn't think he was molesting anyone," Boone said. "If I'd gotten one complaint from a parent, he would have been gone."

'Hi Carl: I Circled the Area That You May Want to Look At'

By the time the 1998–99 school year began at Kokanee Elementary, Leede's behavior had become, in the words of a subsequent legal claim, "essentially predatory," so bold that he was fondling some girls almost every day.

Girls tried thwarting him by wearing loose clothing, or crossing their chest when he approached from behind, or elbowing him in the stomach. One girl dreaded sitting at the computer: "It was like I was trapped," she told an investigator. "There was no place to get away." One student said Leede warned girls not to tell or he'd get them in trouble with the principal. Some doubted they would be believed anyway.

When the 1998–99 school year began, Ed Young was coming off a year spent as the district's interim director of personnel. Now he was returning to Kokanee, where he had been principal for three years. Called in one review "a sincere believer in teacher empowerment," Young presented written goals for the year about letting teachers "think outside of the box in a risk-free environment."

Leede was beginning his fifth year at Kokanee. He taught fifth- and sixth-graders in an alternative program, called PACE, that emphasized parental involvement.

By this time, Northshore principals had already been warned of inappropriate touching by Leede at least a dozen times, personnel files and other records show. At least five warnings had reached Young. When he took the personnel position, Young told his fill-in to keep an eye on Leede, saying there'd been reports of touching, according to school records.

Young canceled an interview for this story and didn't return subsequent calls. Leede, who lives in Seattle, declined comment.

The 1998–99 school year offered one chance after another for the school district to put a stop to Leede.

OCTOBER: A father saw Leede touch his daughter's breast in a school hallway. The newspaper isn't naming the father to protect his daughter's identity, but he gave this account:

He told Leede then and there: "If you ever touch my daughter like that again, one of us is going to the hospital and one of us is going to jail." That night, the father said, "I was in tears for not protecting my daughter better." He met with Young the next day, and Young told him: I'll take care of it. You don't need to put anything in writing. But later, the father said, Young claimed he couldn't do anything without a written complaint.

The girl's mother also met with Young. "Ed said that Carl had a clean file, that ... nobody had ever complained about him," she later told police.

After these meetings, Young sent Leede a note:

Hi Carl,
The personnel office sent us some pamphlets on safe interaction with students. After talking with you last week in regard to [the parents'] concern about you hugging their daughter, I thought that you may want to take a look at it. The pamphlet really helps to clarify what is appropriate or inappropriate. I circled the area that you may want to look at. Thanks again for listening and responding to the concerns.

NOVEMBER: During Thanksgiving week one teacher saw Leede with his hands on a girl's backside. Another saw Leede hug and kiss a girl. Both reported what they saw to Young on Dec. 1. The principal again referred Leede to the pamphlet, according to law-enforcement records.

DECEMBER: The girl who had been called into Young's office in 1996 told a Bothell police detective what Leede had done. That detective called Young, who told police he remembered Leede hugging a girl in the library. He wrote the detective: "I gave Mr. Leede a warning about touching, shared the district's policy on appropriate and inappropriate touching and directed him to not do it again. He agreed and we had no further incidents."

The detective closed the case, and told the girl that her "perceptions of what took place might have magnified the actual contact," according to his report.

(Families filing a claim against the district later seize upon Young's words—"we had no further incidents"—and allege that he "knew this information not only to be misleading but categorically untrue." Instead of protecting students, they say, Young "sought once again to minimize the conduct and instead protect and cover for Leede.")

JANUARY: The father who had met with Young in October turned in a written grievance: "I told him, 'Here's your bloody complaint. Now do something.'" The letter said Leede was still hugging children. Young wrote the father back: "I have spoken with him about your concerns and advised him on the district's policy on safe and appropriate touching. . . . The inappropriate behavior will stop."

Young later described his talk with Leede to a district investigator: "I told him, 'You cannot hug from the front' and showed him the side hug."

MARCH: Because of declining enrollment in Leede's Kokanee class, Northshore was considering moving him to Woodin Elementary next fall. But Woodin's principal had a concern. He asked the district's personnel director if Leede had a problem with touching students, according to a memo the director wrote.

The director got ahold of Ed Young and asked him. "Ed replied that he did not," the director's memo says.

The transfer went through.

A Father Tells Police: 'It All Makes Sense Now'

In April 1999, a seventh-grader began having nightmares about the teacher who had fondled her—"about once a day," in her words—in fifth and sixth grades at Kokanee.

The girl told her mother what Leede had done. "I was scared to death," the mother later told police. "I felt horrible, that I'd blown it as a parent."

The mother began making calls and discovered that Leede had also fondled a friend of her daughter's. "It all makes sense now," that girl's father told police. He remembered asking his daughter: "Why are you wearing this heavy sweatshirt to school on the hottest day of the year?"

This girl's father called the Snohomish County Sheriff's Office—initiating the first comprehensive investigation of Leede, 10 years after Cheryl Cone reported him standing there, hands on a student's breasts.

Police arrested Leede on May 20, 1999. He didn't seem surprised or shocked when told he was suspected of child molestation, according to a police report. "I do hug children," he told a detective. But Leede said there was nothing sexual about it. He considered hugs important to a child's development.

A Mother Writes: 'You Did This. You Live with It'

News of the arrest touched off a series of events colored by secrecy and damage control.

Woodin Elementary parents complained of Leede's pending transfer to their school. A district spokeswoman assured them: "We will not knowingly or consciously place students in an unhealthy environment."

The school district placed Leede on paid leave and conducted an investigation to see if he should be fired. A month after Leede's arrest the investigator completed a confidential report that described how the teacher had repeatedly fondled girls. The report listed eight instances in which administrators had been warned.

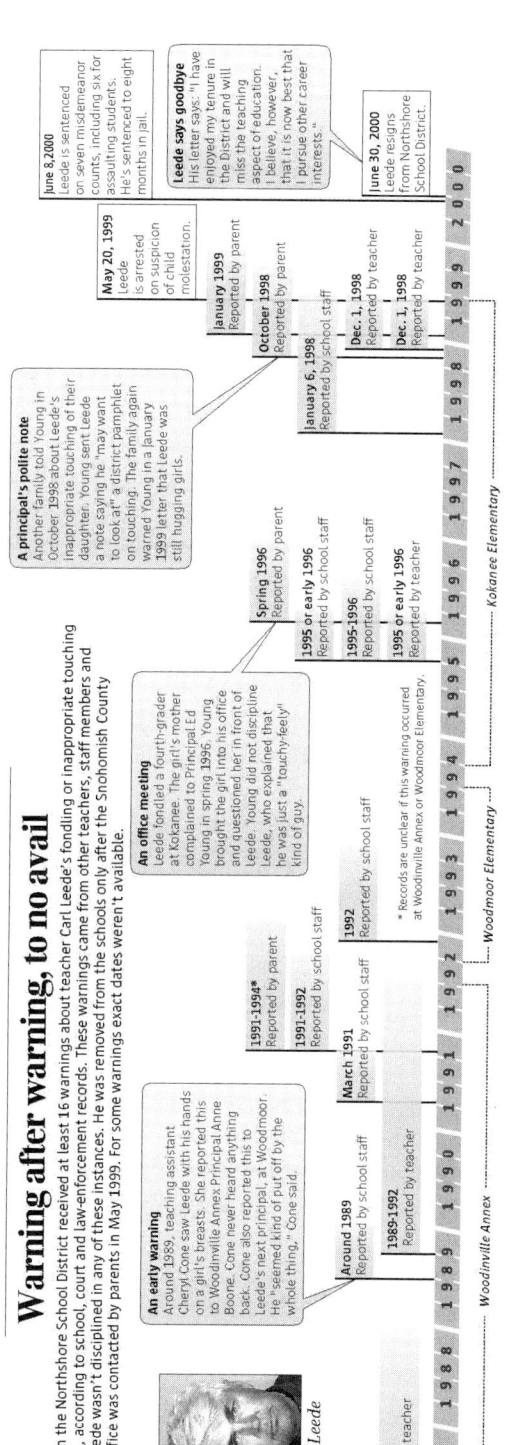

Courtesy of *The Seattle Times*

Still, in news reports afterward, district officials minimized Leede's misconduct and insisted that officials followed proper procedures in dealing with him.

In August 1999, the district's general counsel wrote a confidential memorandum saying the failure of some administrators to document complaints had obscured Leede's "pattern of misconduct." He also cited "inadequate management skills" for what happened at Kokanee, bemoaning how some administrators shy away from confrontation.

A week later, the district reprimanded Young, saying his "inadequate performance" contributed to the district's "failure to appreciate" Leede's "touching issues" earlier. The reprimand blamed Young for inadequate investigation ("You prejudged the intentions of Mr. Leede"); inadequate documentation ("You relied upon recall from memory rather than writing down information at the time"); inadequate supervision; and for failure to report complaints to personnel.

But Young's annual evaluations made no mention of these failings. One praised his handling of a meeting with parents after Leede's arrest. Another lauded "the integrity with which [he] has handled the challenges of leadership and supervision."

In the summer of 1999, the school district announced it had found probable cause to fire Leede. Leede filed a union grievance and demanded a hearing.

The two sides settled, quietly. Instead of firing Leede, the district agreed to pay him $55,000 for another year's work, to be done away from students. He would be paid even if convicted of criminal charges, the agreement says. Leede, in turn, agreed to resign on June 30, 2000.

When the media disclosed the employment settlement in October 1999, the mother of the fourth-grader who had been called into Young's office wrote Karen Forys, Northshore's superintendent:

"Your settlement does not right a wrong. It just begs for it to go away, to be swept under the rug. It tells the victims that the school district does not care and that coming forth to tell the truth, no matter how painful, doesn't result in any justice, so why should they bother? Is this a proud example to set for our students? Does this show principle or expediency? Does this show courage or fear? You did this. You live with it."

Forys wrote back, saying the outcome of any hearing would be uncertain and that fighting Leede's appeal would cost more than settling. Northshore avoided further "stress and pain" for any victims or witnesses, Forys wrote, and the settlement assured Leede would not teach in the district again.

In March 2000, Leede reached a plea deal with prosecutors and was convicted of seven misdemeanors, including six counts of assault.

The sentencing judge received more than 80 letters of support for Leede, from family, friends, parents, students. They said Leede imbued a love of reading and helped kids overcome their fear of public speaking. He learned sign language to communicate with a deaf child. He spent 45 minutes untangling a hairbrush from one student's hair.

But other letters wrote of trust betrayed and damage done. The girl with the nightmares described sitting in the dark, trying to cut the dirt and germs off her body with a serrated knife, and how, at 14, she used black permanent marker to write "ugly" all over her skin.

Leede was sentenced on June 8, 2000, to eight months in jail. His sentence required him to surrender his teaching certificate, register as a sex offender and complete a 36-month program of "psycho-sexual deviancy counseling" that used "controlled electroshock, boredom tapes and negative olfactory stimulation."

Three weeks later, Leede's resignation took effect. His letter said: "I have enjoyed my tenure in the District and will miss the teaching aspect of education. I believe, however, that it is now best that I pursue other career interests."

Destroy Documents, Purge Files, Zip Lips

In December 2000, the families of three girls—the girl called into Young's office, the girl with the nightmares, the girl with the heavy sweatshirts—wrote a "claim letter" notifying the school district of their intent to sue.

The letter predicted a jury would be "incensed" at how the school district and four principals had failed to protect students from Leede.

Soon after, the attorneys for these families learned that Leede was selling his house. To preserve his assets, they quickly filed a separate suit in King County Superior Court and obtained an order attaching his home. The only defendants named in this lawsuit were Leede and his wife.

The claim against the district, the principals and Leede went to mediation and was settled in 2001, with the families receiving $700,000.

The settlement agreement demanded secrecy. It required the families and their attorneys to gather whatever documents they had about their allegations, and turn them over to be destroyed. They also had to "purge all computer records" related to their claim.

Even though the Northshore School District is a public entity—making its finances public record—the agreement forbade the parties from disclosing the settlement amount. It also prohibited any party from disparaging another, and set the penalty for any violation at $10,000.

Spicer, the families' attorney, said his clients consented to secrecy because they wanted to settle. Otherwise, these "very vulnerable girls" would have been exposed to depositions and a possible trial, he said.

The King County lawsuit against Leede was also sealed, based upon a motion that said the parties wanted the outcome to be secret. Court Commissioner Carlos Velategui went along, signing an order that violated the rules governing open court records.

It was this order—the only part of the file kept open—that caught the eye of a *Seattle Times* reporter and led to this story. The newspaper filed a motion and got the file opened this year, and obtained other documents about Leede and the district through a host of public-disclosure requests.

Forys, the superintendent, would not answer questions for this story. Nor would Northshore's general counsel, Joe McKamey.

In November 1999—six months after Leede's arrest—Forys was named Washington's Superintendent of the Year.

Ed Young left the Northshore School District in 2000 to take a job in the Mukilteo School District. He retired there in 2004, leaving as principal of Kamiak High School.

Last year he returned to school administration. He's now principal of Skyline High School in Sammamish, one of the state's top high schools.

Recently, a reporter told the father who complained to Young in October 1998 about the principal's newest job.

"Are you kidding me?" the father said. He laughed bitterly, then paused. "Oh, wow. He's a good politician."

26. What the State Didn't Know About Doctor, Malpractice Suit

DEC. 13, 2006

By Ken Armstrong and Justin Mayo

Since 2001, Dr. James H. Greene has been accused in two lawsuits of negligence that resulted in extreme injury or death. In both cases, Greene's employer, Group Health Cooperative, paid significant settlements to the patients' families—one for $5.5 million, the other for $800,000.

But when health-care regulators filed disciplinary charges against Greene earlier this year, they knew about only one settlement, the smaller one. The state Department of Health wound up giving Greene its lightest possible punishment.

All the while, the $5.5 million settlement was hidden away, improperly sealed by a King County Superior Court judge.

It shows up in a database used by lawyers, but only as Confidential v. Confidential, in county Confidential. The defense attorneys? Confidential. Medical experts? Confidential.

The Seattle Times recently got this lawsuit opened, as part of a continuing investigation of improperly sealed court records.

The public—and state regulators—can now see what's inside.

The suit accuses Greene of not bothering to examine a pregnant woman well past her due date and entering her 25th hour of labor, leading to devastating injuries to a newborn child. While Group Health denied that Greene and other employees were negligent, it paid millions to the baby's family—so long as they kept quiet about it. Let slip the defendant's name, and they could lose the money.

Even now that the case is unsealed, the family and their lawyer can't talk about it.

Theirs is one of at least two dozen medical-malpractice cases sealed in their entirety in King County Superior Court since 1990.

The lawsuit involving Greene—along with two other Group Health cases unsealed through *The Times*' efforts this year—illustrates the dangers of secrecy in medical-malpractice lawsuits. Patients, regulators and hospitals need to know all they can about the people entrusted with the public's health.

A Difficult Delivery

When she was 38 weeks pregnant, an ultrasound showed that her child already weighed an estimated 10 pounds, 4 ounces. The average newborn weighs 7 to 8 pounds, and a full-term pregnancy typically lasts about 40 weeks.

The 35-year-old woman was in the midwife program at Group Health, a nonprofit HMO with more than 500,000 members in Washington and Idaho. Nurse midwives provided prenatal care while doctors handled delivery.

At 40 weeks, she still had not delivered. The child continued to grow.

In June 1999, when she was "42-plus weeks" pregnant, she finally went into labor and was admitted to Group Health Central Hospital in Seattle. After about 24 hours of labor, a midwife contacted the obstetrician on call, Dr. James H. Greene.

But Greene didn't respond by examining the woman, nor did he personally review her chart, according to court records. Instead, he told the midwife to keep doing what she was doing.

About two hours later, the baby's head appeared. The midwife called another Group Health doctor. She arrived but for 10 minutes was unable to deliver the child, according to court records. The baby's shoulders were stuck. A Virginia Mason obstetrician offered his help, and delivered the baby within two minutes.

The baby boy had no heartbeat. Medical workers resuscitated him—but he wound up with brain damage, spastic quadriplegia and a seizure disorder. He struggles to communicate and must be fed through a tube.

In 2001, the child's family sued Group Health, alleging that the midwives, Greene and another doctor were negligent. Group Health's employees should have recognized the risk factors for shoulder dystocia—large baby, long pregnancy, protracted labor—and warned the expectant mother against regular delivery, the lawsuit alleged. Greene, the plaintiffs argued, should have examined her and prepared for a Caesarean section.

Group Health denied its employees were negligent, court records show.

In 2003, the two sides settled, with Group Health agreeing to pay $5.5 million. A confidentiality clause said the boy's parents could not "reveal to or discuss with anyone, including the media," the names of "the parties released"—that is, Group Health.

The mother recently told *The Times*: "Basically, we can't talk to you. I'm sorry."

These boxes in the office of Bainbridge Island attorney Carol Johnston are stuffed with documents from two families' malpractice lawsuits against Group Health. But confidentiality agreements prevent Johnston from revealing the documents. (Photograph courtesy of Mike Siegel/The Seattle Times)

The family's lawyers could publish, or release, the case's facts—but only if the names of the parties, the defense attorneys, the county and the case number were left out. That's why the lawsuit appears in a lawyers' database as Confidential v. Confidential.

The Times asked one of the family's lawyers, Judy Massong, which party wanted the confidentiality agreement. "The defendants," she said. You mean Group Health? she was asked. "I can't say that," she said. The confidentiality agreement won't allow her to say those words.

An attorney appointed to represent the boy's interests also asked that the entire file be sealed, saying this would keep the settlement details confidential. Judge Terry Lukens went along, even though the law doesn't permit such extraordinary secrecy on such slim grounds.

When *The Times* challenged this sealing order, a different judge opened the file. Group Health officials declined to comment on this or any other case, citing concern for patient privacy.

'A Crack in the System'

In Washington, companies that provide liability insurance to physicians must notify state regulators of any malpractice settlement above $20,000.

But the way the Department of Health reads the law, the reporting requirement wasn't triggered in the late-birth case settled for $5.5 million. That's because the lawsuit didn't name Greene as an individual defendant, and it was Group Health's insurers who paid, not Greene's.

But many medical-malpractice lawsuits name only a hospital or HMO as a defendant, even when individual doctors are accused of negligence.

State Rep. Tom Campbell, vice chairman of the House Health Care Committee, said: "This is a classic example of a crack in the system. This was never an intention of the Legislature, I can tell you that."

Campbell said he will propose changing this law in the next legislative session to require greater reporting. He'll also ask for a stiffer penalty. Insurers that violate the reporting law can currently be punished only by a fine—and the maximum is $250.

The Department of Health's records show the $5.5 million settlement was never reported to the state. Because Group Health was self-insured up to $3 million, it paid most of the settlement, according to court records. An outside insurer paid the rest.

But Sally Yates, associate general counsel for Group Health, would not say whether Group Health had filed a report with state regulators.

Greene, 43, declined to comment for this story, referring questions to a Group Health spokeswoman. "That's what I was instructed to do," he said. He now works for Group Health in Tacoma.

'Dr. Greene Will Call You'

In May 1999, Greene performed a cervical biopsy on Deluvina Gonzalez, a seamstress who lived in Seattle. She received written after-care instructions that said: "Dr. Greene will call you."

The biopsy results showed Gonzalez had cervical cancer. But, according to a lawsuit filed by Gonzalez's family, Greene failed for five months to notify Gonzalez of that news.

Gonzalez died in December 2000 at the age of 56. Her family's lawsuit, filed in 2002, alleged that Greene's neglect created a five-month delay in treatment that proved fatal. Medical experts hired by the family said a hysterectomy performed after diagnosis could have saved her.

Group Health denied the allegations of negligence. And its experts concluded that cancer would have killed Gonzalez no matter what.

In January 2004, the two sides settled the lawsuit for $800,000. This settlement included a confidentiality agreement, but the court file itself was not sealed.

This year the state filed disciplinary charges against Greene, stemming from the Gonzalez case. The charges said Greene could produce no contemporaneous notes showing he had tried to contact Gonzalez. The state also accused Greene of other incompetence—saying, for example, that he did not remove the entire tumor during the biopsy.

Greene insisted that he had contacted Gonzalez twice by phone. He also made other attempts to reach her regarding follow-up care, he told the state.

Four months ago, the state and Greene cut a deal, called a "stipulation to informal disposition." Greene did not admit unprofessional conduct but did agree to corrective action.

The deal requires Greene to serve as an example of sorts. He must tell his Group Health colleagues what happened in this case and describe the steps he'll take to notify future patients of a life-threatening diagnosis: alerting the patient in writing, delivering word by certified mail, sending a messenger to the patient's home.

Larry Berg, a staff attorney for the Department of Health, said that when Greene met with regulators to settle the disciplinary charges, his responses were consistent and his demeanor credible. "For the sake of settlement negotiations," Berg said, the state accepted Greene's claim that he had called Gonzalez. But the state "still determined that disciplinary action was appropriate," Berg said, based on Greene's failure to follow up those initial calls.

When the state reached this deal, it knew of two other settlements in Greene's past, one for $250,000, the other for $42,500.

Berg recently searched state files and confirmed that the late-birth lawsuit, settled for $5.5 million, was unknown to regulators when they investigated Greene. "If other complaints were known at the time of settlement negotiations, then they also would have been considered and would have influenced the [state's] decision regarding appropriate sanctions in this case," Berg said.

Yates, the Group Health attorney, declined to say if the HMO had ever taken action itself against Greene: "We do not divulge that kind of information about our staff." But she said Group Health does "rigorous reviews" of its employees every year, including an analysis of any claims or lawsuits filed.

Four Boxes Not to Be Opened

Carol Johnston, a Bainbridge Island lawyer who specializes in medical-malpractice cases, represented Deluvina Gonzalez's family. Johnston also represented another family that sued Group Health, in a lawsuit that was sealed.

A reporter recently visited Johnston in her office. On her floor were four boxes, stuffed with documents from those two lawsuits, including records that were exchanged by the parties but never filed publicly. Johnston said she wanted to share what was inside those boxes. But she couldn't. Confidentiality agreements made that impossible.

In both cases, Johnston said, she and her clients agreed not to discuss who did what, or how much was paid. Such agreements, she said, are "common." Asked who requests them, Johnston said: "The defense—always, in my experience. And it is made a condition of settlement."

Yates, the Group Health attorney, declined to answer questions about confidentiality agreements in any particular case.

But, she said, in general: "Confidentiality clauses in settlement agreements are commonly used by parties in all kinds of civil disputes. . . . They can serve to protect the privacy of individuals involved in a dispute. They can protect families."

Johnston, a former nurse, bristles at these secrecy agreements: "It prevents the public from having access to information that they're entitled to, and which can be used to improve health care."

Demands for confidentiality frustrate her clients, Johnston said. "The vast majority of my clients say, 'All I want is for this to not happen to someone else.'" But secrecy agreements prevent them from helping others, she said, so now they suffer guilt with everything else.

And the incentives to settle are great, Johnston said. Someone may be dying or in immediate need of care. A trial means delay, stress, expense and risk.

Johnston said that because of the confidentiality agreement, Gonzalez's family cannot talk to the media.

They can't even provide a picture of Deluvina.

27. Woman's Coma Leads to Secrecy, Silence

DEC. 17, 2006

By Ken Armstrong and Justin Mayo

Sylvia Lane, a diabetic, lay in her apartment bed in Lynnwood, comatose and alone, her blood and brain in desperate need of sugar.

But the medical device she'd just received instead kept pumping insulin into her body, pumping and pumping, starving her brain and making it more unlikely she would ever wake up.

Lane was 17 weeks pregnant. Her husband was on an aircraft carrier, halfway round the world. Relatives were calling but getting no answer.

The pump, about the size of a cell phone, had a safety feature designed to stop the insulin flow in emergencies like this. But the feature wasn't on. The pump had been shipped to Lane with the option turned off, and the device's instructional video devoted only 15 seconds to it, saying nothing about *why* the feature should be used.

Ultimately, Lane suffered severe and permanent brain damage. Her family sued Medtronic Inc.—the parent company of the pump's manufacturer—alleging the pump was unsafe. Medtronic had already sold 150,000 insulin pumps in the United States.

What happened to Sylvia Lane could have yielded insight into the pump's design and instructions, alerting patients and health-care providers to the importance of this safety feature, originally called a "Deadman's Switch."

But when Medtronic settled the lawsuit three years ago, the entire court file was improperly sealed, hiding every allegation and discovery behind an electronic password.

What's more, Medtronic failed to disclose Lane's injury to the federal government, which uses such reports to spot problems with medical devices and to protect the public.

Lawsuits and regulatory reports allow patterns to emerge and warnings to sound. Here, there was merely secrecy and silence.

The Seattle Times got this file opened three months ago as part of a continuing investigation of improperly sealed court records.

Lane's family also sued the state of Washington, alleging the University of Washington Medical Center committed medical malpractice while instructing Sylvia on the pump's use. The state settled, using taxpayer dollars. But the UW, despite being asked for all its records a year ago, has yet to reveal the amount.

The following account relies on the court file. The lawyer for Lane's family said he cannot comment, nor can the family, because the parties agreed to confidentiality as a condition of settlement. Medtronic also declined comment, citing the settlement agreement and Lane's privacy.

A Pump That Mimics the Pancreas

Michael Lane and Sylvia got married in 1989, then moved about as his Navy career dictated. In 1995, they were living in Naples, Italy. That's when Sylvia learned she had type 1 diabetes.

Her pancreas didn't work. It wasn't producing the insulin she needed.

Insulin, a hormone, counteracts rising blood sugar. When blood sugar goes up, a healthy pancreas releases more insulin. When blood sugar goes down—during sleep, for example—insulin production decreases. The pancreas acts as a regulator, keeping blood sugar from going too high or low, either of which can mean sickness or death.

Sylvia now needed to inject herself with insulin, using a syringe.

The couple moved to Washington in 2000. In August of that year, Sylvia, then 34, learned she was pregnant. Soon after, Michael, a lieutenant, left for duty in the Persian Gulf.

Sylvia lived alone in their Lynnwood apartment.

Because her blood sugar wasn't under control, Sylvia went to the UW's Diabetes in Pregnancy clinic. A doctor there prescribed an insulin pump. Sylvia's insurance helped her buy a pump, a model 508, for about $5,100. The pump arrived in October 2000.

Insulin pumps came onto the market in the 1980s. Today's models weigh just a few ounces and can hold a several-day supply of insulin. A thin tube runs from the pump, worn on a belt or in a pouch under clothes, into the user's stomach. Mimicking a pancreas, the pump steadily releases small amounts of insulin. It can also be programmed to release larger doses—to anticipate a meal, for instance.

Pumps help minimize the highs and lows, reducing diabetes' long-term effects, such as kidney failure, limb loss and blindness.

But pumps also carry risk. If someone's blood sugar drops too much, he can go into a hypoglycemic coma. Hypoglycemia demands sugar, not insulin. But the pump doesn't know that. It keeps pumping insulin—and the user, unconscious, can't turn it off.

MiniMed, the maker of Sylvia's pump, recognized this danger early on. It created a safety feature in the late 1980s that would stop the insulin flow if the user didn't press a button for a set number of hours. Company documents initially called it a "Deadman's Switch." It later became known as the "Auto-Off."

Medtronic, a multibillion-dollar company based in Minnesota, acquired MiniMed in 2001. This took place a year after Sylvia received her pump and a year before her family filed suit.

When Sylvia's pump arrived, the Auto-Off was deactivated. That's how the company ships all its pumps, to this day.

Sylvia's pump came with an instructional video. The video, 48 minutes long, devoted only 15 seconds to the Auto-Off, and that came more than a half-hour into the tape. "A safety feature which can be helpful for every pump user," the video called it. But the video didn't say *why* anyone might want the pump to stop pumping. It didn't say *how* the feature could save users from harm.

That video would become emblematic of this question:

Insulin pumps help diabetics. The 508 appears to be a good pump. The Auto-Off appears to be a smart feature. But how can it be a safety feature if many people don't know why they need it?

17 Calls—And No Answer

On Oct. 25, 2000, a Wednesday, Sylvia met with Emily Holing, a diabetes educator at the UW clinic. Holing hooked up Sylvia's pump and showed her how to use it.

This same afternoon, Holing documented two episodes of hypoglycemia for Sylvia, 15 minutes apart. Each time Sylvia needed to drink orange juice.

Holing didn't activate the Auto-Off on Sylvia's pump. She understood the feature, Holing said later, but didn't think Sylvia should use it. "I don't want the insulin interrupted during pregnancy," Holing said in a deposition. She advised Sylvia to use a "buddy system," with a friend or relative making regular checks on her.

Sylvia had pizza that evening, then drove home. She wouldn't be heard from for three days.

Friends and family tried calling Sylvia on Thursday, Friday and Saturday, leaving 17 messages. Sylvia's twin sister lived three hours away. On Saturday she traveled to Sylvia's and, with another relative, went inside. They found Sylvia on her bed, unconscious, lying in vomit. Her insulin pump was attached and running.

How a pump works

An insulin pump helps diabetics regulate their blood sugar by providing a constant source of insulin. Introduced to the market in the 1980s, the pumps provided an alternative to multiple daily injections of insulin.

Ⓐ The pump – about the size of a deck of cards - weighs only a few ounces and can be worn on a belt or kept in a pouch under clothing.

The pump connects to flexible Ⓑ plastic tubing that delivers insulin to the body.

Users set the pump to give a steady trickle of insulin throughout the day. It can be programmed to release larger doses at meals or at times when blood sugar is too high.

All major models have an Auto-Off feature. When activated, the Auto-Off stops the delivery of insulin if the user doesn't press a button after a set amount of time. This is particularly important if the user becomes unconscious and is unable to stop the pump manually.

Sources: American Diabetes Association, Medtronic MiniMed

MARK NOWLIN / THE SEATTLE TIMES

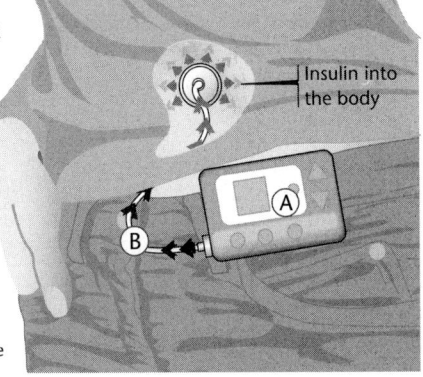

Sylvia was in a hypoglycemic coma. Paramedics injected her with sugar water and transported her to the hospital.

She gradually emerged from the coma but suffered permanent and severe brain damage. Memory, comprehension, reading, writing, walking, problem solving, judgment—all were impaired. Sylvia could speak only in combinations of two or three words, such as, "I'm fine." Medical experts said they expected little improvement. She would need round-the-clock care for the rest of her life.

Doctors terminated Sylvia's pregnancy Nov. 11, at 20 weeks, fearing the unborn child had suffered serious injury.

10 Deaths—With Few Details

In May 2002, Michael Lane filed suit in King County Superior Court, on his and Sylvia's behalf.

The lawsuit named two sets of defendants.

Medtronic, the lawsuit alleged, violated Washington's product-liability law: The pump's warnings were insufficient and its design unsafe. The

Auto-Off should be automatic, not an option, the lawsuit alleged. Had the feature been activated and the insulin cut off, Sylvia could have emerged from her coma and sought help before suffering brain damage, the lawsuit contended.

The lawsuit also accused the UW Medical Center of medical malpractice, saying Holing failed to advise Sylvia adequately on the pump's use and risks.

Christopher Otorowski, a Bainbridge Island lawyer, represented Michael Lane.

A year into the suit, Otorowski cited 15 reports filed with the U.S. Food and Drug Administration (FDA) for a nine-month period ending in March 2003. Although light on detail, the reports disclosed 10 deaths and five injuries suffered by people using Medtronic's insulin pumps.

The reports, Otorowski said, constituted "a trend or pattern of deaths." He said Medtronic should divulge more information about each case. The company, he wrote, was concealing information about the pump's risks "from the public, the medical community and the government."

Before approving a new medical device, the FDA requires clinical studies or testing for safety and effectiveness. But MiniMed had bypassed that step by saying the devices were "substantially equivalent" to a generic infusion pump used for medical fluids, Otorowski said. That general-purpose pump was approved before 1976.

The company made and sold insulin pumps "without anything more than a rubber stamp," Otorowski wrote.

Medtronic defended its pumps in general and the safety option in particular. The Auto-Off "is not some mysterious and nefarious device that dooms unsuspecting pump users to hypoglycemic comas," wrote Douglas Hofmann, a lawyer representing the company.

Medtronic said the role played by Holing, the UW diabetes educator, should free the company from any claims of liability. How could Medtronic be blamed for shipping the pump with the safety feature off, the company argued, when Holing had decided Sylvia shouldn't use it anyway?

The company also said the law does not require it to warn users about risks. The pump is available only by prescription, Medtronic said, so the company's duty is to ensure that health-care providers prescribing the pump understand its features. And in this case, Medtronic said, Holing understood the safety option and chose not to activate it.

Medtronic tested Sylvia's pump afterward and determined that it "performed flawlessly," Hofmann said. The company called any demand for a redesign "manifestly irresponsible."

Medtronic also challenged the relevance and reliability of the 15 reports to the FDA. The reports said little or nothing about the Auto-Off feature. Plus, none of the reports concluded that a pump had *caused* a death or injury, Medtronic said.

Motions That Become Moot

As the October 2003 trial date approached, Otorowski demanded more and more information from Medtronic. He wanted records of other lawsuits; customer complaints; details of adverse-event reports to the FDA; documents on the government-approval process.

Medtronic and Otorowski sparred over what documents the company would have to produce. Ultimately, the judge would have to decide.

In August 2003, the UW settled the claim against it. But the university has yet to disclose what it paid, even though that figure is a public record.

The same month, just before a hearing to determine if there was enough evidence to warrant trial, Medtronic and Michael Lane also settled. The judge had not yet ruled on Otorowski's demands for additional records—so those motions became moot.

Together, Lane, Medtronic and the UW asked for the entire file to be sealed. They said they wanted to keep private Sylvia's medical information and Medtronic's proprietary records; to protect the Lanes from financial predators; and to honor the parties' settlement agreement, which required that the amount remain confidential.

The joint sealing request also made one other argument—a perplexing one, given Otorowski's prior reference to the pump's "insidious danger."

"It is unlikely that the sealing of this court file would be of interest to any other individuals," the request said. "This is a unique case involving the claims of a single individual."

In October 2003, Judge Richard Jones sealed the file.

This year *The Times* challenged that order. Just because the parties want their settlement a secret is no grounds to seal an entire file, the newspaper argued. And where legitimate privacy concerns exist, limited parts of documents can be blacked out.

Jones opened the file back up.

'Tip of the Iceberg'

Manufacturers must file reports with the FDA when they become aware that a medical device has malfunctioned or may have contributed to a death *or* serious injury.

The key word is "or." That's the word used in federal regulations: malfunction or injury.

In the Lane lawsuit, Medtronic acknowledged that it did not report Sylvia's injury to the FDA. A Medtronic director wrote in court documents that the company makes a report "if a malfunction is identified and it meets" reporting requirements.

He used the word "and."

"By making this convenient word substitution, the defendant has created an imaginary loophole," Otorowski wrote. Medtronic's interpretation requires a malfunction—in effect, erasing injury as grounds for reporting, he argued. Lane's lawsuit didn't claim malfunction. It alleged that Sylvia suffered severe brain damage because of a flawed design and insufficient warnings.

Otorowski said Medtronic's reporting practices were "deceptive" and put the company's "credibility squarely at issue."

One of Lane's experts, William Damaska, once directed the FDA's Division of Compliance Operations. The FDA uses "adverse-event" reports to issue recalls, safety alerts and labeling changes, Damaska wrote. Doctors use them to make choices about treatment and medical devices.

Sylvia's injury "clearly" met the reporting criteria, Damaska wrote. Medtronic's failure to alert the FDA, he said, suggested that "what is reported is only the tip of the iceberg."

Medtronic said any suggestion that it had not reported other events was "entirely speculative."

Nationally, other lawsuits have also accused Medtronic of reporting lapses. Medtronic, a Fortune 500 company with annual sales of $11 billion, makes all kinds of medical devices. Other lawsuits have alleged that Medtronic failed to make timely warnings to the public and physicians about problems with implantable heart defibrillators and with the tubing on insulin pumps.

In addition, the company agreed last summer to pay a $40 million fine to settle civil allegations that it provided kickbacks to doctors, to encourage them to use its spinal products. The kickbacks included sham consulting and royalty agreements, as well as lavish trips, the U.S. Justice Department said.

Which Device? The Words Are Blacked Out

Some lawsuits allege a broad threat. But sealing the file can make it nearly impossible to figure out what happened.

When *The Times* began this investigation, it identified 420 sealed civil suits in King County. The names of the parties were available, but little else.

The Medtronic case stood out. The company sells pacemakers, defibrillators, insulin pumps, heart-valve products. Did the lawsuit claim some device was defective? And if so, which one?

Because the UW—a public entity—was also a defendant, *The Times* asked for its records from the lawsuit. A sealing order applies to the courts; it does not suspend open-records laws for other public entities.

In January the university turned over the complaint, a document that lays out the allegations. This provided a first glimpse inside the court file. But the university—citing patient privacy—had blacked out just about every meaningful detail in it.

The complaint said some medical device was unsafe. Which device? That information was marked out.

The newspaper contacted Medtronic. In February, a spokesman said the company couldn't comment on the lawsuit because the file was sealed. But his e-mail added:

"Medtronic and the entire medical technology industry follow strict guidelines and regulations stipulated by the FDA regarding product development, safety, effectiveness and quality. We take those guidelines and regulations very seriously, and must—by law—report any incidents that could potentially harm our patients. Medtronic would not intentionally hide information that could potentially jeopardize patient safety by sealing a court file."

Lawmakers Do an About-Face

The Washington Legislature passed two laws in 1993 to prevent secrecy in product-liability cases.

One barred parties from entering confidentiality agreements that concealed a public hazard. The other kept judges from signing orders that hid such dangers.

But in 1994, lawmakers did an about-face. The former law was repealed, and the latter, diluted.

Gone was the rousing endorsement of the public's right to know about hazards. The new law said the public has two interests: knowing about threats to safety—and making sure that businesses can keep trade secrets. A judge must balance the two before approving secrecy.

The new law has rarely, if ever, been used. A search of published appellate opinions failed to turn up even one case where it has been applied.

But the law still allowed an outsider to challenge a confidentiality agreement as contrary to the public interest. And that's what *The Times* is doing.

The newspaper has asked a judge to void the confidentiality agreement between Medtronic and Michael Lane. Doing so might free the parties to discuss the case and reveal how much Medtronic paid.

The newspaper's motion is still pending.

A conversation with
Ken Armstrong

This edited e-mail interview was conducted by Poynter Institute faculty member and Poynter Online Managing Editor Scott Libin with Ken Armstrong, who was part of The Seattle Times *reporting team with Justin Mayo and Steve Miletich, winners of the ASNE Distinguished Writing Award for Local Accountability Reporting. Armstrong responded for the team.*

SCOTT LIBIN: Where did the idea for the project originate?

KEN ARMSTRONG: When I began working at *The Seattle Times* a few years ago, I noticed that beat reporters consistently complained that they were being denied access to court records. These complaints came from education reporters writing about public schools; business reporters writing about some company or executive; reporters covering sports, religion, politics; even folks covering government agencies—for example, the state's social services agency. Typically, just part of the file was sealed; but it usually was the part of the file you'd most want to see. This seemed to be happening too often to be attributable to chance or circumstance.

So Justin Mayo, a specialist in computer-assisted reporting, and I decided to see if we could figure out how often files were being sealed. Rather than writing about the subject anecdotally—finding a few sealed files and holding them up as emblems of the problem—we opted for a comprehensive approach. We wanted to know: How many files were sealed, in whole or part; who wanted the files sealed, and why; which judges sealed the files; and were the rules restricting secrecy followed in each case?

Where and how did you collect the information?

When starting this project, we knew some files were being sealed but had no way to say how often. The clerk's office at King County Superior Court did not keep a list of sealed cases.

We turned to the state Administrative Office of the Courts, and its massive databases of dockets collected from all counties. State programmers ran computer searches for us, looking for specific docket codes such as "ORSRF" (order sealing record/file) or keywords like "seal." This method turned up more than 10,000 cases in King County alone. Using our own database software, we filtered the list to about 3,000 cases.

At King County Superior Court we entered each nine-digit case number into the electronic court records system. If a case was sealed entirely, a message popped up, denying access. We also checked older files stored on shelves. We walked down rows of files at the clerk's office, looking for yellow, folder-sized markers that indicated a case was sealed and locked away in a separate room. In the end, we found at least 420 civil cases that had been sealed in their entirety.

We knew little about the 420 cases, other than case number, party names and case type. Even these scraps could be a riddle. Case No. 94-2-13372-1, for instance, had John and Jane Doe as plaintiffs, and John and Jane Roe as defendants. The case type was "minor settlement." From those clues alone, there's no telling what happened in the lawsuit.

But the names of the parties usually gave us enough of a clue to start digging and to figure out which cases might be most important to the public. Was the defendant a teacher? A police officer? Some CEO? We ran the party names through dozens of searchable databases, including ones for lawyers, health-care professionals, government employees and state-licensed occupations. We also searched court records and news archives.

Next we gathered the sealing orders, which by law are supposed to be open. The clerk's office helped us gather orders in 383 of the 420 cases. In the other cases, the order was missing from the file, the whole file was missing, or the court said the order was itself sealed. The orders showed which judge or court commissioner sealed a file and whether or not they followed the rules when granting such secrecy. Nearly all were sealed improperly.

The first installment of "Your Courts" was published in March 2006. This story provided an overview of how hundreds of files had been sealed illegally in King County, and gave readers an idea of what kinds of disputes were at the heart of these lawsuits.

The next week, we went to court and began filing motions to unseal individual lawsuits. We ultimately filed 40 motions. Thirty-seven were granted, two were denied, and one is still pending. These motions, filed by top attorneys at leading law firms, cost us about $6,000 each. So if we had filed a motion in each of the 420 cases, we would have been forced to pay about $2.5 million. That was the cost of public access—a cost the courts forced us to pay, even though the problem was of the court's own making.

When we first showed the court's leadership how frequently the judges had been ignoring, or neglecting, the laws restricting secrecy, the court's leaders crafted a plan that would have opened files with minimal delay and expense. But other judges rebelled, saying we should be required to file a formal motion in each case that was improperly sealed.

Not only did this require great expense, but at times it bordered on the ridiculous. In one case, defense attorneys argued that *The Times* should have contacted the plaintiff about unsealing the file. The plaintiff was identified as "J.P." That's all we knew. We were also asked to notify other parties who were identified by pseudonyms, or had names so common they were shared by dozens of people in Washington alone.

Getting a file unsealed was important, but reporting challenges didn't end there. We filed dozens of public-records requests to supplement the court files. For a story of a 13-year-old girl raped while in the state's care, we read through more than 10,000 pages of investigative documents.

Powerful public institutions threw up obstacles. When researching a sealed lawsuit against the University of Washington Medical Center and a medical-device manufacturer, we asked the university for its records. We received heavily redacted documents in which even the medical device at issue was blacked out. For a year, the university withheld details of the settlement agreement it reached with the plaintiff, defying state law.

To keep track of the vast amount of information we were gathering, Justin created a database that allowed us to download what we knew about each case. The database also anticipated questions that we would need to answer about the cases as a group—quantifying, for example, how many cases involved lawyers being sued; or how many used the wrong legal standard for sealing a file; or how many involved a public agency as a litigant.

We brought in Steve Miletich, another reporter, to help gather information about certain cases. Steve has been a reporter in Seattle for decades and has uncanny recall for people and events. Other reporters also contributed, pitching in on individual lawsuits or themes, such as the large number of guardianship files that had been sealed in Washington State.

In all, the project took us about two years—and cost hundreds of thousands of dollars in legal fees alone.

How did you decide what the focus would be—of the series and of its individual stories?

The focus, from the get-go, was on the improper use of secrecy—and how the public suffers when the courthouse curtains are drawn.

Each case we wrote about had to strike that theme. We therefore concentrated on cases where the public interest was clear: lawsuits alleging that a medical device was unsafe; or that principals in a public school had failed to stop a teacher from molesting students; or that doctors or lawyers had committed malpractice; or that the state's social services agency was responsible for the rape of a 13-year-old girl who was being kept in the state's care.

As for the actual writing of the stories, we decided, early on, to speak directly to our readers. We used a lot of pronouns—you, us, our, them. We wanted our readers to understand that they had a stake in this; that the principle of open courts is one that matters to the public at large, and not simply to newspapers. We also used a conversational tone, one that didn't push readers away or create distance.

After a year or so of reporting, we had a lot of numbers (for example, 420 sealed civil suits) and a dense database. But how do you make a large number and a dense database snap to life? We knew that the importance of open courts had to be illustrated through specific examples that were rich with detail and which allowed us to tell meaningful stories. If the principle remained abstract—open courts, good; secrecy, bad—then readers would have tuned us out. So while we provided sweeping context on all these sealed cases in King County and in other parts of Washington State, we also went deep on individual lawsuits and wrote about them separately.

How did you organize your stories—again, individually and as an ongoing series?

We could have held everything back and eventually wheeled out a traditional multi-part series. Instead, we decided to roll the stories out one by one, writing what we knew, when we knew it. Between March and December 2006 we published about 15 lengthy stories, along with a number of sidebars and follow-ups.

We started with a broad opening piece, and closed the year with an update on what we had learned and how entire files were no longer being sealed. In between, we published stories about individual cases, individuals or subjects, as each piece was ready to go.

How many drafts did you do of each story?

Not many. We had done so much work on the front end that the writing, with few exceptions, came together easily. Write, edit, publish. We didn't get hung up. We discussed organization and story outlines with our editor, Jim Neff, before we began writing any piece. And for the longer stories, we painstakingly assembled timelines that were scores of pages long. These timelines cobbled together the most important details from each relevant document and saved us an enormous amount of time once we started writing. We weren't constantly searching for some police report or deposition excerpt. It was all there, in one document. We had so much information to wrestle to the ground, so staying organized was crucial.

What role did your editor play?

Jim Neff, the investigations editor, kept in touch with reporters throughout the process, discussing organization and possible reporting holes early on. He wanted to avoid surprises. So did we.

Jim discussed tone and the need for *The Times* to be transparent about its role in finding these cases and getting them unsealed. He didn't shy away from pronouns or blunt language. Jim also helped work with the lawyers who were filing all the motions on the newspaper's behalf—a task that proved to be extraordinarily time-consuming.

What were the particular challenges of "Your Courts, Their Secrets"? How did the newspaper's role as a stakeholder in this project—as well as its significant financial investment in legal costs—affect your approach?

The newspaper's role in this project helped push us in the direction of clean, transparent language. Readers needed to understand just what the newspaper's involvement was in these cases, and why we were going to such lengths to find and open these files. The newspaper was "we." The readers were "you." The project's title established this tone from the outset: "Your Courts, Their Secrets."

We let readers know how we found these cases; what obstacles we encountered along the way; and what documents we were relying upon to tell each story.

One of the challenges we had in writing these stories was that the voices you'd expect to hear were frequently silent. The plaintiffs, or alleged victims, were dead, physically incapacitated or had signed confidentiality agreements as a condition of settlement. These agreements prevented them from speaking to us, much as they might want to. But we were often able to fill in those voices through other means. We were able to obtain deposition transcripts, or statements to police or victim-impact statements.

We also wrote about many of these plaintiffs without identifying them. Some were minors, or victims of sexual abuse, or both. So we tried to find ways to write about what they had suffered, with considerable detail, but without revealing their identities. We were conscientious about privacy. We didn't want to compound the harm that people had already suffered.

Since publication of your series "Your Courts, Their Secrets," what important changes have taken place in the courts you covered? How would you assess the impact of the reporting project?

We ran a story in December that outlined the project's impact. The most profound difference has been that King County judges have stopped sealing entire files. Another change has occurred in the area of court rules governing secrecy. The Washington State Supreme Court and the King County Superior Court both tightened their rules, making it more difficult for files to be sealed, in whole or part.

Here are some excerpts from that story.

From the top:

> "... since *The Times* began reporting on improper sealing practices in March of this year, such secrecy has evaporated. A recent review of King County court records failed to turn up even one civil guardianship or divorce case that has been sealed in its entirety in the past nine months.
>
> "Instead of being hidden away, files are being opened up.
>
> "King County judges and commissioners have unsealed 42 cases based upon a motion or formal request by *The Times*. In Snohomish County, at least 150 files have been opened—with hundreds more likely to follow. Files in other counties, including Pierce, Spokane and Whatcom, have also been unsealed.
>
> "Even narrow secrecy requests get scrutinized in ways unimaginable a year ago. Before, parties routinely made settlement amounts confidential. The courts typically approved, even though a settlement's terms can provide the public valuable information. Was the amount a nominal figure easily dismissed as a nuisance settlement? Or was it something more?
>
> "Last year the YMCA of Greater Seattle was sued in a case with obvious public interest. A Seattle couple alleged that a teenager working in a YMCA day-care center had sexually assaulted their son and five other children. The YMCA, accused of negligent hiring and supervision, elected to settle.
>
> "At a hearing last month, Court Commissioner Kimberley Prochnau was asked about the possibility of keeping the settlement's terms confidential. Prochnau said things are different now: The parties' mere desire for secrecy is no longer enough to seal any document. The settlement amount—the YMCA agreed to pay

$300,000 to this one family—went into the court file, unsealed.

"Prochnau told the courtroom: 'It's a new day.' "

From a graphic that ran with the story:

Files sealed: Then and now

Between 1990 and 2005, King County judges and commissioners sealed in their entirety:
420 civil cases
266 guardianship cases
692 divorce cases
Total, 1990–2005: **1,378**
Cases sealed since the *Times*' series began: **0**

From the bottom of the story:

"Since the *Times* began reporting on improperly sealed court records, state and federal courts have adopted a number of changes.

"This year the Washington Supreme Court amended its rules, saying, among other things, that the parties' wish for secrecy does not, by itself, justify sealing.

"The U.S. District Court for the Western District of Washington also tightened its rules, saying lawyers can no longer file pleadings under seal without first getting permission from a judge.

"In King County, judges and commissioners now receive extensive training on sealing restrictions. The judges threw out an old sealing form that misstated the law on secrecy, and took the power to seal away from substitute commissioners.

"In Snohomish County, judges initiated an exhaustive review of more than 1,000 sealed cases. They've opened at least 150 so far and are reviewing dozens more each month."

Writers' Workshop

Talking Points

1. Ken Armstrong, Justin Mayo and Steve Miletich say they "decided early on to speak directly to our readers. We used a lot of pronouns—you, us, our, them. We wanted our readers to understand that they had a stake in this." How would these stories have worked in the traditional third person, and when is the less-formal first- and second-person approach more effective?

2. The "Your Courts, Their Secrets" team faced an ironic challenge: writing about openness while protecting the privacy of certain stakeholders. How did the reporters and editors behind this project balance their truth-telling responsibility with their interest in minimizing harm?

3. This series sought to provide a "comprehensive approach" to the issue of court secrecy, "rather than writing about the subject anecdotally," according to Armstrong. How did the stories convey the scope of the problem? How did they make it manageable for readers? Where did the focus of the series go from wide, encompassing great numbers of cases, to tight, zooming in on individuals involved—and how did that work?

Assignment Desk

1. "Your Courts, Their Secrets" is a good example of what The Poynter Institute's Al Tompkins calls "turning the problem into the story"—or, in this case, more than 15 stories. By that, Tompkins means turning attention to the very obstacles that get in the way of reporting, and reporting on those obstacles themselves. The problem in this case—the denial of access to court records—was one that frustrated beat reporters for *The Seattle Times* for years. What similar frustrations have you faced or heard about that could be turned into stories? Which roadblocks could be reported on in your community?

2. Armstrong, Mayo, Miletich and their editors faced the additional challenge of translating esoteric legal language into clear English for readers who aren't lawyers. Find an example in their work of jargon that has been defined and demystified. What words commonly creep

into news copy without the explanation needed to make them understandable? What words have you used without fully sharing—or perhaps even knowing—their meaning?

3. Washington state law was clearly on the journalists' side in the case of "Your Courts, Their Secrets." The newspaper and its attorneys were able to document clear violations in the sealing of certain cases. How does the law in your state compare? What are the requirements for the sealing of court cases? How about the nondisclosure of other information of interest and of importance to the public? What do you know and what do you need to know about the rights of public officials to keep secrets from the public?

Finalist

Fred Schulte and June Arney
ASNE, Local Accountability Reporting
Finalist, Pulitzer Prize, Local Reporting

28. On Shaky Ground

DEC. 10, 2006

Baltimore's arcane system of ground rents, widely viewed as a harmless vestige of colonial law, is increasingly being used by some investors to seize homes or extract large fees from people who often are ignorant of the loosely regulated process, an investigation by *The Sun* has found.

Tens of thousands of Baltimore homeowners must pay rent twice a year on the land under their houses. If they fall behind on the payments, the ground rent holders can sue to seize the houses—and have done so nearly 4,000 times in the past six years, sometimes over back rent as little as $24, *The Sun* found.

More than half of the ground rent suits filed in the past six years were brought by entities associated with four groups of individuals and families, court records show.

Most ground rent holders insist that home ownership is rarely put in peril. But Baltimore judges awarded houses to ground rent holders at least 521 times between 2000 and the end of March 2006, *The Sun* found, analyzing court computer data and studying hundreds of case files to document the trend for the first time. The properties ranged from boarded-up rowhouses to a 7,000-square-foot Victorian in Bolton Hill.

In many cases, ground rent holders used their extraordinary power under state law to oust the owners from their houses and then sold the homes for tens of thousands of dollars in profits. Some homeowners reached settlements to regain their houses, paying legal and other fees many times the amount of ground rent owed, though court records don't make clear how often that happens.

While some of the most aggressive investors have owned ground rents for years, it wasn't until the late 1990s that rising property values in Baltimore City made it attractive to attempt to seize houses. The number of new lawsuits rose 73 percent last year and shows no signs of leveling off.

This activity occurs across Baltimore but has clustered in some areas as they have started to gentrify, including neighborhoods just north of Patterson Park and around Washington Village.

Told of *The Sun*'s findings, outgoing Maryland Attorney General J. Joseph Curran Jr. said he had ordered an immediate investigation, adding that it might be time to phase the system out. "An older couple or a widow could forget this, and for someone to come and take their house, when it's worth so much more than they paid for it, is an outrage," Curran said.

The Sun's investigation also found that:

• In nearly every aspect, the law favors ground rent holders. Homeowners rarely win once a lawsuit is filed. And the longer a case goes on, the more it can cost the homeowner.

• No other private debt collectors in Maryland can obtain rewards so disproportionate to what they are owed. In contrast with a foreclosure, the holder of an overdue ground rent can seize a home, sell it and keep every cent of the proceeds. To prevent a seizure, homeowners almost always have to pay fees that dwarf the amount of rent they owe.

• State law puts the onus on property owners to track down their ground rent owner and make payments, though it's sometimes next to impossible to find that information. No registry of ground rent holders exists, and property deeds typically contain only the barest of details about them.

• Some investors seek out overdue ground rents to purchase, then file lawsuits to take the property built on the land. In some cases, the legal owners of these houses have died, and the law is not clear about whether investors must give relatives a chance to satisfy the debts and keep the homes.

'Business Is Business'

R. Marc Goldberg is a Baltimore attorney and ground rent owner who acts as a spokesman for about two dozen rent holders, including his family and some of the other investor groups that pursue the most ground rent lawsuits, called "ejectments."

He doesn't dispute that clashes over property ownership occur more often these days as investors scramble to reclaim decrepit parts of Baltimore. But he denies that they exploit the ground rent law or charge

> **What Is Ground Rent?**
>
> In much of Baltimore, and in parts of a few counties in Maryland, homeowners lease the land beneath their houses from a person, charity or business.
>
> The amount of rent depends on when the lease was executed. Leases are written for terms of 99 years, renewable forever, though homeowners can buy out most of them under terms specified in state law.
>
> Ground rent can be traced to 1632, when King Charles I of England gave the second Lord Baltimore all the land in what is now Maryland. Cecilius Calvert charged rent to colonists who wanted to build on his land.
>
> After the American Revolution, Maryland's legislature empowered any landholder to demand rent, and starting in the early 1900s developers created ground rents to make rowhouses more affordable for working people. New ground rents are still being created.

excessive fees. Nobody gets in trouble if he pays his rent on time, Goldberg said.

"I'm not looking to put people out and to be mean and nasty," he said. In a series of interviews with *The Sun*, Goldberg repeatedly used the refrain "Business is business."

"I can't deny an economic incentive to make a windfall profit," he said.

Many investors say that while the returns remain attractive, the business is difficult—with many challenges in collecting the rent or tracking down owners of vacant houses. They say they deserve to be paid their rent on time—and that they sue to take homes only after lengthy collection efforts, and because it is their only remedy under the law.

"If you don't pay, you are putting your property at risk," said Lawrence Polakoff, a Baltimore Realtor whose family has filed more than 100 ejectment lawsuits since the start of 2000. "A ground rent owner isn't going to just sit back and say, 'I'm sorry someone's died,' and forget about it."

"You can make a very good living doing this," said Polakoff, adding that the increase in ejectment lawsuits is directly related to rising real estate prices.

Most ground rent holders say they rarely, if ever, try to seize homes. For smaller holders, the cost of pursuing an ejectment can be prohibitive. Some investors are fearful of seizing properties that have lead-based paint or housing code violations. Others say they avoid seizures on principle.

"We would never allow ourselves to be in that position. We are about helping people, not hurting them," said Greg Cantori, executive director of the Marion I. and Henry J. Knott Foundation. The foundation, which supports Catholic charities, owns about 1,600 ground rents but hasn't filed an ejectment lawsuit since 1996.

Landlord Baltimore

Estimates of the number of Baltimore properties subjected to ground rent run as high as 120,000, many of them the familiar red-brick and white-marble-stepped rowhouses.

Ground rents take the form of 99-year leases, renewable forever. All property deeds must note whether there is a ground rent. Rents generally range from $24 to $240 a year; some very old leases are written in shillings.

Their origins can be traced to the summer of 1632, when King Charles I of England gave Cecilius Calvert all the land in what is now Maryland. Calvert, better known as the second Lord Baltimore, did what any self-respecting aristocrat did in those days: He charged rent to the colonists who wanted to build on his soil.

Starting in the early 1900s, developers built miles of rowhouses in Baltimore with ground rents. They saw the system as a progressive way to keep home prices within reach of the working class, because people wouldn't have to buy the land as well as the house.

Charities, foundations, churches, banks and some retirees have held ground rents for years as investments. Investors often buy and sell them from each other, sometimes through classified ads.

More recently, some property owners have created new ground rents—at rates several times higher than the previous rents—when they sell a property. This is allowed by the law.

Homeowners, however, have the right under state law to buy out ground rents created after 1884 under specified price formulas and conditions.

Though there are residential ground rents in other areas of the state, including Anne Arundel and Baltimore counties, they are far more common in Baltimore City. While unusual, ground rents exist in other places; for example, much of Hawaii has them.

"We view ground rent as one of the sticks in the bundle of property rights," said Carolyn Cook, deputy executive vice president of the Greater Baltimore Board of Realtors, adding, "For the majority of the people, it doesn't have much of an impact."

Loss and Gain

Thelma Parks, 56, lived for more than two decades in Druid Heights, just a few blocks from the boyhood home of the late Supreme Court Justice Thurgood Marshall, until losing her house last year in an ejectment case. It was filed by a trust set up by Fred Nochumowitz, whose relatives have long held ground rents.

A distressed Anthony Sims stands amid possessions moved to the street last July after his family's home was seized over unpaid ground rent. Ground rent owners have filed an increasing number of suits against city residents. (Photograph courtesy of Elizabeth Malby/*The Sun*)

Records show that the Nochumowitz trust bought the ground rent on Parks' house in January 2002. Parks couldn't make her payments, which with the fees for the court action came to "about $1,200," she says. With more time, she says, she could have paid off the $1,200.

After taking her property, the trust sold it to an investment company for $70,000 in September 2005. That company resold it about six months later for $128,000. Parks, meanwhile, was forced to rent in another part of town.

"It ruined every one of my plans," said Parks, who works for the federal government. "They all went out the window. . . . I'm going to have to work until I fall apart.

"I can't retire," she said. "Everyone is making a profit from it but me."

Geoffrey Forman, the attorney who handled the Parks case for the Nochumowitz trust, said he wouldn't discuss any cases he was involved in. A woman at Fred Nochumowitz's Boca Raton, Fla., residence identifying herself as Mrs. Nochumowitz said her husband wasn't available for comment and that she didn't know when he would be.

Reporters for *The Sun* witnessed six property seizures stemming from ground rent between early summer and late fall.

Some played out matter-of-factly. Once deputies from the city sheriff's office determined that nobody was home, workers hired by the new owners popped out the door locks and replaced them within minutes. The crew could then empty the house and pile its contents in the street—so long as cars could get through.

In the 2600 block of Mura Street in the East Baltimore community of Berea, electric candles still shined in the front window of the vacant rowhouse, and an Easter wreath hung on the front door as the ejectment crew arrived on the morning of July 26.

Strewn throughout the rooms were personal mementos, from bowling trophies to religious icons to two ticket stubs from an evening showing of "Scary Movie 4" three months previously. The unpaid ground rent was $252, though fees and other costs boosted the bill to $2,118.67.

In three cases, deputies told occupants they had to get out immediately unless they could work out something with the new owners.

On a hot August morning on North Brice Street in the Midtown-Edmondson area, one family lost a rowhouse adjoining the one where it lives. Minutes later, an elderly man told a child about to put his tricycle away in the seized house: "You can't put it in there. It ain't our house no more."

The actions of some ground rent holders upset some traditional investors, such as Cantori of the Knott Foundation.

Cantori says that the foundation relies on the income from ground rent—about $200,000 a year—to help pay its operating expenses, but that it is redeeming or selling dozens every year and writing some off as uncollectible.

Property records show that the Knott Foundation—among other charitable and religious groups—sold ground rents to investors who filed ejectment lawsuits. It typically has sold those leases for their redemption value under state law—for example, a $90-a-year rent sold for $1,500.

Cantori calls the rise in ejectment actions and seizures "unconscionable." He says the foundation sold ground rents because they were delinquent and wanted to "get them off the books" after failing to collect the rent through normal procedures. He says he didn't know that the new owners had sued to seize the properties.

From Owner to Renter

Deloris McNeil still doesn't understand how she went from owner to renter in her West Baltimore house.

Herbert Burgunder III (left), attorney for ground rent holder Houndswood LLC, tries to block a camera from photographing him at a city courthouse. He represented Houndswood in its suit against homeowner Linda McGill (right). (Photograph courtesy of Jed Kirschbaum/*The Sun*)

Court records give only part of the answer.

Fred Nochumowitz, acting as trustee for some family ground rent holdings, filed suit against McNeil in April 2002, asserting that her ground rent—$96 a year—was more than six months behind. McNeil admits that she let the debt slide, but only did so because she was sick. Later, she said, she couldn't afford the legal fees added to her bill, and didn't realize she could lose her house.

McNeil, 59, said she is disabled and suffers from high blood pressure, which she keeps in check by taking seven pills a day. She says she suffered a stroke after her daughter died.

McNeil never tried to defend herself in court, though court records show she was served with legal notice of the suit. She says she couldn't face going to court.

A judge handed over her rowhouse to the Nochumowitz trust. Property records show that the trust sold the house about a year later for $15,000 to Lauren Montillo, who specializes in rehabilitating city properties for resale as rentals.

Montillo, who has bought at least 22 properties from Nochumowitz family interests, says she chose not to rehab the house and evict McNeil, so long as she paid her $550 a month in rent. "I don't have the guts to throw her out," said Montillo. "I have a little bit of a conscience."

Says McNeil, "It would mostly kill me" to move.

McNeil is luckier than others who lost ownership of their homes, but she says she doesn't feel that way.

"Sometimes I feel like screaming at the top of my lungs," McNeil said, seated at her cluttered dining room table, dabbing at tears with a crumpled tissue.

McNeil's loss of her house without a fight is not unusual. *The Sun*'s analysis of court data found that homeowners didn't respond in nearly 60 percent of the ejectment lawsuits in which property changed hands during the past three years.

'Uninformed Public'

There's no single explanation for why this happens, according to a review of hundreds of court records and interviews with more than a dozen people facing ejectment.

Some people say they didn't understand the process, especially the severity of the consequences for failing to pay. Some say they couldn't afford an attorney. Others say they hadn't been contacted. A few people who were owners of boarded-up or abandoned properties didn't seem to care about losing them, even when told that they could be sold for thousands of dollars.

Court officials don't know why so few people respond. As a result, they can't tell whether the lack of response is a growing problem or not. "By itself, that doesn't raise any suspicions," said Judge Evelyn Omega Cannon, judge in charge of the civil docket in Baltimore City Circuit Court.

Some lawyers and people sued say that part of the problem is that, even with all the fees added to ground rent bills, it costs more to hire a lawyer than to pay the amount the lawsuit is seeking.

"If they're not eligible for our services and they can't hire a lawyer and they don't know enough to file a letter with the Circuit Court, then it's all over," said Louise Carwell, senior staff attorney in the housing consumer law unit of the Legal Aid Bureau in Baltimore.

Three years ago, after a Towson lawyer complained about an ejectment suit filed against a 93-year-old client, the General Assembly capped a ground rent holder's attorneys' fees for preparing and filing an ejectment lawsuit at $700. But the law also allows ground rent holders to charge the property owner $300 for searching property titles, and pass on all other costs of collecting the debt—copying, process servers, lawsuit filing fees—plus up to $500 in costs of recovering back rent for periods before the lawsuit was filed.

The best a homeowner can hope for in most cases is that a judge will approve an installment plan for paying off these fees—which can be 20 to 50 times the amount of rent owed—but that happens infrequently.

Reviewing more than 500 case files, *The Sun* found fewer than a dozen in which homeowners won their cases outright.

"Unfortunately, in many of these cases, you're dealing with an uneducated public and an uninformed public," said former Circuit Judge Thomas E. Noel, who heard numerous ground rent cases before leaving the bench in April.

Even a lawyer who represents ground rent holders says his side has a clear advantage. "The people who file these cases know the law inside and out," said J. Scott Morse. "Other people [homeowners] don't have a clue about it."

It Takes a Lawyer

Before filing an ejectment lawsuit, a ground rent owner must send a registered letter to the property owner's "last known address" demanding payment. But if there is confusion over the address, or for any other reason the person fails to receive the bill, problems can result.

Linda McGill, a mortgage broker, got into ground rent trouble over a West Baltimore house she had bought for her grandmother, who later died. The relatives living in the house after her grandmother died initially failed to send the ground rent bills to her, she says.

McGill says she discovered that the rent was overdue when the relatives passed a bill on to her husband. An April bill demanded $1,715—of which the overdue ground rent was $84. McGill sent the ground rent holder, Houndswood LLC, a check for $84, but Houndswood refused to accept it.

For weeks afterward, McGill says, her calls and letters to Houndswood went unanswered—until the day before she was scheduled to appear in court. She got a call from longtime Baltimore real estate investor Jack Stollof, a Houndswood consultant who is a founding director of another large ground rent holder, Jack & Harvey Inc. Houndswood filed 522 ejectment lawsuits between January 2000 and November 2006, making it one of the most prolific filers, court records show.

"In the beginning, he was pleasant on the phone," she said of Stollof. "He hinted at $1,500."

McGill had offered $1,050 in the letter she wrote to Houndswood's attorneys in April—reasonable, she thought, considering the overdue ground rent was $84. But she says Stollof told her that wasn't enough, and that she had no chance in court.

In court the next day, McGill was surprised to hear not only that the bill had grown to $1,837, but also that Houndswood wanted the house—although that demand had been in the lawsuit. "We're asking for the possession of the property, because the payments have not been made," Herbert Burgunder III, an attorney for Houndswood, told the judge.

"You're in a tough spot because they're acting in accordance with the law, and the law does allow them to impose fees," Circuit Court Judge Joseph H. H. Kaplan told McGill. "How much of the $1,837 can you pay?"

"I agree to pay $900," she responded, no matter that she had offered $1,050 earlier. "To me that's fair."

But the judge asked if she was willing to pay more.

"If you pay $1,500, I will allow you to keep the property," Kaplan said. "Will you?"

Stollof at that point acknowledged the phone call to McGill the day before. "I offered this young lady yesterday the chance to avoid this," he said in court.

McGill wrote a $1,500 check immediately after the hearing.

"For $84, your house can be taken," McGill said after court. "I'm a mortgage broker. Half my clients don't know how to contact their ground rent owners. This is going to take place all day long in Baltimore City, and it does."

Stollof declined to discuss his business when approached after the hearing.

In rare cases, property owners have won ejectment suits by arguing that the ground rent holder did little or nothing to find them.

In October 2003, Brent W. Procida got a call from his banker, telling him he was being sued over $38 in back ground rent. The house in Canton that he owed the rent on was vacant and under renovation; Procida was living five blocks away.

The suit, which demanded $1,615, had been filed in August. But Procida said in court papers that he didn't get a copy of the lawsuit until two days after he got the call from his bank. The ground rent bills had been sent to the vacant house, which is why Procida said he never saw them.

Procida sent a check for $57 to the ground rent holder, Jack & Harvey Inc., to cover the overdue and current rent. Jack & Harvey, however, refused to accept the check because it didn't include the attorneys' and other fees, court records show. Procida said in court papers that he also offered Jack & Harvey $800 to settle the case, to no avail.

Unlike most homeowners taken to court, Procida, a lawyer himself, fought back. He argued in court papers that Jack & Harvey didn't try to look him up in the phone book, which would have taken "approximately 15 seconds," just so it could justify "the exorbitant fees on which it has built its business."

Jack & Harvey argued that it was entitled to all of the fees it sought and had sent notices to Procida's "last known address" as required by the law. Circuit Court Judge Stuart R. Berger ruled in Procida's favor.

Burgunder, who represented Jack & Harvey in the case, declined comment.

Attorneys' Fees

The fees in Linda McGill's case are the norm rather than the exception, an examination of hundreds of court files shows.

"The staggering sum of money is the attorneys' fees. It has nothing to do with the ground rent. You only lose your house because the attorney fee is not paid," Noel said. "That's where the problem is."

Noel, the former circuit judge, says he regularly urged settlements when he felt fees were too high. The ground rent system, he says, "should have been investigated 20 years ago."

"Think of how many times judges rendered these judgments in all the courtrooms over all those years," he said. "You're talking about a lot of property. A lot of people were affected by the loss of these houses."

Kim McGavin is an attorney who has advocated ground rent legal reform since a 93-year-old client in a nursing home was sued in an ejectment proceeding.

She and other critics contend that the largest holders tend to do all their legal and title-search work in-house, and can do much of it by computer, making their actual costs minimal.

"Even if you're billing at $200 [an hour], that's three hours, and there's no way it takes that long," she said, referring to the cap of $700 for "reasonable" legal costs. ". . . Even if you sent your paralegal to Calvert Street by camel, it's not going to take that long."

Goldberg, the spokesman for the ground rent owners coalition, says ground rent holders must be able to justify the amounts whenever questions are raised.

"I spend $500 in legal fees, a title search, a judgment report and postage before I even send a letter [demanding payment of overdue rent].

A lot of people don't like that.... Then you get to court and there's that additional level of fees, and people don't like that, either," he said.

"I really don't see [that there is] a problem with gouging. People are never happy to pay a lawyer, especially someone else's lawyer. They should have paid in the first place."

'Land of the Undead'

In most cases, homeowners who have mortgages and are subject to ground rent have little to worry about; their payments are made by their lenders from escrow accounts.

Problems can begin when the mortgage is paid off, making the property owner responsible for the rent payments, or when a mortgage is sold by the lender or refinanced, particularly if the new lender is unfamiliar with Maryland's ground rent system.

Ground rent owners typically send homeowners a postcard or form letter every six months as a reminder that it is time to pay. Because there is no uniform style for bills, and they might bear unfamiliar return addresses, they can be easily overlooked by homeowners or dismissed as junk mail, especially by newcomers to Maryland who have never heard of ground rent.

Some ground rent owners use post office boxes or corporate names that can't be found in any telephone directory or don't include a phone number to call. Some never send bills, or they send them directly to the property address, rather than the owner's home address.

Paul Anderson, chief legal review officer for the state Department of Assessments and Taxation, says that homeowners who lose track of a ground rent owner can find themselves in the "land of the undead," unable to either pay the rent or take steps to buy it out.

Noel, the former circuit judge, says he presided over cases in which a mortgage was sold and the new lender stopped paying the ground rent—unbeknownst to the homeowner. "I'm not suggesting it was anything nefarious. They may not have known who to pay the ground rent to," he said. "The new company had collected this sum of money and they didn't know what the hell to do with it."

Mortgage companies acknowledge that it takes extra vigilance to stay on top of ground rents.

"When a Maryland loan comes in, we identify if there's a ground rent," said Bob Smiley, executive vice president of U.S. Bank Home Mortgage in Owensboro, Ky., which services about 8,500 Maryland loans—about 1,000 with ground rents. "If you don't, it spirals out of control real quickly."

New Rents Bloom

Lauren Montillo and another Baltimore rehabber, Petar Pecovic of Touch of Class Properties LLC, have found seizures to be sources of inexpensive housing for their rehab businesses. Each has purchased about two dozen properties from the Nochumowitz businesses, property records show.

Montillo says she feels for people such as her tenant Deloris McNeil. "It's pretty bad what they [ground rent holders] are allowed to do," she said. "The average person can't afford it. How can they come up with four grand?"

Pecovic says he thinks the system has outlived its usefulness. "People losing their houses like this, it's terrible," he said. "Their families have worked for years for these houses."

Even so, he sometimes creates new ground rents—at $240 a year—on the properties he fixes up and sells.

"The ground rent business is a great business," Pecovic said. "You just have to be ruthless."

Sun *staff researchers Paul McCardell and Doris Johnson contributed to this article.*

HOW THIS SERIES WAS REPORTED

To pry open the secretive ground rent business, *The Sun* obtained computer data from the Baltimore City Circuit Court and identified nearly 4,000 lawsuits filed by ground rent holders against homeowners since 2000. Reporters Fred Schulte and June Arney analyzed this information and pulled hundreds of case files to determine key patterns: who was filing the suits for overdue ground rent, the outcomes of the suits and where the homeowners lived. Many were losing houses as a result of these suits, and Schulte and Arney accompanied city sheriff's deputies on six occasions to observe new owners taking possession. Elizabeth Malby and other *Sun* photographers captured images of these scenes, important figures in the story and events at the courthouse.

Cartographer Christine Fellenz used geographic information software to plot locations, by neighborhood, of homes targeted in ejectment suits.

To learn more about people involved in the ground rent business, the reporters searched state tax and assessment and incorporation records. During nine months of research, *The Sun* conducted dozens of interviews with ground rent holders, homeowners, real estate professionals, legal experts, government officials and judges.

You can read the entire ground rent series at http://www.baltimoresun.com/groundrent.

Lessons Learned

BY JUNE ARNEY

When a family lost a home in Baltimore, over what started as a few hundred dollar "ground" rent debt, the resulting story didn't even make the front page. But Business Editor Bernie Kohn was intrigued by Baltimore's arcane ground rents—a practice dating from colonial days requiring many Baltimore homeowners to pay rent on the land beneath their houses. He wanted to know how many people were losing homes.

"It never happens," I was told again and again by multiple sources on my beat.

There were naysayers even in the newsroom and in the paper's clip file. That mindset held that ground rent was not a problem and lived on as a quirky but innocuous tradition.

But the landscape had changed swiftly while nobody was looking. Responding to market forces, investors had twisted the system to seize homes and make huge profits.

The first lesson: Don't make assumptions.

My inquiries had begun to unravel a system that operated virtually unchecked, right in front of a cast of city officials, lawmakers and judges—the very people charged with protecting homeowners' rights.

Investigative reporter Fred Schulte was called in to establish how many lawsuits had been filed, and we discovered the existence of a whole branch of circuit court few people knew about that was devoted to ground cases where court records showed lawyers had filed suit thousands of times seeking homes over ground rent debts. Fred's task was to create multiple databases to track the way investors profited as ground rent deeds and homes changed hands. We were able to establish that there was a huge growing network of ejectment cases filed. Both of us repeatedly accompanied sheriff's deputies to see the resulting "ejectments" happen firsthand.

The second lesson: Step back, get the big picture and keep taking steps to make sure that it's valid.

Few knew much about the parts of the system beyond their immediate reach. The most savvy seemed to be the handful of investors whose lawyers had brought half the lawsuits. Least informed were the very officials charged with safeguarding the public. It was our exposure of the actions of the ground rent owners and the consequences for homeowners that prompted outrage powerful enough to act like a wrecking ball against Maryland's centuries-old system of ground rent.

One reason the story succeeded was because sufficient background reporting went into the project proposal.

The third lesson: Make sure the story is really there before making a commitment to spend months on it.

Once we knew the enormity of the ejectment filings from court records, fairly early on, we knew every month of time would be worth the final result.

The fourth lesson: It takes persistence, patience and ingenuity to draw out the human angles.

Ground rent is not simple to understand, and the biggest players didn't want to talk. We went back to them repeatedly, sent letters and had doors slammed in our faces. On the streets, victims of abuses were elusive. Family and friends warned them against revealing personal troubles in the newspaper. One woman was so embarrassed about losing her home that she vanished from her neighborhood without telling best friends what had happened. Yet, she eventually confided in me during late-night conversations.

On a bad day, the ideal subject wasn't home or wouldn't talk. On a good day, even the mail carrier cooperated and the payoffs were huge.

Because the stories came together across a year's time and involved two reporters, three editors and a cartographer, managing information was crucial.

The fifth lesson: Download interviews in real time.

We did this while they were fresh and put them in an accessible place, so that everyone stayed up-to-date. Months later, for example, I could vividly recount what had happened in a courtroom. Editors and copy editors benefited too.

The sixth lesson: Stay open to developments even after publication.

The scheduled ejectment seemed redundant coming just days after the series ran. But the paperwork named an owner who records showed as deceased. In keeping with the discipline maintained for months, I made the trip to see what we were sure would be a boarded-up house.

What I found was stunning. Christmas decorations framed a real cat in the window, and the man and his two teenage sons inside had no clue they were at risk of losing their home the next morning.

Vernon Onheiser, whose deceased parents were listed as owners of the row home, couldn't know that he would become the face of ground rent abuse in Baltimore. He couldn't know that the community would rally around him and demand justice. A few months later, Gov. Martin

O'Malley would send a car to carry him to the capital, to take part in what would be the first of several bill signings. In all, the legislature would ban new ground rents and pass seven other reform measures.

June Arney is a business reporter at The *(Baltimore)* Sun. *Previously, she was a staff writer at* The Virginian-Pilot *in Norfolk, Va., where she covered police, courts and juvenile justice and won a variety of state, regional and national journalism awards for investigative reporting and enterprise journalism. Arney was a 2007 Pulitzer Prize finalist and a 1995 Casey Journalism Center Fellow.*

Fred Schulte is an investigative reporter at The Sun. *Previously he was investigative editor at the* South Florida Sun-Sentinel *in Fort Lauderdale, where his projects won dozens of journalism awards. Schulte has received the George Polk Award, the Investigative Reporters and Editors Award, the Gerald Loeb Award, the Worth Bingham Prize for Investigative Reporting and the American Bar Association's Silver Gavel Award. He has been a Pulitzer Prize finalist four times.*

BELLEVILLE NEWS-DEMOCRAT

Finalist

George Pawlaczyk and Beth Hundsdorfer
Local Accountability Reporting

29. Lethal Lapses

NOV. 19, 2006

Fifty-three children died between 1998 and 2005 after state child welfare workers assigned to protect them committed serious errors, made lapses in judgment and ignored their own rules.

Children were beaten, burned, smothered, shaken and starved to death by their parents or other adults, even though the Illinois Department of Children and Family Services was supposed to be protecting them, according to an investigation by the *Belleville News-Democrat*.

In one case, a full-term baby girl—posthumously named Vanessa—died in a ramshackle house in Venice when her mentally ill mother, Jaki Ingram, delivered her into a waste-filled toilet. The DCFS suspended a caseworker and a supervisor for failing to properly assess the case over a five-year period.

In another case, 2-year-old Miracle Moon, of Chicago, died when her mother's boyfriend pushed her head under water because, according to a prosecutor, she was slow at potty training. A medical examiner found more than 50 human bite marks on her buttocks.

State overseers from the DCFS' own Office of the Inspector General investigate child deaths where DCFS worker error or neglect is suspected. The office publishes annual warnings of the consequences of repeated mistakes and offers solutions.

But the newspaper's four-month investigation showed that despite receiving specific warnings regarding the 53 child deaths between September 1998 and January 2005, DCFS caseworkers, child protection investigators, supervisors and contracted private agency workers made repeated errors and failed to properly gauge danger to children.

"No system should tolerate mistakes that can lead to the death of a child," said Bruce Boyer, a law professor at Loyola University in Chicago and director of its Civitas ChildLaw Clinic, which specializes in representing children.

"It makes you wonder what they might be doing wrong in cases where kids don't die."

Bryan Samuels, former director of the DCFS, declined repeated requests for an interview for this series. Samuels resigned Friday.

Investigations of child deaths, which are published one to three years later in inspector general's annual reports, detail department worker errors but do not contain the names of victims, caseworkers or references to where and when a death occurred.

To put a face on these children, the *News-Democrat* compared these anonymous child death reports to news accounts, police and coroner's reports and other documents.

As a result, the newspaper identified 41 of the 53 children who died and linked errors to actual cases.

The newspaper found that DCFS and private agency workers:

• Repeatedly got suspected abusers' names wrong when making criminal background checks, resulting in false "clean" reports.

• Accepted the word of a suspected child abuser that his son was sleeping and couldn't be disturbed. The caseworker left without seeing the boy, who died an hour later from a beating by his father.

• Failed to fully investigate a scalding case because a state-supplied thermometer did not come with batteries. The child later died of asphyxiation.

• Left a sick, 5-month-old baby boy in the care of a 7-year-old girl. A caseworker said she was in a hurry and didn't have time to wait for the mother to return.

DCFS records are not subject to the state's Freedom of Information Act. This overall confidentiality prevents publicity that could reduce errors by holding DCFS more accountable, said Patrick T. Murphy, a Cook County domestic court judge.

"Kids get tortured and brutalized, and all we ever get is some sanitized report without names, dates or places," said Murphy, who as a public guardian in the 1990s fought to protect children in state care. Murphy said the way to decrease errors is to open the agency's records to public scrutiny.

Kendall Marlowe, deputy chief of communications for the department, said top administrators are aware of worker errors.

"It's a matter of setting up procedures, policies and practices, and monitoring supervision so that if an employee does a bonehead thing, there's somebody right there that catches it before it affects the child," Marlowe said.

Children Still Die

Despite these procedures, children continued to die during and after botched DCFS child abuse investigations. According to inspector general's reports:

- In Aurora, near Chicago, a child abuse investigator allowed 4-month-old Daniel Bowie's mother to smoke crack cocaine as long as she agreed to first drop the baby off next door. The caseworker accepted this arrangement as a "child safety plan" and allowed Daniel to remain with his mother. A few weeks later, the baby died from a beating in his home. No one was charged.
- In Southern Illinois, 5-month-old Dakota Jean Hedger of Carrier Mills went to the emergency room with "friction burns on her nose, a bruise on her ear, a puncture wound on her foot, a split lip, fingertip bruises on her back and a tear on the underside of her tongue," according to a child death report. A department supervisor sent the baby and her mother to live with a relative, but the two returned to the baby's father without approval. A caseworker could not then locate the family for three days. On the fourth day, a sheriff's deputy called to say the infant was dead. The father is serving 25 years for murder.
- In Chicago, 6-year-old Alma Manjarrez died after her mother's boyfriend punched the girl in the stomach on Christmas Day and left her outside in the snow. A DCFS investigator failed to check with police about a previous episode involving the boyfriend that could have alerted her to potential danger to Alma. The investigator said it was inconvenient for her to talk to the police officer because he worked nights and she worked days.
- In Blue Island, a department investigator was assigned to determine whether it was safe to allow 3-year-old Kenya Riley to remain at home. But the investigator, who was supposed to contact the family within 24 hours, failed to locate them. He finally got word of Kenya's whereabouts six weeks later when a coroner called to say the little girl died from head trauma.

In September, stories about a young East St. Louis mother whose unborn fetus was cut from her womb and whose three children were killed and stuffed into a washer and dryer emphasized the importance of DCFS' duty to protect at-risk children.

The mother had been involved with DCFS as a child, as were her three children.

The inspector general's office does not investigate most deaths of children involved with the DCFS. During the period examined by the newspaper, 780 children died while wards of the state or while having some involvement with the department. Most of these deaths were due to medical problems or accidents.

The inspector general's investigators conducted full probes into 77 child deaths during this seven-year period. The 53 deaths involved cases where the newspaper found significant caseworker error or neglect. In the other 24, there were few or no serious errors on the part of DCFS workers, even though these cases ended with the death of a child.

In many of the child death reports, the newspaper found a combination of errors, instances of neglect and questionable judgment on the part of DCFS workers.

The newspaper's review showed that state child protection workers who commit serious errors are sometimes disciplined, transferred or counseled, but seldom suspended and almost never fired.

In 50 child death cases (two cases involved more than one child), no department employees or private agency workers were fired. Five employees resigned, 12 were counseled and 14 were disciplined or reprimanded.

In 26 cases, the department took no action against any worker after a child's death.

In one case, 7-month-old Edgardo Martin died in January 2005 in a fire at his family's mobile home in Fairmont City. A DCFS investigator noticed three space heaters hooked up on a single series of extension cords, but failed to warn the family and accepted the word of a Spanish translator that it was OK, according to an investigative report. Three weeks later, Edgardo died in a fire the state fire marshal's office attributed to an electrical overload in the series of cords.

The caseworker received no dicipline, while two supervisors received counseling, the report stated.

Finding Solutions

Child welfare advocates say openness, increased staffing and less reluctance by prosecutors to bring child abuse cases to court are the keys to reducing worker error.

"In the private sector, if someone makes an egregious error, you could probably discharge them. In systems where you have a Civil Service setting and personnel rules . . . you can't do that," said Jess McDonald, who was director of the DCFS from 1990 to 2003.

McDonald acknowledged that while children die under DCFS' watch, including after worker errors, many are helped.

"Thousands and thousands of children over these same number of years have been protected from abuse," he said, adding that eliminating potentially lethal mistakes is probably a matter of increasing supervision and vigilance.

"You know what they say when you walk along the beach," said McDonald. "Don't turn your back to the ocean because that one in a million rogue wave may get you. It's the same with worker error."

Most current and former department workers contacted for this series did not want to be identified or talk on the record. They described the work as stressful and said the department, especially in the East St. Louis office, does not have enough workers.

Gary Guadagano, a former DCFS child abuse investigator, said the department pays caseworkers to make "very chancy decisions."

"I found the job excruciating," he said. The state of constant worry about whether he made the right decision led him to leave his DCFS job.

"It's the worst thing. You worry that something might happen to a kid you saw," said Guadagano, who works as a court liaison for the department in St. Clair County Court.

A study released earlier this year by Council 31 of the American Federation of State, County and Municipal Employees, which represents DCFS workers, found that despite an 11 percent increase in child abuse investigations from 2001–05, the department lost 23 percent, or 747, of its "frontline" staff statewide.

Murphy, the Cook County judge, said the agency's strict emphasis on confidentiality leads to a lack of accountability and increased caseworker error. He favors making all details in child death reports public except for the names of people reporting the abuse and psychiatric records, unless a judge reviews them.

"They want to keep the whole thing secret, like this investigator who let the mom smoke crack. That stuff goes on across the board. I've seen it repeatedly," Murphy said.

Court Involvement

DCFS Inspector General Denise Kane said one of her top concerns is the practice of allowing children to remain in the home in the face of obvious or repeated abuse.

She warned that accepting a parent's word without verification and giving too much consideration to their promises to do better is "fraught with difficulties."

"If a parent is using (drugs) and keeps getting high, there's a risk to those children," she said.

DCFS often tries to steer family drug cases into court, but many state's attorneys won't take them, Kane said.

"Our office says that's not correct. You should take them, even if it's only for an order of supervision," she said.

An order of supervision allows a judge to force a mother into court, where she can be ordered to accept drug treatment or lose custody of her children and forfeit state benefits.

In order to remove a child from the home, a judge must find "an immediate and emergent need." That's a problem, Kane said.

"If a mother smokes crack on Monday, but word doesn't get to the judge until Thursday, he will probably decline to place the children in protective custody because the immediate need was when the DCFS worker actually saw the mother taking drugs," Kane said.

But Guadagano, who makes recommendations to judges about whether a child should be removed, said most judges are willing to put a child into foster care if there's any chance that leaving them at home will lead to injury.

"Most people will err on the side of caution," Guadagano said. "Who wants to take a chance like that?"

When to intervene and get a court order to remove someone's children is the most difficult part of the job, said Michael Davis, a member of the Illinois Child Welfare Ethics Advisory Board. The investigative office turns to this board for broad answers about why children die in DCFS' care.

"When somebody actually dies, a lot has to go wrong," he said, "because DCFS has . . . a number of back-up systems in place.

"There are egregious errors," he said, "which is why they ended up in the reports. Our view is that (child deaths) indicate problems . . . and we try to figure out what the underlying cause is."

But in some cases, the DCFS allowed children who were obviously being abused to remain in dangerous situations.

In Harvey, Ill., 9-year-old Shanecia McClellan, who suffered from cerebral palsy, starved to death, despite 33 visits to the home by DCFS caseworkers, according to a child death report.

The girl's mother, a cocaine user who refused free drug counseling, told police that Shanecia had died three days earlier, but she hadn't called authorities because she was "too busy to deal with that."

Waiting Too Long

William Adams didn't survive childhood, though there were many warning signs that he was in danger.

In April 2002, 3-year-old William died in a Centreville house fire. His mother had a long history of drug use and neglect during years of involvement with DCFS, yet her children were allowed to remain in her care, according to a child death report.

The mother, Rosie Rainey, gave birth to three children before William was born. Two tested positive for cocaine at birth, according to the state report. Three weeks after the birth of her second child, Rainey took her 3-year-old daughter to a hospital emergency room where the infant was found to be suffering from gonorrhea.

Authorities never charged anyone with sexual assault of the toddler.

William also tested positive for cocaine at birth. The DCFS referred the mother to a drug treatment program, but she attended only sporadically and was kicked out, the report stated.

In August 2000, Centreville Police Officer Pat Reliford found Rainey's four children home alone. He found the oldest child, a 6-year-old girl, cooking for her younger siblings. Police charged Rainey with child endangerment.

As required by state law, Reliford called the state child abuse hotline. DCFS took the children into protective custody but later returned them and assigned a second caseworker to the family.

The state investigative report on William's death stated that the 14-month tenure of the second caseworker "was characterized by ineffective assessments and lapses in critical judgment."

According to the state report, the caseworker was not concerned about the threat of fire from the use of space heaters and general disarray of the house ". . . because the mother did not smoke cigarettes."

But Rainey did use drugs, and one afternoon, while she slept, William's older brother found a lighter and accidentally set some blankets on fire, according to a police report.

The older boy tried to awaken his mother to help William escape the smoky and burning bedroom, but Rainey, who admitted to using crack a few days earlier and smoking marijuana the night before, slept on.

Finally, she awoke and tried to rescue the trapped boy, but it was too late.

"I heard William screaming in the room," she told police, "and I kept calling to him to 'come to Momma, come to Momma.'"

You can read the entire "Lethal Lapses" series at http://www.bnd.com/lethal_lapses.

Lessons Learned

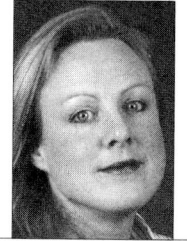 

BY BETH HUNDSDORFER AND GEORGE PAWLACZYK

It wasn't unusual to hear complaints about Illinois' child protection system.

Complaints from family members, police officers, coroner's deputies and caseworkers who deal with abused children were difficult to verify because they were off the record and lacked specific information.

While vague, the message was disturbing: The child protection system was flawed with rampant mistakes and limited accountability. State confidentiality laws kept it all secret.

In March 2006, we learned that dull gray books resembling state audits contained details of child protection worker blunders compiled by the Illinois Department of Children and Family Services' own Office of the Inspector General. One of these books surfaced in the newsroom when a reporter was cleaning out a desk.

Dozens of sanitized accounts of horrific deaths are printed annually in these unassuming publications. The reports, often not published until years after the deaths, contain no names and don't say when or where the children died.

Casually glancing through the book, we recognized a case from our area of a baby girl born in a waste-filled toilet and left to die. Six months earlier, we did extensive research about her mentally ill, transient mother who wandered neighborhoods where crack cocaine was sold on corners—with her little boy in tow. We didn't know how we were going to use the information, but the story resonated with us.

It was instantly clear from reading this account, though anonymous, that it was about the story we investigated. The report documented missed opportunities to help this woman and her children. We thought we could link more of these anonymous reports to real children.

We knew that detailed stories about flesh-and-blood children who died after workers made mistakes or ignored obvious problems could lead to public outrage and demands for accountability.

In reading other cases, we found outrageous details: a girl with dozens of bite marks on her buttocks; a girl thrown into the snow on Christmas Day; a teen who was allowed to starve to death.

We realized those details would be enough for a definite identification if we could discover where, among Illinois' 102 counties, the death occurred.

We figured local police and coroners must have heard about these things. We knew that nothing beats knocking on doors, so that's what we did.

The Social Security Administration's death records, available online, also provided children's names—if there was an approximate date of death. With a careful review of annual anonymous death reports, we discovered that in a majority of the cases a very brief "child death summary" published earlier provided the county name that could then be connected to the lengthier, final reports.

Linking the time and county of death in the summary to the final report was invaluable. The better we knew our material, the easier it became to verify names in the anonymous death reports.

The anonymous books that lay ignored in an unused desk drawer became our path into otherwise sealed case histories. This led to a swift lesson: Don't overlook what is right in front of you.

As we progressed, we tried repeatedly to get answers from DCFS Chief Bryan Samuels, including sending registered letters to his home and office. We got few answers and no response to questions about why basic errors on the part of state caseworkers continued. Our FOIAs were rejected or modified. But by persisting in our investigation, we learned about avenues to circumvent DCFS' denials.

We found out that some of the relatively few suspensions given to child protection workers were challenged during hearings before the state's Civil Service Commission. If offered as evidence, confidential records, including caseworker notes, psychiatric and medical records and the DCFS Inspector General's field reports, became public records during these hearings.

During a visit to the commission, we asked for the latest appeals and were given access to a 35-page confidential field report on the mother who gave birth to a girl in a toilet—the tragedy that focused our interest in abused children.

We agreed to allow a secretary extra time to photocopy our request, then mail copies. However, this agreement allowed a DCFS lawyer to step in the next day and block their release. But the threat of a lawsuit and pressure applied by the Civil Service commissioner was enough to get the information released the next day.

Here, too, we learned another lesson: Never leave without the documents.

George Pawlaczyk is a general assignment reporter specializing in investigative reporting at the News-Democrat. *Beth Hundsdorfer joined the* Belleville News-Democrat *in June 2001. Hundsdorfer and Pawlaczyk teamed in 2001 for the series "Subject to Inspection," which exposed discriminatory enforcement practices of Belleville's occupancy code requirements. The series was a finalist in the Investigative Reporters and Editors contest. Hundsdorfer covers the police and courts beat at the* News-Democrat.

PART 5

Reporting and Writing Editorials

WINNER
Jane Healy
ASNE, Editorial Writing
Finalist, Pulitzer Prize, Editorial Writing

Orlando Sentinel

Jane Healy combines a sharp, reportorial eye for details with a flair for passionate, precise prose. The combination results in evocative editorials that convict and convince.

In her *Orlando Sentinel* editorial series, "Florida's Shame," Healy convicts politicians, developers, bureaucrats, commissioners and others of opting for growth at the expense of Florida's environment. She pulls back a curtain that reveals how laws passed to manage growth went ignored, or were simply violated. She creates clever scenarios that enable the reader to engage with, and understand, the historical, legal and environmental complexity involved. She uses direct, unvarnished language that exposes the people, and the laws, for what they are.

Healy convinces the readers of her opinions with facts and details. She clarifies the issues by using common language that readers can grasp immediately. She uses old-fashioned, shoe-leather reporting. She shows up in person at events, visits growth management sites, and talks directly with the people involved. Her words sound solid because she knows firsthand what she's talking about.

Consider Healy holistic in her journalism. She combines the best features of a news reporter with those of an editorial writer.

Her wholeness comes from practicing on both sides of the editorial divide. She spent several years on the news side as a metro reporter and a frontline editor. Then she became an editorial writer. It was during that time, under John Haile, who was editorial page editor then, that she found herself pushed to document her opinions.

"In my first 'Florida's Shame,' he is the one who insisted I have airtight examples for each problem we were writing about. I was ready to strangle him during the editing process, but the editorials came out better because of his tough editing," Healy said.

After a dozen years on the editorial page, she went back to the news side as managing editor. Then, when she was offered the opportunity to be editorial page editor, she leapt at it.

"I loved [being managing editor] too but didn't want to do it forever. It's a job that can burn you out, though I wasn't burned out yet," Healy said. "In 2001, we had a new editor, and I had an opportunity to go back to the editorial page as its editor. I jumped at it, realizing it is something I could be happy doing for a long time."

Healy, who began her career in 1973, still sees journalism "as an exciting profession." She followed in the footsteps of her father, who worked as a Washington journalist for 35 years. He prompted her to shine a spotlight on injustice and unfairness.

Now one of her sons wants to become a journalist.

"I think that's great. I can't think of any better profession. It's changing but there still will be journalism, just maybe not in the same form," she said.

And what would she like to leave behind as her journalistic legacy? "That my journalism made Central Florida a better place to live."

The "Florida's Shame" series was a finalist for the 91st annual Pulitzer Prize in editorial writing.

—Aly Colón, co-editor of "Best Newspaper Writing"

30. Losing Paradise

APRIL 2, 2006

By Jane Healy

We feel duped. How about you?

SPRING 1974: Florida declares that the Green Swamp in Lake and Polk counties won't be paved over for the next get-rich-quick scheme. Hallelujah! In putting this swamp in the same category as the Everglades, legislators must have recognized even then that this was exactly what was needed to preserve it. Central Florida's Everglades, if you will. Not only does it intersect five major river systems, this 560,000-acre swamp between Orlando and Tampa teems with rare plants and animals. The scrub jay, the wood stork, the black bear. Even the elusive Florida panther roams its forests. Name an endangered species in Florida, and you can bet you'll find it here. Quite a stand for a state that usually bends over backward to accommodate every fast-buck artist who shows up at the state line. Must be real precious land.

SUMMER 2005: Wait a minute. What's this we hear about the Lake County city of Groveland fighting to allow a megadevelopment in this very swamp? The developer even has the nerve to call itself Banyan, the name of a popular Florida tree. The developers will plop down as many as 532 homes in a part of the swamp that was slated for 57 homes. Do the math: It means that developers stand to make almost 10 times more than if the 361 acres remained rural. Didn't 72 percent of Groveland just vote to ban so many homes in the swamp? Why, yes, but Groveland commissioners will have none of that. They actually went to court to get around their own voters and gain the right to help kill the Green Swamp. So much for the Legislature's 1974 vision.

And you wonder why we feel duped. Bet it's nothing compared to how 72 percent of the Groveland voters feel. And this commission is supposed to be looking out for them? Come again? Our only comforting thought is that this is an isolated incident for Central Florida.

Or is it?

NOVEMBER 2004: Seminole County voters approve a referendum that says the County Commission has the right to protect areas such as the Black Hammock, an oasis for endangered critters and plants just on the edge of Winter Springs and Oviedo. The voters know full well that

Seminole has precious little land left to protect. And they don't want politicians to destroy the very things that drew them to Florida in the first place. Well, that's a nice thought, but not good enough for Winter Springs. It apparently reads the same playbook as Groveland and sets the stage for a scheme to put at least nine times as many homes in that area as now allowed. By this time, we're getting pretty good at developers' math. Winter Springs, too, drags a case against the Seminole vote into court. A copycat killing? Sure sounds like it. Winter Springs now is saying it won't turn Black Hammock into a subdivision. Well, pardon us if we're not celebrating just yet. The city still is bulldozing ahead with its court case to strip the County Commission of its right to preserve the Black Hammock.

Surely, this isn't going on in Orange County, is it? Hasn't Orange learned time and again that caving in to big-time landowners and developers betrays the voters' trust?

Apparently not.

JAN. 10, 2006: Surprising as it is, Orange County actually comes up with a decent plan for developing so-called Innovation Way in east Orange County. The idea is to create an area where high-tech jobs can exist alongside homes. Work, live and play all in the same area. Terrific. But what are all those Gucci loafers doing in the commission chambers the day Innovation Way is coming up for an initial vote? Please, tell us it isn't true that this snarl of lobbyists is going to use Innovation Way to promote the next big scheme. Some innovation. Can't anything just be left alone? Well, we might want that, and so might the voters. But four county commissioners—Bill Segal, Homer Hartage, Mildred Fernandez and Bob Sindler—disagreed. They turned to the lobbyists and, in effect, said, "Let's see if we can maul another 10,000 acres of wilderness." Who cares that this land has nothing to do with Innovation Way except that it's next door? It's a great excuse for a huge, new subdivision. Isn't that the only thing that really matters in Central Florida?

So why would these commissioners do this? It's just a first step, they said, nothing to get all huffy about. They just wanted to see what state regulators think. Well, yeah, we do feel a bit huffy. Why do they want to hear what the state has to say about a project their own county planners didn't even support? Could they be fishing for a few kind words? Words that could give them an excuse to approve this project when it comes up for another vote in May? Surely not, we think. Hasn't Orange gotten better about these things? But then we realize that we can't remember any project that has gotten this far only to be rejected. By the way, Commissioner Segal says he has had a change of heart, and he's not for the project after all. Pardon us if we're not cheering this either. His vote allowed this scheme to take off.

Something else: This land sits next to the Econlockhatchee River, the one that 15 years ago the Orange commission vowed to protect.

So has nothing changed? Will Florida remain forever the butt of the jokes, the place where elected officials treat developers as royalty rather than people to regulate? Unfortunately, in too many cases, yes. In the next four days, we will explore why Florida remains such a mess of traffic jams and crowded schools. We will show you a state law passed 20 years ago that was supposed to fix things, only to be doomed in its first few years. We also will tell you more about the new villains—the cities such as Groveland and Winter Springs, whose panting for growth is upending any responsible thoughts that voters harbored. We will tell you about the Kissimmee River. Taxpayers are spending $578 million to restore it to its roots, only to have Osceola County poised to OK megadevelopment after megadevelopment that could help destroy the waterway and endanger the eagles that nest there.

But all is not for naught. There still is time to do things right, even in the fiascoes detailed above. Only, though, if our elected officials grow some backbone.

31. Failure to Launch

APRIL 3, 2006

By Jane Healy

Did you enjoy your commute this morning? Neither did we.

Seems to get worse every day whether you're coming or going. But don't you wonder why this is? Those of you here in 1985 probably remember hearing legislators tout a new law that said, once and for all, that subdivisions won't be approved if the roads aren't in place to handle them.

As everyone can see, the traffic got worse, not better. And if you think it's bad now, grab your steering wheel. The seven-county area with 3.5 million people now will grow to 4.6 million in 2020, 7 million by 2050. This isn't a matter of growth or no growth. There's no way to stop it, nor should we. But there are ways to manage it, ways that our elected officials have pretty much ignored.

Oh, the lawmakers pass tough laws. It's just that it takes only a Florida minute for them to fall apart when elected officials start understanding it means they actually would have to start turning down developments—or forcing developer pals to come up with more money. To heck with that.

So from the get-go, they found ways around it. Take the "landmark" law requiring governments to have a responsible plan for growth. Turned out, it was just that—a plan—one that usually never saw the light of the commission chambers. For its part, Orange County waited only six months before it turned 3,000 acres that was supposed to stay rural into an industrial park. The joke was on the rest of us. When other governments saw that Orange could get away with this, they fell right in line. After all, there's big money at stake here, for the developer anyway. Let a developer put four homes on an acre rather than one on 5 acres and the cash register starts clanging. Let the rest of us stew on I-4.

But, wait a minute. Weren't state officials supposed to stop all this? Aren't they the ones who had the power to say no? Well, yes. Problem is that they instead said, "Fine, go right ahead." So Florida wasn't serious after all.

Don't think it ended there. Once developers saw an opening, they pounced. Now that they had decimated the 1985 law, they turned to a new prey. Their victim was a law that gave regional planners a legal avenue to challenge a megadevelopment. Developers hated that law. It had them shaking in their Guccis because regional planners didn't accept campaign contributions. So what happened next?

SPRING 1993: The Legislature decides that regional planners can't appeal these developments anymore—that they can only make "recommendations." Wonder why you never hear about regional planners anymore? That's why.

But at least we had Gov. Lawton Chiles, the one who stood up for the people against the special interests, right? Now that the regional planners had been put in their place, surely he would push the state to crack down. Wrong again. Read on.

By this time, St. Lucie County in South Florida had gotten the word loud and clear that it could put the developers ahead of everyone else. Must have heard about Orange County. So it said "Be my guest" to a developer who wanted to plop his citylike development right in the middle of a rural area. This was too much for even state planners, who had been more than happy to rubber-stamp every fast-buck scheme that came out of Orange. But this time, they said: Enough. End of story, right? Not quite. The story in Florida never ends with an unhappy developer. So his next stop was back to the politicians: Gov. Chiles and the Cabinet. Surely, Mr. Chiles would back his own agency, wouldn't he? Actually, no. On a 4–3 vote, Mr. Chiles signaled the end of any hope that the state might be there for its residents.

Now fast-forward to Gov. Jeb Bush. Mr. Bush is a smart man. He understands that Florida can't continue like this, right? Well, Mr. Bush apparently hadn't been in Florida long enough to realize how it works here. Only a few years ago, the governor believed that things would get better if governments simply calculated the real cost of sprawl. Being shocked—shocked!—at how much it cost, the politicians then would turn down the developments. Well, give him credit for understanding the costly effects of sprawl, how inefficient it is to pay for new sewer lines and new roads in the countryside when they're needed somewhere else. He understood that while this allows the developers to get exactly what they want—cheap land—it sticks the rest of us with jammed roads and schools everywhere else. But was the governor so naive as to believe that passing a law making governments come up with this information would really stop anything?

Maybe Mr. Bush hadn't been paying enough attention to what was going on in the Legislature. Otherwise he would have realized that every few years, the lawmakers trot out a new "growth-management bill." It supposedly cracks down "once and for all." Want to know the best indicator that a growth law is worthless? A unanimous vote of approval. That tells you right off the bat that it's not going to do anything other than give every lobbyist a new Lexus.

But, as we said, Mr. Bush is a smart man. It took him a while, but now he recognizes nothing will get better here until governments actually turn down developments if the roads and schools aren't available for the growth. So he got behind a new law, one that really will work—if it's enforced. That's certainly a leap of faith in Florida.

Indeed, legislators watered down even this one in the last legislative session as soon as the development industry and its legislative pals got their gloves on it. Nevertheless, it could make things better—but only if our elected officials have the will to make it work. Finally, finally can't they just say no if the roads and schools aren't there to accommodate it? What actually is so hard about that? Stay tuned. The legislative session is only half over.

32. Dollars For Dummies: For Aspiring Developers—Five Easy Steps to Get Rich Quick

APRIL 4, 2006

By Jane Healy

Lesson 1: Find an attractive project like Orange County's Innovation Way to latch on to. Remember the new buzz words: living, working and playing, all in the same area. That's what Innovation Way would do. But don't exactly do Innovation Way. That's much too expensive. Instead, find some rural land next door.

That's right. It's that easy. In Florida, you can always find enough commissioners to fall for this. (Don't mention that this would mean the county would have to provide roads, schools and water for thousands of new homes that it hadn't even planned on.) But don't think words alone will convince these savvy commissioners. So:

Lesson 2: Find the most expensive lobbyists around. Can't afford them? You must have forgotten lesson 1: You never lose if you have the politicians right along with you. Always remember to buy the cheapest land possible. And here's the beauty of that: You never have to worry about its initial cost because the commissioners rezone the land before a mortgage payment ever comes due. It's always worth 10 times as much by then.

Here's how those developers did it in Orange County: First, they called their development "Camino Reale." Good start. Makes it sound like something you can't say no to. Then they hired the very best: former Speaker of the Florida House John Thrasher. Next they added another important component: someone who just recently was a big shot in the state agency that has the final say. Here in Florida, that would be Oscar Anderson.

OK, you now have on board the powerful former politician and the former agency honcho—who's next? Down Orange County way, it's almost always Hal Kantor. Not a name everyone has heard of, but he sure is popular around the commission chambers. He gets in on about every big deal that rolls through the pasture.

Now for the execution:

Lesson 3: Tell them to visit the newest county commissioners first. (These three already know this, but it will make you sound authoritative.) In Orange's case, that would be Commissioners Bill Segal and Mildred Fernandez. They both are pretty new and don't yet know that they're seen as suckers. Here's the trick: Tell them you just want the project "transmitted" to the state. The big word sounds good, and they have no idea what it means. But we do. We asked about the record books in the past 20 years and found that whenever an Orange County project is "transmitted" to the state, it gets approved.

Oh, yes, there was one project rejected, something on University Boulevard 10 or 15 years ago, but everyone has a tough time remembering any details. Must have had the wrong lobbyists.

But you can't be too sure here. The newbies might think they have to ask some questions. So:

Lesson 4: Have your lobbyist tell the commissioners that a more popular commissioner—or mayor—is going to vote for the project. Again we're back to Orange. Can't help it. It's a great teaching lesson. Bill Segal fell for it. When the lobbyists told him—or at least strongly implied—that Mayor Rich Crotty was going to vote for Camino Reale, he figured it was good enough for him, too. (Wonder what Crotty thought when he heard that one? Turns out Crotty voted against having Camino Reale latch on to Innovation Way.)

Start counting those dollars, ladies and gentlemen. Now is the time to go for the close—the final two votes:

Lesson 5: Set your sights on the commissioner who never seems to know what he's voting on. You can get those guys to do the wildest things. In Orange's case, that would be Commissioner Bob Sindler. All it took was one visit from the lobbyists to get his vote. And now he's telling people he never really voted for it. Remember that for the next time. Get commissioners to deny they ever did it.

OK, now for the kill: the fourth vote, the vote to riches. That would be Homer Hartage. And what brought him around? Don't know. He's not talking. But it doesn't matter. His vote's still good.

Congratulations! You have figured out Central Florida.

One last piece of advice: Get out of town! That's right, get out of town before people figure out what you did, in this case, to the Econlockhatchee River. Forgot to tell you, but this easy money means that thousands of rare critters will have to move somewhere else. We know, there might not be anywhere else for those scrub jays, wood storks and eagles. But, heck, you've made your pile of money already, right?

A note of caution: Sometimes a commissioner may change his or her mind. In this case, it's Bill Segal, who now realizes the lobbyists might have been having their fun with him. He's saying he won't go along with the gig when Camino Reale comes up for another vote May 23.

Final lesson: Don't give up. That next vote is still seven weeks away. Messrs. Kantor, Thrasher and Anderson are ready and available. Their price may go up, but it will be worth your while. If nothing else, just remember one lesson: All you need is four people—doesn't matter which ones—to turn precious land into the next subdivision.

33. The New Villains

APRIL 5, 2006

By Jane Healy

Like happy endings? Then you might not want to read this.

NOV. 2, 2004: What a great day for Seminole County residents. Hurrah. By their votes, they were actually going to protect precious land against the sound of the bulldozer. Not many other counties in Central Florida could claim that, now, could they? After all, who in Seminole hadn't made the trek to the Black Hammock?

It's hard to believe that just a few short minutes from their subdivisions with homes cheek-to-jowl, they could sit at a fish camp on the shores of Lake Jesup. Residents could sip a drink and watch gators slip through the water while a snowy egret, maybe even an eagle, soared above. Nearby they might spot an endangered wood stork making its way through the dark swamp. And they knew they could take a look at something called the cuplet fern, a plant so rare that this is the only place in the continental U.S. where it can be found in the wild. Now this is more like it. This is why they stay in Florida.

They also knew that the Black Hammock, with its dripping Spanish moss hanging from the water oaks that fill the swamp, was only the beginning. It was the gateway to rural Seminole County. Lake Harney, the Econlockhatchee River, the St. Johns River. They all now would be protected from citylike subdivisions. Finally.

NOV. 16, 2004: No, this can't be happening. The city of Winter Springs, which sits right next door to the Black Hammock, is in court to stop the voters' bid to save the hammock and the rest of rural Seminole County. Please say no. Was their vote just some sort of bad joke cooked up by a prankster? Why else would Winter Springs' lawyers be marching into the courthouse with a piece of paper arguing that the voters had somehow violated the city's rights? The county can't tell the city what to do, it says.

Then we come to our senses. We realize we shouldn't have been surprised. Winter Springs was the reason that Seminole commissioners asked voters whether they wanted to keep the area rural. And can you blame them? Winter Springs was making moves to put sewers—sewers—in the hammock even though it wasn't even in the city limits. Anyone who has been in Florida more than 10 minutes knows what sewers mean. They mean subdivisions and plenty of them. All Winter Springs needed to do now was bring the land into the city, a simple feat in Florida. Even worse, Winter Springs wins the first round in court. It may actually win the right to prevent the Seminole commission from protecting the rural area. Pardon us if we're not cheering. But Winter Springs doesn't stop there. It also supports a bill gaining steam in the Legislature that would allow Winter Springs to ignore county voters who want to protect land. The Winter Springs cheerleader for all this is City Manager Ron McLemore, who has backed one scheme after another for the Black Hammock.

Ready for the punch line? The Winter Springs commission now says it doesn't even want to put a subdivision in the hammock. It just wants the right to do so.

So let's take Winter Springs at its word: It's not going to develop Black Hammock or other wilderness in eastern Seminole. Why does it want to give other cities the right to? Why does it want to leave this precious land victim to any developer who can sweet-talk the next new commissioner? We all know how those conversations turn out. And what about the next Oviedo City Commission? That city also sits right next door to Black Hammock.

Well, it can't be that bad, can it? Can a win for Winter Springs really destroy Seminole's way of life? Well, yes it can. Here's the ugly truth: If cities are allowed to fill rural eastern Seminole County with subdivisions, that area alone will have more residents than the entire city of Orlando has now. It would house even more residents than presently live in Osceola County. All told, it could mean 80,000 new houses, 240,000 more people. Wonderful. Houses replace the critters. Now are you happy, Ron McLemore?

But at least in Seminole there is some hope. Maybe Winter Springs will come to its senses and drop its suit. Or maybe it will stop backing the bill in the Legislature.

In Lake County there is one case that has no hope. There, Groveland went to court against its own city voters to pave the way for a subdivision in the Green Swamp. Yes, that's the same swamp the state 30 years ago vowed to protect against just this sort of development. The 560,000-acre swamp is filled with waterways and endangered animals that need plenty of space. Groveland too had a city manager—Jason Yarborough—engineering the assault. Thankfully for the Green Swamp, he's no longer there. But his big reason for supporting this Banyan subdivision is that the developer might donate a park. Welcome to the new Florida. Do whatever you want as long as you donate a park or a school. Works every time.

That was last July. So has Groveland gotten its park? Not yet, says the new city manager. They are still working on it.

34. Eagles For Sale?

APRIL 6, 2006

By Jane Healy

Want to hear another great thing about living in Central Florida? Right near Kissimmee, at the Osceola and Polk county border, we have the richest concentration of bald-eagle nests in the U.S. Even richer than Alaska. That state has far more bald eagles than we do, but we have more eagle nests close to one another: 329 in both counties.

It's not hard to imagine why so many eagles settled near the Kissimmee Prairie. Bald eagles always want a waterfront view so they can see where their next meal is coming from. In this case, that would be Lake Tohopekaliga and the Kissimmee River. This area is so attractive to the eagles that their numbers have been increasing every year. Last year alone, America's birds built 15 nests for their eaglets in the two counties. No small feat when you consider that the nests are about 5 feet wide, 3 feet deep and can weigh more than 1,000 pounds. Isn't Central Florida great?

By now you've probably guessed that this isn't going to be a happy tale of a threatened species being able to survive peacefully amid the bulldozers and asphalt. And you're right. It's not. Guess who else covets this waterfront view? Right again. It's the developers, who want to plop five megadevelopments in the very area where many of these eagles nest. All told, these subdivisions will account for almost 100,000 new residents, nearly half the number living in the entire county right now. Politicians such as Osceola Commissioner Atlee Mercer will tell you that there's nothing to worry about, the eagles will do just fine. Wish we could be so confident. Problem is, subdivisions always mean fewer trees. And fewer trees can mean fewer eagle nests. The nests there now can't be touched. And for good reason. Just think how long it took for the U.S. to bring the eagle back from near-extinction. But what about more eagle nests for the future? And what happens in the next hurricane? The last hurricanes destroyed 70 percent of Florida's eagle nests. Because there were still plenty of longleaf pine trees around—the best for nesting—80 percent of those nests came back.

But it's not too late for the eagles. Politicians such as Mr. Mercer could insist that developers preserve enough trees to protect and help increase America's bird. But Osceola isn't doing this. And don't think it's just about these megadevelopments. Even worse will be the smaller subdivisions popping up along the lake's shore as Osceola explodes with growth. And you thought Florida had changed? Wrong again.

If that isn't enough to get you concerned about what's going on in Osceola County, its new subdivisions might destroy the Kissimmee River, which taxpayers are spending $578 million to restore. This is the river that government channeled in the 1960s to control flooding. Didn't do much except ruin a river and a lot of animals and plants. Now we're bringing back the river's curves, along with wildlife. Great idea. But we might as well throw the money into the old ditch if the politicians don't insist that enough of this land be kept free of houses. By keeping a lot of the land open, water can remain there during the wet periods. Otherwise, it will flood somewhere else. And guess what happens then? We're right back to digging channels and polluting the water. Who cares about $578 million?

This isn't about rejecting these developments. They can end up just fine if the Osceola County Commission would just develop some backbone. But here's the scariest part: Two weeks ago Ken Shipley, vice chair of the Osceola commission, stood before a group of business leaders to brag that the county will be a "model" for managing growth. Sounds good until you realize that a week earlier, the state sent back Osceola's plan for growth with a 64-page litany of problems. Basically, the state couldn't figure out how Osceola was going to provide all the roads to support its new residents or even where the homes would be located. Has nothing changed? Except commissioners now know enough to say they are a "model" and hope to get away with it.

Actually, Commissioner Shipley is one of the good guys. He may be delusional about Osceola being a "model," but he says he will push for more protections for the eagles and other critters. He doesn't want the politicians to destroy the very things that make Osceola special.

A personal plea to elected officials in Osceola County: You actually can be a model if you want to. We are pleading with you to learn from the mistakes of the other counties in Central Florida, mistakes that we have detailed in the past five days. Most of your growth is in the future. Don't ruin what you have by putting quick bucks for the developers ahead of all the things that folks appreciate about Central Florida. You can insist that these subdivisions keep enough trees and open land to allow the eagles and the waterways to thrive. You also could launch programs that allow owners to trade land in such sensitive spots for more intense development somewhere else. Maybe even join with other nearby counties to do so.

Be a model. For generations to come, Central Florida will thank you.

X-RAY READING   By Roy Peter Clark

Jane Healy is a journalist who did not let an early Pulitzer Prize go to her head. In 1988, she won the big prize "for her series of editorials protesting overdevelopment of Florida's Orange County." It's inspiring to see that, nearly two decades later, she's still at it. During that time Healy has been one of America's best and most productive editorial writers. To borrow an adjective applied to economics, editorial writing can be a "dismal" craft, weighed down by institutional purpose and an omnivorous solemnity. Healy keeps it sharp and light, an audience of real readers always in her mind.

This editorial offers a splendid example of Healy's cleverness and originality. The topic is complex and recurring—land fraud in Florida. But Healy's approach is simple and popular. She borrows the voice of the snake oil seller and creates a five-lesson curriculum—a kind of school for scoundrels. In American lore, this is the language of the huckster, the used car salesman or the late-night infomercial gadfly. Beneath this borrowed voice is the real Healy, who has dedicated her life to protecting citizens by holding the powerful accountable for their actions.

Once you've read the editorial, without reference to my notes in the margins, read it again with these elements in mind:
1. The transparent structure of the lesson plan
2. The writer's adoption of cheesy marketing language
3. The ways in which she incorporates real evidence within a playful frame
4. Her methods of achieving clarity, such as the use of short sentences
5. The way she targets the accountable and names names

Learn and enjoy.

reference to the popular how-to book series

irony—noble word for ignoble pupose

language of the sales pitch

makes the structure transparent

sentences average nine words

Dollars For Dummies: For Aspiring Developers—Five Easy Steps to Get Rich Quick

Lesson 1: Find an attractive project like Orange County's Innovation Way to latch on to.

editorial will become a language lesson	Remember the new buzz words: living, working and playing, all in the same area. That's what Innovation Way would do. But don't exactly do Innovation Way. That's much too expensive. Instead, find some rural land next door.	sentences average nine words
picks up infomercial pitch	That's right. It's that easy. In Florida, you can always find enough commissioners to fall for this. (Don't mention that this would mean the county would have to provide roads, schools and water for thousands of new homes that it hadn't even planned on.) But don't think words alone will convince these savvy commissioners. So:	she embeds the technical argument
		crisp transition
expensive and cheapest— clever parallel constructions	**Lesson 2:** Find the most expensive lobbyists around. Can't afford them? You must have forgotten lesson 1: You never lose if you have the politicians right along with you. Always remember to buy the cheapest land possible. And here's the beauty of that: You never have to worry about its initial cost because the commissioners rezone the land before a mortgage payment ever comes due. It's always worth 10 times as much by then.	fake conversation; more pitch talk
another language lesson		another technical argument
	Here's how those developers did it in Orange County: First, they called their development "Camino Reale." Good start. Makes it sound like something you can't say no to. Then they	sentence fragment reinforces informality

hired the very best: former Speaker of the Florida House John Thrasher. Next they added another important component: someone who just recently was a big shot in the state agency that has the final say. Here in Florida, that would be Oscar Anderson.

OK, you now have on board the powerful former politician and the former agency honcho—who's next? Down Orange County way, it's almost always Hal Kantor. Not a name everyone has heard of, but he sure is popular around the commission chambers. He gets in on about every big deal that rolls through the pasture.

Now for the execution:

Lesson 3: Tell them to visit the newest county commissioners first. (These three already know this, but it will make you sound authoritative.) In Orange's case, that would be Commissioners Bill Segal and Mildred Fernandez. They both are pretty new and don't yet know that they're seen as suckers. Here's the trick: Tell them you just want the project "transmitted" to the state. The big word sounds good, and they have no idea what it means. But we do. We asked about the record books in the past 20 years and found that whenever an Orange County project is "transmitted" to the state, it gets approved. <!-- she's telling us a story -->

Oh, yes, there was one project rejected, something on University Boulevard 10 or 15 years ago, but everyone has a tough time remembering any details. Must have had the wrong lobbyists.

But you can't be too sure here. The newbies might think they have to ask some questions. So:

Lesson 4: Have your lobbyist tell the commissioners that a more popular commissioner—or mayor—is going to vote for the project. Again we're back to Orange. Can't help it. It's a great teaching lesson. Bill Segal fell for it. When the lobbyists told him—or at least strongly implied—that Mayor Rich Crotty was going to vote for Camino Reale, he figured it was good enough for him, too. (Wonder what Crotty thought when he heard that one? Turns out Crotty voted against having Camino Reale latch on to Innovation Way.) <!-- naming names; she sets the record straight -->

Start counting those dollars, ladies and gentlemen. Now is the time to go for the close—the final two votes: <!-- helps us see the ending -->

Lesson 5: Set your sights on the commissioner who never seems to know what he's voting on. You can get those guys to do the wildest things. In Orange's case, that would be Commissioner Bob Sindler. All it took was one visit from the lobbyists to get his vote. And now he's telling people he never really voted for it. Remember that for the next time. Get commissioners to deny they ever did it.

OK, now for the kill: the fourth vote, the vote to riches. That would be Homer Hartage. And what brought him around? Don't know. He's not talking. But it doesn't matter. His vote's still good. *[sentences get shorter and shorter, building a comic suspense]*

Congratulations! You have figured out Central Florida. *[sarcastic exclamation points]*

One last piece of advice: Get out of town! That's right, get out of town before people figure out what you did, in this case, to the Econlockhatchee River. Forgot to tell you, but this easy money means that thousands of rare critters will have to move somewhere else. We know, there might not be anywhere else for those scrub jays, wood storks and eagles. But, heck, you've made your pile of money already, right? *[three examples stand for the whole]* *[the birds become the back-up singers for her argument]*

A note of caution: Sometimes a commissioner may change his or her mind. In this case, it's Bill Segal, who now realizes the lobbyists might have been having their fun with him. He's saying he won't go along with the gig when Camino Reale comes up for another vote May 23.

Final lesson: Don't give up. That next vote is still seven weeks *[final accountability]* *[secret message to readers: there's still time to act]* away. Messrs. Kantor, Thrasher and Anderson are ready and available. Their price may go up, but it will be worth your while. If nothing else, just remember one lesson: All you need is four people—doesn't matter which ones—to turn precious land into the next subdivision.

> secret message to readers: there's still time to act

Roy Peter Clark is senior scholar and vice president of The Poynter Institute.

A conversation with
Jane Healy

This edited e-mail interview was conducted by "Best Newspaper Writing" co-editor Aly Colón with Jane Healy, winner of ASNE's Distinguished Writing Award for Editorial Writing.

ALY COLÓN: Where do the ideas for your editorials come from?

JANE HEALY: Generally, from news stories. But sometimes they just come from my expertise on a subject. Whatever it is, it should be a subject of significant community interest. In the case of "Florida's Shame," it came from my expertise over the years.

What prompted you to write the "Florida's Shame" editorial series?

I began writing "Florida's Shame" in 1984, when news produced a "Florida's Shame" special section. That section focused more on the tackiness of Florida, rather than on serious growth issues. On the editorial side, we decided to focus instead on the fact that Florida and Central Florida were being overrun with unmanaged growth at the behest of developers.

I continued writing those series until 1990, usually once or twice a year. They touched on different aspects of Florida's growth problems. But all had to do with government caving in time and again to the development interests or big landowners.

In each of the series, I used the same approach of citing hard, fresh examples to illustrate the problems. The idea was to have examples so compelling that they argued the case to the readers. Of course, to do that took a great deal of reporting. Sometimes I would think an example would work, but then it would fall apart. The exhaustive reporting—not just interviews, but poring over land-development documents—gave me the authority to write without attribution.

You focused on different elements affecting growth. How did you decide what aspects to zero in on?

I wrote this set of editorials after having spent eight years . . . as managing editor. I came back to the editorial page in 2001. During the next couple of years, I noticed from briefings and discussions on various growth matters that the laws I pushed for during the '80s were not being enforced. It became more and more apparent to me that I needed to get back into the subject in a big way. That's why I did last year's "Florida's Shame." I couldn't resist.

Sometimes editorials emanate almost completely from reporting done on the news side. In your case, you engaged in original reporting of your own. What caused you to do that? And what portion of the series came from your reporting as opposed to reporting done by others?

From the beginning, my "Florida's Shame" editorials have almost all been based on original reporting. As I mentioned above, my consistent device was using hard, vivid examples to make the case of things gone very wrong—showing rather than telling. I can't remember any example I used that was used in a news story in a major way. News generally would write about a development being approved, but it didn't usually connect it to the big picture, as these editorials did.

My editorial "Eagles For Sale?", for instance, was almost entirely from my reporting. I discovered that our neighboring county had the richest eagle nesting area in the world that was about to be destroyed by new lakefront homes. While news had written here and there about the proposed developments themselves, they hadn't made the connection with the eagles' nests.

"Dollars For Dummies," about the commissioners and the lobbyists, was entirely reported by me.

It's not surprising that news isn't chronicling every development approval—there are too many of them. What I was able to do was find the most egregious and then connect the dots on the trends.

What steps did you take to collect the information you needed?

I visited the endangered sites by airboat, helicopter and jeep. I attended county commission meetings. I met with planners and residents. I even attended a business reception in Osceola County where I could talk to some of the county commissioners making the decision on the eagles. That's when I heard one—whom I called "delusional" in the editorials—say the county was a "model" for growth.

How did you decide the focus of the editorials in your series?

When I had finished weeks of reporting, I sorted out the most important issues. There were dozens of directions I could have gone because this issue is so complex. When I took time to really think about what I had, I realized that the community was being duped. We had been told one thing, but elected officials were doing something very different.

In the editorials used in this book, you zero in on particular time periods, or use succinct lessons, as techniques to encapsulate and capture your theme. In "Losing Paradise," for example, you time travel from "Spring 1974" to "Summer 2005." And in "Dollars For Dummies" you write concisely about five lessons readers need to learn from. What prompted you to use those two approaches?

Using specific dates is a device I have employed since I wrote my first "Florida's Shame" series in '84. It seemed particularly effective for these editorials because it showed that no sooner had politicians passed laws, they were violating them.

I decided on the "Dollars For Dummies" approach after I interviewed all the county commissioners on why they voted for a huge, new development in a sensitive rural area. I had gotten ahold of the lists of lobbyists' visits to commissioners so I was able to confront them with that information.

My interviews had astounding results—one commissioner tried to deny he even voted on it. Another said he thought the mayor also was voting for it because the lobbyist told him so.

I knew this information shouldn't be told in a straightforward way. So after thinking, thinking and thinking about the best approach, I came up with "how to get rich quick in five easy steps."

Then I figured a parody of the "Dummies" book would work. It was devastating to the commissioners involved. But it got the point across that they were being duped by lobbyists. That also played into the theme of everyone being duped. Of course, they are elected officials and should have known better.

How did you decide how to organize this series of editorials?

First, I wanted to give readers an overview of the series and my theme that politicians were duping the public with their unenforced laws. Then for the second editorial, I wanted to give them some historical perspective. That's why I took them back to the '90s when things started unraveling. Then I went into the specific examples in each of three counties.

How did you decide to organize each editorial?

As I have done with all my "Florida's Shame" editorials, I always wanted to begin with an example. If the example is compelling enough—and that takes lots of reporting to find—it grabs the readers and makes your argument at the same time. You pull the reader along with you. I also wanted to sprinkle persuasive facts throughout the editorials so that they would unfold. I then wanted a punch line at the end, so readers would end up wanting more.

How did you decide what your lead would be for each of these editorials?

When I looked at all my reporting, I concluded that the community was being duped. So I decided that would be the voice—that we, too, are part of that community being duped by our elected officials. It was intended to be the voice of a betrayed community.

In almost all of the editorials in the five-part series submitted for the ASNE Award, you begin with a question. Why?

That was part of making readers feel part of our outrage over what was happening. I wanted to immediately bring them into the fold so they would share the feelings with us.

How did you determine what your ending would be?

For the endings, I wanted to draw some sort of conclusion about the problem at hand, or end with some sort of kicker that summed up the problem. The ending that I believe worked best was the one in "The New Villains" in which a city had been promised a park if it allowed development of a swamp. But now it's still waiting for the park. Again, this was an example gleaned through my reporting—an interview with the city manager . . . allowed me to do this.

What elements do you think must be included in an editorial to make it effective?

First of all, an editorial must have something to say. There must be an actual opinion the editorial will put forth, rather than an analysis or observation. There is precious little real estate on editorial pages. It shouldn't be wasted with pieces that don't argue for some sort of change.

I also believe you need facts to argue your case. Show rather than tell. And that you should always bring up the strongest argument on the other side and then refute it. The point of our editorials is to persuade readers of what we think is in the community's best interest.

In "Florida's Shame," I tried to bring up the opponents' arguments in a conversational way so that it didn't ruin the flow of the piece. For instance, in day one, the editorial said that county commissioners said their vote "was nothing to get all huffy about." And then we responded that, yeah, we are huffy and explained why.

That was a different approach to answering the argument without disturbing the voice of a community that has been duped. Of course they didn't use the word huffy, but it was a good description of their response rather than "Commissioner Segal responded that . . . "

What's most important, too, in editorials on complex issues is to absolutely not use jargon or bureaucratic terms. If I had filled these editorials with terms like "infrastructure, or comprehensive planning amendments," they would have been deadly. No one would have read them. And then they would have had no effect.

What I tried to do with these editorials is have readers enjoy reading about a complex issue.

Is there a particular structure, or approach, that you think works well in editorial writing?

I don't think an editorial generally should go more than a graf or two without readers knowing where you are headed on the opinion. They always should be persuading readers of something, much like taking one side in a debate. And the argument should be airtight, or there's no reason to waste the space.

Of course in something like a "Florida's Shame" series, the formula is different because I'm using examples to argue. It can take longer for readers to understand the opinion.

How many drafts do you do when you write your editorials?

I did several drafts for "Florida's Shame" because I wanted to get just the right tone with the right examples. I had way more information than I could use, so I tried to pare it down to the strongest ones.

What role does your editor play in your editorial writing?

I report to the publisher. The editor plays no role. The publisher, Kathy Waltz, and I talked all this out before I started reporting the series. She's a good sounding board.

Do you envision a particular type of person when you write an editorial?

In editorials like these, I envision regular citizens, since they are the ones who have to put up with all the traffic problems and polluted waterways because of politicians' spineless decisions.

What role do you believe an editorial writer plays in a newspaper?

I believe they play a more crucial role than ever because they can give a voice to the voiceless that so often gets lost these days. And they can play a leadership role in the community by writing strongly from a disinterested point of view. The newspaper is one of the very few institutions these days that can cross geographic and political boundaries, and simply care about community interest in general.

The bottom-line question for all our editorials is: What is in the community's best interest? The community isn't always the local community, but may be the state or even the nation, depending on the issue. When we endorse for president, the question to us is: What is in the nation's best interest?

What about voice? Whose voice does the editorial represent? The institutional newspaper's voice? The writer's voice?

It is the institutional voice, but the writer has a lot of leeway in that. It doesn't mean that the voice has to be boring.

Your editorials deal with complicated issues. What do you do to keep your writing clear, simple and precise?

I try to avoid any bureaucratic terms. That is deadly in growth issues, but many editorials do that because they don't really understand the issues. If you haven't done the reporting to truly understand the issue, you will just end up parroting the planners and other bureaucrats in their language. I try to use active voice and to use as few as possible adjectives or adverbs. I like to vary the rhythm of the sentences. I don't use weasel words. I try to say things in a straightforward manner so readers don't have to wonder what we're saying.

What editorial writers, or writers in general, do you admire and what have you learned from them?

Two editorial writers I learned a lot from are Richard Argood, who used to write for the *Philadelphia Daily News* and Paul Greenberg from Little Rock. I liked Argood's conversational style and his enthusiasm about jumping head first into a controversial issue. Greenberg critiqued our pages years ago and suggested that you have an opinion right away. That was great advice and I insist on it with my writers for every piece.

What would you advise someone who wants to be an editorial writer? What kind of skill, talent, drive and disposition does such a job require?

An editorial writer needs all the same skills as other journalists—intense curiosity about almost everything, good writing skills, ability to work under pressure and backbone to stand up to controversy. But an editorial writer also needs to feel comfortable with opinion and have the ability to quickly grasp complex issues. They also need an ability to look at every issue fairly and not jump to conclusions before both sides have been heard.

Is there anything you would like to add or re-emphasize?

I think editorials in general need to be far more conversational and sound like they are having a conversation with the reader. Too many editorials in the area of growth, for instance, are deadly because the writer doesn't understand the issue in the first place. So then they can't really use voice to get their point across. The authority is missing. But growth, in Florida at least, is the most important daily issue there is to readers because it affects too many things—traffic, schools, recreation and the environment. I also think editorials need to be far more hard-hitting than most are. Weak positions misuse an editorial page.

What happened as a result of your editorial series?

The Orange County Commission backed off its approval of opening up 10,000 sensitive rural acres to development. Developers in Osceola County moved their developments away from the eagles after it was clear the commissioners would force them to. And the city of Winter Springs agreed not to allow development in the sensitive Black Hammock, which also would have opened up the entire eastern Seminole to subdivisions.

Writers' Workshop

Talking Points

1. In Jane Healy's editorial "Losing Paradise," she opens with a three-word opinion followed by a three-word question. Then she documents her view using dates and facts. Discuss the effectiveness of her technique and approach.

2. Throughout her "Florida's Shame" editorial series, Healy uses language that identifies with the reader: "We feel duped. How about you?" . . . "Did you enjoy your commute this morning? Neither did we." . . . "Like happy endings? Then you might not want to read this." Talk about how this approach differs from the more prescriptive tone used in some editorials. How does her writing style affect the way you view the issues she raises?

3. Healy uses a variety of approaches, including blunt language and exhaustive reporting. Compare her editorials to those in your newspaper. How are they similar? How are they different? Which works better for you? Why?

Assignment Desk

1. Jane Healy tries to put herself in the reader's place when she writes her editorials. Think about an issue that matters to your community. What questions would you ask if this issue affected you personally?

2. Healy not only asks questions, she answers them. She does so based not only on what she thinks but what she learns firsthand. Identify sources and do some reporting to find answers to the questions you asked in number 1 directly above.

3. Study the structure of Healy's editorials. Identify her focus. Examine her arguments. Notice how concise she is. Now write an editorial using her voice. Compare yours with hers. How are they similar? How are they different?

The Boston Globe

Finalist

Lawrence Harmon
Editorial Writing

35. A Child Teaches

APRIL 18, 2006

No one who saw the prominent picture of 5-year-old Kai Leigh Harriott weeping on the stand last week while giving a victim impact statement will soon forget the image. Kai, paralyzed from her chest down, offered her forgiveness to Anthony Warren, the 29-year-old man who shot her on July 1, 2003, while he was menacing her neighbors with a .38-caliber handgun. In the Bronx, N.Y., there will never be an impact statement from David Pacheco Jr., age 2. He was killed on Easter Sunday while riding in his family's minivan in the Morris Heights section. The stray bullet that passed through the boy's chest was one of at least four fired at a group of men nearby.

Some of the young men who fire their weapons with abandon on city streets may be sociopaths, devoid of empathy. But that didn't appear to be the case with Warren, who apologized to Kai and her family after sparing them a trial by pleading guilty to multiple charges. Then, in a monumental act of compassion, Tonya David embraced the man who shot her daughter. Yet it is the photo of Kai seated in her wheelchair, her hair adorned with bright beads and her face wrenched in sorrow, that transfixed an entire city.

Certain photographs speak with unconstrained power to injustice. That was the case with the 1976 photo of an anti-busing protester at City Hall who tried to spear Theodore Landsmark with the pole of an American flag. What, asks the viewer, can be done to eradicate such mindlessness? The same question must be asked when looking at a photo of Kai Harriott, whose spine was severed because of some foolish dispute among adults.

Five-year-old Kai Leigh Harriott weeps on the stand while giving a victim impact statement. (Photograph courtesy of David Goldman/*The Boston Herald*)

The Menino administration and community groups, desperate to remove guns from the street, are designing a gun-buyback program. Hardened criminals aren't likely to disarm. But there is hope that sensible friends and relatives may intercept so-called community guns that circulate through some neighborhoods. City leaders might want to ask if Kai and her family would be amenable to placing her photo on the buyback announcements.

"What you done to me was wrong," Kai told Warren. "But I still forgive him." Those are the words of an amazing girl of 5, the age when most children are just starting to become sensitive to the feelings of others and beginning to understand the concept of right and wrong. Some people never reach this stage of development, and some of them are carrying guns.

Lessons Learned

BY LAWRENCE HARMON

"DBI" or "Dull But Important" is the shorthand used by editorial page editor Renee Loth for some of my offerings on diversifying municipal revenue, bond bills and auto insurance reform. But editorial writing is not a bloodless business in Boston.

The shooting of Kai Leigh Harriott changed the chemistry of the city. The picture of this little girl with the shattered spine froze *Globe* readers. Then they melted on reading Kai's words of forgiveness for the man who shot her. Physicians are trained to suppress their emotions. But editorial writers need to feel the burn if they hope to mobilize readers and push policymakers into making the expensive choices that keep communities livable.

I try to avoid writing commentary solely off the stories that appear in the morning paper. Often I'll re-report the work of good reporters. There's always something new to uncover or interpret. It's a little strange, therefore, that I was honored by ASNE merely for describing my feelings on seeing a pool photo. This editorial is based on raw emotion rooted in the fact that a year rarely passes here without a child being caught in a deadly crossfire. The editorial page doesn't let such crimes pass without comment. Sometimes the editorial focuses on gun control laws or police deployment practices. But I search often for some detail that gives the reader a sense of what was taken from this particular child. It can be something as simple as the upcoming reading list for the class that the slain child would have attended in the fall.

As a lifelong Bostonian, I try to make historical connections for readers that they might not have the time or background to explore. Comparing Kai's photo to a 30-year-old image that captured anti-busing protesters attacking an innocent man on City Hall Plaza allows me to make a universal point about injustice while grounding readers in their city.

In "A Child Teaches," I tried to focus primarily on the personal responsibility of the perpetrator. But policy concerns underlie all of our work. Our readers are politicians, police officials, bankers, business leaders, legislators and philanthropists. They can provide summer jobs, protect witnesses, stabilize communities through investments and write laws that limit the availability of handguns. Part of my job is to make sure that they are always moved by a child's tears.

Lawrence Harmon has been covering urban policies and Boston neighborhoods for the editorial page as an editorial writer since 1992. Before joining the Globe *in 1992, Harmon edited several community newspapers, including the* Jewish Advocate *and the* Citizen Group *papers. Harmon won the Benjamin Fine Award for outstanding education reporting in 1995. He is the co-author of "The Death Of an American Jewish Community: A Tragedy Of Good Intentions."*

Arkansas Democrat Gazette

Finalist

David Barham
Editorial Writing

36. Mighty White Of Ya

AUG. 11, 2006

The numbers are in. And they've been crunched. What you thought was true has been confirmed: You can't swing a dead *gato* in Arkansas without hitting somebody of Hispanic descent.

The U.S. Census released estimates on Arkansas' population last week, and our own Daniel Nasaw got knee-deep in the numbers. His story last Friday said that, since 2000, Arkansas' Hispanic population grew more than 12 times faster than the state's population as a whole. Evidently attracted by jobs—who isn't?—Arkansas' Hispanic population grew 51 percent to more than 130,000 people.

At this rate, Arkansas will have as many people who identify themselves as Hispanic as it does folks with a trace of Cherokee. Gosh, is there a space on the form for Cherokee? Half of Arkansas might be entitled to bragging rights. Or are the Cherokee just subsumed under American Indian/Alaska Native? The way Hispanic covers Cubans, Mexicans, and Castillians. Much like Filipinos and Chinese are considered Asians, along with Koreans and Vietnamese. Yep, the state of the statistical art in these matters can be far from perfect. Happily, it's all based on self-identification, and isn't that what counts in America, in this New World where we can all be what we want to be?

However vague the numbers, it's pretty clear why all these newcomers are putting up buildings and gutting chickens and so productively on in Arkansas. They're following the money. As do most people. And there's nothing like a booming economy to attract folks. Have you noticed the huge increase in tax revenues the state has been rolling up lately? Officials are projecting a $721 million surplus at the end of the fiscal year.

* * *

People who uproot themselves, leaving family and familiar surroundings behind, and move to a strange new land with a strange new language, tend to do it because they don't intend to stay poor. They, too, want their chance at the American Dream, and to attain it, they're willing to work the night shift at a poultry plant, or do whatever else the locals won't. Immigrants are not only a sign that the economy is growing; they add to that growth. By producing, buying and generally trying to move up in the world. In short, what we've got here is one more chapter in the history of American immigration—and American reaction to it.

Because now, of course, we're going to get all those letters to the editor asking the familiar question: Just what part of ILLEGAL don't you understand?

We understand the word just fine, thank you. That's why we'd like to see a sensible, humane, and rational legalization program put in place for all these folks as part of a comprehensive approach to fixing this country's immigration system.

Our question is: What part of ECONOMIC GROWTH don't you understand?

All of which brings us to the race for lieutenant governor in Arkansas. On the very day the Hispanic population story appeared on the front page, this story appeared on 1B:

Holt, Halter
wrangle
on services
for illegals

In a battle of dueling press releases, the Republican in the race, Jim Holt, rapped the Democrat, Bill Halter, for being insufficiently mean.

Jim Holt, state senator and demagogue-in-training wants to deny ILLEGAL ALIENS! state services that aren't required by the feds. Like what? Like prenatal programs, for starters.

What kind of far-seeing leader—what kind of person—would withhold money for *prenatal programs*? Lord have mercy. Has anybody told Jim Holt that once these little suckers are born they're going to be full-fledged, pure-Dee, native American citizens—even if their parents aren't? And if these kids are born sickly, they'll need more taxpayer-paid health care services. Quite aside from the Christian charity of it, prenatal care is one of the best investments a provident nation can make.

Jim Holt's website says he's pro-life. *Hmmm*. How can he be pro-life but anti-baby? Or is he just anti-healthy baby? Or is he just anti-healthy Hispanic baby?

Surely not. Jim Holt may be one of those strange ideologues all wrapped up in his own theoretical world (he does tend to ramble on) but he can't be that cruel. Does he think pretending to be will improve his chances of beating Bill Halter? (A recent poll by a TV station shows him trailing his opponent, 48 to 39.)

In our story, Senator Holt noted that the Department of Health and Human Services (note: *Health* and *Human* Services) had underestimated the cost of a prenatal program for ILLEGAL ALIENS!, and that Arkansas is only one of nine states to have such a program. He also noted that Arkansas ranks 49th in per-capita income.

Jim Holt didn't note that Arkansas is projecting a surplus in state coffers along the lines of $721 million. And that last year, the prenatal program cost the state all of $6.5 million. Can you think of a better expenditure, or one with a more satisfying return? As for us, we love to see healthy little babies gurgle and smile and grow stronger by the day. Every one of them adds to this state's, and this nation's, promise.

Is $6.5 million too much to ensure that these future citizens are going to be healthy future citizens? How much more do you think it'd cost to deny them prenatal care, then send them to doctors and emergency rooms and specialists for problems that could've been prevented with a little care—and love—before birth?

Let's not find out.

Lessons Learned

BY DAVID BARHAM

What can an aspiring editorial writer learn from this piece? Just look at the headline. That headline would've never made it past a committee. Some member of an editorial board would have put the kibosh on that headline right quick. Editorial writers are almost always better when they write without having to appease every member of a board.

The year 2006 in Arkansas was—as they say in the military—a Target Rich Environment. When you have somebody like Jim Holt running for statewide office, and he claims to be pro-life, but wants to deny prenatal programs to certain people, namely, The Other, editorial writing gets very easy.

One of the first rules of writing decent editorials is: Pick a topic you like, or dislike, or that just plain drives you nuts. Your fingers can hardly keep up with your thoughts when that happens. Arkansas has had no shortage of demagogues over the years, and still puts out its fair share. Arkansas' newspapers also have a history of taking on those demagogues. And, happily, it looks like we'll continue doing so.

Another helpful hint: Spend as much time on the headline as you would any particular sentence in your editorials. "Mighty White Of Ya" probably got the attention of a lot of people who would normally not read an editorial. I think that headline probably got more attention than something like "Jim Holt Is Wrong on the Subject of Prenatal Programs For Aliens." Headlines like that—which are too common on editorial pages in America—just beg somebody not to read the article.

We always try to make the editorials for Arkansas' only statewide newspaper SOUND like they were written for Arkansas' only statewide newspaper. In other words, we don't want our editorial to sound like the editorials in Kansas City, or Chicago, or New Orleans. We always want to find that Arkansas slant. (Every newspaper, in every city, ought to try for a hometown flavor.) Thus the part about Arkansas folks identifying with Cherokee Indians. Just a little something you wouldn't find elsewhere.

We also like to spice up our editorials with words and phrases you'd find in Arkansas, like "pure-Dee" and "swing a dead *gato*."

We always try to take our editorials to a Second Level, by which we mean finding a moral to the story. It'd be one thing to criticize a politician for being against prenatal programs. But if you can write a moral to the story, and do it while explaining consequences, and do all that in such a way that your readers enjoy your writing, then you've just hit on the Great Editorial Experience.

David Barham is an editorial writer at the Arkansas Democrat-Gazette. *He worked in Louisiana for 10 years as an editorial page editor, political reporter, cops reporter and general assignment reporter. His work appeared in "Best Newspaper Writing" in 2003 and 2005. He won the National Headliner Award for editorial writing in 1999.*

Part 6

Covering War At Home and Abroad

WINNER
Anne Hull
Batten Medal

Chronicling life comes naturally to Anne Hull. Her grandmother kept a journal. So did her mother. And Hull picked up the habit when she was about 12. She feels like she's been writing all her life.

"Diaries were big in my family. Not just the pink leather-bound versions that little girls receive but spiral notebooks and journals meant for recording the day's events," Hull wrote during an e-mail interview for this book.

She kept her mother's and grandmother's journals. When she reads them, she sees how these two women "captured and defined their surroundings as well as any newspaper reporter." Hull shows that same skill in her award-winning writing.

Hull worked for 15 years at the *St. Petersburg Times,* where she was the paper's national correspondent from 1995 to 2000.

"I learned journalism by being thrown into the whirring blades of a newsroom," Hull wrote when asked how she became a reporter at the *Times.*

When she joined the *Times,* after high school, she started out in a variety of jobs, including "copy kid, city desk clerk, telephone-answerer and obit-taker." She described the *Times* then as "home to many of the best king-dog reporters who were pushing the boundaries of news feature writing. These reporters were driven by news, tension, social injustice and life's odd turns.

"They were restless and hungry and self-doubting, always mumbling and plagued by, 'How do I best capture the story in a way that serves the subject and not me? How do I harness the reporting, shape the material and most importantly, stay out of the way?' They reported exhaustively and obsessed on the material. This is the way they did it, and the way many of us at the *St. Pete Times* learned to do [it]," she noted.

Hull moved to *The Washington Post* in 2000, where she is an enterprise reporter on the national staff. At the *Post* she continues to push boundaries and bring issues and people to life. She says she is able to do this because of what her editor, David Maraniss, teaches by example: "Be rigorous, do your homework and that will give you latitude to fly."

"Some of it comes down to a way of seeing life—how do you pay attention to life?—and the impressions you have from those observations," she wrote. "And yet those observations are almost always gained from exhaustive reporting and time in the field."

For years, Hull's work has won recognition for her as a Pulitzer Prize finalist. And the American Society of Newspaper Editors has twice awarded her distinguished writing prizes.

The winning entries that this year garnered the Batten Medal reflect the evolution and expansion of the journal-writing skills Hull developed in those spiral notebooks so many years ago. She honors her mother and grandmother in her meticulous, detailed and sensitive depiction of lives lived, especially in relation to the Iraq War and its impact on the home front.

In "When Mom Is Over There," Hull reports the personal journey that she, her brother and her brother's children experienced when she spent time with them while "Mom" served in Iraq. Her involvement in the story, and first-person account, offers nuances and context that deepen and enrich the reading experience. Her eye for detail provides the factual framework from which to assess what happens, and why.

Hull said she stays in journalism "because people need to know things."

What does she like the most about her work?

"The best part of the job is still the internal and often ghastly death match of writing a story," she wrote. "It's a competition on many levels—against yourself, against the claims of your subject, against your knowledge of the material, against another newspaper or against a government or corporate institution that's trying to thwart you.

"The stakes always feel high," she added. "Every morning, coffee in hand, you step off an elevator into a crammed hell-pod of cubicles and tilting piles of documents, and in that terrible fluorescence, you still feel as if you might be able to make something right."

—Christopher Scanlan, Senior Faculty in Reporting, Writing and Editing, and Journalism Adviser to NewsU (www.newsu.org), The Poynter Institute

The Batten Medal honors reporter, editor and newspaper executive James K. Batten and is intended to celebrate the journalistic values for which he stood: compassion, courage, humanity and a deep concern for the underdog.

37. When Mom Is Over There

JAN. 8, 2006

By Anne Hull

I am driving a hulking Expedition with a yellow ribbon on the bumper that says "Support Our Troops." In the grocery store parking lot, a man nods at me. I'm walking to the shopping carts when it hits me. He thinks I'm a kindred spirit in a country that is losing its nerve. I should turn back and tell him that the truck isn't mine, to clear up his misconception, but I don't.

For one week I find myself pulled into the war effort. I am in Florida to help my brother juggle single parenthood while his wife is serving in Iraq. Jim lives in a cul-de-sac community outside Tampa where the garage doors flip up every night at 6 and swallow incoming cars. His girls are 10 and 9. We spend the week eating Cocoa Pebbles and watching "The Incredibles." We hold dance parties in a bedroom where the stuffed animals are giving way to dreamy teen idol posters. We go to the mall and to the dentist. One night while I make dinner, the girls ride bikes outside in the waning winter dusk. It is a relief to be away from Washington, where politicians in marble hallways proclaim righteousness though they have never carried a canteen. Here in this linoleum kitchen, there is just a crayon calendar on the refrigerator marking the days until Mama comes home.

The yellow ribbon on the truck is the most outward sign of where this family stands on the war. And, of course, the quiet absence of Master Sgt. Angela Hull from the house.

In a breathless choreography of necessity, my brother cooks, cleans, folds mountains of laundry, carpools, grocery-shops, works full time as a technical writer for a defense contractor and tries to distract his daughters with amusing weekend activities like Celebration Station. He is trying to distract himself as much as the girls. "Worrying is not productive," he says. Normally, I would tease him about such a statement. I would make a case for worry and why it's only human. But I don't dare now. I am too in awe of his composure. One morning I go into his bedroom closet to get the laundry and I'm greeted by the scent of Angela's perfume, still on her clothes. I touch her blouses. How does he do it?

Angela is chief controller of the air-traffic control tower at Kirkuk Regional Air Base in northern Iraq. She did not graduate from the Air Force Academy or come from a long line of military heroes. Angela was

22 and working at the Stouffer's frozen-food factory in her home town of Gaffney, S.C., in 1987 when she rebelled against the smallness of her life and joined the Air Force. She advanced the slow, hard way, from refueling aircraft at 30,000 feet to learning air-traffic control to commanding towers. In Kirkuk, she supervises 10 controllers in the base tower while serving as first sergeant to a squadron of 48.

Angela never uses the macho language of war or the slogans favored by those who took us there. She works 16 hours a day, six days a week and sleeps in a pod. In a photo she sent home, I can see her office and a chalkboard where someone in her unit has written, "Sgt. Hull, take a day off!" She earns $54,000 a year.

I don't know where Angela stands on the war because we never talk about it. I remember once when Jim, Angela and the girls came to visit me in Washington not long after the United States invaded Iraq. It was a cold spring weekend, wet and gray, but we were excited tourists. We walked down to the White House to take pictures. Crossing through Lafayette Square, we came upon an antiwar protest. There were people shouting and jabbing signs in the air, and one of the sticks hit my niece, frightening her. I was furious at the protester, at the carelessness of his selfish passion. My brother, who is 6 feet 6 inches tall, wanted to slug the guy. Angela—calm and strong Angela—simply rounded us up and moved us along.

* * *

Jim says it's good to keep a routine. The week of my visit, the holiday lights blink in the darkened Florida balm. Palm fronds brush against the plastic snowmen and wise men propped up in the cool night grass. At the kitchen table, my nieces dream up Christmas lists to e-mail to their mother, as if she will trudge out into the sands of Iraq and find a Wal-Mart.

Jourdan is 10 and long-legged. My brother seems not to notice that she is wearing cocktail outfits to school. Jourdan is spending hours in front of the mirror, hypnotized by her own reflection as Hilary Duff and Kelly Clarkson channel messages to her at ear-shattering decibels.

In the bedroom next door, childhood still reigns supreme. Chrislyn is barely 9 and a devout fan of SpongeBob and teddy bears that she names Zack and Champ. Chrislyn is as earnest and innocent as Jourdan is sophisticated and enterprising.

When Angela received her orders for Iraq last spring, my brother boiled down the situation this way: "There are bad people over there trying to hurt Americans and Iraqis," he said. "Mommy has special gear that keeps her safe." The girls were accustomed to Angela leaving for short stints but they

Master Sgt. Angela Hull maintains a phantom presence over her house. Her husband, Jim, tends to their girls, Jourdan, 10, left, and Chrislyn, 9. (Family photos; illustration courtesy of Patterson Clark/*The Washington Post*)

knew this was different. In the way that children often seize on a grain of sand, they fixated on Angela's living quarters. "Will you sleep in a hard tent?" Chrislyn asked, her blue eyes clouded by worry. Angela promised that she would be sleeping in a very hard tent. On the morning of her departure, the girls went to school and Angela went to Iraq.

Routines. We wake at 6 each morning, eat our breakfast and get ready for school. Usually my brother drops the kids on his way to work but now I do it, watching the girls' colorful backpacks disappear in the sea of others. I ride around town in the truck with the yellow ribbon on the bumper. Jim says to check out the YMCA, a sprawling new facility for the sprawling new communities devouring the pastures. A woman on a stair climber is reading a book titled "What Would Jesus Eat?" We discuss Biblical dining habits and then I tell her that I'm from Washington. "State or D.C.?" she asks. A look of pity crosses her face. Quickly, I volunteer that I'm visiting my brother, whose wife is in Iraq. This wins her back.

All week, strange moments of charade occur. A neighbor across the street is waxing his car when he sees me coming out of the house. "Welcome home," he says, waving his cloth in the air. He has mistaken me for Angela. I'm just the sister, I say. I wonder if Angela's homecoming will be like this—a friendly neighbor welcoming her back as if she's been away at a conference.

Her absence is banal and profound. She maintains a phantom presence over her motherless house. E-mails and digital photos zip back and forth. In one of the photos, Angela notices a lump on Jourdan's forehead. She and my brother discuss the lump, and it's decided that Jourdan needs to see a pediatrician.

On the morning of the appointment, my brother gulps down cereal while CNN reports that 10 Marines were killed outside Fallujah, blown up by a homemade explosive. Jim curses and says the insurgents are picking away at us with bombs set off with 25-cent oven timers. He lets the dog out. Pop-Tarts are toasting in the toaster. The first Hilary Duff song of the day is playing in a bedroom. I look at the TV, relieved not to hear the word Kirkuk.

Of all the postings Angela could have received, Kirkuk was among the least dangerous, but lately things have gotten testier. ("Sportier," as Angela says.) The 101st Airborne Assault Division arrived at the base in October and has been deftly thwarting rocket attacks ever since. For safety reasons, Angela has yet to venture off base. Explosions rumble the furniture in her office. I wonder what worries her most today—the explosions or a small, shiny lump on the forehead of her 10-year-old.

I take Jourdan to the pediatrician's office. She sits on crinkly white paper in an exam room. A nurse practitioner named Miss Yvonne looks at the lump. Using a rubber hammer, she checks Jourdan's reflexes and then turns on a penlight and tells Jourdan to follow the beam with her eyes. "Tell me about these headaches you've been having," Miss Yvonne says.

"I think they're because I don't drink enough water, and I am growing at a really fast rate," Jourdan answers. Miss Yvonne finishes her exam. She doesn't think there is anything to worry about. The minute I'm outside the office, I call my brother at work, and I can hear him typing an e-mail to Angela as we speak.

It's mid-morning and we are late for school. We decide to stop at a convenience store on U.S. 301. We are not sticking to the routine. We go inside and peruse glossy teen magazines and the selection of snack cakes. The packaging is in Spanish because of all the Mexicans and Guatemalans who pick strawberries and tomatoes in the fields nearby. I share the sociology lesson with my niece. "Oh," she replies, feigning interest. She picks up a double-pack of coconut creme-filled snowballs. Next, a big Coke, her eyes wandering to meet mine as she reaches inside the cooler. Her mom's at war. What the hell.

School is an L-shaped set of flat buildings shaded by oaks. The office is in front. Jourdan and I stand there in the bright fluorescence with our sugar-crusted mouths. "See you at 3:30," I say.

* * *

My brother is three years younger than me. He watches NASCAR and trades barbecue tips with someone on the Internet named Jurassic Pork. He washes the truck and cuts the grass on Saturday afternoons. Order is very important, which is funny, because as a boy he was gangly and calamitous, with an uncombed thicket of blond hair. Once he slipped from a boardwalk into a swamp full of alligators. Another time, he lit the gas stove and, whoosh, he had two charred haystacks for eyebrows.

We grew up in rural central Florida, when flocks of white birds would fill the sky as they left the backs of cattle that stood in soggy pastures. Our father worked in citrus. He couldn't keep a job. After our mother decided to leave with us, I remember being so broke that we ate meat only once a week—Sunday—but what Jim remembers is how delicious Sunday dinners were, and that would be the difference between us our entire lives.

At 19, he joined the Air Force and saw the world, and now he is back beneath the dripping Spanish moss that shrouded our childhoods. His house is in a subdivision near the Alafia River in eastern Hillsborough

County. The river is tannic and winding and beautiful but surrounded by subdivisions that keep hatching and expanding, beige on beige. One day I'm returning home with the girls and I pull into what I believe is our driveway. My nieces inform me that their house is in fact three doors down. "Do these houses all look alike?" I ask.

"Our light is different," my younger niece says.

My brother loves the stability and sameness of these communities, a clue that he has not forgotten everything from our childhood. In Oklahoma they lived on Altus Air Force Base in a windswept brick ranch house with brown carpet, and every night an anemic bugle would sound taps over loudspeakers. During a bad plains drought, my brother torched his and a neighbor's lawns during a barbecue mishap. Three Halloweens ago in Virginia, in a neighborhood of Special Forces, Navy and Air Force members, I remember all the children flying around the cul-de-sac in vampire and Shrek costumes as their dads prepared for the invasion of Iraq. The night was starry and perfect, for these children.

Now, Angela is there. Patience, President Bush says on the news, patience. Stay the course. His twin daughters are about the same age that Angela was when she was working at the Stouffer's frozen-food factory and decided to enlist because good jobs were scarce in Gaffney, S.C. Now, Angela is high in a tower over the northern desert of Iraq, watching the red trails of rockets flare off in the distance. Patience, Angela, patience.

It is nearly bedtime. My brother turns off the TV. The sliding glass door is open and he pulls it closed, the small click of a lock echoing between us. One last time for the night, he goes to the computer to see if there is any news from Angela.

* * *

"Hey, baby," my brother shouts into the phone on my last Saturday afternoon. Knowing it's their mother, the girls come running.

"Mama," Chrislyn says, "I got a new bear."

Jourdan shares with her mother a dark tale from "Chicken Soup for the Preteen Soul." It has come to Angela's attention, through more digital photos, that Jourdan is wearing blue eye shadow to school, and a mother-daughter conversation follows.

My brother gets back on the line, and the kids start arguing. He cups his hand over the phone and yells at them sharply, drawing a rebuke from Angela.

"Dammit, Ang," Jim says, "I'm here with them 24-7 and you're in the peace and quiet."

We have to laugh at that one.

We decide to take a walk on the nature trail around the subdivision. Frogs grunt from the sludge of the creek, like kettledrums sounding off from the depths of the soupy algae. Jim tells the girls to stay on the paved trail. I whisper to him, "When we were kids, we played hopscotch over rattlesnake nests."

The sky is obscured by palms and oaks; it feels as if we are alone in Florida's last forest, until we hear the rush of the nearby interstate, cleverly hidden by landscaping. The girls race ahead. I have told them to bring their swimming suits. The subdivision has a pool, and though it is unheated, the gate is unlocked. We change into our suits. No one is saying the obvious, that the water is cold and that Angela would never allow this. But Angela is not here. We leap into the pool, cannonballs and jackknives. With chattering teeth, we make a pact never to tell Angela we went swimming in December.

We are warm and dry by the time we eat dinner. The girls sit at the kitchen table to write letters to their mother. Chrislyn picks up a pencil and stares out the window. A dreamer and sensitive soul, like her father when he was a boy. She looks down at her blank paper and begins. *Dear Mom: If you read this carefully, you might actually hear my voice.*

Since the war began I have read the U.S. casualty lists published in newspapers. When the photos of the dead are published in newspapers, I study the faces that are laid out like yearbook photos filling the pages of an endless year. Every picture has its own story but no future. The brim of an olive cap shields the impish eyes of a young Marine, now gone. Why do the names of their home towns seem so poetic? Mineral Bluff, Ga. Spooner, Wis. Angelina, Tex. Mechanicsville, Iowa. Zanesville, Ohio. Evening Shade, Ark. Valentine, Neb. When I see these photos, I imagine the knock on the door.

My brother never reads these lists. He never looks at the photos. Seeking out memorials is for those of us who live around the edges. Instead, Jim stands over his girls as they say their bedtime prayers, the same singsong prayers they have repeated since they could talk, about grandmas, papas, Todd their cat and baby Jesus, with one new addendum to their pajama pleadings. "Please keep Mama safe."

38. Call to Duty

APRIL 9, 2006

By Anne Hull

MERIDIAN, MISS.—Blake Johnson is almost 18. Tan and muscular, he plays third base for the Clarkdale High School Bulldogs. He is a B student who says "Yes, sir" when his coach corrects his batting stance. Wisps of brown hair fall above his green eyes, and a rope choker is clasped around his neck. He lives in a mobile home with his mother and younger brother on Old Highway 80 on a piece of land that never quite dries.

On the afternoon before the opening of baseball season, a balloon floats inside the cab of his truck, a gift from one of the Diamond Girls at school, with a note that says, "Go Big Senior!" But any poetry about the waning days of youthful abandon feels false in this part of central Mississippi, where the bridge to Iraq is a short one.

"Welcome home, 155th!" a road sign announces, heralding the return of Mississippi Army National Guard units recently back from Iraq. At the country mini-mart where Johnson stops for candy bars and gas, a handmade memorial honors a local 19-year-old Marine killed in Iraq. So far, 36 Mississippians have died in Iraq—15 of them members of Army National Guard units. From these red clay hills, it sometimes feels as if joining the military is less a choice than the inevitable march of life.

Now it's Johnson's moment to enlist, and the pull is hard.

Toby Keith's "American Soldier" rocks the inside of his pickup. The Marine Corps recruiter tells him he's a born leader and that his athletic skills would make him an ideal Marine. He imagines himself in uniform, and wonders what it would be like, "just actually being a part of something you can feel proud of."

And yet Johnson—a decent shot with a hunting rifle, with a Bible on his nightstand—is resisting what feels like his fate. He lives within a mile of two young men killed in Iraq, and the deadly geography is giving him pause. As he says, with honest yearning:

"I want a family and kids and stuff."

A Patriotic Place
Short on Money, Long on Pride

When President Bush calls for sacrifice in Iraq, this is a place that listens. Here, where the gnats swarm and the magnolias blossom, and where locals pin their hopes on a Kia Motors Corp. assembly plant that would bring 2,500 jobs to the sagging economy, only to have it go to another state instead.

Military recruiters talk of Mississippi being a special place, a patriotic place and the envy of other states. The recruiting battalion commander for the Mississippi Army National Guard says his state's force is as large as the one in Georgia, which has triple the population. Patriotism aside, bleak demographics make the state a ready labor pool. More than 30 percent of high school students fail to graduate. The median household income—$32,397—ranks lowest in the nation. When the Cooper tire plant in Tupelo cuts employee hours, the Mississippi Army National Guard experiences a bump in enlistees.

A few weeks ago, some mail came for Blake Johnson. A cold front had blown through the working-class community of Meehan Junction, outside Meridian, and the daffodils of early spring shivered in the wind. Sticking out of the mailbox across the road from Johnson's trailer were two recruiting letters, one from the Army and the other from the National Guard—the Guard offering a $10,000 signing bonus. All of Johnson's senior year, the local recruiters have come after him; the national mailers were the latest enticements.

As his mother said, as she placed them on the counter, "That's a whole lot of money when you are in the 12th grade."

Square-chinned and tranquil, with a deep Dixie drawl, Johnson understands the vague isolation of his rural existence. There is one mall in Meridian, "and it don't even have a Gap," he says. He watches "Viva La Bam" on MTV while a train whistle blows in the distance. On Friday nights, he and his friends hang out at the Sonic drive-in until the waitresses chase them off, and when there is really nothing to do, they meet at the boat ramp where they stand around a 55-gallon drum and burn trash.

"Pretty redneck, huh?" he says, smiling.

The men in his family operate cranes, install cable and lay telephone lines. His father was mostly absent from his childhood. His mother held the family together, going back to college for her two-year degree. She now works as an IT specialist at Peavey Electronics. They live in a mobile home on two acres of cleared land that cost $3,000. A house would be nice, but Diane Johnson is afraid more manufacturing work will shift to China, leaving her with a mortgage payment and no job.

Such fragility makes the military the best job going, but there are also cultural forces. Johnson jokes about being a hick, but the powerful realities in his life are hunting, church, Confederate soldier memorials and American flags. His public school has brightly painted "Prayer Request"

One of the war casualties from the area was Pfc. Christopher D. Mabry, 19, who died five weeks after being sent to Iraq in 2004. (Photograph courtesy of Andrea Bruce/*The Washington Post*)

boxes in the hallways. Students held a Godapalooza on campus this year, and 170 souls stepped forward to be saved. Unlike some schools around the country, Clarkdale warmly welcomes military recruiters.

"Not to feed a stereotype of the South, but the people here believe in God and country," says Roy McNeill, the high school principal. "For the most part, they believe the president has their best interest in mind. These are not high-and-mighty government thinkers; they are young men and women who just want to help their country."

For such notions, they pay a price. The football field at Clarkdale is named after a 2003 graduate who joined the Marines and was killed in Iraq. This is the same field where Blake Johnson played quarterback this year, and the same field where he suffered a knee injury that hurt his chances for a college scholarship, which is what led him to meet with the military recruiters.

"If you don't have a college degree, you have to work on the railroad or [the oil rigs] offshore," Johnson says. "Or get a cashier job that don't pay nothin'. Around here, people are like, 'Why don't you go to the military?'"

And yet the weeks and months of his senior year roll by and he does not sign the paperwork to enlist. One night as baseball season gets underway, he goes to the mall and runs into a Clarkdale graduate wearing a red

Marine Corps T-shirt. Wiry and taciturn, Matthew Addy pulls up his sleeve to show off his tattoo.

"I'm still studying up on Navy SEAL karate," he tells Johnson, standing outside the food court. "In a bar, I can't even throw the first punch. Being with the martial arts and being a Marine, I'll get charged with attempted murder."

Johnson nods. "You're a dadgum deadly weapon," he says.

Addy rides him for not committing to the Marines, and he delivers a message from some of the recruiters: "They told me to tell you they don't like you for [wimping] out."

Preparing to Ship Out
'There Is Danger in Anything You Do'

The redbuds are starting to flare along the roadsides. Spring is here, and graduation is not far behind. Young Marine recruits are receiving their ship dates for basic training at Parris Island. One warm Saturday afternoon, 10 young men gather for an orientation at a recruiter's house in Meridian. The house is in a new subdivision and is palatial by the standards of many in Mississippi. Gunnery Sgt. Mark Ramos likes to bring recruits here to show them what they can have if they become Marines.

No one gathered in his living room mentions Iraq, but privately Ramos says that getting deployed there is no more perilous than normal, everyday life. "There was a young man at the mall here—he got injured and killed on a hatrack," he says, of a recent freak accident at a hat store. "There is danger in anything you do. War is all around us. We will not send a Marine into harm's way unless they are properly trained."

The recruits—all white except for a Native American—gather in Ramos's back yard. Several parents have tagged along. They stand at the side, watching their sons compete in the grass with ropes and obstacles. The boys pant and sweat as the recruiters shout encouragement. One drill is called dizzy-izzy. Recruits race to a baseball bat lying 20 yards away. They stand it upright, place their foreheads down on the butt of the bat and spin 15 rotations. Then they are supposed to sprint back to the finish line, but most are so disoriented they stumble in slow motion toward a stand of pine trees or the side of the house.

One of the fathers watching is John Rue. His son is slender and pale, with scruffy chin hair and shiny blue warm-up pants. "Come on, boy, pick it up, let's go!" he yells, clapping his hands.

Rue's own dream of joining the Marines was thwarted by his mother when he was 18, and now his son is fulfilling the dream. Rue says he has

"Around here, people are like, 'Why don't you go to the military?'" said Blake Johnson, who is approaching his 18th birthday. (Photograph courtesy of Andrea Bruce/*The Washington Post*)

tried to teach his son America's true purpose in Iraq. "We need to show honor and commitment," he says, wearing a Marine Corps T-shirt. "You always love these people. You are not ever there to destroy them. We are trying to make a point: There's a better way." Rue's son wants to be a mechanic in the Marines, but Rue has tried to explain the wider possibilities. "You are gonna have to do some killing on your own," he told his son.

After the sit-up contest, the recruits finish with their drills. They pile barbecue, rice and watermelon on paper plates, and eagerly talk about boot camp.

"I ship July 2nd," one says. "When do you ship?"

"The 10th of July."

Absent from the group is Blake Johnson, an absence that pains one of the recruiters.

"Now, that's a Marine," says Staff Sgt. Jay Wyatt, describing the first time he met Johnson. "Just how he walked into the office. He has the basic leadership qualities we are looking for. He's a quarterback, pitcher and third baseman. These are leadership positions. He is a very determined individual. His scores would qualify him for any job he wants."

Wyatt watches the other recruits chow. "It gets me personally," he says. "There's really not a whole lot of prosperous opportunities around here. We do offer opportunities."

A Mother's Struggle
Pondering Other Options

There is no other option in Johnson's life that offers such a full package. All he has to do is sign the papers and the next five years are paved with a job, housing, education, medical care, paid vacations, physical supremacy and honor.

His mother supports the war and has voted for George W. Bush twice. "Terrorism is scary," Diane Johnson says. "We need to protect what we have." But now that her son is almost 18 and the president is calling for more sacrifice, she's having second thoughts.

"I'm not sure I'm willing to give up my son," she says.

This surprises Blake. He listens to her talk one evening. They are at a Mexican restaurant after baseball practice, and he is wolfing down quesadillas and guzzling sweet tea as his mother explains her reversal. She makes a case for another option besides the Marines. They could trade in his gas-guzzling truck and buy a smaller car so he could commute to classes at Meridian Community College, and he could work part time.

Unsettled by her own feelings, she calls a friend later that night to talk. She finds out the woman's son has signed with the National Guard. "I feel guilty, not wanting Blake to serve," she says. "I want freedom, but I'm not willing to do anything for it. I'm sorry if that's two-faced."

A few days later, she is in her living room folding laundry. A light rain falls on the roof. Her son is getting his baseball uniform ready. "Mama, did you dry my pants?" he shouts.

"He's a good kid," Diane says, of her middle son, the high achiever who somehow transcends his overheated trailer with a cologne called Fierce and button-down shirts that suggest he is a legacy from Ole Miss, and not these hills that are covered in green and loss.

"Two houses down from where we live there's Glenn Pugh," Diane says. "His son got the Silver Star on Saturday. Another mile down the road is a young man who died in Iraq, Chris Mabry. I used to give him a ride home from football practice. I don't want a flag. I don't want a star. I want my child."

She is cautious making such a declaration in public. One afternoon she's at a family gathering at her sister's place. Her son is out in the yard tossing a football. Some of the other boys are buttoning on camouflage to hunt turkey. Several of the women are in the kitchen talking. Johnson expresses relief that Blake is leaning toward community college instead of joining the Marines while the country is at war.

One mother says how good she'd feel if her son enlisted.

"Wouldn't you be upset?" Johnson asks.

"I would be upset," says Wendy Stephens. "But I would just be so proud. Bo has such a big love for America."

Johnson is quiet. What she wants to say is, "Bo is only 10 years old. Your attitude might change when he gets a little closer to joining time." But she says nothing.

One Family's Loss
A Marine Sent to the Front Line

Sweet gums and pine trees lead the way to the Mabry place. Everyone knows it by the Marine Corps flag flying in front. Inside the mobile home is Frances Mabry and the china cabinet she carefully pulls open.

"This is the global war on terrorism medal," she says. "This is his good conduct medal. And, of course, his Purple Heart. Here is the Silver Star. He was shot four times.

"This is him on prom night and graduation night. The prom was at the Howard Johnson in Meridian. This is another picture." She pauses. She stares at the six-foot blond with freckles scattered across his nose. "He always had a clear, direct way of looking at you," Mabry says. "If you would have known him. He was so young. So well-thought-of. He loved life. He took to life."

The china cabinet is what's left of Christopher Mabry, the grandson that Frances Mabry raised since he was a boy. His bedroom is down the hall, now darkened. She pulls out his letters from Iraq. In one, he asks if she could please send Pop-Tarts, trail mix and razors.

> *I appreciate everything ya'll have done for me. I wish I was still at home, too, or at least in the states. I hate this place with a passion. You worry about getting blowed up or stabbed or shot in the back.*

After her grandson was killed, faraway postmarks and fancier stationery kept arriving in her mailbox in the small Mississippi town of Chunky. There is the official Marine Corps letter from a Capt. C.J. Bronzi.

> *It is with the deepest regret and my most heartfelt sympathy that I write this letter to you.*

And a letter from the White House, signed by President Bush. In her trove of memorabilia, Mabry also has a photo of herself with the president last year when he visited the Nissan plant. She holds the picture with particular pride. "He said, 'God bless your family, this country owes you,'" Mabry recalls. "When he learned that Chris's cousin was over there, too, big tears welled up in his eyes."

Chris Mabry knew he wanted to be a Marine from the time he was a junior at Clarkdale. In preparation for boot camp, he'd run up and down the highway wearing headphones. He'd run on the blistering track at school while the maintenance man cut the grass in the dead of summer. Seeing him out there made everyone feel proud because they knew he was determined to vault over the circumstances of his life and become a Marine. The only anger that Frances Mabry holds is toward the Marine recruiter who she says stood in her living room and said it was unlikely that Chris would be sent to Iraq. Of course, six months after boot camp he was in Iraq, and five weeks later he was dead at 19.

"The snipers set up an ambush," Mabry explains. "The Marine captain said they were outnumbered. Where they were, they really didn't have a chance. An ambush was set up. Chris was shot through the left thigh. His left arm was literally blown off, according to the autopsy report. He was shot through the right abdomen. The bullet that killed him went through the sixth and seventh rib, through the liver, the lung and apex of the heart. He survived for six hours."

She is reading from the autopsy report. A retired nurse, she wanted to know the details. Now she closes her china cabinet.

"The only way to preserve our freedom is to fight for it," she says. Her voice has a quiet dignity but also the weariness that comes with grief. "I feel like our president has done the best he could. I can't fault him because of Chris's death. Every bit of improvement we can make in their lives over there, try to reason with them to see that there's a better way, well, I'm for it."

A Different Path
Decision Comes Gradually

Blake Johnson is standing on the foul line with the Clarkdale Bulldogs in the late afternoon light. The bleachers are full, and hamburgers are grilling. When Faith Hill's voice begins singing the national anthem, hats are removed and hands are placed over hearts. Diane Johnson arrives by the third inning, after work. The Bulldogs lose but hold their own against a formidable team Blake Johnson describes as "rich preps who drive way nicer trucks than ours."

After the game, Johnson throws his bats into his truck, and guns into town with his friend Tanner Street, the right fielder. Street announces that he's signing with the Army Reserve.

"I'm going," Street says. "Nothin's gonna change my mind."

"That girlie might," Johnson says, of Street's longtime steady girlfriend.

"Not even that girl will change my mind," Street answers. His father, a retired sheriff's deputy, has just left Mississippi to take a better-paying job in Iraq training police officers. Street fumbles through a stack of CDs. The interstate lights bounce off his boyish face and brown bangs. "If I have to go over there and fight, that's fine with me. Hey, Blake, you got any George Strait? That song, 'Cross My Heart,' man, that's gonna be my wedding song."

Johnson listens to his friend, only 17 and already planning his wedding and his war. Johnson won't be enlisting. The decision doesn't come in a lightening-bolt moment. It occurs gradually, seeping in. While the death of Chris Mabry inspired some boys at his school to enlist, it sent Johnson's mind in another direction, focusing him less on pageantry or revenge and more on what happened that day in Anbar province.

"He was on watch," Johnson says, of Mabry. "There was a building. You know how the Alamo looks? Some stone-lookin' little house? He got shot through the stomach. I guess some Iraqi dude did it. They were taking him back to the hospital when he died."

Johnson's tone is reverent. His own path will be different. Instead of boot camp after graduation, he'll try to find a job—"anything I reckon"—and start community college in the fall.

39. The Army Vs. Spec. Richmond

SEPT. 24, 2006

By Anne Hull

GONZALES, LA.—Eddie Richmond's son got back from the war in June. He wanted nothing in the way of a homecoming, no yellow ribbons tied around trees, none of the piles of boiled crawfish that sent him off.

While other sons came home from Iraq with duffel bags that spilled sand from the desert, 22-year-old Edward Richmond Jr. carried release papers from an Army jail.

Edward had been among the first soldiers to be sent to prison for killing a civilian in the Iraq war, and among the first to walk out of prison. What waited for him was a parole officer in heat-struck Louisiana.

Ascension Parish was the same—green and mossy lowlands afloat with Whataburgers, Starcuts, daiquiri drive-throughs and gas stations that sell hot shrimp by the pound—but Edward was different.

He didn't like anyone standing too close. He slept on the floor instead of the bed. When he went through a box the Army had sent home, he found his uniform, infantry badges and ribbons. The vestments of a soldier's life. Edward put all of it in the trash.

His release coincided with a wave of investigations into U.S. soldiers killing civilians in Iraq. After an incident at Haditha, more than a dozen Marines are being questioned in the deaths of as many as two dozen civilians. Some blamed the fog of war or the stress of combat. Others said they only did what they were trained to do.

"War is not a pretty thing," Edward's father often said. "Things *happen* in a war zone."

The Army had trained his son to kill. Then Edward went to Iraq, and the Army decided he had killed someone the wrong way.

For two years now, his father has asked the Army why his son was prosecuted.

Even after Edward's release from prison, the 52-year-old Richmond's war rages on. He owns an air conditioning and heating business, and as he changed out compressors in the mosquito-rife back yards around Baton Rouge, sweating and heaving, Iraq was with him. He cited page numbers and footnotes from his son's case, like a record needle dropping down mid-song: "In Captain Morgan's statement on the 28th . . ."

Edward was a casualty of something, and so was his father.

In Gonzales, a large American flag hangs outside the Richmond house on two shaded acres. If the family feels any shame or anger, they keep it to themselves.

Eddie Richmond strolled into a coffee shop one afternoon and proudly told the owner, "Edward's home, he's healthy as a mule, he's just getting settled."

But many in Gonzales know about the father's crusade against the Army. It is an awkward fight for someone who drives a truck with a decal that says, "Home of the Free, Because of the Brave." Eddie gets his news from Fox and his accent from the rural hills of north Louisiana. His own father was a decorated Marine disabled in the Korean War. He served three years in the Air Force.

What fueled his frustration was a cache of confidential Army documents he had gotten his hands on that described how another soldier in Edward's brigade with the 1st Battalion, 27th Infantry Regiment, had shot and killed unarmed civilians. But Edward was the one who went to prison.

There seemed little left to fight for. Edward had served his time, been dishonorably discharged, lost his right to vote or carry a firearm, and couldn't leave the state without permission from his parole officer.

The general who commanded the 1st Infantry Division in Iraq and convened Edward's court-martial, retired Maj. Gen. John Batiste, said he has faith in the military justice system. "If I were Dad, I would be focused on Donald Rumsfeld and his leadership, which took our great military to war without a strategy, with insufficient troops on the ground, which allowed chaos to rein in early 2004," Batiste said.

So Iraq was a mess and Edward was folded into the mess. This was unacceptable to Eddie Richmond.

Father and son shared the same name, but it was the elder Richmond who went by "Eddie" and his son the more formal "Edward." The son was always the guarded one in life, and he came home from prison burning with mistrust. At Fort Sill, Edward spent much of his time in a segregated cell for discipline violations. "You gotta understand, he didn't believe he belonged there," said Charles W. Gittins, a civilian lawyer handling his appeal.

It is impossible to know whether Edward wanted his name cleared as much as his father. He refused to be interviewed for this story.

His second week back, Edward got a job at a foundry outside Gonzales. He woke at 4 each morning and spent the next 10 hours near a furnace so hot that his boots smoked. One day his boss called him "jarhead." People knew his story.

While Louisiana sweltered and beer signs blinked in the windows of the bars where the Blind River Outlaws played "brain-busting, spine-tingling Southern metal," all Edward did was work.

His schoolteachers had always imagined that the exceptionally bright boy would be a mathematician or an engineer. His parents liked to say he joined the Army after 9/11, but Edward was less a twin towers avenger than an 18-year-old who needed a fresh start.

As a boy, he preferred playing computer games to hunting squirrels with his dad. He took medication for attention deficit hyperactivity disorder. He competed on the math team and was described as a "genius" by two former teachers.

But Edward refused to follow instructions if he thought they were pointless. His father made many trips to meet with administrators at East Ascension High School, including assistant principal Gwynne Pecue, who found him overprotective but struggling to understand his son. At the start of 11th grade, Edward announced that high school had nothing more to teach him, and he dropped out.

He was involved in an altercation with some local boys the next year, and he was charged with resisting arrest and disturbing the peace. His next run-in was more serious. A few months shy of his 18th birthday, Edward was arrested with crack cocaine and marijuana in an undercover drug sting. After deputies swooped in, he punched an officer in the chest and tried to run. He was charged with possession of cocaine with intent to distribute, possession of marijuana, battery of a police officer and resisting arrest.

Edward did a 30-day stint in rehab, passed his GED and enrolled at Louisiana State University, but he still faced felony drug charges. The military was his answer.

"There was the understanding that if you don't do this, the DA will prosecute you," said his attorney, Carl E. Babin of Baton Rouge. A soldier was born. The prosecutor did not seek a conviction.

A recruiter who worked in the Gonzales office at the time said Edward scored high on his tests and said he wanted to serve his country. "He had some problems, but it wasn't anything that we couldn't put him in the Army for," said the recruiter, who was not supposed to discuss Edward and asked that his name not be used.

From basic training, Edward shipped to Schofield Barracks in Hawaii, home of the 1st Batallion/27th Infantry Regiment of the 25th Infantry Division. He broke his jaw in a bar fight and joined the headquarters company mortar platoon. In "Lightning Thrust Warrior" training exercises, Edward was chosen as best gunner and "hero of the battle."

Edward Richmond Jr. hugged his mother the day before he left for Iraq. Edward was a mortar man, and was one of the better soldiers in his platoon, according to his sergeant. (Photograph courtesy of Charlie Varley, freelance photojournalist)

His father counseled him about challenging his superiors. "Regardless of whether they are right or not, they are wearing stripes," he said.

"Daddy," Edward answered, "dumb people are hard to deal with."

For a kid from the middle-class suburbs, he could trash-talk like a thug, "but when he put on those glasses and buried his nose in a book, his whole attitude changed," said Sgt. Shaun Mittler, Edward's squad leader in Hawaii.

Sometimes he came off as a know-it-all. By the time his mortar platoon got its orders for Iraq, "everybody turned on him," said his buddy, Pfc. Frederick Sidney. "He would speak out. Everybody else was trying to suck up."

Spec. Richmond went home to Gonzales before deploying. Yellow ribbons were tied around the oaks in his yard. A photograph shows Edward at a picnic table giving his little sister a playful headlock. In another shot he is shirtless and handsome, with deep-set eyes and vacation stubble, staring steadily into the camera.

"I'm ready," he told his mother.

'Frightening and Chaotic'

Iraq was cold and rainy when the mortar platoon got there in February of 2004. The mud was frozen around Forward Operating Base McHenry, a primitive outpost south of Kirkuk. To fend off sniper attacks, a 10-foot mound of dirt, topped with triple-stand razor wire, surrounded the base. Beyond the wire were outlying roads littered with bombs, especially on the way to Hawija.

"We didn't know anything about the people or their land," said Mittler, the sergeant. "We all had our finger on the trigger. It was frightening and chaotic."

Late one night, according to Army court documents, Edward's squad was briefed on a mission. Word came that high-level insurgents were hiding in the village of Taal Al Jal, possibly with weapons. The plan was for Alpha Company to perform the raid while Edward and the mortar guys set up a security checkpoint outside the mud wall of the village. Sgt. Jeffrey Waruch relayed their orders: Shoot any males fleeing the village, but check with him if possible before firing.

The raid started at daybreak. Edward could hear screaming in Arabic and English, and shotguns blowing the locks from doors. After the sun was up, cow and sheep herders from the village made their way into the fields with their animals.

A call came over the radio to detain all males leaving the village. Edward saw a cow herder in a field about 200 yards away. Waruch would later testify that Edward asked if he could shoot the man; Edward said he asked if he was supposed to shoot the man.

Waruch said no and set out for the cow herder, telling Edward to come along.

The man wore sweat pants, a baggy top and a head scarf. As the two soldiers approached with rifles and plastic flex-cuffs, the Iraqi became angry and began pointing back to the village.

Waruch pantomimed for the man to put his hands in the air. As the soldiers came within three yards of the Iraqi, Waruch told Edward to stand guard with his rifle while he handcuffed the man. Waruch did a quick upper-body search. As he tried to pull the man's wrists down to handcuff him, he resisted, and Waruch ordered Edward to raise his weapon to "high ready."

Edward would later say that Waruch told him to "shoot him if he moves," a statement Waruch would deny making.

Edward was at close range, but he flipped his rifle scope up, training its red dot on the cow herder's head.

The man stopped resisting as Waruch cuffed him, and the sergeant turned to lead him back to the road. As they walked on the uneven field, the man lost his balance and stumbled into Waruch.

A single shot from Edward's M4 rang out. The Iraqi dropped. Waruch squatted down, covering his ears.

Edward was pale and holding his rifle with one hand. He said the Iraqi had jumped at the sergeant.

Brain matter was seeping from the man's eyes. His cows were wandering away in the field.

Another soldier came up. Seeing the dead man's bound hands, he said to Edward with profane prescience, "You are f——."

Edward had been in Iraq less than three weeks.

A Soldier's Trial

Eddie Richmond bought a $1,700 ticket from New Orleans to Kuwait, then caught military transports the rest of the way in. A hot, sandy wind swirled through the Black Hawk helicopter that carried him to the 1st Infantry Division's headquarters in Tikrit. Edward's battalion, normally with the 25th Infantry Division, fell under the command of the 1st Infantry Division in Iraq.

As the months had passed, Eddie felt sure that the Army would drop its case against Edward. "I know my son, and he would not just shoot someone," he said. "How many of our kids over there hesitate and die?"

But the Army charged Edward with unpremeditated murder and scheduled his general court-martial in Tikrit in August. He faced life in prison.

The trial was held in one of Saddam Hussein's former palaces near the Tigris River. At night, father and son slept in a room with some special operations soldiers. Eddie found it surreal: The same Army that was his gracious host was prosecuting his son.

He sat behind Edward in the makeshift courtroom. When the prosecution showed photos of the dead cow herder on a projection screen, Eddie felt a knot in his stomach. The man's name was Muhamad Husain Kadir. Part of his head was missing.

The key witness against Edward was Waruch. The sergeant testified that after he handcuffed Kadir, he patted him on the shoulder and said to Edward, "He's good, let's go." Waruch said he even saw Edward lower his rifle. Then came the blast.

Edward took the stand, wearing his desert camouflage and glasses. His accent dripped like the river parish he came from.

Edward testified that Waruch ordered him to shoot Kadir if he moved, so he raised his rifle and aimed at the man's head. Looking through his scope, he was unable to see Waruch put the handcuffs on. When he saw

Eddie and Darce Richmond's son spent two years in an Army detention center for killing a civilian in Iraq. Another soldier in his unit was not prosecuted in the death of an Iraqi girl. (Photograph courtesy of Charlie Varley, freelance photojournalist)

what looked like Kadir lunging at Waruch, he believed that his sergeant's life was in danger.

The defense tried to keep out a statement Edward gave a month after the incident, admitting that he was pumped on adrenaline and "had to know" that Kadir was cuffed "before I shot him but it just did not register in my mind at that time." Edward signed the statement after an agent with the Army Criminal Investigation Command (CID) told him he flunked a polygraph; he really hadn't.

Prosecutors goaded him. Hadn't it been obvious that a herder walking in a field with cows was not fleeing the village?

"You don't look at everybody as Saddam Hussein himself, sir, but until it is clarified otherwise, you have to be suspicious," Edward answered. "I mean, people are dying every day, so you have be suspicious of everyone, sir."

"Answer the question," the prosecutor said. "Did you or did you not assume that Mr. Kadir had escaped from the village?"

"I knew he had come from the village, sir," Edward said. "I didn't know. I hadn't formed an opinion based off that."

Two of Edward's fellow soldiers testified that he often talked about wanting to kill an Iraqi. But under cross-examination, they said most soldiers did. Edward's sergeant said he was one of the better soldiers in his platoon.

Waruch's credibility was also on trial. Staff Sgt. Marcus Warner testified that Waruch was a "compulsive liar." His nickname was "Shady Jay."

Eddie Richmond watched his son, admiring his confidence. Edward never second-guessed himself. "Daddy, I've done my job, and I did what I thought was right," he said. He believed he would be acquitted.

He was only partly right. The jury found him not guilty of unpremeditated murder but guilty of voluntary manslaughter. The prosecution was recommending eight years in prison and a dishonorable discharge.

Edward had one chance to address the court before sentencing. Instead of asking for mercy, he expressed a vague regret.

"If I had known everything then that I know now, it wouldn't have happened, and I am sorry that it had to come to this," he said.

The jury gave him three years, a demotion in rank and a dishonorable discharge. He was shipped to the Fort Sill Regional Correctional Facility, an Army prison in the hills of Oklahoma, where he was diagnosed with post-traumatic stress disorder.

Sadness Turns to Anger

His father went home to Gonzales.

"You could see the mourning," said his friend Marvin "Bud" Ragland, a retired rice farmer. "His son—his oldest child—went to war for his country and was branded by that country as a murderer."

But Eddie received something in the mail that would shift him to outrage. Inside an envelope with no return address were confidential Army documents. One page was stamped "Serious Incident Report." It was part of an Army investigative file, known as a 15-6. The subject was Sgt. Jeffrey Waruch.

Eddie sat in his kitchen and began to read. Waruch had shot three female civilians, one of whom died. Eddie vaguely remembered the sergeant being asked about it at Edward's trial, but the judge had limited the questions. Edward never mentioned it to him. The documents Eddie held in his hand—sworn statements by Waruch and several other soldiers—laid out what happened in detail.

Ten days before Edward shot the cow herder, the mortar platoon was riding in a convoy to Al-Abassi when a roadside bomb exploded. Soldiers began firing from the sides of their vehicles. No one was seriously hurt by the bomb, but orders went out to stop any Iraqis fleeing the area.

Waruch began running across farmland after a group of several Iraqis in the distance. After crossing a muddy stream in pursuit, he fired warning shots in the air and screamed for them to stop.

According to his written statement, Waruch said he was 200 yards away when one of the Iraqis knelt down with what looked like a tube-like object, possibly a rocket-propelled grenade. Waruch fired about five times, knocking down two bodies. This subdued the group, but as he moved closer, two other Iraqis suddenly started to run toward him, with one reaching into her clothes. He fired five more rounds.

Arriving at the group in the field, he saw that a girl was shot in the head and her pulse was gone. Another female was hit in the thigh and going into shock. Another was shot in the knee.

Waruch had fired on a mother and her two daughters, killing a 14-year-old. The survivors would later tell a reporter that they had been weeding a bean field and had started to run as the Americans ran toward them.

Waruch was initially cleared of any wrongdoing, but a second review found that he had violated the rules of engagement. The girl had been trying to surrender when she was shot. No weapons were found.

As a result of the shootings, the battalion commander ordered that the soldiers be retrained: no spraying of bullets, aimed shots only, and only when under hostile intent.

Eddie felt his eyes burning with tears. Whoever sent him the file wanted him to see that the prosecution's key witness against his son was under investigation for his own civilian casualties. As he studied the documents, he saw that one soldier had escaped punishment and that another was needed to pay for the platoon's mistakes.

Eddie wrote to members of Congress and the Army CID. When a reporter from the *Dayton Daily News* in Ohio called, researching a story on civilian deaths in Iraq, Eddie shared his documents and pushed the Army for more. Eddie wanted the same spotlight that burned on his son to burn on Waruch.

In May 2005, more than a year after the incident, the CID opened an investigation into the shooting of the three female civilians. Waruch left the Army early this year. The investigation remains open. Attempts to reach Waruch for comment for this story were unsuccessful.

Edward turned 22 in prison. He subscribed to *The Wall Street Journal*, gorged on science fiction novels and built muscle. He refused to bend to the will of Fort Sill, spending much of his time in a segregation cell for discipline violations.

"It's a mental war," he wrote his parents. "I'll be fine."

Eddie contacted Defend the Defenders, an organization that raises funds for the legal defense of soldiers and Marines accused of crimes in combat. It was founded by Merry Pantano, whose son, Marine 2nd Lt. Ilario Pantano, was charged with murdering two Iraqis but was acquitted last year by the Marine Corps. Pantano agreed to fund Edward's appeal.

Eddie slapped his truck with "Defend the Defenders" stickers and wore the group's T-shirt that said, "Who's Got Their Backs?" The war in Iraq roiled on, but for Eddie it was frozen on two days, 10 days apart, in February 2004.

Then came a break. In April, the Army's clemency board granted Edward parole.

When he was released in June, he had served nearly two years of a three-year sentence. He called from the airport in Lawton, Okla., and told his parents, "I'm a free man." They picked him up in Baton Rouge. He was pale but rock-hard from exercise, and still had a grunt's haircut.

He soon received a congratulatory call from Ilario Pantano, the Marine acquitted of murder. In a sense they both belonged to the same fraternity of the misunderstood.

Edward told his father he didn't want anyone feeling sorry for him. He wanted to start over. But his father could not let go so easily. After Edward put his Army uniform and ribbons in the trash, Eddie retrieved them and took them to the charity bins behind the grocery store in town.

In Iraq, the Army has tried to make up for the tragedies.

The family of Muhamad Husain Kadir was paid $1,000 for his death.

The Army paid more than $4,000 to the family of the girl killed by Waruch, among them her wounded sister and mother, whose leg was amputated. The 1st Battalion commander wrote a sympathy letter to the family. "I ask for your continued support as we attempt to provide a safe and secure environment," wrote Lt. Col. C. Scott Leith. He closed by quoting the Koran: "We belong to Allah and to him we shall return."

The former 1st Infantry Division commander in Iraq, Batiste, is now the president of a steel company.

Edward is earning $10 an hour at the foundry.

The chapter was closing, but not for Eddie Richmond.

"I just want the truth to come out," he said. As summer turns to fall, he wears his Defend the Defenders T-shirt, waiting for word on his son's appeal.

Staff researcher Julie Tate contributed to this report.

X-RAY READING   By Roy Peter Clark

I have known Anne Hull since she was a young feature writer for the *St. Petersburg Times,* and it has been a pleasure to watch her grow into one of the most honored newspaper writers of the past decade. Hull is a ferocious learner and an eager reader. When she reads something that moves her, she wants to know how the writer achieved such poignance so that she can incorporate that writer's tools into her own workbench. Now you can ponder this same question as you read Hull's work.

"When Mom Is Over There" marks a departure for Hull. She shares a traditional inhibition against use of the capital letter "I," but in this story it comes into play not just as a personal pronoun but as the first letter in Iraq. Oddly, this brilliant observer has to observe herself as she witnesses the liturgies of the home front, standing in for her sister-in-law, who is off to war. This point of view, sometimes called "participant observer," has produced works as disparate and interesting as John Howard Griffin's "Black Like Me" and George Plimpton's "Paper Lion."

Read this piece once through without reference to my notes in the margins. Then, read it again with these recurring maneuvers in mind:

1. Hull delivers information at key points, but this is primarily a story. Notice the techniques she uses over and over to build your vicarious experience. These were enumerated famously by writer Tom Wolfe in the 1960s: Hull builds her story around pivotal scenes, some of which are so concise they qualify as anecdotes. There are few quotes, which are static, and more examples of dialogue, which move the story forward. Action happens in settings, not in bland backdrops. The writer is a compass, always positioning her characters and telling us readers where we are. And you will find status details galore: brand names, titles, products, possessions, curious names that define character and invite the reader to connect.

2. On the level of style, Hull keeps her work in motion. By that I mean phrases, sentences, paragraphs, whole sections move, move, move. They move up and down the ladder of abstraction, from words that define meaning to words that exemplify it. Sometimes she shows. Sometimes she tells. More often she shows *and* tells so that we can think about the consequences of war and also see them. Hull has one favorite move that I like to call the "Buffy the Vampire Slayer" technique. That is, she likes to join two things that don't sit comfortably side by side—like the name Buffy and the title Vampire Slayer. This strategy reinforces the story's most powerful cultural inversion: we live in a time when a mom can be sent off to war while a dad must stay home and mind the kids.

Learn and enjoy.

When Mom Is Over There

I am driving a hulking Expedition with a yellow ribbon on the bumper that says "Support Our Troops." In the grocery store parking lot, a man nods at me. I'm walking to the shopping carts when it hits me. He thinks I'm a kindred spirit in a country that is losing its nerve. I should turn back and tell him that the truck isn't mine, to clear up his misconception, but I don't.

For one week I find myself pulled into the war effort. I am in Florida to help my brother juggle single parenthood while his wife is serving in Iraq. Jim lives in a cul-de-sac community outside Tampa where the garage doors flip up every night at 6 and swallow incoming cars. His girls are 10 and 9. We spend the week eating Cocoa Pebbles and watching "The Incredibles." We hold dance parties in a bedroom where the stuffed animals are giving way to dreamy teen idol posters. We go to the mall and to the dentist. One night while I make dinner, the girls ride bikes outside in the waning winter dusk. It is a relief to be away from Washington, where politicians in marble hallways proclaim righteousness though they have never carried a canteen.

Here in this linoleum kitchen, there is just a crayon calendar on the refrigerator marking the days until Mama comes home.

The yellow ribbon on the truck is the most outward sign of where this family stands on the war. And, of course, the quiet absence of Master Sgt. Angela Hull from the house.

In a breathless choreography of necessity, my brother cooks, cleans, folds mountains of laundry, carpools, grocery-shops, works full time as a technical writer for a defense contractor and tries to distract his daughters with amusing weekend activities like Celebration Station. He is trying to distract himself as much as the girls. "Worrying is not productive," he says. Normally, I would tease him about such a statement. I would make a case for worry and why it's only human. But I don't dare now. I am too in awe of his composure. One morning I go into his bedroom closet to get the laundry and I'm greeted by the scent of Angela's perfume, still on her clothes. I touch her blouses. How does he do it?

Angela is chief controller of the air-traffic control tower at Kirkuk Regional Air Base in northern Iraq. She did not graduate from the Air Force Academy or come from a long line of military heroes. Angela was 22 and working at the Stouffer's frozen-food factory in her home town of Gaffney, S.C., in 1987 when she rebelled against the smallness of her life and joined the Air Force. She advanced the slow, hard way, from refueling aircraft at 30,000 feet to learning air-traffic control to commanding towers. In Kirkuk, she supervises 10 controllers in the base tower while serving as first sergeant to a squadron of 48.

Angela never uses the macho language of war or the slogans favored by those who took us there. She works 16 hours a day, six days a week and sleeps in a pod. In a photo she sent home, I can see her office and a chalkboard where someone in her unit has written, "Sgt. Hull, take a day off!" She earns $54,000 a year.

I don't know where Angela stands on the war because we never talk about it. I remember once when Jim, Angela and the girls came to visit me in Washington not long after the United States invaded Iraq. It was a cold spring weekend, wet and gray, but we were excited tourists. We walked down to the White House to take pictures. Crossing through Lafayette Square, we came upon an anti-war protest. There were people shouting and jabbing signs in the air, and one of the sticks hit my niece, frightening her. I was furious at the protester, at the carelessness of his selfish passion. My brother, who is 6 feet 6 inches tall, wanted to slug the guy. Angela—calm and strong Angela—simply rounded us up and moved us along.

* * *

Jim says it's good to keep a routine. The week of my visit, the holiday lights blink in the darkened Florida balm. Palm fronds brush against the plastic snowmen and wise men propped up in the cool night grass. At the kitchen table, my nieces dream up Christmas lists to e-mail to their mother, as if she will trudge out into the sands of Iraq and find a Wal-Mart.

Jourdan is 10 and long-legged. My brother seems not to notice that she is wearing cocktail outfits to school. Jourdan is spending hours in front of the mirror, hypnotized by her own reflection as Hilary Duff and Kelly Clarkson channel messages to her at ear-shattering decibels.

In the bedroom next door, childhood still reigns supreme. Chrislyn is barely 9 and a devout fan of SpongeBob and teddy bears that she names Zack and Champ. Chrislyn is as earnest and innocent as Jourdan is sophisticated and enterprising.

When Angela received her orders for Iraq last spring, my brother boiled down the situation this way: "There are bad people over there trying to hurt Americans and Iraqis," he said. "Mommy has special gear that keeps her safe." The girls were accustomed to Angela leaving for short stints but they knew this was different. In the way that children often seize on a grain of sand, they fixated on Angela's living quarters. "Will you sleep in a hard tent?" Chrislyn asked, her blue eyes clouded by worry. Angela promised that she would be sleeping in a very hard tent. On the morning of her departure, the girls went to school and Angela went to Iraq.

Routines. We wake at 6 each morning, eat our breakfast and get ready for school. Usually my brother drops the kids on his way to work but now I do it, watching the girls' colorful backpacks disappear in the sea of others. I ride around town in the truck with the yellow ribbon on the bumper. Jim says to check out the YMCA, a sprawling new facility for the sprawling new communities devouring the pastures. A woman on a stair climber is reading a book titled "What Would Jesus Eat?" We discuss Biblical dining habits and then I tell her that I'm from

Washington. "State or D.C.?" she asks. A look of pity crosses her face. Quickly, I volunteer that I'm visiting my brother, whose wife is in Iraq. This wins her back.

All week, strange moments of charade occur. A neighbor across the street is waxing his car when he sees me coming out of the house. "Welcome home," he says, waving his cloth in the air. He has mistaken me for Angela. I'm just the sister, I say. I wonder if Angela's homecoming will be like this—a friendly neighbor welcoming her back as if she's been away at a conference.

Her absence is banal and profound. She maintains a phantom presence over her motherless house. E-mails and digital photos zip back and forth. In one of the photos, Angela notices a lump on Jourdan's forehead. She and my brother discuss the lump, and it's decided that Jourdan needs to see a pediatrician.

On the morning of the appointment, my brother gulps down cereal while CNN reports that 10 Marines were killed outside Fallujah, blown up by a homemade explosive. Jim curses and says the insurgents are picking away at us with bombs set off with 25-cent oven timers. He lets the dog out. Pop-Tarts are toasting in the toaster. The first Hilary Duff song of the day is playing in a bedroom. I look at the TV, relieved not to hear the word Kirkuk.

Of all the postings Angela could have received, Kirkuk was among the least dangerous, but lately things have gotten testier. ("Sportier," as Angela says.) The 101st Airborne Assault Division arrived at the base in October and has been deftly thwarting rocket attacks ever since. For safety reasons, Angela has yet to venture off base. Explosions rumble the furniture in her office. I wonder what worries her most today—the explosions or a small, shiny lump on the forehead of her 10-year-old.

I take Jourdan to the pediatrician's office. She sits on crinkly white paper in an exam room. A nurse practitioner named Miss Yvonne looks at the lump. Using a rubber hammer, she checks Jourdan's reflexes and then turns on a penlight and tells Jourdan to follow the beam with her eyes. "Tell me about these headaches you've been having," Miss Yvonne says.

"I think they're because I don't drink enough water, and I am growing at a really fast rate," Jourdan answers. Miss Yvonne finishes her exam. She doesn't think there is anything to worry about. The minute I'm outside the office, I call my brother at work, and I can hear him typing an e-mail to Angela as we speak.

It's mid-morning and we are late for school. We decide to stop at a convenience store on U.S. 301. We are not sticking to the routine. We go inside and peruse glossy teen magazines and the selection of snack cakes. The packaging is in Spanish because of all the Mexicans and Guatemalans who pick strawberries and tomatoes in the fields nearby. I share the sociology lesson with my niece. "Oh," she replies, feigning interest. She picks up a double-pack of coconut creme-filled snowballs. Next, a big Coke, her eyes wandering to meet mine as she reaches inside the cooler. Her mom's at war. What the hell.

School is an L-shaped set of flat buildings shaded by oaks. The office is in front. Jourdan and I stand there in the bright fluorescence with our sugar-crusted mouths. "See you at 3:30," I say.

* * *

My brother is three years younger than me. He watches NASCAR and trades barbecue tips with someone on the Internet named Jurassic Pork. He washes the truck and cuts the grass on Saturday afternoons. Order is very important,

---

- even as an aunt, she is reporting
- repeat of word, with new meaning
- great gooey details
- details reveal character of brother
- scene directly observed, not reconstructed
- first-person plural shows her role in the family
- bit of dialogue
- aunt is indulgent
- details appeal to the senses
- punch line at end of sentence

which is funny, because as a boy he was gangly and calamitous, with an uncombed thicket of blond hair. Once he slipped from a boardwalk into a swamp full of alligators. Another time, he lit the gas stove and, whoosh, he had two charred haystacks for eyebrows.

We grew up in rural central Florida, when flocks of white birds would fill the sky as they left the backs of cattle that stood in soggy pastures. Our father worked in citrus. He couldn't keep a job. After our mother decided to leave with us, I remember being so broke that we ate meat only once a week—Sunday—but what Jim remembers is how delicious Sunday dinners were, and that would be the difference between us our entire lives.

At 19, he joined the Air Force and saw the world, and now he is back beneath the dripping Spanish moss that shrouded our childhoods. His house is in a subdivision near the Alafia River in eastern Hillsborough County. The river is tannic and winding and beautiful but surrounded by subdivisions that keep hatching and expanding, beige on beige. One day I'm returning home with the girls and I pull into what I believe is our driveway. My nieces inform me that their house is in fact three doors down. "Do these houses all look alike?" I ask.

"Our light is different," my younger niece says.

My brother loves the stability and sameness of these communities, a clue that he has not forgotten everything from our childhood. In Oklahoma they lived on Altus Air Force Base in a windswept brick ranch house with brown carpet, and every night an anemic bugle would sound taps over loudspeakers. During a bad plains drought, my brother torched his and a neighbor's lawns during a barbecue mishap. Three Halloweens ago in Virginia, in a neighborhood of Special Forces, Navy and Air Force members, I remember all the children flying around the cul-de-sac in vampire and Shrek costumes as their dads prepared for the invasion of Iraq. The night was starry and perfect, for these children.

Now, Angela is there. Patience, President Bush says on the news, patience. Stay the course. His twin daughters are about the same age that Angela was when she was working at the Stouffer's frozen-food factory and decided to enlist because good jobs were scarce in Gaffney, S.C. Now, Angela is high in a tower over the northern desert of Iraq, watching the

out of the mouth of babes—best quote ever

dialogue

setting for anecdote

abstract "stability and sameness" follows concrete example on previous page

Buffy technique

but not for their parents

repetition hooks beginning and end of paragraph

embedded editorial

red trails of rockets flare off in the distance. Patience, Angela, patience.

It is nearly bedtime. My brother turns off the TV. The sliding glass door is open and he pulls it closed, the small click of a lock echoing between us. One last time for the night, he goes to the computer to see if there is any news from Angela.

* * *

"Hey, baby," my brother shouts into the phone on my last Saturday afternoon. Knowing it's their mother, the girls come running.

"Mama," Chrislyn says, "I got a new bear."

Jourdan shares with her mother a dark tale from "Chicken Soup for the Preteen Soul." It has come to Angela's attention, through more digital photos, that Jourdan is wearing blue eye shadow to school, and a mother-daughter conversation follows.

My brother gets back on the line, and the kids start arguing. He cups his hand over the phone and yells at them sharply, drawing a rebuke from Angela.

"Dammit, Ang," Jim says, "I'm here with them 24-7 and you're in the peace and quiet."

We have to laugh at that one.

We decide to take a walk on the nature trail around the subdivision. *Frogs grunt from the sludge of the creek, like kettledrums sounding off from the depths of the soupy algae.* Jim tells the girls to stay on the paved trail. I whisper to him, "When we were kids, we played hopscotch over rattlesnake nests."

The sky is obscured by palms and oaks; it feels as if we are alone in Florida's last forest, until we hear the rush of the nearby interstate, cleverly hidden by landscaping. The girls race ahead. I have told them to bring their swimming suits. The subdivision has a pool, and though it is unheated, the gate is unlocked. We change into our suits. No one is saying the obvious, that the water is cold and that Angela would never allow this. *But Angela is not here.* We leap into the pool, cannonballs and jackknives. With chattering teeth, we make a pact never to tell Angela we went swimming in December.

We are warm and dry by the time we eat dinner. The girls sit at the kitchen table to write letters to their mother. Chrislyn picks up a pencil and stares out the window. *A dreamer and sensitive soul, like her father when he was a boy.* She looks down at her blank paper and begins. *Dear Mom: If you read this carefully, you might actually hear my voice.*

— great swamp of language

— an important sentence gains power from brevity

— a profound sentiment for a child

— telling

— showing

Since the war began I have read the U.S. casualty lists published in newspapers. When the photos of the dead are published in newspapers, I study the faces that are laid out like yearbook photos filling the pages of an endless year. Every picture has its own story but no future. The brim of an olive cap shields the impish eyes of a young Marine, now gone. Why do the names of their home towns seem so poetic? Mineral Bluff, Ga. Spooner, Wis. Angelina, Tex. Mechanicsville, Iowa. Zanesville, Ohio. Evening Shade, Ark. Valentine, Neb. When I see these photos, I imagine the knock on the door.

My brother never reads these lists. He never looks at the photos. Seeking out memorials is for those of us who live around the edges. Instead, Jim stands over his girls as they say their bedtime prayers, the same singsong prayers they have repeated since they could talk, about grandmas, papas, Todd their cat and baby Jesus, with one new addendum to their pajama pleadings. "Please keep Mama safe."

- the most important phrase lands at the end of the paragraph
- another difference from sister
- another common liturgy
- power of place names to evoke American culture
- always get the name of the cat
- most important phrase in the final power spot

Roy Peter Clark is senior scholar and vice president of The Poynter Institute.

A conversation with
Anne Hull

This edited e-mail interview was conducted by Poynter Institute senior faculty member Christopher Scanlan with The Washington Post's Anne Hull, *winner of ASNE's Batten Medal.*

CHRISTOPHER SCANLAN: The three stories from your award-winning entries chosen for this edition of "Best Newspaper Writing" tell the story of the Iraq War by focusing on the home front. What were the origins of these stories?

ANNE HULL: The country was in the fourth year of war, but it was like background music or faded wallpaper for lots of Americans. Like a lot of reporters, I wanted to bring it center stage. A friend of mine said, "Is it always your job to bring everyone down?" But it was important to chip away at the heavy varnish of "patriotism" pushed particularly hard by this administration and write about people who were actually paying the price. It's a primitive motivation, but it's the answer. Of course, woven into the story of war is the story of class.

You seem unafraid to step back and draw conclusions about the places and people you write about. For instance, in the second paragraph of "Call to Duty," you write: "But any poetry about the waning days of youthful abandon feels false in this part of central Mississippi, where the bridge to Iraq is a short one." What is it about the work you do that makes it possible to write with such authority and precision?

I studied casualty databases, and the number of troops killed from Mississippi was high. Mississippi is one of the poorest states in the country and historically the military has offered a route to escape poverty. Now there is a war going on and kids you know who live down the street are coming home in coffins, and yet you are STILL weighing the merits. The recruiters come to your high school during senior year and entice you with a $10,000 signing bonus. You attend the funeral of a young Marine who played football for your team. Imagine these colliding and competing thoughts in your head when you are just a senior in high school. These were the thoughts that preoccupied Blake Johnson, the senior I wrote about. So, Iraq felt very close, as if it were breathing down the neck of Meridian, Miss.

Sense of place plays a big part in your stories. Why and how do you create "the where" in them so evocatively?

Place is a character. It's the stage upon which the drama is set. It informs the people who move across the stage. Language evolves from place and so does a sensibility about life. One of the best examples of "place" is in Melissa Fay Greene's work "Praying for Sheetrock." The trick is not to laundry-list the characteristics of a place (132 Baptist churches, seven freshwater lakes, a million tourists a year) but to acquire all these facts and then knit them into the writing. Connect the facts to the soul of the place and put them in the right context. Read Kate Boo. She makes you feel as if you are stepping off a train in another land. You are there. You are connected to the people. You can smell the food and hear the music. Most importantly, you begin to understand the choices they make.

Most reporters I know would prefer a libel suit to writing in the first person. But "When Mom Is Over There" begins this way: "I am driving a hulking Expedition with a yellow ribbon on the bumper that says 'Support Our Troops.' " You've told me before that this was the first time you'd written in the first person. Why did you do so?

I had something to say. Living in Washington, D.C., your ears hurt from the righteousness of politicians who talk about sacrifice when in truth they never served in the military, nor do their children serve, and yet they call on others to do it. This is a very simplistic reduction on my part. And wrongheaded, according to friends in the military, who say it doesn't matter if the president served or not; they have a job to do. But for me, this hypocrisy pushed me to write about my sister-in-law marching off to Iraq and the sacrifice required of her family. It was a jagged appreciation.

How difficult or easy was it for you to write in the first person?

After the initial shock of typing the letter "I," the piece flowed. The best writers of first person minimize their presence, as they minimize sentimentality or indulgent detours. And they appear as foils or refractors. I tried to be the train tracks and let the larger story be the train. My presence had one explicit purpose: to convey the pulsing and uneasy sensation of having mixed feelings about the war, proud of my family, conflicted about being associated with war. Like writing any story, you have scenes and pacing, you move from humor to poignancy, from pointillist detail to a larger sense of sweep and keep it humming toward a precise ending. In an ethereal way, I think this story is about wistfulness, for things gone.

How do you report a story when you, the reporter, are a character in it? How is that different from all the stories you've written in third person?

It's more liberating to work from memory than from a notebook. You don't have to report out emotions, because they are yours. In terms of reporting, I know my family. No research needed. I can scroll from the past to the present, like a dream sequence because these are how memories play in our heads. I did ask my family for permission to include certain intimate details. And I spoke with my brother about framing our childhood in a way that was less than Hallmarkian. The piece also was made easier by the fact that it was set in a very familiar place—Florida, where I grew up—so that the twin feelings of childhood and extinction played off each other.

What advice would you give a journalist trying to write in the first person?

First person is a loaded gun. Only those who've been to the shooting range should try it, which is why I have always avoided it. But I would say start small and try it. Read the best newspaper columnists out there to get a feeling for the role of self. Read William Maxwell to learn how to avoid sentimentality. And find a topic that is within you that might play off something in the news. (We are a newspaper, after all.) The most important thing is that you have to have something to say, something you MUST say. Also, unless you can use a critical eye on yourself and those close to you, it's not worth doing. No one wants a love letter or tribute that doesn't feel real. Think of "About Alice," Calvin Trillin's elegy to his wife, which is perfect because of the imperfection of the two characters.

What surprised you the most about the reporting, writing and publication of "When Mom Is Over There"?

How some things are bottled inside us for a long time and they don't come out until the right moment. You can't rush them. They stay submerged for a reason. In this case, it took my sister-in-law going to war to get me to write about childhood. As for the most jarring aspect of publication, it was seeing my family's photos in the newspaper. I felt protective and even a little frightened by the exposure and was reminded of the risks that everyday people take with reporters when telling their stories.

What did you learn from the experience?

It's vital to keep taking risks as a writer and as a reporter. You know the old saying: If it scares you, do it.

These stories are about turning points, including your own writing in the first person. What advice, encouragement or counsel did you get from your editor, fellow writers or your family? How important was that?

There was no larger chorus at work here. The hardest part was saying to my editor, "I want to try writing about the war, my family, childhood in some impressionistic way that pivots off a visit I had with them. Can I have three days to try it?" (Of course, all the while, the internal voice is shouting, "What do you have to say that's unique?") Luckily my editor is David Maraniss, and he said: "Go for it." Given the personal nature of the material, his support was necessary. If he had expressed doubt, it would have played into my own self-consciousness about writing first person and I never would have attempted it.

The next step was: How do I do this? When it comes to first person, some writers are naturals. I quickly read a bunch of first-person newspaper stories. My friend Hanna Rosin wrote a piece about her immigrant childhood in Queens. She just hammered it out and it raced along with grace and humor. In a fit of heartbreaking urgency, Maraniss wrote about the unexpected death of his sister. For both of these writers, the stories poured out quickly because there was something bottled in them that they needed to be heard or that they felt might pay tribute or give permanence to a memory. I felt similarly. Also, when sitting down to write I tried to remember, "This isn't 'To Kill a Mockingbird'; it's a story in a newspaper that costs 35 cents."

What ethical challenges arose as you produced this story? How did you deal with them?

No ethical challenges other than the moral questions that have to do with memory, recall and authenticity. To ensure factual accuracy, I let both my brother and sister-in-law read the story before it ran. But I was also wary of what my brother might have to say about my recollection of childhood. Certain events are more significant for me than for him, and vice versa. Our lives are shaped by truths, but at some point those truths slide or blur into mythologies or "stories" that we rely on to define us.

Your stories resonate with details. Blake Johnson and his family live "on a piece of land that never quite dries." How do they make the journey from reporting to writing?

Every time I stepped out of my car onto Blake's front yard my shoes got muddy. His mom complained about the wet property, despite trucking in gravel to sop it up. The wet property was a constant reminder of never having enough money to make things right. Whatever effort was expended by the family, it was never enough. It's the feeling of people trying hard but not quite pulling it off. Practically speaking, take a factual detail and ask yourself, why is this so and what does this mean?

What is your benchmark for choosing which quotes, details and other reporting make it into your stories?

Different standards are used for different stories. In a news story, you are more concerned about making sure all the stakeholders have their say and are given equal time. But in general, reporters often use quotes when they could paraphrase. In some ways, using quotes sparingly makes more work for the reporter because it forces the reporter to have a stronger command of the material.

I like to use quotes to show how someone speaks. I love language and malapropisms and English-as-a-second-language mistakes and surfer slang and all manner of linguistic mash-ups. (But keep in mind that language should be used to explain the fullness of individuals, not to ridicule them.) Too often we sanitize, and thus homogenize—not to mention sabotage—realness. Take 20-year-old infantry soldiers in Iraq. Compare the way newspaper stories quote them and describe their experiences versus how the soldiers talk on their MySpace pages.

If a reporter or editor were to approach you and ask, "How can I learn to collect such details so they can make my stories richer?", how would you answer?

Most journalists are focused on the essentials of the subject at hand. This is understandable. They see the other details but don't include them in their stories, or they don't know how to use them. You can train yourself to be observant. Jot down on your notebook as a reminder: sights, sounds, smells, feelings, voices, bumper stickers.

The harder part is weaving the details in such a way that they contribute to the larger point of the story. Read writers who do this well (Joan Didion, Tom Wolfe, David Remnick, Gay Talese, Kate Boo, Susan Orlean, Wil Haygood, David Finkel, Adrian Nicole LeBlanc) and study how they do it. Part of me thinks you can't teach this stuff—it has to be natural, like singing—but part of me also thinks that a lot of this *can* be learned, which is why singers take singing lessons.

Let me make one unexpected argument here for minimizing details: Sometimes they get in the way. They distract and don't contribute to the meaning of the story. They create a detour from the events. Sometimes, especially in news writing, the simpler the better, with a killer detail here or there so that that one detail sears. David Von Drehle has a great saying: "Nuance is the enemy of bright lines."

How did readers respond to your home front stories, especially "When Mom Is Over There"?

The stories require an investment from the reader because
- none of the stories are news;
- they are long;
- they are truly excursions into the gray; and
- they don't take a particular side.

All of these factors can cut into the number of readers, especially in this "American Idol" and "Iron Chef" age when America wants a winner and a loser and a finite conclusion. So, given the atmospherics of the age, I really appreciate the support of the *Post* to let me write such stories and of readers who find reason to keep reading.

Some reporters throw bloody chum into the water to get the sharks circling. I tend to do the opposite, and so the response to my stories is different.

Who are your models for the reporting and writing you do? Who and what inspires you?

Some writers I read over and over. And some stories I read over and over. (Many of the names already mentioned.) If on deadline, I think of Dan Barry's work out of New Orleans or Anthony Shadid in Iraq or David Finkel from the war zone or David Von Drehle on funerals. Different stories call for different inspirations. I keep a drawerful of clips, some so worn that they are as thin as 20-year-old recipes. I pick up Raymond Carver to remember the importance of flow and simplicity. My models are the spare Spartans of writing. Though Kate Boo can be as intricate as origami, she knows how to sear the soul as well as Carver.

Writers' Workshop

Talking Points

1. Anne Hull's stories show the impact of the Iraq War on American enlistees. How does her integration of family and community insights help readers understand and appreciate the reality of military service?

2. In "Call to Duty," young Blake Johnson is struggling with a decision: Should he enlist? How does Anne Hull illustrate the twin forces—patriotism and economics—that have made Meridian, Miss., a prime recruiting ground for the military? How do those forces affect Johnson and his decision making?

3. "When Mom Is Over There" is written with few allusions to romance, yet on several levels, it is a love story. How does Hull's writing convey this?

Assignment Desk

1. Anne Hull has a gift for providing readers with a sense of place. Her eye for regional detail is remarkable: "green and mossy lowlands afloat with Whataburgers, Starcuts, daiquiri drive-throughs and gas stations that sell hot shrimp by the pound." Write a paragraph about your neighborhood or community that brings its unique qualities into equally sharp focus.

2. The Iraq War has brought pain and problems to the main subjects of each of Hull's stories. Consider the challenge of writing these complex personal accounts without reducing them to anti-war opinion pieces. List the values that should guide the journalist.

3. We are drawn into "When Mom Is Over There" because it is Hull's first-person account of helping "my brother juggle single parenthood while his wife is serving in Iraq." One of the challenges of the first-person writing style is moving the spotlight carefully from oneself to the others in the story and back again. The story is about more than you, but readers are seeing it through your eyes and experience. Think about a time you stepped in to help others. Write a short, first-person account of your experience.

WINNER
C.J. (Chris) Chivers
Individual Deadline News Reporting

The official *New York Times* biography of Chris Chivers says he has been a Moscow correspondent since 2004, with additional service covering war zones in Iraq, Afghanistan, Central Asia, Israel and the Palestinian territories. It cites his earlier work in Metro, writing the stories that bled from the 9/11 attacks. It notes that he came to the *Times* after working at *The Providence Journal* in Rhode Island, and that he served as an infantry officer in the U.S. Marine Corps, honorably discharged with the rank of captain in 1994.

But it is the *Times*' ASNE award-nomination letter for Chivers that brings his bio to life: "To carry out his compact with his readers, he is willing to go to the most dangerous places on the planet, to push himself harder than even the toughest editor would ever dare to and to use every journalistic, intellectual and artistic tool at his disposal.... The most extraordinary thing about Chivers' coverage is that it is almost always done on deadline, though his writing is as carefully crafted as if he had all the time in the world."

Chivers is married, the father of three sons and a daughter. He earned a bachelor's degree in English from Cornell University and was the 1995 valedictorian of Columbia University's Graduate School of Journalism. He is a graduate of the U.S. Army's Ranger course.

When contacted for this edition of "Best Newspaper Writing," Chivers e-mailed that he faced a challenge responding to our questions about his award-winning work: He was to leave for Afghanistan the next day, once again joining up with patrols. He wrote: "Between now and when I depart I have to finish two stories for the *Times* and a book review for a Moscow newspaper. I also have to pack my gear and restock my first-aid kit. And today is my oldest son's birthday, so I'm taking a few hours at home on a Sunday."

Despite all that, and true to his reputation, Chivers delivered on deadline.

—Jill Geisler, Leadership and Management Group Leader,
The Poynter Institute

The Jesse Laventhol Prize for Deadline News Reporting by an Individual is funded by a gift from David Laventhol, a former Times Mirror *executive, in honor of his father.*

40. Medic Tends a Fallen Marine, with Skill, Prayer and Fury

NOV. 2, 2006

By C.J. Chivers

KARMA, IRAQ, Oct. 30—Petty Officer Third Class Dustin E. Kirby clutched the injured marine's empty helmet. His hands were coated in blood. Sweat ran down his face, which he was trying to keep straight but kept twisting into a snarl.

He held up the helmet and flipped it, exposing the inside. It was lined with blood and splinters of bone.

"The round hit him," he said, pausing to point at a tiny hole that aligned roughly with a man's temple. "Right here."

Petty Officer Kirby, 22, is a Navy corpsman, the trauma medic assigned to Second Mobile Assault Platoon of Weapons Company, Second Battalion, Eighth Marines. Everyone calls him Doc. He had just finished treating a marine who had been shot by an Iraqi sniper.

"It was 7.62 millimeter," he continued. "Armor piercing."

He reached into his pocket and retrieved the bullet, which he had found. "The impact with the Kevlar stopped most of it," he said. "But it tore through, hit his head, went through and came out."

He put the bullet in his breast pocket, to give to an intelligence team later. Sweat kept rolling off his face, mixed with tears. His voice was almost cracking, but he managed to control it and keep it deep. "When I got there, there wasn't much I could do," he said.

Then he nodded. He seemed to be talking to himself. "I kept him breathing," he said.

He looked at Lance Cpl. Matias Tafoya, his driver, and raised his voice. It was almost a shout. "When I told you that I do not let people die on me, I meant it," he said. "I meant it."

He scanned the Iraqi houses, perhaps 150 yards away, on the other side of a fetid green canal. Marines were all around, pressed to the ground, peering from behind machine-gun turrets or bracing against their armored vehicles, aiming rifles at where they thought the sniper was.

The sniper had made a single shot just as the marines were leaving a rural settlement on the western edge of Karma, a city near Falluja in Anbar Province.

The marines had been searching several houses on this side of the canal, where they found five Kalashnikov assault rifles and bomb components, and were getting back into their vehicles when everyone heard the shot. It was a single loud crack.

No one was precisely sure where it had come from. Everyone knew precisely where it hit. It struck a marine who was peering out of the first vehicle's gun turret. He collapsed.

Petty Officer Kirby rushed to him and found him breathing. He bandaged the marine's head as the vehicle lurched away. Soon he helped load the wounded marine into a helicopter, which touched down beside the convoy within 12 minutes of the shot.

Once the helicopter lifted away, he ran back to his vehicle, ready to treat anyone else. He was thinking about the marine he had already treated.

"If I had gone with him," he said, and glanced to where the helicopter had flown away, over the line of date palms at the end of a field. His voice softened. "But I'm not with him," he said.

He turned, faced a reporter and spoke loudly again. "In situations and times like this, I am bound to start yelling and shouting furiously," he said. "Don't think I am losing my mind."

He held his bloody hands before his face, to examine them. They were shaking. He made fists so tight his veins bulged. His forearms started to bounce.

"His name was Lance Cpl. Colin Smith," he said. "He said a prayer today right before we came out, too."

"Every time before we go out, we say a prayer," he said. "It is a prayer for serenity. It says a lot about things that do pertain to us in this kind of environment."

The only sounds were Doc's voice and the vehicle's engine thrumming.

He recited the prayer. There was a few moments of silence. "It's a platoon kind of thing, if you know what I mean," he said.

He listened to his radio headset and looked at Lance Corporal Tafoya, relaying word of the marines' movements. "Right now the grunts are performing a hard hit on a house," he said. He turned back to the subject of Lance Corporal Smith, 19.

"The best news I can throw at anybody right now, and that I am throwing to myself as often as I can, is that his eyes were O.K.," he said. "They were both responsive. And he was breathing. And he had a pulse."

He listened to his radio. "Two houses they've hit so far have both been swept and cleared."

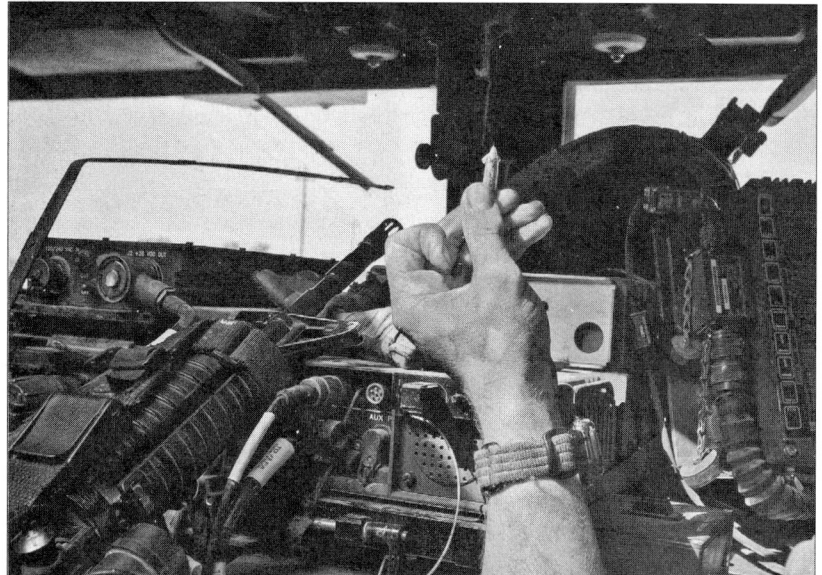

Petty Officer Third Class Dustin E. Kirby, an American medic, with the sniper's bullet that wounded a member of his platoon in Iraq. (Photograph courtesy of Joao Silva/The New York Times)

He looked at the reporter beside him. "Do you pray?" he asked. "Do that. I'd appreciate it."

After a few minutes he started talking again. "You see, having a good platoon, one that you know real well, it's both a gift and a curse. And Smith? Smith has been with me since I was . . ."

He stopped. "He was my roommate before we left," he said.

He refilled his lungs and raised his voice. "His dad was his best friend," he said. "He's got the cutest little blond girlfriend, and she freaks out every time we call because she's so happy to hear from him."

He sat quietly again. A few minutes passed. "The first casualty we had here—his name was James Hirlston—he was his good friend."

"Hirlston got shot in the head, too," he said.

He said something about Iraqi snipers that could not be printed here.

Then he was back to the subject of Lance Corporal Smith.

"I really thank God that he was breathing when I got to him, because it means that I can do something with him," he said. "It helps. People ask you, 'What are you doing? What are you doing?' It helps, because if he's breathing, you're doing something."

There had been many Iraqi civilians outside a few minutes before the sniper made his shot. Most of them had disappeared. Now an Iraqi woman walked calmly between the sniper and the marines, as if nothing had happened.

She passed down the street.

Petty Officer Kirby began to list the schools he had attended to be ready for this moment. Some he had paid for himself, he said, to be extra-prepared.

In one course, an advanced trauma treatment program he had taken before deploying, he said, the instructors gave each corpsman an anesthetized pig.

"The idea is to work with live tissue," he said. "You get a pig and you keep it alive. And every time I did something to help him, they would wound him again. So you see what shock does, and what happens when more wounds are received by a wounded creature."

"My pig?" he said. "They shot him twice in the face with a 9-millimeter pistol, and then six times with an AK-47 and then twice with a 12-gauge shotgun. And then he was set on fire."

"I kept him alive for 15 hours," he said. "That was my pig."

"That was my pig," he said.

He paused. "Smith is my friend."

He looked at his bloody hands. "You got some water?" he said. "I want some water. I just want to wash my wedding band."

He listened to the tactical radio. The platoon was sweeping houses but could not find the sniper.

The company started to move. It stopped at another house. The marines were questioning five Iraqi men. Doc watched from the road, waiting for the next call.

"I would like to say that I am a good man," he said. "But seeing this now, what happened to Smith, I want to hurt people. You know what I mean?"

The marines had not fired a shot.

They took one of the men into custody, mounted their vehicles and drove back to Outpost Omar, their company base, passing knots of Iraqi civilians on the way. The civilians looked at them coldly.

Inside the wire, First Lt. Scott R. Burlison, the company commander, gathered the group and told them that Lance Corporal Smith was alive and in surgery. He was critical, but stable. They hoped to fly him to Germany.

Doc had scrubbed himself clean. A big marine stepped forward with a small Bible, and the platoon huddled. He began with Psalm 91, verses 5 and 11.

Petty Officer Third Class Dustin E. Kirby, at far left in foreground, and members of his platoon prayed for Lance Cpl. Colin Smith, who was wounded by a sniper. (Photograph courtesy of Joao Silva/*The New York Times*)

"Thou shall not be afraid for the terror by night, nor for the arrow that flieth by day," said the big marine, Lance Cpl. Daniel B. Nicholson. "For he shall give his angels charge over thee, to keep thee in all thy ways."

Then he asked for the Lord to look after Lance Corporal Smith and whatever was ahead, and to take care of everyone who was still in the platoon.

"Help us Lord," he said. "We need your help. It's the only way we're going to get through this."

Doc stood in the corner, his arm looped over a marine. "Amen," he said. There were some hugs, and then the marines and their Doc went back to their bunks and their guns.

A conversation with
Chris Chivers

This edited e-mail interview was conducted by Poynter Leadership and Management Group Leader Jill Geisler with Chris Chivers, winner of the Jesse Laventhol Prize for Deadline News Reporting by an Individual.

JILL GEISLER: You see so much as a reporter on the front lines of this war; why was this story, this incident, important to you to write? What inspired you?

CHRIS CHIVERS: Your question assumes we have a choice. We don't. When you go on a raid or a patrol with an infantry unit, you don't know what will happen any more than anyone else does. This story fell from a previous decision: Joao Silva and I accompanied the Marines on the raid in Karma's outskirts as part of an intention to live with the enlisted Marines for a month or so and capture a sense of their daily lives and living conditions. By doing so, we hoped to get an intimate view of the counterinsurgency in Anbar Province—its tactics, its frustrations and its successes—and to reflect the experiences of the people engaged in it.

It was simple enough: I hoped to draw on my own knowledge as a former Marine infantryman and shadow these guys and get it down on paper. We were open to whatever would happen and had no larger plan. Joao's an old hand and wanted to do the same thing with his cameras. We saw this approach, potentially, as a complement to the wider coverage from the bureau.

The raid that morning had all but ended and we were getting back into the vehicles when the sniper shot Lance Corporal Smith. Joao and I had been assigned by the Marine company commander, who led the raid, to ride with "Doc" Kirby. We were with Doc when we heard the shot. We had just walked by Smith and taken a seat two vehicles away. I had put down my notebook and was opening one of the Granola bars Doc had been handing out. At a moment like that, everything shifts. Up to that point, we had been making a record of the raid and the search for two insurgents, which ended with the discovery and confiscation of weapons and bomb-making gear. From the instant of the shot, what followed flowed naturally.

We watched Doc lock in and followed him through his work, and then, after Smith was flown away by helicopter, we essentially just listened and watched. The company was busy trying to find the sniper, and Doc was following that, too. But an understanding of the significance of his friend's injury, and of the circumstances, was rippling through him.

He was amped up and speaking almost in a stream of consciousness for several minutes afterward, and it often was not clear to whom he was talking. Sometimes it was to his driver, sometimes it was to himself. Occasionally, he addressed Joao or me directly. I had my notebook and wrote much of it down, trying to keep up while also watching the scene as it unfolded around us.

At the time, I was fully involved in getting it down without getting in the way. I had less of an idea what I would do with the notes as I gathered them. As I began to think about writing, later in the day, I understood that this material would not work as a standard newspaper story. The wounding of one Marine, in a month when three or four service members were dying in Iraq each day, would not get 1,500 words in an international newspaper. It would hardly make the daily wrap-up.

But once we got back to the company's position, I thought that showing the incident and its effects on Doc and the platoon in an intimate, immediate way could capture something more universal about life in the infantry, about service in this war and about the feelings these men have for each other.

That was exactly why Joao and I had come. There was no choice, really, once the value of the notes sunk in, and they did quickly after we were clear of the incident. Everything up to that point was habit: When you're in an intense event, you start making a record, which is what Joao and I had done. Habits and training kick in and take over. Then you call the desk.

Your story's strength is built on its use of vivid, visceral detail. What's your method for capturing all the obligatory data and those extraordinary fine points as you report? How do you collect information?

I use a notebook and a small digital camera that can also capture video. (My pictures and video usually are terrible, but they're useful to me later as documents. I use the camera as a visual tape recorder, which is much different from what Joao and his peers do with the real photography skills.) As for this story, in an event like that, visceral details are self-evident and abundant; you will discard more than you will use. To get them into the memory, when you're there, you slow your thoughts down, way down, and watch and listen and write things quietly, methodically, without interfering. Taking a little video, or a few stills, now and then can also be helpful, as it records the scene and details you might miss but will see later on a quick replay. It can also give you something to do while you're not speaking. It's important not to talk too much. When things are happening, let the people around you fill the silence unless you have a pressing question. There is no secret to any of this. The main element is in the first step: You have to be there.

This story could have been told through any number of lenses. How did you decide to focus on young Petty Officer Kirby?

At one point, I thought, but only for an instant, of rushing off and trying to run around with the other Marines. But I realized that Doc was the intersection of all of this emotion and activity. And that his state of mind was important to record because much of the perils and emotions of the infantry life were all there. He also wore a radio headset and kept speaking out these staccato updates he was hearing. Thus the larger event was also compressed around him. I was learning of the situation around us by listening to him. I also knew that if anyone else were to be injured, Doc would go there as well, and be in the thick of it if the violence flared. So it seemed obvious to stay beside him and make a record. There's an old line from fishing that applies to reporting: *Never leave fish to find fish.* Later, I realized that the story could be framed around Doc, too. But at the time he was my subject because he was my subject; he offered a clear view.

We ask winning writers how they organized their stories. Could you tell us about your approach to story organization, and more?

The story was built on an old formula. Take a story and think of it chronologically. Then take one scene out of the sequence—any scene that captures the story as a whole—and open with it. When gathering the notes about an event, think 1-2-3-4-5. You need 1 through 5 in your notes. When writing, think 3-1-2-4-5, or 4-1-2-3-5 or something along these lines. Other than that, once you line up the story as a draft, you tuck in a little background and context here and there, where they're needed, and where they fit. This is not specialized work. If you have the notes, you have the story.

To be sure of my notes, that evening I sat with Doc in his bunkroom and we talked through the event together. A few Marines gathered around. One gave me a digital picture of Lance Corporal Smith, which I downloaded into my laptop and which we would later publish. The Marine who led the prayer session let me read his Bible, so I precisely quoted the version of the psalm he had read. I told them I was writing the story and described what shape it was taking, and I told them that I wanted to check my facts. They helped me. They were very gracious, and also very interested in letting the story get out.

Under what physical conditions were you reporting and writing that day?

Joao and I were living with the Marines, and they had generators. That's all we needed to get the material out—electricity. We carry satellite gear and laptops and chargers. Once we get "juice" and a satellite link we can talk to our bosses and we can e-mail our work to the desk. If you have electricity, you're in touch with the editors and you're filing. If you don't have electricity, your batteries die on you quickly and you're failing. When your work needs are boiled down to essentials, once you have your material, access to a few hours of electricity is the physical condition that matters most. Everything else is less important.

How many drafts did you do, and what kinds of revisions did you make?

I wrote the story through once and then went back and changed the top, trying to figure out what section to start with. I don't remember what I had up there at first. But I settled on the helmet because I vividly remembered Doc running back with it and showing it, and then the bullet, to his driver, who wanted to hear news of Lance Corporal Smith. The rest had fallen into place pretty much chronologically. I recall inserting a line about the Marines not firing a shot, because that sole line signaled something important about their discipline, even in such an intense situation. It was economical and essential.

What role did your editor play?

My editors had supported the idea of opening a line of coverage focusing on the young Marines in Anbar. This was with the thought that Joao and I would accompany small units within a single battalion through their patrols and raids and stand post with them, and try to show counterinsurgency and tactics from the bottom up. It was a significant investment of time and money, and the editors freed me from daily coverage so I could take on the assignment. I didn't read the wires or newspapers while I was there, or worry over other lines of coverage. Uncoupling ourselves from the news cycle allowed Joao and me to immerse ourselves and make a small record of a small piece of this war. When we called the story in to New York, the editors were ready to run it as it was. That's the kind of editing we all hope for. The editors also supported the writing approach. This story was not written according to the so-called inverted pyramid, which, while valuable, is overused and can deaden copy. Can you imagine this story in that form? To the editors' credit, they couldn't either.

What should we know about covering this war that will help us better understand your work and that of other journalists in Iraq?

As for me, I already hinted pretty strongly that I don't believe in magic formulas or think there is any special way to do the job. I stick to the basics. You go to where things are happening. You get the notes. You fill your head with the background (hopefully much of this is already done). Then you write to the length your editors give you and until the time the story is due, or until you have to move on. It's the same wherever you are, whether you cover a stickup at an ice cream truck in Queens, a debate about a school curriculum before a school board or a walk with the grunts through Iraq. Yes, the living conditions change. And yes, some stories are riskier and more intense than others. And of course Iraq often imposes limits on movement and access. But the work is still the work. It's fundamentals, fundamentals, fundamentals. As for my colleagues, I don't pretend to speak for other journalists in Iraq. I'd say only this: Many of them are doing extraordinary work under conditions of regular risk and sustained personal sacrifice. I admire them, and am grateful for them, as a reader and as a citizen.

Conversations about CONVERGENCE with Chris Chivers, Joao Silva and Eric Owles

These edited e-mail interviews were conducted by Poynter Online Editor Bill Mitchell with New York Times *Moscow correspondent Chris Chivers,* Times *contract photographer Joao Silva and* Times *chief multimedia producer Eric Owles regarding the online slide show prepared to accompany the print version of "Medic Tends a Fallen Marine, with Skill, Prayer and Fury."*

BILL MITCHELL: Please give us a sense of how the online audio slide show came together. How long after writing your print story did you start work on the audio?

CHRIS CHIVERS: I would like to tell you that the slide show was somehow part of a well-oiled process in the field, but in truth, for those of us on the ground the process is very informal. In this case, after filing, I called the desk and was connected to Eric Owles, who interviewed me on the satellite phone.

In addition to your notes, what guided your script?

I had no script, no special microphone or software for audio editing on the ground, and only my notes, which were hard to read in the dark. I just talked, working principally from memory, although I remember that I took care to read the psalm word for word so as not to make a mistake.

What guided your tone of voice?

Nothing guided my tone of voice except that I was tired and Eric wanted me to speak slowly and clearly because the connection was not great.

How did you settle on a pronunciation of Iraq as EYE-rack as opposed to IR-rack?

As for pronunciation, I gave it no special thought. Anyone who has been to Iraq has heard the word Iraq pronounced all sorts of ways by Arabs, Kurds, Americans and Europeans, and I don't know that there is one best way, one way that is correct. Think about it: *eye-ROK, ee-ROK, ee-RAK, eye-RAK, EE-rok, EYE-rak,* etc. I could give you a similar list for all the ways I've heard people—including local people—say Iran or Afghanistan. Pronunciations are malleable even inside each of these places, depending on local dialect, accent and language. Who is to say which is right? In any event, I didn't think about it. I have no radio training, and I sound like I sound, and on that night I was just talking into a telephone on the ground in the darkness in Anbar. After we finished my first run-through of my memories, Eric asked a few more questions and had me repeat a few sentences, because they were garbled or I stumbled over words. But by that time I was pretty run down and I don't remember it all.

In your interview with Jill Geisler (pp. 398–402), you describe your stories about this unit's work in Anbar Province as a complement to the bureau's wider coverage. In what ways do you see the audio slide show as a complement to the story and photos published in print?

We do these slide shows now and then, and they are another task in the day, and I don't commit each motion to memory. They are always roughly the same: I dictate my memories, and Eric keeps me going with questions and then edits the answers into something coherent. We always have a side conversation, too, in which I will sometimes suggest particular photos, or share information about maps or graphics so we can pinpoint things for the readers and Web site visitors. But I don't have any more involvement in the process than that and never see the slide shows or hear the final audio until after they are posted on the Web.

Where did you record the audio?

I found a fairly quiet place at the position where I was living with the Marines. It had to be outside, because the satellite phone only works in direct line of sight to the satellite. Eric had me move around a little until there was a minimum of background noise because there was a generator running and he could hear it on his end in New York. The best place was just outside the first bunkers, and so I lay down on the dirt in the darkness and he interviewed me. My role was limited to that. I did not have my laptop because it would have thrown off light, and the infantry did not want that. I simply narrated what happened from my immediate recollections, telling the story as I would tell it to you in a bar, but remembering to keep my pace a little slower and not to use foul language or military slang. Eric by then had read the story, so he asked questions that kept me focused, or as needed to fill in holes.

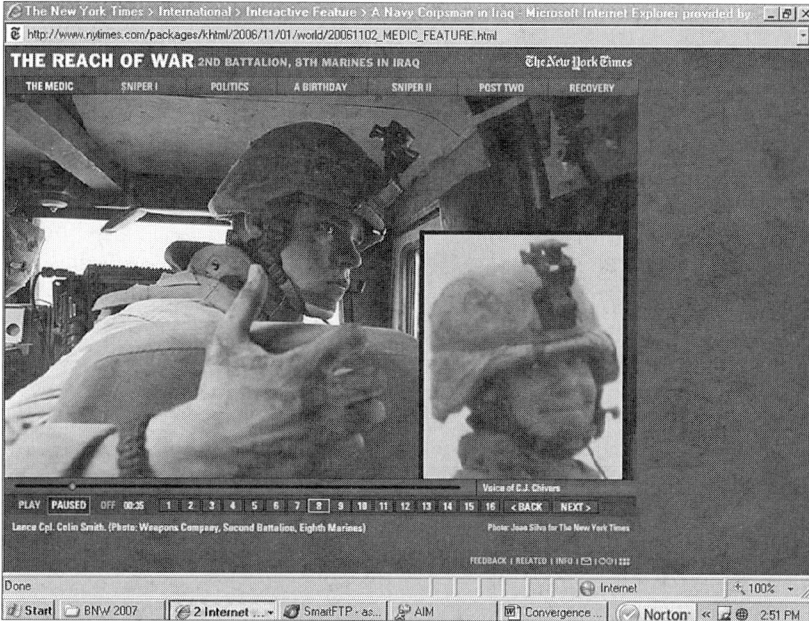

To view this image and others in the slide show, navigate to http://www.nytimes.com/packages/khtml/2006/11/01/world/20061102_MEDIC_FEATURE.html.

What's the response been from readers and Web site visitors?

I received a few hundred e-mails for the pieces and the slide shows, and almost all of them were very positive. I also received a lot of feedback from Marines on the ground, who, almost to a person, appreciated that their work and hardship and sacrifice were being portrayed realistically and unflinchingly. The e-mails came from all walks of life, in and out of the military, from veterans and spouses and parents of service members, and from old friends I hadn't heard from in years and from priests and doctors and teachers. Not all of the feedback was supportive, though. A few people were intensely negative. A few blogs contrived descriptions of how Joao and I had worked, essentially making up their own accounts of the process and then commenting angrily and self-righteously. The lies and the hate mail were usually anonymous or posted under Web names. One guy wrote to tell me that I'm an ignorant yahoo. Another guy wrote that he wished that I had been shot. This sort of thing accompanies newspapering these days, and I've grown used to it, I suppose.

* * *

BILL MITCHELL: Please walk us through the reporting stage of your work as the photographer on this story. How did you prepare for the assignment?

JOAO SILVA: It was the beginning of a three-week-long embed with the 2nd Battalion, 8th Marines (2/8) in Karma, Anbar Province, Iraq. During one of our first outings (if not the first) with the Weapons Company 2/8 Marines, an operation to search several houses in West Karma, Lance Cpl. Colin P. Smith was shot by a sniper.

When embedded with the U.S. military, a journalist or photographer falls into the unit's schedule. When they go on patrol, for instance, you have the choice to join them, and at times you have to be ready to deploy at a moment's notice. With scheduled events, you are usually notified several hours before.

But I think that being embedded automatically readies you for that. Your gear is ready, your camera batteries charged, and in the back of your mind you know that anything could happen, and if it does you want to be prepared.

What equipment did you bring? What did you use?

I work with Canon digital cameras. During that time I had a Canon EOS 5D and a Canon 1D. My backup camera body, which lives in my luggage, is a Canon 30D. It never sees the light of day but is there if needed. I work with a 16 mm–35 mm f2.8 wide-angle zoom lens, a fixed 24 mm f2.8 and a 70–200 mm f2.8 lens. My backup lenses are a wide-angle f2.8 zoom and a medium-to-long f2.8 zoom. They also live in my luggage. On that day I was carrying a 1D with the medium-long zoom and the 5D with wide-angle zoom. The images were taken with the 5D.

What were some of the challenges you faced in making these photographs? How many photos did you take during your time with Petty Officer Kirby that day?

We had traveled in "Doc" Kirby's vehicle to the weapons sweep and only returned to it as the operation was coming to a close. That's when the sniper attacked. So until that point my images were of the operation. Our vehicle, with Doc in it, rushed to the vehicle where Lance Corporal Smith lay bleeding, where Doc launched himself out and went to the assistance of Smith. When he returned to our vehicle he was emotional and his hands were covered in blood.

I started photographing as Doc described what had happened while clutching at a bloodied helmet. He then showed us the bullet. I am not sure how many pictures I took inside the vehicle as I do not have the raw take with me.

A while later, we were allowed to leave the vehicle and I continued to photograph the Marines, who had been busy with a search for the sniper. I photographed Doc again during a prayer meeting that was held for Smith.

Please walk us through your edit. How many images did you upload to New York for editors to consider for the print edition? For the slide show?

I filed 16 pictures on the day we reported the story, including photos of the search for weapons, three of Doc inside the Humvee and two of a prayer meeting, one that included Doc. Four total of Doc.

What do you see as the relative pros and cons of still images in a slide show versus video on stories such as this?

There is a place for both on the seemingly infinite World Wide Web, and at times they can complement one another. Photographs look great on the Web if well displayed and if the quality is good, and in most cases the slide shows are accompanied by a voice-over. Video has sound, which gives power to visuals, but due to bandwidth restrictions and technological limitations most videos lack in quality. Very different mediums, but they both have their place and worth.

Any lessons learned from this story—and/or its accompanying slide show—that you'll carry with you to future assignments?

Not sure. I would like to say that we learn from all experiences, but as a professional I made images of what was presented to me, and I did what I could with those moments. While we were in the vehicle, the Marines were fanning out into the surrounding buildings in search of the sniper, and I was frustrated at being stuck in the vehicle, but then Doc opened his heart to the two journalists sitting in the back seats. Maybe that's the lesson.

As for the slide show, our Web design people do a great job if they have the material to work with. So as a photographer on the ground you do the utmost to produce as much visual variety as possible in case a slide show is planned.

* * *

BILL MITCHELL: Please walk us through the process of producing "The Medic" slide show. When did you first learn about the story? How did you begin framing what the slide show might look like? When did the slide show go online vis-à-vis publication of the print story and photos?

ERIC OWLES: I knew Chris was going to be embedded with the Marines, and I heard the unit came under fire on Oct. 30. He filed his article on Nov. 1 and Joao filed photos that same day. I ordered the photos chronologically and then called Chris on his satellite phone. We arranged a time to talk and, based on his article and the photos, I asked him to take me through the events of the day. The article starts with the shooting, but the audio is more straightforward. It just makes the piece easier to follow. We usu-ally write a script, but in this case we just talked over what Chris should say for the introduction, and then he did the majority of the audio on the fly with a few prompts from me.

How many images were you working with as you made your selection of 16? What guided your selection of those final 16?

Joao filed 16 photos and we used them all. I'll usually keep a photo on screen for about 10 seconds in a slide show. In this case we used one photo about every 17 seconds.

What guidelines did you provide to Chris for the audio (length of recording, etc.)? How did you capture the audio?

No guidelines. We've done this together for years so he knew the drill. (His interactive on the 2004 school seige in Beslan, Russia, is really great.) He had a video camera, but we couldn't get any video out in time transmitting over a satellite phone (very slow). So he called me and we talked for about 20 minutes and I cut it down to 4:40. I took out my voice and edited down comments from Chris, but really this piece didn't need much editing. I didn't want it to sound too polished, so when I had a question about leaving something in or out I usually left it in.

What equipment did you use to edit the photos and the audio? How long did it take?

We used Photoshop for the photos and I used ProTools and cleaner for the audio. We recorded sometime in the afternoon New York time (late at night Iraq time), and I finished the editing around 11 p.m. in time to have it ready for posting the article on the Web site.

How do you envision Web users taking in the various elements of the slide show, i.e., images, audio, captions?

I think most just view the images and listen to the audio. We spend a lot of time on the captions, but I don't think most people read them while listening to the audio, so we try to keep them short for the most part.

How many users have viewed the text story online?

375,000-plus.

How many users have viewed the slide show?

328,000-plus. (We kept adding chapters to the audio slide show, so I'm not sure how many viewed the whole thing.)

If I failed to address something you think readers would find interesting, please answer any questions I wasn't smart enough to ask in the first place!

This was a really simple piece from a multimedia standpoint. The images don't flash quickly across the screen, the audio for the story isn't rushed and there is no interactive element at all. It has a very slow pace, but the subject matter is so serious that it doesn't need any distractions.

We've done lots of pieces like this when reporters and photographers go out on an embed, including Dexter Filkins' "Farewell to a Soldier," Damien Cave's "Return to Haifa Street" and Michael Kamber's "A Deadly Search For Missing Soldiers."

For links to material mentioned in these interviews, see the following page.

Links to Material Mentioned in "Conversations about Convergence"

- **"The Medic"**
  slide show:
  http://www.nytimes.com/packages/khtml/2006/11/01/world/20061102_MEDIC_FEATURE.html
  story:
  http://www.nytimes.com/2006/11/02/world/middleeast/02medic.html

- **2004 Beslan school siege**
  slide show:
  http://www.nytimes.com/packages/khtml/2004/09/14/us/20040904_RUSSIA_FEATURE.html

- **Dexter Filkins' "Farewell to a Soldier"**
  slide show:
  http://www.nytimes.com/packages/khtml/2006/06/29/world/20060629_SOLDIER_FEATURE.html

- **Damien Cave's "Return to Haifa Street"**
  slide show:
  http://video.on.nytimes.com/?fr_story=FEEDROOM197131

- **Michael Kamber's "A Deadly Search For Missing Soldiers"**
  slide show:
  http://www.nytimes.com/packages/khtml/2007/05/22/world/20070523_SEARCH_FEATURE.html

Writers' Workshop

Talking Points

1. "Medic Tends a Fallen Marine . . ." has a narrow focus: one sniper, one victim and one medic. How does this close-up view help readers understand the nature of military service in the Iraq War?

2. Chris Chivers writes this story with vivid detail, some of which may be painful to read. How did you react as Petty Officer Kirby, known as "Doc," described his medic training on the anesthetized pig? Why do you think the writer made that episode an integral part of the story?

3. Throughout the report, in quote after quote, we hear the voice of Petty Officer Kirby. Chivers doesn't incorporate reactions to Kirby's statements, not even a response when Kirby asks a question. What impact does the use of quotes in this manner have on the story?

Assignment Desk

1. Look at the headline of Chivers' story: "Medic Tends a Fallen Marine, with Skill, Prayer and Fury." It pinpoints the sharp focus of the report. Go back to the story and identify those elements that prove the claim made in the headline. Where do you find evidence of skill, prayer and fury? How did the writer make this clear and compelling?

2. Chivers sees the carnage of war. Reporting combat's graphic reality can present a challenge—a struggle between truth and taste. How much detail is too much, or too little? Why? Think about a time you witnessed something graphic. Try writing a paragraph that presents the reality of the scene in a meaningful way.

3. What has happened to Petty Officer Third Class Dustin E. Kirby and Lance Cpl. Colin Smith since this story was published? Use your reporting skills to find out. To appreciate the challenge of writing an important story on deadline, give yourself no more than three hours to gather the freshest information and write a minimum three-paragraph update on the men.

San Jose Mercury News

Finalist

Mark Emmons
Nondeadline Writing

41. Frank's Fight

DEC. 13, 2006

Who had Frank Sandoval become?

Where was the tough soldier who wouldn't quit?

Michelle Sandoval broke down in tears, her brave front shattered as she tried to describe the man her husband had been before that awful day.

Frankie was someone who never gave up. He wouldn't make excuses and he didn't accept them. He always encouraged their young daughter by saying: *I don't want to hear you say, "I can't." Just do it.*

Now, she was watching him cry and plead those haunting words: *I can't.*

Frankie never would have done that before.

It was late January, and they had just arrived at the Veterans Affairs hospital in Palo Alto. Frank could sit up in his wheelchair for only a few minutes. He couldn't feel or control much of his left side. His speech was nearly unintelligible.

And there was the more obvious evidence of his terrible wound: The right side of his head was sunken like a deflated basketball.

Frank now was a face of the modern war casualty. He had suffered a traumatic brain injury—the emblematic wound of the fighting in Iraq and Afghanistan. These devastating injuries have forever altered the lives of hundreds of U.S. soldiers and Marines, leaving their futures uncertain.

Like Frank's.

It wasn't his physical impairments that upset her most, a tearful Michelle told Harriet Zeiner, a VA neuropsychologist. It was that Frankie seemed not to remember who he really was.

That, Zeiner believed, could be the cruelest part of a brain injury. Losing a sense of who you are.

No one knows how the journey of Frank Sandoval will end. But this is how it began.

He joined the Army in the aftermath of Sept. 11. Part of it was patriotism. But he also wanted more for his new family than a job managing a pizza parlor in Yuma, Ariz., could provide. A former high school wrestling team captain and a big fan of Superman, Frank saw the military as a springboard to college and a career in law enforcement.

Those goals were the only things that could pull him away from the two lights of his life: Michelle and their daughter, Joelena.

That's how, on Nov. 28, 2005, Cpl. Sandoval came to be on a stretch of hilly, barren terrain in northern Iraq that baked under the midday sun. He manned the .50-caliber machine gun on a Humvee.

When Lt. Maurio Smith received the assignment to train Iraqi soldiers, he handpicked 12 men from his artillery battery to accompany him. Sandoval, 25, was his first choice. That's why he was atop Smith's lead vehicle. When you went down a dark alley, you wanted Sandoval covering your back.

And now, on an unfamiliar road in the middle of nowhere, as their small convoy slowed to cross a narrow bridge, everyone sensed danger.

Cpl. Randy Radant, in the last vehicle, had been counting holes in the road—ominous evidence of the deadly improvised explosive devices used by insurgents. In the second Humvee, Sgt. Nardello Keith heard Smith's warning over the radio to be ready for anything. Keith saw Sandoval turn and give a thumbs-up sign, indicating that the way looked clear.

Then there was a flash and a loud bang, followed by a mushroom cloud of dust and debris. A roadside bomb had ripped through the lead Humvee.

The three men inside the vehicle—Smith, driver Cpl. Jeff Neville and an Iraqi interpreter—were left stunned by the explosion. As Smith and Neville regained their senses, they called up to Sandoval, who had been standing in the gunner's hatch, his upper body exposed to the blast. He didn't respond. After racing up the road to safety, Neville scrambled on top of the Humvee to Sandoval. He was slumped back, unconscious.

He was bleeding, but Neville couldn't find the source—until he removed Sandoval's Kevlar helmet. Shrapnel, blown upward in the blast, had torn into his skull, just below the helmet's rim.

At the top of a hill, where they had driven to call for a rescue helicopter, the soldiers formed a protective cocoon around Sandoval. The minutes felt like years as they waited for the Black Hawk. Sandoval, a muscular man who could bench-press 300 pounds, roiled with seizures. Neville, Radant and Keith struggled to calm him.

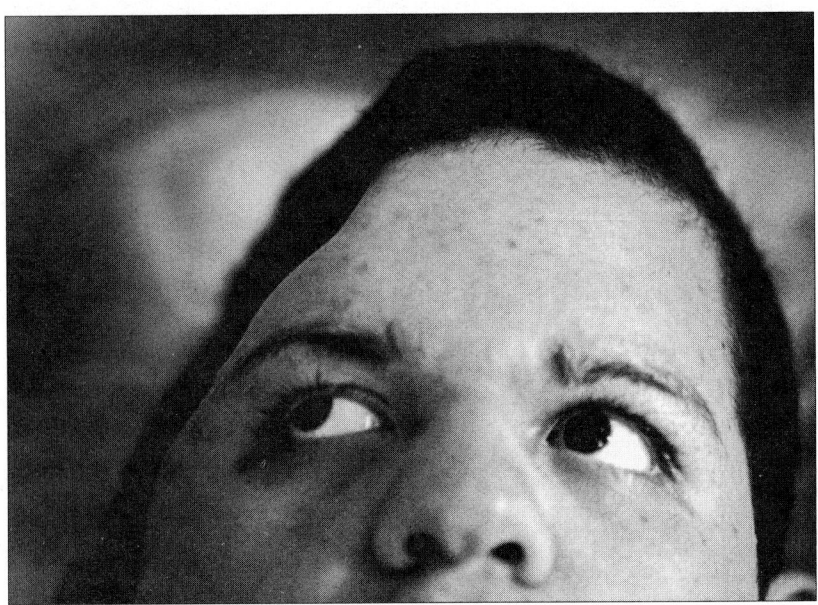

Doctors had to remove part of Cpl. Frank Sandoval's skull after a roadside bomb in Iraq sent shrapnel flying up under his helmet. (Photograph courtesy of Pauline Lubens/*San Jose Mercury News*)

Keith remembered sharing a sandwich with Sandoval at lunch, just an hour earlier. Now he was fighting back tears, cradling Sandoval's bloody head in his lap, cleaning vomit from his friend's face, not daring to look under the bandage.

Stay with us, Frank. Help is on the way. Think about your family. You're gonna make it.

Smith wasn't so sure. Neither was Radant, who had seen a ball bearing lodged in Sandoval's exposed and broken skull.

Back at the battery's home base in Mosul, 120 miles north, Capt. Tom Caldwell looked on as reports came into the operations center that one of his men had been wounded. Not Sandoval, he thought. Caldwell always believed that with a unit full of Sandovals, he could take over a small island.

Caldwell gathered some of his soldiers. They began to pray.

A Phone Call
Frantic Flight Overseas Before It's Too Late

In Arizona, 12 hours later and 8,000 miles away, Michelle Sandoval was picking up her younger sister from school. Her cell phone had kept ringing during her shift at a coffee shop, but every time she answered, the call would drop.

Michelle's mother had told her someone from the military had called at home, but that he would talk only to Frank Sandoval's wife. Michelle, increasingly anxious, had expected something bad.

It was.

Your husband suffered a serious head injury. He is out of surgery and will be transferred to Baghdad for the flight to a military hospital in Germany.

Michelle went numb. The only words she could focus on were: *He's alive.*

Back home at her parents', Michelle had become so frantic that she was scaring 3-year-old Joelena. After telling her father what had happened to Frank—the only boyfriend her dad had ever liked—Michelle disintegrated. She locked herself in the bathroom and sobbed for 15 minutes.

And then, she was done. Michelle decided there could be no more crying, no more negative thoughts. She would get through whatever came next.

By 7 the next morning Michelle was in Phoenix, where she had rushed to get a copy of the birth certificate she needed for an emergency passport. Her phone rang again. This time it was a doctor at Landstuhl Regional Medical Center.

If you're not here within 24 hours, Mrs. Sandoval, you might be too late.

She traveled to Germany on commercial flights with Frank's parents, Bea and Ricky. Ten days earlier, Bea had dreamt that Frank, the third of their four children, had been hurt. The premonition so unnerved her that she had e-mailed Frank, who was in his second deployment in Iraq, to make sure he was safe.

Don't worry, he responded.

Now, she was living that nightmare.

Ricky, a Homeland Security official along the California-Mexico border, had used his contacts to arrange for someone to sit with Frank, someone to whisper that they were coming.

He didn't want his son to die alone.

A Long Vigil
Risk Of Death Recedes; Hospital Is His New Home

When Michelle first saw him, Frank appeared to be sleeping peacefully. He had no cuts or bruises—only the bandage wrapped around his head. But it hid the severe injury that has become the signature wound of the war.

In clinical terms, he had suffered a penetrating brain injury that required a right decompressive craniectomy with a partial temporal and parietal lobectomy.

In layman's terms, surgeons had removed a section of his skull bigger than a softball—both bone destroyed by shrapnel and undamaged bone to relieve the pressure caused by massive swelling of his brain. In addition to brain tissue lost in the operation, both of his frontal lobes had been traumatized by the powerful blast, and he was suffering from aspiration pneumonia because he had inhaled vomit into his lungs.

When Frank arrived at Landstuhl, the doctors initially believed he would die. Instead, as the hours passed, his condition stabilized. Still, he was critical, and even if he did survive, he might be blind and partially paralyzed. Or he could remain in a vegetative state for the rest of his life.

Yet although Frank was in a coma, tears trickled down his face as Michelle and his parents spoke to him and held his hand.

The following weeks melted into one long vigil at Frank's side. Just four days after he was wounded, Frank, Michelle, Ricky and Bea flew on a transport plane that served as an airborne intensive-care unit to Andrews Air Force Base outside Washington, D.C. He was taken to the National Naval Medical Center in Bethesda, Md., where Michelle, after talking to an optimistic doctor, became convinced that Frank would survive.

But he remained a very sick man. He developed other infections. Frank was kept heavily sedated because he was on a ventilator, yet he still would become agitated and disoriented. He had to be restrained so he wouldn't hurt himself. Ricky thought his son's mind was still on the battlefield.

Even after he was transferred to Walter Reed Army Medical Center in Washington in mid-December, Ricky, Bea and Michelle barely ate or slept.

But slowly, Frank improved. He became more alert. On Christmas Eve, he left intensive care. A general came to award him a Purple Heart—the same honor his late grandfather, also named Frank Sandoval, had earned in the Korean War.

Although he was plagued by severe headaches, dizziness and nausea, doctors decided a few weeks later that he was ready to begin more extensive rehabilitation. On Jan. 23, he and Michelle arrived in Palo Alto, home to one of the VA's four polytrauma centers that treat traumatic brain injury, or TBI.

He had no memory of what happened to him and didn't seem to understand why he was in a VA hospital in Northern California.

In Palo Alto
A Painful Struggle Even For Small Things

Frank's temporary home was a room in Acute Care Ward 7D. Military rank had no place here. All patients were equal and shared the same plight. Everyone was trying to reclaim his or her life.

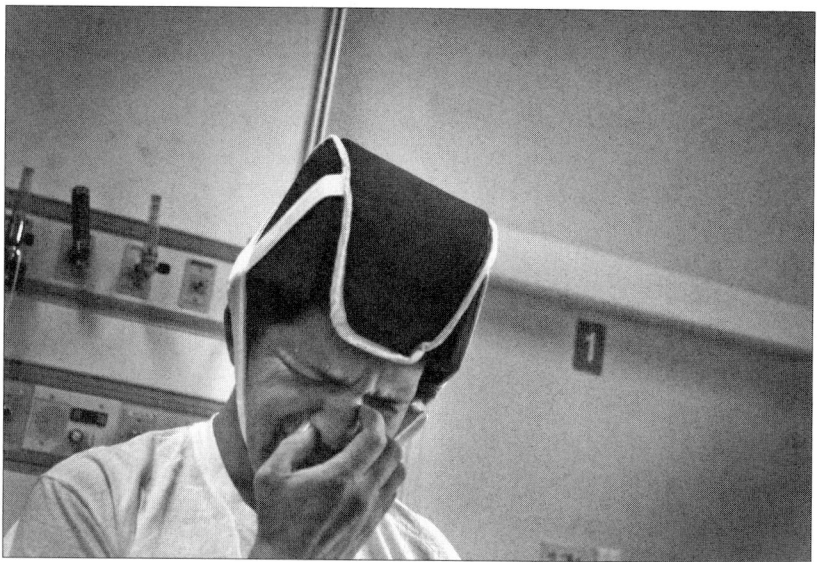

After a hard day's work, Frank begins to cry in his room at the Palo Alto Veterans Affairs hospital. The ward's chief neuropsychologist, Harriet Zeiner, says his crying is the only way he can express himself when he is tired, frustrated or overwhelmed. (Photograph courtesy of Pauline Lubens/*San Jose Mercury News*)

This was how that process started for Frank: He sat in a wheelchair, struggling to hold his head up for a few minutes of physical therapy.

He could barely do it.

Frank wanted to go back to bed. But Beth Pittman, a physical therapist, reminded him of his goal. If he wanted to walk again, he needed to regain his endurance and strength. That meant fighting through the fatigue.

Wearing a T-shirt, pajama bottoms and a protective helmet that made him look like a hockey player, Frank pounded his right fist on the wheelchair armrest. His face contorted into a look of sheer anguish—the way a young child appears in that silent moment before unleashing a scream of pain. What emerged from Frank's mouth was a whimper.

A photo on the wall, taken in Iraq, showed the brawny, intense-looking soldier he had been two months earlier. The man crying in the wheelchair had now lost more than 40 pounds and shared only a passing resemblance to the one in the picture.

His left arm and hand hung limp in his lap. He could move his left leg and foot only fractions of an inch.

He understood what was being said to him, but Frank's short-term memory lapses meant VA staff members had to repeat things like their names and the day of the week to him, over and over.

A weakened tongue and muscles of the mouth made swallowing difficult, so he tended to drool. His diet was limited to pureed food and thickened liquids. Because he ate so little, Frank had a feeding tube for nutritional supplements and 12 vitamins and medications—everything from an anti-seizure drug to Ritalin, which kept him calm.

His words were so difficult to comprehend that even speech pathologist Karen Kapolnek had trouble understanding what he said.

Except for one thing. Whenever his wife was not in the room, Frank repeatedly asked a question that everyone understood.

"Where's Michelle?"

Hidden Feelings
Would Frankie Ever Be the Same?

She no longer saw his disfiguring wound. All she saw was her Frankie.

Michelle seemed older than someone who was a few months shy of 22. She and Frank always had been an inseparable couple. Now, Michelle had moved into a nearby hotel and was living in a strange city, far from their daughter, who stayed with grandparents in Yuma.

She settled into a routine. Michelle arrived at the VA hospital most days at midmorning, always taking care to look her best, and she wouldn't leave until early evening. Michelle accompanied Frank to his therapy sessions, absorbing everything the VA staff said. And often they addressed her, not Frank.

Since her breakdown in the bathroom, Michelle had resolved to be strong for both of them. This would be the low point of their lives. Someday, they could look back and say: Can you believe how far we've come?

But she also was consumed with anxiety and doubt—feelings she didn't dare to display in front of Frank. That's what came tumbling out of her in a flood of emotion the day that Zeiner, the ward's chief neuropsychologist, asked about her husband's personality and who his therapists were trying to recapture. Michelle feared Frankie never would be the same.

A small, cheerful woman, Zeiner had worked with brain-injury patients for nearly 30 years. But since the fighting in Iraq and Afghanistan had begun, the ward was seeing an influx of more young wounded, along with their often-distraught loved ones. Improved body armor and life-saving techniques meant these soldiers had survived grievous wounds. Now Frank, like every other patient who came to the polytrauma center, faced the struggle of trying to rebuild his life.

Zeiner said Frank's condition was fairly typical for someone who had just suffered such a severe wound.

Frank's wife, Michelle, will also face profound challenges throughout their long struggle to rebuild a meaningful life in the wake of his grievous brain injury. When she first learned he was wounded, she locked herself in a bathroom and cried for 15 minutes. Then it was over—she decided there could be no more crying, no more negative thoughts. She decided they would get through whatever came next. (Photograph courtesy of Pauline Lubens/*San Jose Mercury News*)

His crying wasn't the result of depression. It was the only way he could express himself when he was tired, frustrated or overwhelmed. And sensory overload was common in TBI patients. Zeiner used this old-fashioned analogy: His mind was operating at 45 RPMs in a 78 RPM world.

His damaged brain would begin rewiring itself and create new connections to his body. Most of his improvement would occur within two years. How quickly he emerged from the fog of post-traumatic amnesia—this period when he was confused because his brain was unable to store or process new information—would be an indicator of how much he could be expected to recover.

Nothing, though, was guaranteed. No matter how hard a patient worked, sometimes there was just too much damage. As of Oct. 31, 1,652 American soldiers and Marines in Iraq and Afghanistan had been treated for brain trauma, ranging from mild to severe, according to the Defense and Veterans Brain Injury Center. Of those, it's estimated at least 250 are in assisted-living facilities, unable to care for themselves.

All Zeiner could promise was that she and the staff would help Frank return to the highest level of function possible.

"You can't have the life you had before, because you don't have the brain you had before," Zeiner said later. "But the trick is you can still have a meaningful life. Our job is to make sure hope stays alive."

Mental Struggle
Frank Finally Asks What Happened to Him

It would be weeks after their arrival in Palo Alto before Frank first asked Michelle about that day in November.

By then he had endured hours of physical, cognitive and emotional therapy—each session a painful ordeal. Some days were good, when therapists pushed his fragile body and mind to do just a little more than he thought possible. Other days, he mostly cried and begged to return to bed.

Nothing came easily. A simple tongue exercise—sucking on a LifeSaver that Kapolnek attached to a string to prevent choking—left Frank exhausted. Even basic memory drills, such as reciting the alphabet and counting backward from 20, inevitably resulted in a headache because just thinking drained his limited energy.

But he also had begun to propel his wheelchair around the ward for short distances. Occasionally, when Michelle was close by, his stoic demeanor—usually devoid of any expression—brightened.

"We know it's going to be a long path," Michelle said one afternoon, sitting next to Frank's bed. "It will be slow, but we'll get there."

It had been a few days earlier, during a trip around the VA grounds as Michelle pushed his wheelchair, when Frank finally wanted to know what had happened.

Michelle told him what she knew. About how he had been given only hours to live, and how she refused to believe it.

He became quiet and looked sad.

Michelle was sad, too.

She knew she probably would have to repeat this story to him many more times. He wouldn't remember.

42. The Signature Wound

DEC. 14, 2006

By Mark Emmons

The longer Dr. Elaine Date studied the medical file of Cpl. Frank Sandoval, the more certain she became: In any previous war, he never would have survived.

Shrapnel from a roadside bomb blast in Iraq had broken open his skull and damaged portions of his brain last November.

Yet here he was, alive and struggling to recover from what has been called the signature wound in the Iraq and Afghanistan conflicts:

Traumatic brain injury.

A sudden, blunt blow to the head can cause TBI, which in severe cases leaves people unable to perform even basic cognitive and physical functions. Military and VA doctors describe a perfect storm of contradictory factors that have contributed to a spike in the number of brain injuries compared to other recent conflicts.

Improvements in combat medicine and body armor, which protects vital organs, mean that fewer soldiers die on the battlefield. About 86 percent of all U.S. casualties have survived their injuries—the highest percentage in the history of warfare. In contrast, about 75 percent of all casualties survived in both the Persian Gulf War 15 years ago and the Vietnam War.

That blessing comes with a terrible catch. The survivors of these once-deadly wounds are returning home with devastating and disfiguring injuries that can require months of therapy and sometimes a lifetime of care.

Brain injury has become so prevalent because of the insurgents' primary weapon—the homemade bombs known as improvised explosive devices. Kevlar helmets only do so much to protect the brain's soft tissue, which is vulnerable to both flying shrapnel and the powerful force of the blasts.

Sandoval was critically injured by such a device, resulting in brain damage and forcing the removal of nearly a third of his skull. On this spring morning, 10 weeks after arriving at the Veterans Affairs hospital in Palo Alto, he was undergoing intense rehabilitation, trying to regain his ability to walk and speak. He aspired one day to be able to care for himself without assistance—and even go to college.

"He had a very severe brain injury," said Date, head of the Palo Alto VA's polytrauma center, one of four U.S. facilities that treat patients with TBI. "But I've been just amazed at the recovery of some of these guys. You never really know how far they can come back because there's still so much that we don't understand about the brain."

Pioneering Work
Doctors Still Learning Secrets Of Brain Trauma

Away from the battlefield, TBI is common but misunderstood. According to the Centers for Disease Control and Prevention, 1.4 million people in the United States sustain brain injuries each year. They range from mild, seeing-stars-type concussions to catastrophic injuries that result in permanent disability or death.

Now, the military and VA are on the front lines of TBI research and treatment.

Modern guerrilla warfare—where insurgents use suicide bombers and IEDs—has sharply increased the proportion of brain injuries suffered by American troops. By one 2005 estimate, 68 percent of all injuries sustained in Iraq and Afghanistan at that point were the result of IED blasts.

By Oct. 31, 1,652 soldiers had been treated for brain injuries since January 2003, according to the Defense and Veterans Brain Injury Center, based at Walter Reed Army Medical Center in Washington, D.C. Half of those injuries were moderate to severe, and of those, at least 250 ended up in assisted-care facilities.

As of July, doctors at Walter Reed, where many of the most seriously wounded are treated, had found that 28 percent of their patients suffered from a brain injury.

"The body armor saves lives but still leaves the brain at risk," said Dr. Barbara Sigford, the VA's national director of physical medicine and rehabilitation. That's because, Sigford added, the face and parts of the skull around the helmet are still exposed to shrapnel, and the brain remains susceptible to the blast force.

When Sandoval was wounded, shrapnel just missed his helmet's rim and struck his head. His brain also was damaged by the blast shock wave, which caused massive swelling and limited blood flow. Like many casualties, his life probably was saved by swift evacuation and emergency care. He was in surgery within hours in Balad, Iraq, then in a hospital in Germany the next morning and in Bethesda, Md., just four days after the explosion.

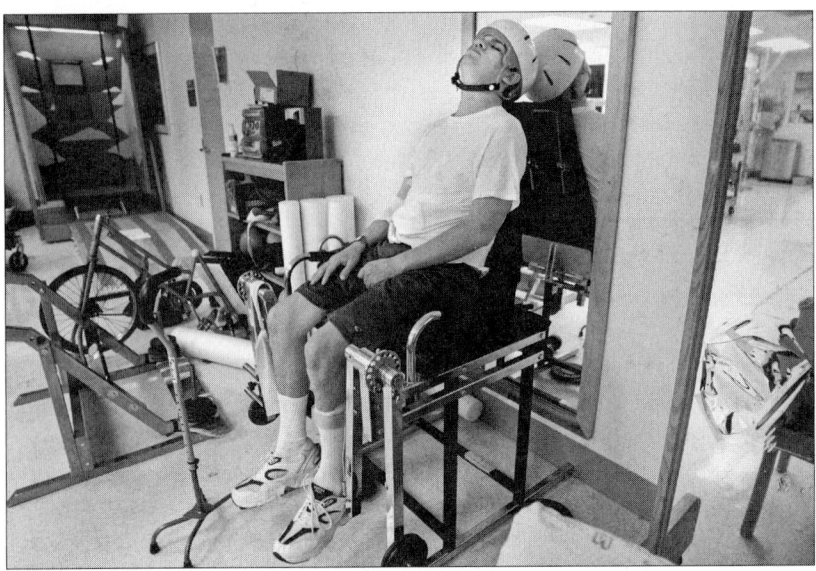

Sgt. Frank Sandoval—promoted from corporal while recovering from traumatic brain injury caused by a roadside bombing in Iraq—takes a break from physical therapy at the Veterans Affairs hospital in Palo Alto. The intensive rehabilitation is grueling and, at times, painful. (Photograph courtesy of Pauline Lubens/*San Jose Mercury News*)

Sandoval's injuries are so severe that they are apparent to anyone who encounters him. But the military system has struggled to deal with another type of TBI, called a closed-head injury, which can be harder to detect. That's why TBI has acquired another moniker:

The invisible wound.

Silver Lining
The Military's Experience May Advance Medicine

VA experts say an untold number of soldiers who seem to survive IED blasts without injury are actually being seriously hurt. They suffer concussions as their brains are slammed violently against the insides of their skulls. That's a concern because a severe concussion, or the cumulative effect of multiple milder concussions, can result in permanent brain damage.

For the military, the vexing question is determining when soldiers are healthy enough to return to the field. For the VA, brain injuries are presenting enormous challenges.

VA facilities are discovering more previously undiagnosed cases of mild brain injury after people have left the service—often when family members complain about a loved one's memory lapses or chronic irritability.

In Palo Alto, an average of eight veterans a month who served in Iraq or Afghanistan are diagnosed with previously undetected brain impairments when they come in for screenings.

Meanwhile, seriously wounded active-duty soldiers such as Sandoval are transferred to Palo Alto and the other VA polytrauma centers because the main military hospitals, such as Walter Reed, are not equipped to deal with long-term brain-injury rehabilitation.

That's why Palo Alto's center has seen a steady flow of mostly young soldiers with TBI. These patients also often have other severe blast-related wounds such as amputations and spinal injuries.

As of mid-November, the brain-injury unit had cared for 116 service members who did tours in Iraq or Afghanistan—more than half hurt in the war zone, the rest after returning home, often in car accidents.

Some VA staff members wonder whether that second group of victims, once out of the war theater, were more likely to be in traffic accidents because they were used to driving faster and more recklessly in Iraq to avoid IEDs. Date, the Palo Alto polytrauma center chief, theorizes that some might have suffered a brain impairment in Iraq that later contributed to their car wrecks.

The VA has struggled to deal with the sudden influx of people suffering from this wound of 21st-century warfare. Injured soldiers receive VIP care at the polytrauma centers, where no expense is spared. But the VA has faced criticism that it was slow to expand its overall treatment of TBI. A July report by the Department of Veterans Affairs' inspector general concluded the VA needed to provide better long-term health care for this unprecedented wave of patients.

Dr. Michael Kussman, the VA's acting undersecretary of health, said it has reorganized, creating 21 smaller regional centers to provide better treatment. But Kussman added that some frustration by families may be unavoidable. Having seen the military "save" their wounded loved ones, they expect the VA now to "restore" their lives.

"But the reality is, that might not be possible," Kussman said. "They may be too severely injured and might end up in assisted care. We have to deal with families who feel like we failed them, and they lash out at us. I'm not saying they're wrong to do so, but that can be very hurtful."

And there have been some families, Date said, who thought the Palo Alto VA hadn't done enough.

But Kussman and others believe that if there is anything approaching a silver lining, it is that better research and treatment in the military sector eventually will improve civilian care for brain-injury victims as well.

Renee Kawahara gives Frank water therapy. He finds it relaxing, and it provides a low-impact way for him to work his leg muscles. (Photograph courtesy of Pauline Lubens/*San Jose Mercury News*)

"We've heard people say, 'You're saving people who would have died in the past, but is that the right decision?'" said Dr. Michael Kilpatrick, a deputy director in the Department of Defense's Office of Health Affairs. "Well, when you have a survival success and you ask them if we made the right decision to save them on the battlefield, the answer is pretty obvious."

Sandoval had his answer. He planned to go to his church, Immaculate Conception Parish in Yuma, Ariz., when he returned home.

"To thank God I'm alive," he said, his words difficult to understand. "This makes me appreciate life more."

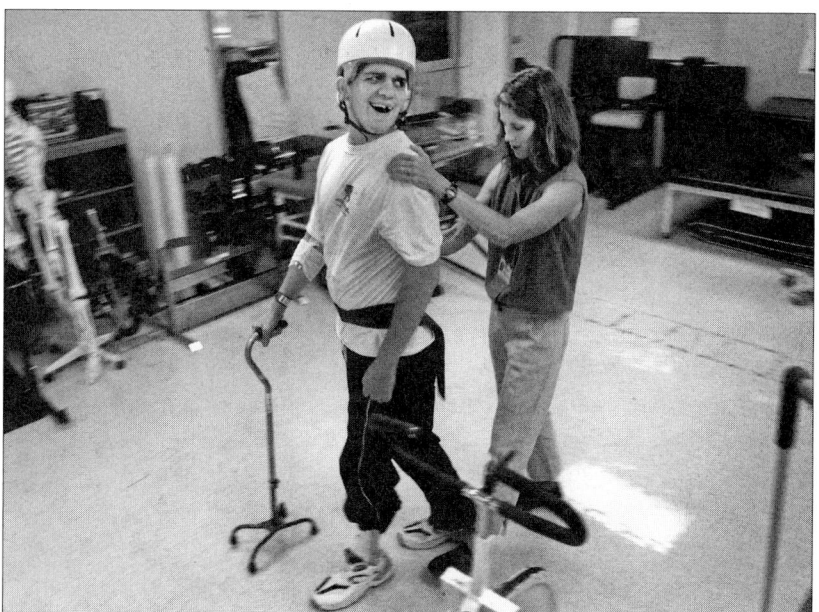

Frank is feeling pretty good about his progress as he works with physical therapist Debbie Pitsch at the VA hospital. His left arm, hand and leg need a lot of work because of brain and nerve damage. He hopes one day to be able to care for himself without assistance—even to go to college. (Photograph courtesy of Pauline Lubens/*San Jose Mercury News*)

After a pause, he added:
"I'm not a quitter."

Pushing Limits
Moving Inches At a Time, Frank Learns to Walk Again

Three months after he arrived in Palo Alto, the newly promoted Sgt. Sandoval took his biggest step yet.

He walked.

With his weak left arm strapped onto a walker, and with a VA staff member behind him, supporting him with a strap around his waist, Sandoval could stand tall and shuffle slowly around the gym. Every step was an unbalanced stagger. He had to be constantly reminded to lift his left foot.

But each day, he went just a little farther. His longest walk to date came on a June afternoon as physical therapist Sae Lowe helped him down a long hallway from the gym to his room. Two-thirds of the way, Sandoval stopped, cried out in pain and shook the walker with his right hand.

"I know you're tired and I know you hurt," Lowe said. "But you can do this. We're almost there."

After a moment, he straightened up and started moving again, just inches at a time. When he reached his room, he slumped into his wheelchair. Lowe, dripping with sweat, gave him a high-five. But Sandoval showed no happiness at his accomplishment—only exhaustion.

He had walked for 17 minutes.

The Human Toll
Soldiers Reflect on How They Were Hurt

A few weeks later, the human toll of war was on display at Acute Care Ward 7D. Everyone gathered for a Friday barbecue that some of the polytrauma center's patients had planned and were helping to serve.

Sandoval rolled his wheelchair over to a picnic table and pulled up next to Tim Jeffers, a 22-year-old Marine from Fountain Valley who had lost both legs, an eye, an ear and a finger and wore a helmet similar to Sandoval's to protect his head.

"How did you get hurt?" Sandoval asked.

"IED," Jeffers answered.

"Me too," Sandoval said. "I was in a Humvee."

"I was on foot," Jeffers said. "I got out of the Humvee to look for the IED. But it found me."

Their conversation was so matter-of-fact that they could have been discussing the weather. Then, they both silently returned to eating their lunch.

43. The Home Front

DEC. 15, 2006

By Mark Emmons

On the day they had been anticipating for months, Sgt. Frank Sandoval pulled his wife Michelle close and asked her to do something for him.

"Pray for me," he said.

Frank was about to have surgery that would restore his head, disfigured by a roadside bomb in Iraq, to its normal shape.

He was scared, but Michelle hoped this would be the turning point in Frank's recovery from a traumatic brain injury.

Doctors and therapists at Palo Alto's Veterans Affairs hospital thought the operation might reduce the headaches that had contributed to a plateau in his progress. They also were certain it would improve his self-image.

He had become increasingly negative about his appearance. He had told Michelle: I'm a monster. Another time, as he stared at himself in a mirror, Frank said bitterly that they were like Beauty and the Beast.

Michelle responded: But the Beast becomes a handsome prince at the end of the story. She believed that after this day, June 28, her prince would begin to re-emerge.

There are pivotal moments in the recovery of every severely wounded service member, moments when the future—for both the wounded and their families—seems to hang in the balance. For Frank and Michelle, who had staked so much on this surgery, there was a sense that they had arrived at their own crossroads.

Later, after the three-hour operation, Dr. Stephen Skirboll came into the waiting room and said he had successfully implanted the artificial "bone flap"—a prosthesis that replaced the portion of his skull lost in a November explosion. Michelle, surrounded by family who had made the trip from Yuma, Ariz., was giddy with excitement.

"When you see Daddy, he's going to be a new person," she told their 4-year-old daughter, Joelena.

But Michelle's elation evaporated when she saw him in the intensive-care unit. She came out moments later, distraught. Frank was suffering a seizure.

Michelle looked stunned as she slowly sat down on a waiting room couch. She put her head on her mother's shoulder and began to weep quietly. Joelena climbed into Michelle's lap and wiped away her tears.

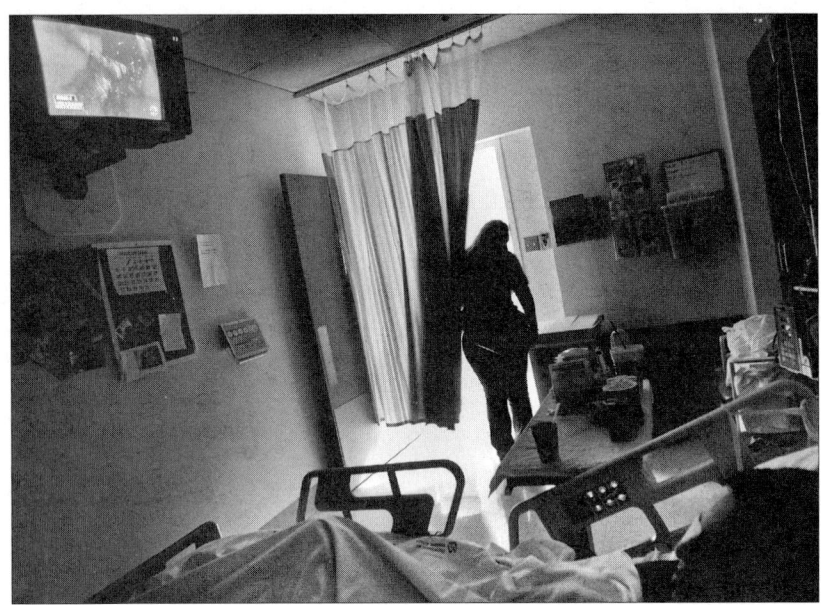

Michelle Sandoval leaves husband Frank's room at the VA hospital in Palo Alto to spend the night in her hotel room. (Photograph courtesy of Pauline Lubens/*San Jose Mercury News*)

"Why are you crying, Mommy?" Joelena asked. "Is Daddy dead?"
Michelle sobbed even harder.

Finding Direction
First Fatherhood, Then the Army

They had met when Michelle applied for a job in a pizza parlor. Frank, four years older, was the manager. He was smitten by the girl with the long dark hair. She was intrigued by the guy who had been a wrestling standout.

The pregnancy her senior year of high school was unexpected, but they had already talked about getting married. And the birth of Joelena profoundly changed Frank's life. He was somebody who knew what beer tasted like and had been in his share of fights—although by his telling they were only for the right reasons, such as sticking up for one of his siblings.

But fatherhood gave him direction. The wedding was four months after Joelena was born. A few weeks later, in July 2002, he was at Army boot camp. Frank thrived in the military, becoming the guy other soldiers looked up to because he seemed to have his act together.

The only thing Frank disliked about the Army was being separated from the two people whose names were tattooed over his heart: Michelle and Joelena. He had been through one deployment in Iraq when, in late

July 2005, he was preparing for a second tour. He already was nervous about returning to Iraq.

As they were driving from Yuma to Fort Sill in Lawton, Okla., where he was stationed, Frank lost control of their sport-utility vehicle during a rainstorm. They hit a guardrail and flipped. Joelena, whose injuries included a facial cut that required 30 stitches, and Michelle's younger sister, who hurt her arm, were airlifted to a Phoenix hospital.

Frank thought the Army would delay his deployment so he could stay with Joelena. It didn't. A week later, he was back in Iraq.

The next time the family was together, in December, Joelena sat at his bedside at Walter Reed Army Medical Center in Washington, D.C.

The Rock
Michelle Is Holding the Family Together

Frank had no more seizures.

But the morning after the surgery, he moaned in pain. His head was swollen so much it looked like a pumpkin. The staples holding together his scalp gave the appearance of a horseshoe-shaped zipper in his shaved head.

Michelle had regained her confidence that this would mark a new beginning for Frank.

"Of course, you're in pieces when you see something like that," she said of Frank's convulsions. "But you have to look forward, and he's going to get better."

Michelle never could have imagined being able to deal with all this. She always had thought of herself as "overly dramatic and weak." In their marriage, she had been content to follow Frank's lead.

Now, she was the family rock and decision-maker—the one who dealt with the bills and military paperwork involving Frank's care. She helped dress him, wiped drool from his chin, helped him use the bathroom.

The weight of their world rested on her shoulders. And every day seemed to present some new challenge.

There were times she felt so despondent that she would start to pray, saying: God, please, I can't take much more. But she would stop herself. Somehow, it didn't seem right to be asking for so much when she had never been very religious.

Because she lived in a hotel with no close friends or family in the area, she would spend hours on the phone with her mother. When she felt overwhelmed or frustrated with Frank, Michelle also would turn to VA neuropsychologist Harriet Zeiner and her graduate student, Soyoun Park, for support, or just a good cry.

One low point, early in Frank's stay in Palo Alto, came as he struggled with positional vertigo that left him feeling constantly ill and dizzy. Michelle began to steel herself for the possibility that this was going to be their life, that Frank always would be this disabled.

But then the vertigo began to subside. It reinforced Michelle's belief that if she just stayed positive, they could have a happy ending that included buying a house and having another child.

"I am young," Michelle said. "I'm only 22. But I'm also mature. I know what I have to do, and being young has nothing to do with making sure that I get it done. I love Frankie and I wouldn't be here if I didn't want to be.

"This experience is changing us. But it's changed me for the better."

This much was certain: Frank was completely dependent on her. And whenever Michelle was not around, he wouldn't stop asking for her.

Zeiner said at least part of the reason for that was his anxiety that nobody would want this "damaged" guy—and that one day she wouldn't come back.

For a badly injured Iraq veteran, it was not an unwarranted fear.

When Love Dies
Many Can't Face Role Of Lifetime Caretaker
Eric Cagle, a medically retired Army staff sergeant from Tucson, had been partially paralyzed and lost his right eye when shrapnel from a roadside bomb penetrated his brain in October 2004. His wife divorced him a year later. He was devastated. She had been his motivation, Cagle said, to "not be a cripple."

On his first day in Palo Alto, it had fallen to Zeiner to break the news that she was leaving.

One day, Cagle was talking to Michelle. "I wish I had a wife like you who stuck around," he said.

About 60 percent of the patients treated at the Palo Alto polytrauma center were seeing their marriages dissolve, Zeiner said. Typically, the breaking point for spouses would not occur at Walter Reed, right after their loved ones had been severely wounded.

"It happens at acute rehab facilities like this one, when they see the improvement ending," Zeiner said.

And reality sets in. Young spouses—and that included husbands, because women with brain injuries also were treated on the ward—found they had lost something precious, too: their vision of married life. Many had been unable to accept a new future that might include assuming the role of permanent caretaker.

That could explain why it was just as common to see parents on the brain-injury ward as it was spouses. Other ward patients spent their time alone.

Zeiner was careful not to judge, saying that people can never know what choices they would make unless faced with a similar situation. But she believed that the success of a marriage depended on the reasons the couple married in the first place.

"Michelle married Frank because she thought he was a good man who could provide for their family, but not because she wanted to be taken care of," Zeiner said. "Her opinion hasn't changed. They both believe in obligations, and that's exactly what can hold a family together."

But the stress was taking a toll on Michelle.

Fog Is Lifting
Intelligence, Memory, Flashes Of Darkness

Since he returned to the ward after his surgery, Frank's helmet had sat on the floor, unused. He received compliments on how handsome he looked. He was quicker to smile, and hints of a playful sense of humor were resurfacing. Although he was still self-conscious about his speech and had developed a habit of responding to most questions by saying, "I don't know," it was becoming clear that Frank in fact did know the answers. The fog inside his mind was fading, and his intelligence and long-term memory were emerging intact.

He had begun walking with a four-pronged cane—as a physical therapist supported him with a strap around his waist. His headaches had lessened.

Yet for all those improvements, his mood also could swing dark whenever he became frustrated. And he had become more prone to vent his anger on the person closest to him—Michelle. Sometimes his spirit could drain away almost instantly and he would tell her: Why don't I just die?

Michelle knew he didn't mean it. But other comments Frank made felt like daggers to her heart.

You're just going to leave me anyway. You don't really love me.

"I'll be like, 'How dare you say that to me!'" she recounted. "It makes me feel like everything I'm doing is for nothing. I just feel like lashing out at Frankie. But I know I can't, because that doesn't help either one of us."

There was a contributing factor to his growing anger. Frank was getting sick.

In late July, his head began swelling again and became red. Michelle was the first to notice something was wrong. Tests confirmed that he had contracted a dangerous bacterial infection known as methicillin-resistant Staphylococcus aureus, or MRSA, which is common in hospital settings.

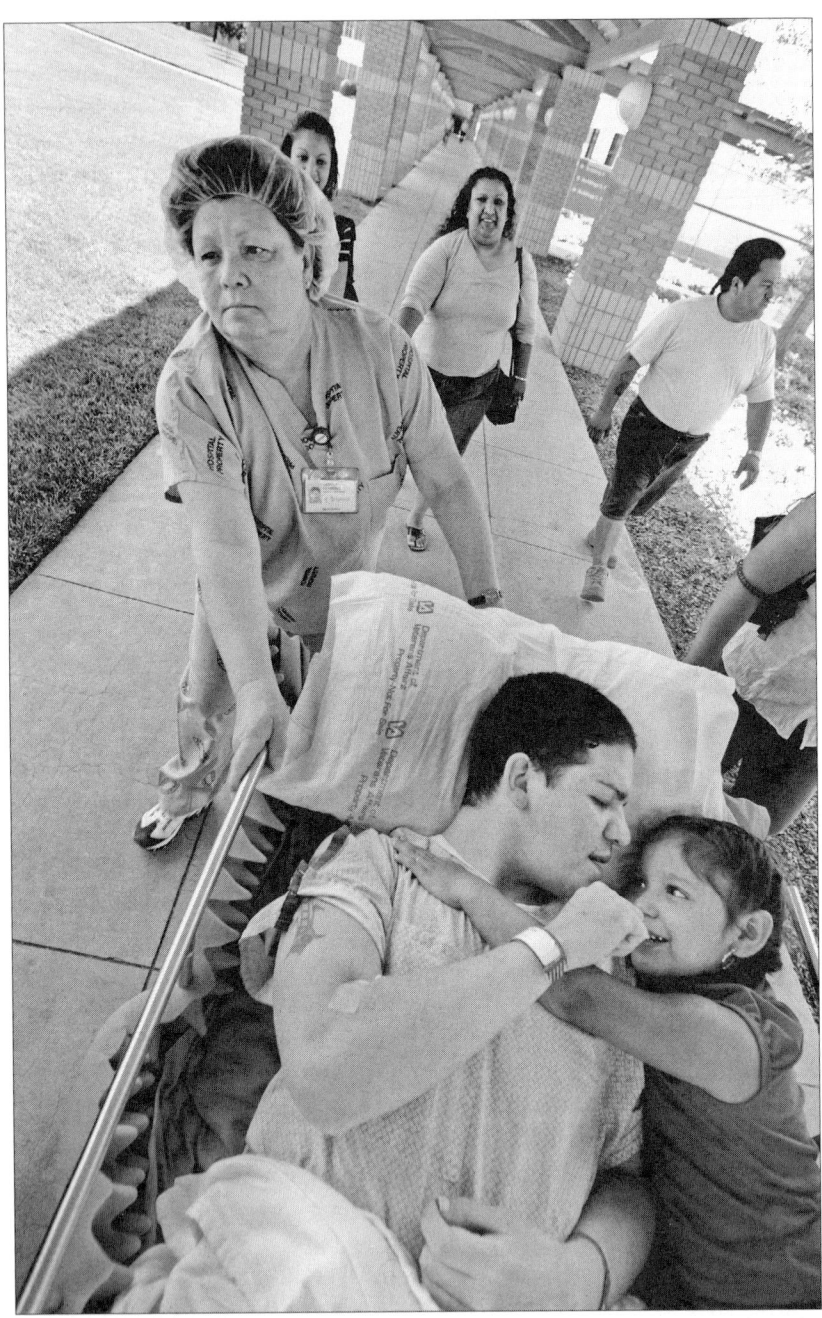

Frank and his daughter, Joelena, give each other a reason to smile as Frank heads for the operating room where doctors will put in a "bone flap" meant to restore his head to its normal shape. (Photograph courtesy of Pauline Lubens/*San Jose Mercury News*)

The bone flap might have to be removed.

"I know this isn't what you want to hear and I'm really sorry," said Dr. Angie Boparai, breaking the news. "But I don't want you to give up hope. This is just a little step back."

When she left the room, Frank turned to Michelle.

"I can't go back to surgery," he said.

She was too distraught to speak.

Staying Strong
Emotionally Drained, Forced to Wait Again

A week later, on Aug. 2, in a darkened VA hospital, Michelle was a forlorn figure as she sat in the same waiting room. Frank was undergoing brain surgery again.

Emotionally drained, she began to talk. The words came slowly at first, and then began rushing out in a torrent. About how she hated being away from her daughter. How it hurt to see Frank losing the strength that he had worked so hard to build. How his despair was wearing her down.

But something else bothered her, too. Another couple she had met on the ward had just split—two years after the husband had suffered a brain injury.

"I can see families breaking apart early, like now, when we're going through something like this," she said. "But not after two years. They've come too far to let it happen."

Michelle stopped and thought about what she had just said.

"Of course I can break anytime," she added. "There are times when I wonder if my body can handle any more. But I'm trying to keep strong for my husband. I intend to stay true to my wedding vows. When you say something, you should mean it."

A tired-looking Skirboll, the surgeon, arrived and told Michelle that he had removed the infected bone flap. In six months, they could put in another prosthesis. Until then, Frank's head once again would have a sunken appearance, and he would have to wear the helmet to protect his brain.

It was nearing midnight when Michelle visited Frank in an intensive-care unit that was silent except for the beeping of machines. He was still unconscious.

She found a washcloth and gently began wiping his face.

44. The Turning Point

DEC. 16, 2006

By Mark Emmons

One of the first signs that Sgt. Frank Sandoval's mind was beginning to reawaken came during a summer visit by a Marine Corps general.

It had been a rough day, with Frank complaining of fatigue and asking the nurses to put him back in bed. Frank seemed less than impressed that a three-star general wanted to stop by his Palo Alto Veterans Affairs hospital room. Yet he perked up as Lt. Gen. John Sattler, an exuberant presence, marched in and drew Frank into a real conversation—something he usually avoided because it was so difficult for him to speak.

Sattler placed a hand on Frank's shoulder and said: "We need your warrior spirit because you are what keeps the rest of us strong."

Frank's eyes moistened. And even after the general left, Frank remained so animated that neuropsychologist Harriet Zeiner and speech pathologist Karen Kapolnek looked at each other as if to say: *What just happened here?*

"When you have a leader like that," Frank told them, "you're willing to die for him."

The next week, Frank took part in a mock talk show in the brain injury ward's lunch room—an event arranged to help him work on his speech.

He answered questions about his favorite sport, boxing. Frank had fought bouts in the Army, earning the nickname "Sandman" because it was said he put his opponents to sleep by knocking them out. He even demonstrated how to throw punches and showed the 5-foot-1 Zeiner how to get into a proper boxing stance.

Laughing and smiling, he looked like a different man. It was as if Frank, eight months after suffering a severe brain injury in a roadside blast in Iraq, had begun remembering who he was: a soldier, and something more.

A fighter.

"I can take a punch and most guys can't," Frank said a few days later. "But I never thought I could get hurt like this. I've never been knocked down this bad before. Now I'm trying to get back up."

Quiet Heroes
He's Come So Far, There's So Far to Go

VA staff members often would talk about the bravery of their patients. It wasn't because they had volunteered for the military and suffered horrible wounds, but rather for the quiet heroism they displayed in the daily ordeal of therapy. They saw the often-heartbreaking sight of mostly young men, grievously injured, still finding the will to try to reclaim their lives.

Frank, in particular, was widely admired in the hospital's polytrauma center because of how far he had come and how much effort it still took him to do the simplest tasks. Even swallowing pills was a struggle.

Just days after the surgery to remove the artificial "bone flap" that temporarily had restored his head to its normal shape, Frank had once again resumed his regimen of physical, cognitive and emotional therapy. In a single day, he could meet with as many as six therapists—a schedule that would leave him exhausted.

Most days followed a common pattern. He would start each session strong but, as pain and fatigue set in, he would begin to complain—sometimes pounding his fist—and plead to return to bed. Relentlessly upbeat therapists would try to coax him into just a few more minutes of work.

Smita Shukla, an occupational therapist whose role was to help Frank return to normal daily living, had a knack for getting the most from him. One of her tactics, when Frank started to balk, was to stop and ask him to rate his pain level on a scale of 1 to 10. (Frank, for some reason, usually said "6.") She would give him a minute to rest, then resume the session as if nothing had happened.

Early in his stay, Frank had begun to bond with Shukla, a native of India who arrived in the United States in 1987 as a student and became a citizen so she could work at the VA. He clearly trusted her. When the 5-foot-11 Frank stood, he would lean on her for support even though Shukla's head came up only to his shoulders.

Frank was the first patient injured in Iraq with whom Shukla had worked, and she was proud to be able to help a soldier regain the use of his body.

That was evident earlier in the spring during a dedication ceremony for Palo Alto's Fisher House, which provides free lodging to families of VA patients. When the national anthem began, Frank—then still using a wheelchair—popped up, stood at attention and put his right hand over his heart.

The display of determination had been inspiring and completely unexpected.

As Shukla stood next to him that moment, she began to cry.

Endurance
French Toast For Joelena

As the weeks passed and Frank's endurance grew, Shukla showed him how to move safely around the ward kitchen and cook with one hand, because his left arm and hand were still so weak. (It was Frank's dream, when he

With an aide to help him, Frank Sandoval and his wife, Michelle, spend part of their last full day in California, Sept. 14, in Santa Cruz. After a departure from the VA hospital that feels like a graduation ceremony, they face the hardest challenge yet—the real world. (Photograph courtesy of Pauline Lubens/*San Jose Mercury News*)

returned home, to cook french toast for his daughter, Joelena.) When he and his wife, Michelle, began to venture out on day trips, Shukla sometimes would rearrange her schedule so she could accompany them to help.

On a shopping trip to Mervyns, Shukla helped Michelle pick out clothes for Frank. And she calmed Michelle, who became frantic when they left the store and found cars parked next to her sport-utility vehicle—giving her no room to get Frank in the passenger seat. Shukla suggested pushing Frank's wheelchair under a tree in an empty part of the lot and driving over to him.

"These are the kinds of things that both of you have to think about when you're back home," Shukla told Michelle.

But there were times Frank didn't want assistance, and he would vent his anger on Shukla. One day in August, she was pushing him particularly hard as they walked in the lunch room. Frank suddenly took a few steps—without any support—as he headed for a chair. He was wobbling as Shukla caught up with him. She told him, bluntly, that he had put himself at risk.

Frank yelled: *Stop lecturing me!*

He later apologized and made sure Shukla knew he considered her "my friend." And Shukla, who had been embarrassed by his outburst, came to look on the incident as a positive sign. Frank was almost ready to go home.

Brain-injury patients stay on the ward as long as they continue to make progress. Frank's physical recovery had produced mixed results. While he was regaining control of his left leg and foot, his left arm still was mostly numb and hung limp at his side.

Because of the location of his brain injury, VA staff members thought it was unlikely Frank would fully regain fine-motor control in his left hand. He also seemed more interested in putting his limited energy into walking.

Still, Shukla thought he could be strangely resistant to putting in the effort needed to regain even some use of his hand, and that worried her. The less he could do, the more burden would be placed on Michelle.

"Motivation and drive will take him as far as he goes," Shukla said. "He can become mostly independent. But it has to come from within. There's no magic. It's all up to him."

Counseling Session
Frank, Michelle Try For a United Front

Frank seemed surprised when, in a counseling session, Zeiner told him how he had "put Michelle through a few weeks of hell." As Frank's skull prosthesis became infected, he had taken out his frustration on the person he loved the most.

Hearing that, his first reaction was to reach for Michelle. Lack of impulse control is one effect of frontal lobe brain injuries, and Michelle often was uncomfortable with Frank's habit of grabbing for her. Michelle, still upset over how she had been treated, definitely didn't want to be hugged now.

"I was mad," he told Michelle.

"Frank," Zeiner said, "not everyone thought you would come this far. But Michelle always did. You need to remember that it's always going to be you and Michelle against the brain injury. You are allies. You always need to stay united against the real enemy in this war—the brain injury."

"I'm sorry," he said to Michelle, with real contrition.

These daily sessions had become a mix of marriage counseling and real-world preparation. When Frank left the VA, Zeiner told him, he would have to adjust to a society that would make few allowances for his brain injury. People would make instant assumptions about him based on his appearance, the way he talked and his memory lapses.

Zeiner also wanted Frank to understand that he would be setting himself up for disappointment if he expected perfection from himself.

"Your speech, your memory, your walking is all going to improve," she said. "But I suspect it's never going to be what it was before the IED. Are you going to be OK with that?"

"No," Frank answered.

"Well, that might have to change," Zeiner responded. "That decision was made the moment the bomb went off. You were lucky to survive. But there was a loss. . . ."

Said Frank: "I want to be better. I want to go to college. I want to work for the DEA," referring to the Drug Enforcement Agency.

"You will be better," Zeiner continued. "Just don't be focused on becoming who you were, because that's the wrong goal. Let's just concentrate right now on getting you home as a functioning, independent person."

In the following weeks, Frank and Michelle began acting more like a normal couple. They went to movies. One weekend they stayed in a specially designed apartment on the ward. It gave them a taste of being on their own—with nurses still just down the hall. When that went smoothly, Frank spent the next two weekends with Michelle at her hotel.

That trial run of independence gave Michelle confidence that she would be able to take care of Frank when they returned home. The privacy also allowed them their first opportunity for sexual intimacy since he had been wounded. But that effort was stymied, Michelle said later, because Frank wasn't yet quite able to move his body the way he wanted.

"But that's the least of my worries," Michelle said. "And I know that sounds strange."

Going Home
Last Test, and Good News: It's Graduation Day

On Sept. 13, Frank was standing in his hospital room, between Michelle and his father, Ricky, when Dr. Angie Boparai entered. The last roadblock to his departure was confirmation that he had been successfully treated for the infection that led to his third brain surgery. For days, Frank and Michelle—tired of dreary hours of therapy, pills and bad hospital food—nervously had awaited the final test results.

After a dramatic pause, Boparai said: "You get to go home!"

Frank jumped with excitement, no small feat for a man doctors initially thought might never walk.

Two days later, staff members and patients gathered for going-away cake. As Frank proudly walked into the lunch room, using his cane and Michelle for support, he basked in their applause.

"When we got the worst news possible last year . . . ," Michelle said, her voice cracking. "And to see him now and how far he has come, I just want to say thank you."

Then Frank stood. He tried to speak loudly so he could be heard, but that made him more difficult to understand. So Michelle repeated his words:

"To the other soldiers, keep fighting. Don't give up."

Then, more than nine months after he had escaped death, Frank left the VA. He had undergone something of a rebirth. The moment had the feel of a graduation ceremony. But in truth, Frank's most difficult challenge was just beginning—the real world.

Left behind in Frank's empty room was a message from Michelle on a small white board.

"Thanks to all the staff that helped through our process. See ya all soon. Sandovals."

Family Lore
Message from the Past Gives Him Inspiration

On the drive home to Yuma, Ariz., Frank told his father of a vision he had sometime after he was wounded.

It was part of the family lore that Frank's grandfather, who earned a Purple Heart in the Korean War, had felt the presence of his deceased father watching over him on the battlefield.

Now, Frank recalled his grandfather, who had died in 2003, appearing to him.

Go back, he had told Frank in Spanish.

It's not your time yet.

45. Coming Home

DEC. 17, 2006

By Mark Emmons

Lunch diners at the bustling Mexican restaurant occasionally would steal quick glances. They looked at his helmet, or watched him repeatedly wipe saliva from his mouth.

If Sgt. Frank Sandoval noticed, he didn't say anything.

"It is a little weird when we go someplace and people will stare, but I don't pay any attention," his wife, Michelle, said. "He's a hero. He served in the war. But they don't need to know that. The only thing that matters is that we know."

Truth was, many people in their hometown knew all about Frank. His September return, after months of recovery from a severe brain injury suffered in Iraq, was well-publicized. People might have been curious, but they also were respectful.

One day, a woman came up and insisted on paying for their meal. When they went shopping for a mattress, the store owner told them it would be an honor to give them one for free. During those first weeks, people would approach Frank just to shake his hand.

"I can tell that Frankie feels good when that happens," Michelle said. "It makes him feel important."

Frank shrugged his shoulders when asked if he felt a little like a celebrity. He seemed more content to be out of Palo Alto's Veterans Affairs hospital and back home. Most of all, Frank said, he enjoyed just being around family.

"Especially Joelena," he said.

Although at this moment, their 4-year-old daughter Joey—as Frank liked to call her—was antsy. Frank said something indecipherable in a stern voice.

"What are you saying, Dad?" she asked.

"Listen closely so you can understand him," Michelle said.

Frank repeated himself, this time more slowly and with a rhythmic cadence: "Behave, Joey."

After paying the bill, Michelle helped Frank maneuver out of his chair and slowly head toward the door with his cane. Some in the restaurant silently watched them leave.

In early October, the temperature still approached 100 degrees in Yuma, located just across the California state line. But Frank said the hot, desert climate did not remind him of Iraq—even though helicopters from nearby Marine Corps Air Station Yuma sometimes passed overhead.

For now, they were living with Frank's parents, who had just moved into a new house. Frank liked staying with them because he was close to his father, Ricky, a Homeland Security official along the California-Mexico border.

Michelle, though, was nervous about moving in with her in-laws. There had been some past friction between Michelle and Frank's mom, Bea. And when Frank was wounded, it had been difficult for Bea to let Michelle take the lead in the recovery of her youngest son.

But while there still was a little tension, the women had an unspoken agreement: They would focus on Frank.

"We've never been that close," Bea said. "But I really admire how she has been there for Frank."

She also knew how tight their bond had become. One day after their return to Yuma, Frank wondered aloud to Bea whether it would be better for Michelle to leave him—if that's what would make her happy.

Frank, his mother had told him, I think she's happy being with you.

Dream House
Michelle's Deepest Wish Is to Be on Their Own

Where Frank and Michelle eventually wanted to be was in a place of their own. For months, Frank had been asking Michelle what he could get her to show his appreciation for everything she had done.

"What kind of jewelry?" Frank had asked once, when they were still in Palo Alto. "A ring? Bracelet? Necklace?"

"You know what I want," Michelle said.

"Earrings?"

"A house, Frankie."

The dream of a home had helped sustain Michelle during the low points of Frank's excruciatingly slow recovery. But they faced some hurdles. Michelle's full-time job was taking care of Frank and Joey. It wasn't clear what exactly Frank's monthly benefits would be because he hadn't yet been medically retired by the Army.

Frank had received $100,000 from the military's traumatic injury insurance program—the maximum amount. Ricky also had done some fundraising.

Michelle had been pre-approved for a loan big enough to buy a nice tract home. But before she could go house-hunting, the loan officer called

Frank cries as he is reunited with his grandmother, Rosa Sandoval, in Yuma. Her late husband, Frank said, appeared to him when he was wounded and told him it wasn't his time to die. (Photograph courtesy of Pauline Lubens/*San Jose Mercury News*)

back. Frank's name was still on the title of a house he had once shared with his brother, who now was behind on payments. They couldn't get the loan until that was resolved.

Meanwhile, Michelle found herself trapped in the military's health care bureaucracy.

Waning Support
Outside the Hospital, No More VIP Treatment

Frank might not have missed the hospital food in Palo Alto, but there was a downside to being out of the VA. They no longer were receiving VIP treatment.

His recovery was like a rock hitting water: At first there was a big splash and lots of attention. But as the ripples radiated out, they gradually became weaker. Now, months after his injury, Frank's support system was waning.

In Palo Alto, whenever Michelle had a problem, she could always turn to Sly Williams, their social worker. If he didn't have the answer, he quickly got it. Also, there was a uniformed soldier on duty—the polytrauma center's sole armed-services presence—who acted as liaison with the military.

But in Yuma, Michelle was left to navigate the system alone, and she had trouble getting Frank's therapy restarted. It had taken her a month just to get approval from Tricare, the military's health insurer. Even then, Michelle had to fight for his speech therapy.

Swallowing continued to be a struggle for Frank. There were times when even Michelle didn't understand what he was saying. While driving to her parents' house one afternoon, Michelle became exasperated as Frank was talking.

"Frankie, I'm not even going to try to listen if you don't start moving your damned lips," she said.

"I'm trying," Frank responded, this time clearly.

A Step Backward
Red Tape Is the Enemy and Now, Michelle Is Fighting

Michelle knew she sometimes could be short-tempered. But now, having assumed the role of primary caretaker, she was trying to prevent Frank from becoming, in her description, "lazy." It wasn't just that she hoped to lessen her own burden. She believed that as he did more for himself, his self-esteem would grow.

She knew that helping him get dressed and use the bathroom was a blow to his dignity. The only way he would be able to do those things for himself was if she kept pushing him.

But in those first few weeks home, Frank spent a lot of time watching TV. What did improve, though, were his walking and stamina, because he would accompany Michelle whenever she visited family or went on errands.

In that way, he literally had begun to regain his footing.

"We're getting there," Michelle said, watching him eat a hot dog at a Wal-Mart. "I don't want people to feel bad for us. It's just going to take us some more time to get through this."

Three weeks later, Frank broke his leg.

They were getting ready to leave a pizza place when Frank's wedding band slipped off his finger. In Palo Alto, Frank had begun wearing the

Frank and Michelle Sandoval lounge around with Michelle's brother Alex in her parents' living room. Their daughter, Joelena, plays on the floor. (Photograph courtesy of Pauline Lubens/*San Jose Mercury News*)

ring on his good, right hand. But because he had lost so much weight, it fit loosely.

As Frank leaned down to his left to pick it up, he lost his balance and fell out of his chair. Before Michelle knew what had happened, he was on the floor.

His first reaction was to keep apologizing to Michelle. (This was nothing new for Frank, who often told her that he was sorry for getting wounded in Iraq.) Frank insisted he wasn't hurt. But emergency room X-rays revealed a break in his left femur, near his hip.

The surgeon who inserted a metal pin in his leg thought the reason for the break probably was that he didn't have enough muscle to help protect the bone.

If that weren't bad enough, Michelle had trouble getting approval from Tricare to have Frank transferred to the Yuma Rehabilitation Hospital, where he could begin his other delayed therapies. Instead, it looked like Frank would recover in a nursing home.

Michelle was furious.

"There's no way that's going to happen," Michelle said. "I'll take him home and take care of him. A nursing home is where people go when there's nobody to take [care] of them."

For days she tried in vain to resolve the problem. She even went to the local Marine base, which has its own health clinic. Clerks told her there was nothing they could do because Frank was not a Marine.

Michelle responded: Well, it didn't matter whether he was in the Army or the Marines when he was sent to Iraq.

She refused to take no for an answer until she talked to the officer in charge. After Michelle explained the problem, he said: Sign him over to me. Within 15 minutes, Michelle had what she needed to transfer Frank to the rehab center.

But as she recounted the story, Michelle sounded weary.

"There's so many really bad people in the world who don't have bad things happen to them," she said. "Then there's us. We try and try, and still we get the bad end of everything. This is just another thing we have to deal with."

So, Frank missed Joey's first day of preschool because he was in the hospital. He couldn't celebrate Halloween with her, either.

He no longer could walk, even with a cane.

And yet, just before he was released in mid-November, Frank was in good spirits. He was much more alert. His speech was better and his memory had improved to the point that he now knew Michelle's phone number—which he constantly called.

"I'm showing more initiative," he said.

Frank was excited about getting out of the hospital—again. He bantered with Michelle about how he hoped to be healthy enough to one day drink a beer, and about how they could solve their home loan dilemma.

"Just wait until I'm back on my feet," Frank said, smiling. "I can't wait until I can take care of you again."

Bronze Star

His Doctor Says Frank Has Much to Learn—And Teach

In the following weeks, he learned that he would be awarded a Bronze Star for valor. Friends from his artillery battery, back from Iraq, were sent to the nearby Yuma Proving Ground for training exercises, and Frank was able to spend time with them. After a gathering at his parents' house, an emotional Frank told Michelle that he wanted to leave with his fellow soldiers.

Seeing them was a bittersweet reminder of who he used to be, she said.

And on Nov. 28, a year to the day after Frank was wounded on a dusty stretch of road in northern Iraq, he sat in a Sears Portrait Studio—posing with Michelle and Joey for their Christmas card photo.

Frank wore his formal Class A uniform. He spent extra time making sure his beret was perfect.

Frank takes a good look at the mirror while getting dressed on his first full day back home. Michelle continues to push his recovery, believing that someday he can do more of such tasks on his own. (Photograph courtesy of Pauline Lubens/*San Jose Mercury News*)

Sometime early next year, he will return to Palo Alto for another cranioplasty to restore his head to its regular shape. He said he is eager "to look normal again."

VA staff members also plan to teach him to use a "memory prosthesis"—a handheld computer that some patients refer to as their portable brains. It might help Frank eventually be able to attend community college.

Frank recently said that he was only "halfway there" in his recovery. Brain-injury patients typically show the most improvement in the first two years. Harriet Zeiner, Frank's VA neuropsychologist, said she expects him to show continued progress over the next 12 months.

He won't have the post-military life he had envisioned, Zeiner added. But she admired how Frank was finding in himself the ability to keep fighting, to build upon this different life.

"Frank can be a teacher to all of us," Zeiner said. "He knows what it's like to be knocked on his rear end multiple times and yet still get back up. He can tell us how to take pain and disappointment, and not give up.

"Most importantly, he can teach us to still have hope."

One afternoon after he first returned to Yuma, Frank sat on the couch watching TV news coverage of the fighting in Iraq. He talked about how he was proud to have served.

"Somebody has got to do it," he said.

Then he added:

"I have no regrets."

ABOUT THIS SERIES

Reporter Mark Emmons and photojournalist Pauline Lubens spent nearly 11 months following the recovery of Army artillery soldier Frank Sandoval—most of it at the Palo Alto Veterans Affairs hospital. In reporting the series, they interviewed family members, doctors, therapists, nurses, soldiers in Sandoval's unit, friends, as well as military and VA officials. Any direct quotes come from interviews conducted by the reporter and photographer, or from conversations that occurred in their presence.

Lessons Learned

BY MARK EMMONS

It was my birthday. My wife, Sandy, and I had just opened a bottle of wine and settled in to watch a DVD from Netflix when the phone rang. My colleague, *Mercury News* photojournalist Pauline Lubens, was on the line saying that Sgt. Frank Sandoval was undergoing emergency brain surgery at the Palo Alto Veterans Affairs hospital. Pauline and I already had spent seven months following the uncertain recovery of Sandoval, who had been severely wounded by an improvised explosive device in Iraq. The wine went into the refrigerator and we headed to the hospital. Once there, we found Frank's wife, Michelle, sitting alone in a sterile waiting room.

Michelle, Frank and VA officials had granted us extraordinary access. Pauline and I had been allowed to witness every facet of Frank's recuperation. We had spent countless hours at the VA watching Frank make incremental progress in regaining portions of his life. I had become a fly on the wall, quietly filling notebooks as I witnessed the often heartbreaking scenes of struggle, despair and hope. Pauline was doing the same with her cameras and audio equipment. I knew we were capturing a powerful, rarely told story of what life is really like for a badly wounded soldier. But it wasn't until this night that I fully understood the level of trust that Pauline and I had been able to create with the Sandovals. With her husband on the operating table, Michelle began to talk, sharing her fears and concerns about Frank's health, their marriage, their future.

This was no longer about being a reporter. This was simply about being human. The notebook stayed in my pocket. I tried, in some small way, to be a comfort to a young wife and mother who was watching her world turn upside down.

We all learn early, either in journalism school or very quickly on the job, that there is a line that must never be crossed. We are journalists. They are sources. We may cooperate, but we do not collaborate. And yet at some point, this became more than "just" a story for Pauline and me. Frank's successes became our successes. Frank's bad days became our bad days. My wife came to feel like she knew Frank and Michelle because their struggle was what we would discuss at the dinner table. I would talk about the Sandovals so much with my ever-patient editor, Rachel Wilner, that it was she who had the true epiphany that crystallized the direction of the series long before the first word ever was written: The Sandovals' lives depended utterly and completely on Michelle and the decisions she would make.

So, yes, I did learn—or maybe relearn—a lesson while working on "Frank's Fight." Access is not the same thing as trust. Pauline and I might have witnessed the same scenes, but we probably wouldn't have fully understood what Frank, Michelle and the VA staff truly felt if they hadn't been secure enough to talk to us freely and honestly. I hesitate to call getting this close to sources a technique because it certainly wasn't planned. And I certainly wouldn't recommend it for every story. But on a series such as this that required such depth of reporting, I don't know how it could have been done any other way.

It's one thing for a reporter and photographer to tell subjects how you intend to go about telling their story. But it's another thing, I believe, to actually do it. We promised nothing other than, to the best of our abilities, we would tell their story accurately, fairly and with as much sensitivity as possible. I think the reason this series turned out the way it did was because slowly, over time, Pauline and I were able to show everyone involved that we intended to be true to our word and that this wasn't just a story to us.

Since the series was published, Pauline and I have been blessed to receive honors such as this one from ASNE. But I have to say, the recognition we both feel most proud about was given by Michelle and Frank when they told us that the series did indeed capture their journey.

Frank's fight had a tragic end. On June 18, 2007, Frank Sandoval was declared brain dead after he failed to awaken following further brain surgery at the Palo Alto Veterans Affairs hospital. Six of his organs were donated. "I really hope someone can use this heart," his wife, Michelle, said through tears. "And if any other man can love a woman as much as he loved me, that would make me very happy."

Mark Emmons has been a newspaper writer for 25 years, working in sports, features and news departments. He joined the Mercury News *in 2000 as a staff writer for the Sunday magazine,* SV, *before moving to the sports section in 2002 as an enterprise writer. Before coming to the* Mercury News, *Emmons held writing positions at the* Orange County Register *and the* Detroit Free Press *and was a sports columnist at the* Mesa (Ariz.) Tribune. *He is the author of "The Last Chance Ranch: A Story About Football, Gang Members and Learning to Play by the Rules."*

The Boston Globe

Finalist

Kevin Cullen
Nondeadline Writing

46. Rakan's War

FEB. 26, 2006

On Jan. 18, 2005, as dusk fell in Tal Afar, a scruffy city in northwest Iraq, Rakan Hassan was riding in the family car, heading home after visiting his uncle. His father, Hussein Hassan, a clerk in the local electricity office, was driving faster than usual, trying to beat the curfew, because, after nightfall, in a town crawling with insurgents and U.S. troops, anything could happen.

From the back seat, where he was crammed in with three of his sisters, his little brother, and a cousin, Rakan saw the dark figures up ahead, waving.

"Look!" Rakan shouted, pointing.

But it was too late. A patrol of U.S. soldiers, jumpy after recent attacks, thought the worst and opened fire. Rakan says it sounded like pops. The windshield splintered, and something punched him in the stomach. In an instant Hussein and his wife, Kamila, were dead in the front seat, their blood splattering the children in the back.

The Opel sedan drifted, "almost like a dream," Rakan recalls, until it rolled dead, against a curb. As it did, his sisters broke the silence, screaming hysterically.

It was the sort of horrifying accident of war that would normally go unrecorded. But Chris Hondros, a photographer for Getty Images, happened to be embedded with the patrol and captured it all in a series of haunting, indelible images.

The children spilled out of the back seat, as the U.S. soldiers shouted "Civilians!" and realized their mistake, Hondros recounted. Rakan, his spine pierced by a bullet, flopped on the pavement. He couldn't feel his legs, only a searing pain in his midsection.

Given how many shots were fired, it seemed incredible that only Rakan, among the six children, was wounded. Even his wound was initially thought to be superficial.

But the scene was hellish: the children's hair mottled with blood; the mournful wailing; the soldiers cursing their mistake. Jilan, Rakan's 14-year-old sister, cried out in their native Turkoman language, "Why did they shoot us? We were just going home!"

The U.S. Army acknowledged its mistake immediately. But the soldiers from the 1st Brigade, 25th Infantry Division who were involved in the shooting were not allowed to dwell for long on what had happened. They had to focus on surviving a yearlong tour in Iraq. During their deployment, which ended in September, the brigade's 4,200 soldiers suffered heavy losses: 34 killed, 632 wounded. They faced more than 3,000 enemy attacks, including 84 suicide car-bombers, and 1,335 improvised explosive devices. Five of the suicide attacks occurred in the two weeks prior to the shooting of Rakan's family.

Rakan's uncle, Falah Abbas, recalls that a U.S. officer turned up at the family's home the next day, to apologize and to offer compensation.

"He was crying," Abbas said.

The family did not accept the apology.

"There is no apologizing for such a thing," Abbas said.

The family was given $7,500 in compensation. In the Byzantine calculus of war, the payment for the car—$2,500—was the same as the recompense for the dead.

Rakan spent a week in a small, rundown hospital in Tal Afar before being transferred to a bigger hospital in Mosul, a city about 40 miles to the east, where his siblings had been taken in by his oldest sister, Intisar, 25, and her husband, Nathir Bashir Ali. In a country where, even in the best of times, there is limited access to rehabilitative care, Rakan was deemed beyond help. The only thing he took home from the hospital was bedsores. His limp legs had withered from disuse. His family was told his only hope was to get out of Iraq, to get the medical care he needed.

Rakan remembers feeling that his plight was dismal.

"I was just in bed," he said, shrugging. "I didn't get out of bed. I watched TV. I played video games. I'd call my sister for food."

Most of the time, he didn't feel like eating.

No one knows how many innocent bystanders in the Iraqi conflict, like Rakan's family, have been casualties of American or other forces' fire. But civilian deaths are a tragic commonplace in this war, as in all wars. In December, President Bush estimated that about 30,000 Iraqi civilians had

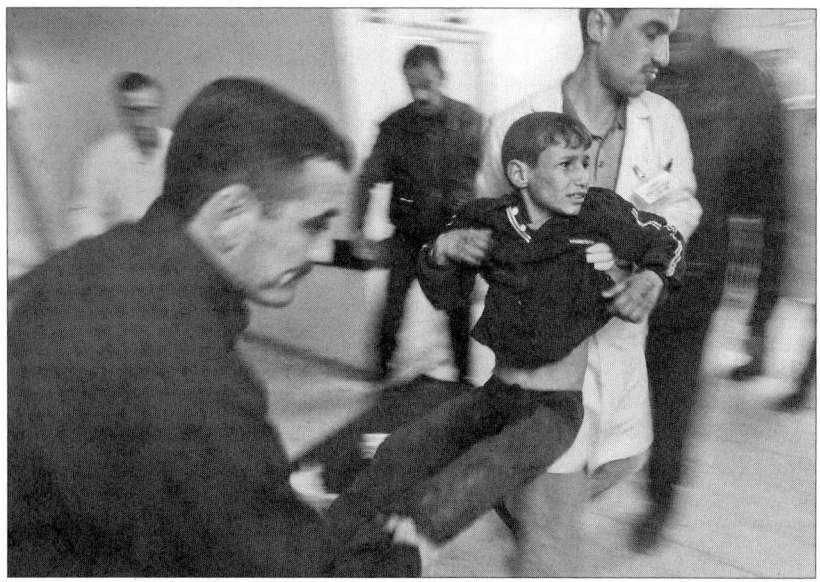

After the shooting, Rakan was rushed to a hospital in Tal Afar, Iraq. At first he was thought to have a superficial wound, but doctors later found that a bullet pierced the base of his spine. (Photograph courtesy of Chris Hondros/Getty Images)

been killed. A similar figure is cited by a British-based, antiwar group, Iraq Body Count, which estimates that about 37 percent of those deaths have been the result of actions by U.S. forces.

But if Rakan had plenty of company in his misfortune, he was also more fortunate than most. Hondros's dramatic pictures appeared in *Newsweek* magazine and *The Times* of London, drawing attention to his plight.

And Hondros, deeply affected by what he had witnessed, tried to interest others in Rakan's situation. His friend, Marla Ruzicka, an American humanitarian worker in Iraq, took up the case. At 28, Ruzicka was an idealist with a practical streak, an accomplished schmoozer who knew how to get officialdom to take an interest in Iraqi civilians, especially children, injured in the war. By April, she had lined up a doctor in San Francisco to help Rakan, and was cajoling U.S. diplomats to help get him into the United States. On April 12, Ruzicka sent a plaintive e-mail to two State Department officials, begging them to speed the visa.

"If we don't get him treatment soon he may never be able to walk again," she pleaded.

Four days later, as she awaited word on the visa, Ruzicka and Faiz Ali Salim, her colleague at the Campaign for Innocent Victims in Conflict, were killed when a suicide bomber blew himself up on the road to the Baghdad airport. The bomber was targeting a U.S. military convoy.

Rakan's relatives, who had been encouraged by Ruzicka's efforts, were devastated by her death.

And Rakan, his thighs and backside covered with bedsore ulcers the size of quarters, was wasting away.

* * *

Sitting in front of his computer in his Rockland, Mass., home, Adam Burnieika, a 57-year-old disabled postal worker suffering from throat cancer, read a news account about Marla Ruzicka shortly after her death. Moved by Rakan's situation, and by Ruzicka's compassion, Burnieika typed out a three-line letter to U.S. Senator Edward M. Kennedy, enclosing the news story, and urging him to finish her job.

"You have the power to help," he wrote.

With those few words Burnieika triggered a remarkable series of events.

Of the hundreds of constituent letters that arrive in Kennedy's Boston office every week, this one was plucked from the pile and made it all the way to the senator's hands. Kennedy, who has opposed the war in Iraq from the outset, said his reaction was personal, not political.

"This one got to me," he said, sitting in his private office on the third floor of the Capitol Building.

Kennedy called Raymond Tye, the United Liquors magnate and philanthropist, who agreed to pay for Rakan's treatment. Tye, in turn, called Dr. Laurence Ronan, a Massachusetts General Hospital internist, asking him to get Rakan out of Iraq and oversee his care. Ronan is a protégé of the late Dr. Thomas Durant, a Mass. General physician and legendary, globe-trotting humanitarian. Ronan, 52, a Chicago native who came to Boston in 1973 to attend Harvard and never left, inherited from Durant a passion for the Red Sox, and for parachuting into the world's trouble spots. In Ronan's spartan sixth-floor office at Mass. General, Durant's photo hangs next to his Harvard College and medical school diplomas.

Tye hung up before Ronan could say, "I've got to check it out with my bosses first." But then Ronan was used to abrupt telephone conversations with Tye.

Six months earlier, Tye had called Ronan for the first time, out of the blue, moments before the doctor left Boston to help victims of the tsunami in Indonesia. Tye had marked his 80th birthday, in 2002, by creating a $2.5 million foundation to pay for medical care for hard-luck cases. It was a commitment made stronger the following year, when Tye's son,

Michael, died of cancer at 49. As Ronan glanced at his watch, trying to figure out if he'd make his plane, this total stranger told him that if he found anyone who needed life-saving care, he'd pay for it.

A couple of weeks later, on a hospital ship in Banda Aceh, Indonesia, Ronan came across a 3-year-old boy with a large tumor on his liver and recalled the offer. Ronan brought the boy to Mass. General, Tye covered $300,000 in medical expenses, and the boy recovered.

"All the money in the world couldn't save my Michael," Tye explained, sitting in the Braintree office where he presides over his liquor distribution business. "But it can save others."

Ronan had been to Iraq once before, in February 2004, for a conference with Iraqi doctors. But the on-ground situation had deteriorated dramatically since then. He needed someone who could marshal the power of the U.S. military, to pluck Rakan out of a hostile environment with precision and discretion. He knew just the man: Fred Gerber.

Gerber had spent 31 years in the U.S. Army, retiring as a colonel with the 82nd Airborne Special Forces two years ago to become the Iraq coordinator for Project Hope, a Virginia-based humanitarian organization. Ronan had been impressed by Gerber's logistical genius during the tsunami relief efforts coordinated by Project Hope. Among the many hats Ronan wears is chief internist for the Boston Red Sox. After three weeks onboard a hospital ship in Banda Aceh, it dawned on Ronan that he was supposed to be in Fort Myers, Fla., when spring training opened. Gerber dispatched a U.S. Marines helicopter for the first leg of an elaborate evacuation. Ronan made it to spring training on time.

"That's when I knew Fred was good," said Ronan.

Working with Kennedy's office was not an easy fit for a career military man.

"Let's just say me and Ted Kennedy wouldn't see eye to eye on many things," said Gerber. "But this was about a little boy."

Gerber, relentless and persnickety, and Kennedy's staff, especially Emily Winterson and Bethany Bassett, masters at cutting through red tape, worked together well, becoming friends. Gerber said more than 60 Iraqis, most of them children, have been airlifted to the United States for medical treatment over the last three years. He has overseen many of the evacuations.

"Every kid like Rakan needs a champion," said Gerber, who after three decades as a spit-and-polish officer now cuts a more rakish figure, his brown hair spilling over his collar. "Once you find the right people, it's not that complicated."

But getting to the right people can take an extra push. After requests to get Rakan out of Iraq had languished for a couple of months in the Beltway bureaucracy, Gerber suggested that Kennedy appeal directly to Defense Secretary Donald Rumsfeld, to have Rakan declared a "secretarial designee" for evacuation through military channels. Rumsfeld and Kennedy agree on little, but in the case of Rakan, they put aside long-standing political differences.

When it looked certain that Rakan would come to the United States, a grateful Kennedy asked if there was anything he could do for Gerber, and Gerber said yes, as a matter of fact, there was. He is now the proud owner of an autographed photograph of the senator, inscribed with these words: "To my favorite Republican Airborne Ranger Special Forces officer, thanks for helping our Iraqi friends."

On the ground in Iraq, United Nations officials from Egypt had persuaded Rakan's relatives that the child needed to go to the United States for treatment, and to entrust him to an army they had every reason to fear. Although bitter over what had happened, the family accepted it was an accident, according to Rakan's uncle, Falah Abbas, who was chosen by the family to accompany Rakan to the United States.

Rakan, still angry and heartbroken, greeted with equanimity the news that he would be spirited out of Iraq by U.S. troops. "I was not afraid," he explained, months later, "because I knew they were taking me to get better."

* * *

Flying somewhere over the Atlantic Ocean, in the pre-dawn hours of Sept. 10, 2005, in the belly of a C-17 transport, Rakan lay on a litter, wide-eyed, listening to the dull hum of the engines and the occasional moans of wounded American soldiers. One of the soldiers was missing a leg, another an arm. Ronan sat next to Rakan, worried that what the child was hearing and seeing would further traumatize him.

A soldier in the bunk above Rakan awoke and slid his legs down to the floor, mumbling in a morphine haze that he had to go the bathroom. A nurse tried to take the soldier's helmet, but he held it tightly to his chest, pointed to a jagged hole in its side and said it was the only reason he was still alive and that he'd be damned before he gave it up.

The soldier, a big country boy with wide shoulders and a deep shrapnel wound in his back, looked at the small, emaciated Iraqi child beneath him, and turned to Ronan, who had met Rakan at the U.S. military hospital in Landstuhl, Germany, and was bringing him back to Boston for treatment.

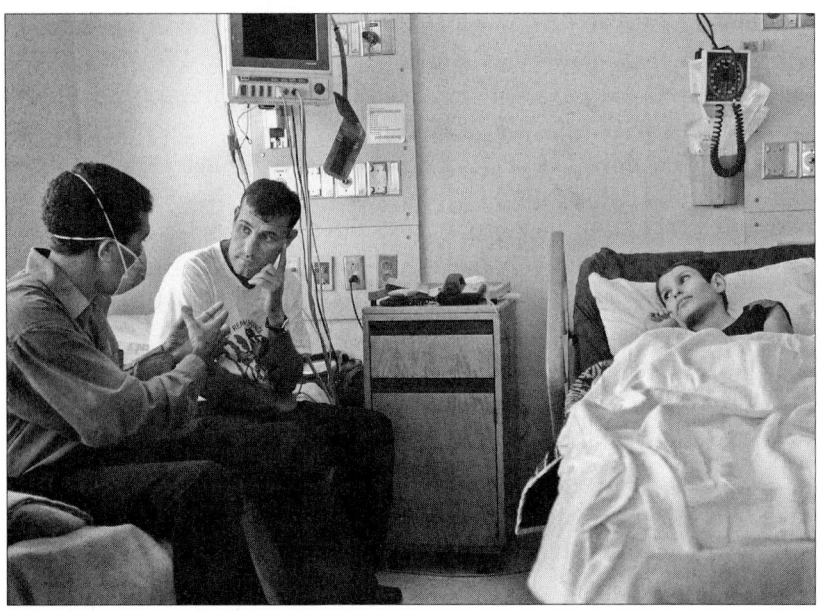

Rakan's uncle, Falah Abbas, listened to Aomar Nait-Talb, one of the translators who helped bridge the language gap between Rakan, an ethnic Turkoman, and the hospital staff. Because Abbas and Rakan had just arrived from Iraq, Nait-Talb, a Mass. General housekeeping worker, wore a mask as a precaution against infection. (Photograph courtesy of Michele McDonald/The Boston Globe)

"What happened to him?" the soldier asked, as Ronan recalls it.

Ronan repeated the story: a speeding car, a jumpy patrol, a family devastated.

The soldier bent down, wincing in pain, and stroked Rakan's head. "I'm sorry, kid," the soldier told him. "I'm really sorry."

Rakan looked at him, intrigued.

Still clutching his helmet, the soldier dug into his duffel bag with his free hand and pulled out his U.S. Army cap and handed it to Rakan. Rakan smiled up at him.

Ronan turned away, his eyes welling up.

Later, he tried to explain.

"Every military person I've dealt with in this says the same thing: what can I do to help? All these guys know they could have been the one who pulled the trigger."

* * *

Rakan's first hospital room was on the 18th floor at Massachusetts General Hospital. It was private, offering sweeping views of Beacon Hill, where the State House's Golden Dome dominated the horizon, shining like a light bulb.

With his infectious smile, Rakan became the darling of the pediatric ward, especially when the nurses and whoever came to his bed read the chart that, in a few dry words, explained he was an orphan from Iraq.

For the first couple of weeks, Rakan said little. His uncle did all the talking, occasionally translating questions to Rakan in their native Turkoman. Hospital officials were unable to find a translator who spoke Turkoman, so language became a huge barrier. Rakan would look back and forth at his uncle, the translators, and the hospital staff, as if he was watching a three-way tennis match, often amused at the cacophony and confusion.

But there was no mistaking the challenge facing Rakan and his caregivers on the afternoon of Sept. 22, when Dr. Nwanneka Okolo, a cheerful neurosurgeon, clapped her hands, saying, "Let's have a look," and pulled back the blankets that covered Rakan's legs.

Rakan was shrunken, almost birdlike. He weighed just 48 pounds, was just over 4 feet tall, and appeared far younger than 12. The muscle mass in his calves had disappeared from atrophy, making his legs appear stick-like. His face was drawn and angular, his almond eyes, doleful and intense.

But the real damage was out of view.

The bullet had pierced his spine, causing neurological damage that left him unable to control his bowels or bladder. There was also nerve damage to his right ankle, but most of his inability to walk was chalked up to the atrophy. His hamstrings had shortened and were painfully tight. His hips were weak.

Okolo stood Rakan up, and his legs wobbled. He held onto her tightly, like a child on ice skates for the first time. He looked like he would shatter if he fell.

"You're in a good place," Okolo said, pulling the blankets back over his legs.

Rakan flashed her the grin that made everybody want to help him.

After two weeks, Rakan was transferred to the Spaulding Rehabilitation Hospital's pediatric unit, on the 10th floor of the Massachusetts Eye and Ear Infirmary. With just 15 beds, its corridor walls lined with prints of idyllic scenes of Boston—Durgin Park bathed in snowfall, the Charles River at dusk—the unit is small, warm, and self-contained. It would become Rakan's world for four months.

Anne Dodwell, program director of the pediatric unit, was confident her staff would meet Rakan's physical needs. But she worried about the things they could only guess at.

"I was lying in bed last night, and I couldn't get all these questions out of my head," Dodwell confided, standing outside her office a few days after Rakan arrived. "What's going on in his head? What things did he see? Is he going to go home? Is someone here going to adopt him? What does he want? What's ultimately in his best interest? How will we ever know?"

47. As Healing Begins, a Painful Decision

FEB. 27, 2006

By Kevin Cullen

On Oct. 6, just as 12-year-old Rakan Hassan steered his wheelchair out of his hospital room, President Bush appeared on the television hanging above his bed, saying the United States must stay the course in Iraq. Moments later, Rakan was on his stomach, on a blue-padded therapy table, in the pediatric unit of Spaulding Rehabilitation Hospital, hiding a timer from his physical therapist, Alison Tate.

"Where is that thing?" Tate said, hands on hips, looking side to side.

Rakan flashed a conspiratorial glance at others in the room, arching his eyebrows twice, before pulling the timer with great flourish from beneath a white towel he had tucked under his chin.

"You!" Tate said, wagging a finger at him.

Moments earlier, Tate had been stretching Rakan's hamstrings, trying to lengthen the muscles that had tightened like taut rubber bands as he lay untreated for months after he was shot by mistake by U.S. troops in Iraq. The stretching was painful, and Rakan's squinting eyes glistened, but he refused to cry.

"Rakan rest?" Tate asked.

"No," Rakan replied, resolutely. "Rakan PT, PT, PT."

Tate put heat packs on the back of his legs and set the timer for 10 minutes.

"A lot of kids don't like this," Tate said. "Rakan just does it."

When Rakan was evacuated from Iraq and brought to Boston in early September, his doctors believed surgery was urgently needed to repair the damage that a bullet had done to his spine, bladder, and bowel. But that plan was quickly abandoned when Dr. William Butler, a neurosurgeon at Massachusetts General Hospital, determined that Rakan wasn't permanently paralyzed, as doctors in Iraq had concluded. Butler and other doctors feared they could do more harm than good by excising the bullet fragments. So the surgery was shelved and most of the responsibility for getting Rakan back on his feet and walking fell to Tate.

Tate, 31, grew up in Marlborough, working her way through Simmons College by waiting tables at Charley's in the Back Bay. Her bubbly personality belies a toughness when it comes to pushing her patients. She would cuddle Rakan one moment, then press him to the limit the next.

But, mostly, she worried about him, even as she tried not to spoil him.

On Oct. 11, as the news ticker on CNN in Rakan's room reported that a suicide bomber had driven into an open-air market in Rakan's hometown of Tal Afar, killing 30 people, Tate sat at her desk, trying to navigate the maddening bureaucracy to obtain a customized wheelchair for him.

The next day, as Rakan ate lunch with the other children in the dining room, unaware of the carnage in a town where a year before he kicked a soccer ball through dusty streets, Tate was a few doors down, staring up at a television screen, which showed people scurrying around in the aftermath of still another bombing in Tal Afar.

"What are we sending him back to?" she asked, almost in a whisper, shaking her head.

There are six pieces of shrapnel in Rakan's midsection, the largest the size of a dime, lodged in his abdominal wall. The metal has settled deeply in.

"At first, we thought the shrapnel compromised his nervous system," said Dr. Laurence Ronan, the Mass. General internist who oversaw Rakan's care. "But it's like a tree trunk in a dam: if you take it out, it causes more damage than if you leave it in."

Ronan sat in the Dodd Room, an open, dimly lit space in Mass. General where computer terminals used to review X-rays and CAT-scans throw off an eerie glow.

The bullet struck Rakan's sacrum, the triangular bone at the base of the spine, slicing it in two and causing the neurological damage that left him incontinent and unable to walk.

"He was lucky," Ronan said, pointing to the fragments. "If the bullet was slightly higher, he would have been paralyzed from the waist down."

From the beginning, those caring for Rakan felt confident that they could treat Rakan's physical wounds, but worried whether they could heal the mental and emotional damage they believed must be there. But Dr. Patrick Brennan, the pediatric unit's chief physician, said Rakan showed no obvious sign of post-traumatic stress.

"No nightmares. He's not jumpy," said Brennan.

Still, his therapists and nurses were concerned because Rakan regularly used crayons and magic markers to draw tanks with turrets dripping blood and other combat scenes. Despite regular assessments indicating that Rakan's mental health was fine, they worried that their inability to communicate with the child in his native language was masking some lingering psychological hurt.

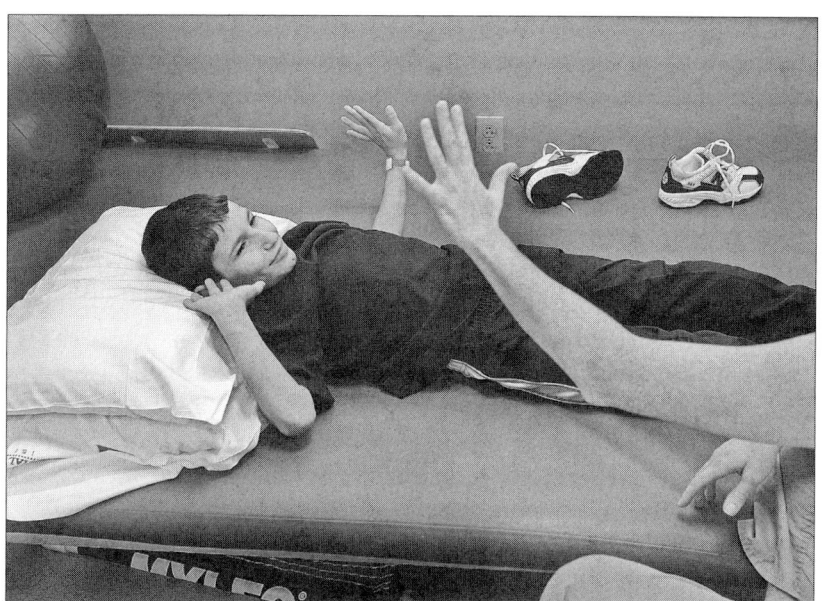

Five more times, physical therapist Alison Tate signaled Rakan, whose muscles had atrophied. He was an eager patient. When asked if he wanted a rest, he replied, "PT, PT, PT." (Photograph courtesy of Michele McDonald/*The Boston Globe*)

On most days, Rakan was upbeat, willing to do whatever was asked. But, sometimes, Rakan would think back to what had happened to him, and his endearing smile vanished.

"I just showed him this picture," said his uncle, Falah Abbas, who accompanied him to the United States. The dog-eared snapshot showed Rakan's parents, his older sisters Intisar, Sosan, and Jilan, his younger sisters Samar and Rana, and his baby brother, Muhammed. Rakan's parents were killed and he was wounded when U.S. soldiers, fearing an insurgent attack, opened fire on the family's car by mistake. His siblings escaped injury in the shooting, but were badly traumatized.

As his uncle named those in the photo, Rakan sat in a wheelchair, by the window, staring out over the brownstones of Beacon Hill.

There were tears, dripping slowly down his cheeks.

* * *

Healing Rakan also meant understanding Rakan, and here, language became a bigger barrier than ever imagined. Rakan is an ethnic Turkoman, about 500,000 of whom live in Iraq, mostly in the north of the country. He understands some Arabic and Turkish, but his native tongue is a distinct language with Turkish roots. His uncle, who speaks Arabic, became as much an interpreter as a guardian. Finding a translator who spoke fluent Turkoman proved impossible. But gradually, a stable of Arabic speakers, some of them professional translators, many of them students at Harvard, MIT and Boston University, was assembled.

From the outset, Aomar Nait-Talb, a Moroccan who works on the housekeeping staff at Mass. General, became a regular visitor. He dropped by almost daily, translating for the medical staff, offering companionship to Abbas, giving Rakan someone to talk to besides his uncle. He also became Rakan's barber.

"Uncle Aomar!" Rakan sang one day in October when Nait-Talb showed up with his haircutting kit.

Only weeks after arriving in Boston, Rakan had begun to change noticeably. The shyness that seemed to envelop him when he arrived melted away. He put on weight. His sunken cheeks filled out. He flexed his once scrawny arms into a muscle. Tate had him up, walking on a treadmill.

Already, too, he had experienced things other Iraqi children could only imagine. He went sailing on the Charles River. He ate popcorn watching the Ringling Brothers circus. He went apple-picking at a farm in Peabody on a warm autumn day. And, having said just about nothing the first few weeks, he had become a veritable chatterbox. Just by listening to those around him, he picked up a remarkable amount of English. He would tease Tate by repeating her demands of him in affected, pidgin English.

"You crazy," he would tell anyone who amused him.

Abbas, meanwhile, was going crazy. He was bored, unable to communicate with Rakan's caregivers, and increasingly homesick. He slept on the bed next to Rakan's, in a hospital ward that was, for all intents and purposes, the domain of non-Muslim women, nurses and therapists, some of whom dressed and comported themselves in ways he found shocking. His one pleasure was Camel Lights, but even these he had to beg money for from the unit's social worker, Amy Simpson.

One day in October, he sat in Rakan's room, complaining that he needed to get home, to make money driving his taxi. Rakan and his siblings were a burden, he said. Rakan sat in his wheelchair, glumly listening to his uncle's lament. The television was tuned to CNN, with the sound off.

Saddam Hussein appeared on the TV screen. He was on trial.

"Do you remember Saddam?" Rakan was asked.

"Yes," Rakan said, turning a small blue basketball over in his hands.

"What do you think of Saddam?"

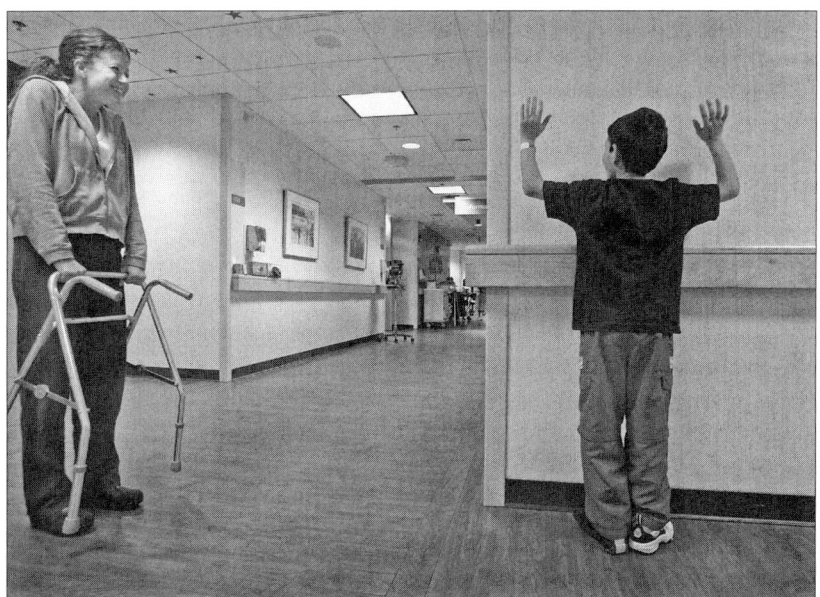

Two months into treatment Rakan showed off how far he had come to physical therapist Alison Tate. He could stand without support. Walking unaided would be his next challenge. (Photograph courtesy of Michele McDonald/*The Boston Globe*)

"I love Saddam," Rakan said, his voice betraying no emotion, staring at the screen.

"He is programmed to love Saddam," his uncle explained. "He is afraid to say anything else, even here. He fears that Saddam would jump through the TV."

* * *

Abbas's clamor to go home posed a problem—for Rakan, and for his caregivers. Ronan was adamant that, under the terms he agreed to when bringing Rakan here for treatment, the boy and his uncle were an inseparable package: if one had to go home, so did the other.

Homesickness wasn't the only issue with Uncle Falah. He had been the source of some turmoil, behaving boorishly with some of the women on the floor.

"It's a good thing he didn't touch me," Tate said, folding her arms. "I would have decked him."

He had also accidentally caused even more pain for Rakan. One day in late October, he spilled a cup of water he had boiled for tea on his nephew, severely scalding his ankle and foot. The burn set Rakan back for weeks, and it became, for the staff, the clearest sign that Abbas's continued, reluctant presence was holding the boy back.

But how much worse would it be if Abbas took Rakan with him, months before he was physically prepared to go? Ronan saw that, but also saw no alternative.

Rakan's caregivers were crushed.

"He's not even close to ready," Tate said, angrily. "He is going to lose everything he's gained this far. . . . To show him what was possible, and then to take it away from him, that's worse than cruel."

Ronan grasped for alternatives. At one point, he proposed making a physical therapy training video for Rakan's relatives. Then he asked an incredulous Tate if she'd volunteer to go to Iraq or Jordan to train Rakan's sisters in some rudimentary therapy skills. But Ronan gradually discerned the rebellion in the ranks, and concluded that Rakan needed to stay, even if Abbas had to go. He called Rakan's brother-in-law, Nathir Bashir Ali, the family leader, in Iraq, and got him to agree to temporarily grant guardianship of Rakan to Richard F. Ready, a Wellesley-based lawyer who is also trained as a registered nurse.

Then Ronan sat Abbas down and laid out a deal: he would give him some money, to help defray the wages Abbas lost not driving his taxi for two months, and Abbas would agree to leave Rakan behind for further treatment. Abbas agreed, shaking hands.

"I don't know if I could have done what you have done," Ronan told him.

Next, Ronan and the medical team went to the therapy room, where Rakan sat in his wheelchair, his furtive glances suggesting he knew something momentous was about to happen.

Ronan explained the dilemma; his uncle was miserable and wanted to go home. Rakan needed more time to recuperate and heal and grow strong. Could Rakan stick it out, alone, for another month?

Rakan said he knew his uncle was homesick. So was he.

"But if he is going to go home and take care of my sisters and my brother, then I say yes," Rakan said. "He can go."

Deb McSweeney, one of the therapists, covered her mouth with both hands and left the room, overcome by Rakan's selflessness.

Abbas, meanwhile, tried to take advantage of the moment. As a taxi was summoned to bring him to the airport in the first week of November, he announced that he needed more money.

By now, Ronan had gained a fragmentary feel for Iraqi mores, a process greatly aided by Iraqi colleagues, including Dr. Ayad Abrou, who worked at Tufts-New England Medical Center, and who sometimes dropped by to visit Rakan and translate. When Abbas tried one last shakedown, Ronan folded his arms and stood his ground.

"We had a deal," Ronan said, as Abrou translated. "If you don't honor this deal, you are not a man."

Abbas's eyes widened. Then he nodded.

"I gave you my word," he said, shaking Ronan's hand. "As a man."

As Abbas collected his bags for the airport, Abrou leaned toward Ronan and whispered, "Perfect."

Rakan and his uncle kissed each other on the cheek three times and said goodbye. There was genuine affection between them.

Though they were relieved to see Rakan's uncle gone, Rakan's caregivers also worried that his departure would lead the boy to regress, psychologically and physically. He had come so far. The silent, spindly boy who had arrived in September had grown robust, mischievous, outspoken, engaging. Tate had managed to get him out of his wheelchair. He was walking with crutches.

But now he was on his own.

A few days after his uncle went home, Rakan sat in his room, in his wheelchair. He fingered a soccer book, and looked longingly at a photo that showed a member of Iraq's national team. Before he was shot, Rakan was known in his neighborhood as a good soccer player, nimble and quick.

"Some day, I play, again," he said matter-of-factly, looking up, betraying no obvious emotion. "I play, in Iraq."

It was hard to say whether even he believed that.

Thumbing through another book, he pointed to a skyscraper and said he wanted to jump off of it.

48. Restless Patient, Agonizing Choice

FEB. 28, 2006

By Kevin Cullen

After three months in Spaulding Rehabilitation Hospital, 12-year-old Rakan Hassan had gained one critical preteen skill—popping wheelies in his wheelchair. It scared the hell out of his nurses and therapists, who feared he might fall over backward and crack his skull.

Their dismay delighted the imp in Rakan.

And so, on Dec. 12, as he rolled down the hall to take his weekly telephone call from his family in Iraq, it was wheels up all the way. The calls were the treasured highlight of Rakan's time in the hospital, which had become drudgery. He was especially looking forward to this call, because, by his calculations, he should be returning to Iraq in a couple of days.

"Home," he said, smiling, holding his arms out like an airplane's wings.

His smile vanished almost as soon as he put the phone to his ear. On the other end was Nathir Bashir Ali, Rakan's brother-in-law, who had taken custody of Rakan and his siblings a year ago, after their parents were killed and he was wounded, in a tragic accident, by U.S. troops. Bashir Ali said that he and his wife, Intisar, Rakan's oldest sister, had spoken with the doctors and learned that Rakan needed to stay longer, maybe a month, maybe more. And, another thing, he said: They had been told that Rakan was not listening to his caregivers in Boston.

Rakan began to protest, but Bashir Ali cut him off.

"You will do as you're told," he said.

During each previous call home, Rakan had been joyous and animated. Now he was crying.

The average stay in Spaulding's 15-bed pediatric unit is less than 30 days. Rakan had already been there three times as long, watching other kids arrive, get better, and leave. By December, he didn't really need to be in the hospital. But the conditions under which he had been allowed into the United States made it no easy thing for his caregivers to place him, as they would have liked, with a temporary foster family.

After hanging up, Rakan sat on his bed, wondering aloud if he would ever be allowed to go home.

"I don't want to stay here," he said, burying his head under a pillow.

* * *

After his uncle, Falah Abbas, who had accompanied him to the United States and spent the first two months with him, returned to Iraq, Rakan seemed to flourish. His quirky personality, a bit subdued in his uncle's presence, emerged. He was upbeat, joking constantly with his nurses and therapists. But he was sometimes more difficult. Where, in his uncle's presence, he had obediently followed orders, he now sometimes ignored his caregivers, perhaps because nearly all of them were women. For a couple of weeks, he refused to get out of bed in the morning.

By word of mouth, and especially by e-mail, it became known in the local Muslim community that an Iraqi orphan who had been wounded was being treated in Boston. An ad hoc group of Muslim students began appearing at Rakan's bedside, keeping him company, talking to him in Arabic or Turkish, bringing him the kebabs he preferred to hospital food. A Turkish couple from Cambridge, Hesna and Himmet Taskomur, visited often and took him to their home. Amy Simpson, the unit's social worker, noticed she was spending more time organizing Rakan's calendar, scheduling his regular forays outside.

"He has a busier social life than me," she said.

After his uncle left, Rakan got a roommate: 11-year-old Will Parr from Salem. Will was Rakan's first peer, the only boy close to his age, who had been in the pediatric unit. They hit it off immediately. Rakan began attending Will's therapy sessions, encouraging him to push through the pain.

"Before, I look like this," Rakan told Will, pulling his legs to his chest, crunching himself into a ball. "But now, PT, PT, I look like this," he said, straightening his legs, puffing his chest out.

A group of therapists stood clustered around the main desk, complaining that because Will and Rakan were staying up so late, talking, even after lights out, the boys were too tired to get up in the morning.

"But," said a perplexed Dr. Ayad Abrou, an Iraqi physician, "they don't speak the same language."

"Yes, they do," said Anne McGrail, an occupational therapist. "They speak 12-year-old."

As Rakan became more settled and continued to make progress in therapy, his caregivers increasingly worried about his approaching return to Iraq. Would he relapse, given the inevitable uncertainties of care in a war zone? Was it fair to send a boy who still struggled to walk from the safety of Boston to the daily hazards of home?

Raymond Tye said he would pay whatever it took to keep Rakan in the United States. Rakan, lounging nearby, was in no mood to listen. (Photograph courtesy of Michele McDonald/*The Boston Globe*)

There were times, indeed, when even Rakan sounded like he was conflicted about it.

Early in December, he and his physical therapist, Alison Tate, had finished a particularly grueling session. Tate sensed that he was trying to cram in as much stretching and exercise as possible before he left. He was hanging around the therapy gym after his sessions were over, asking to do more.

"Maybe," Rakan began, speaking in the pidgin English he had become proficient in, "I no go back to Iraq."

Tate was stunned. She turned slowly and looked at Rakan, who sat on a padded bench.

"Maybe," he continued, "I stay here."

But where, Tate asked, would you live?

"I stay at your house, on your sofa," he said, propping his feet up on an imaginary couch, putting his hands behind his head. "Play video games, do my PT."

He seemed to be kidding, and he probably was. But throughout Rakan's stay, the risks inherent in his eventual return to Iraq had been the elephant in the therapy room, impossible to ignore, impossible to resolve. Most of the people who were caring for Rakan had talked about it, to themselves, to their colleagues, and concluded that it was for the best, that he missed and loved his siblings.

Who were they, they asked, to impose their culture, their beliefs, on this sweet, mischievous child from a place they knew so little of.

But then, they would confess: They were kidding themselves. They didn't want him to go back to Iraq, didn't believe Rakan would be better off living in a war zone, with a family that had to worry as much about day-to-day survival as about the follow-up care Rakan would need.

Rakan told Tate he wanted to return to Iraq without the crutches, which he needed to walk around the house, and without his wheelchair. She sensed that he knew he couldn't expect the quality of care he had received to continue in Iraq, and also that he hoped, above all, to avoid the stigma of returning home disabled.

It wasn't just Rakan's caregivers who resisted the idea of sending him home. Fred Gerber, the Project Hope official who organized Rakan's airlift out of Iraq, was adamant that Rakan should stay and eventually be adopted. Gerber knew the dangers of Iraq first-hand. Two years earlier, while still a colonel in the 82nd Airborne, he had been shot in the head and seriously wounded in Baghdad. He believed that, however much Rakan's family loved and wanted him, sending him back was irresponsible at best and immoral at worst. He said only a handful of Iraqi children had been adopted in the United States after coming here for medical care.

"This kid has a shot," Gerber said. "Why take it away from him?"

Gerber considered moving Rakan to the National Rehabilitation Hospital in Washington while he looked for a family to adopt him.

Dr. Laurence Ronan, the Massachusetts General Hospital internist who was overseeing Rakan's care, was sensitive to the pressure from those caring for Rakan, and from Gerber. But he also felt his ultimate duty was to his patient.

"Rakan wants to go home," Ronan said. "Is it better to be a person who is sick or with disabilities in America than Iraq? You bet it is. But it's not what he wants. And contrary to what some people think, a 12-year-old boy is capable of making that decision. If you listen to him talk to his family on the phone, there's love there. There's attachment. There's longing."

Ronan paced next to a computer bank outside his office. He called up an e-mail from Gerber. It was another plea.

"Larry," it began, "I'm not fighting you on this, but . . . "

Ronan began pacing again.

Ray Tye doesn't outrank Fred Gerber. Tye was an MP during World War II. But he speaks with the authority of a self-made millionaire who

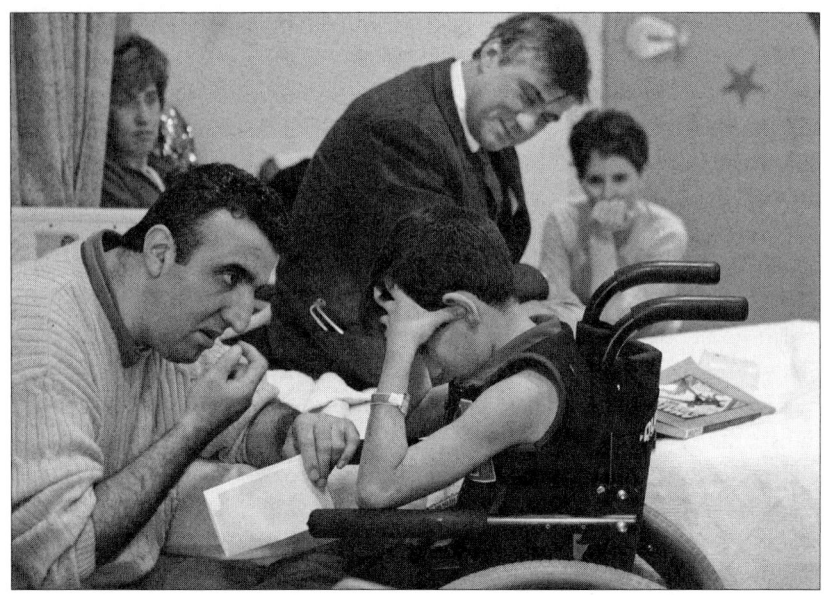

With weeks of therapy still ahead of him, Rakan grew frustrated. He wouldn't cooperate with caregivers and plugged his ears as Himmet Taskomur, a Turkish friend from Cambridge, tried to reason with him. Dr. Ronan, pediatric social worker Amy Simpson, right, and Deb McSweeney, a physical therapist, left, listened as the negotiation continued. (Photograph courtesy of Michele McDonald/*The Boston Globe*)

grew up in a three-decker in Haverhill. He wears a U.S. flag pin on his lapel and his heart on his sleeve.

"Why can't we keep him here?" Tye asked Ronan.

They were sitting in the lunchroom of the pediatric unit, while Rakan lounged in a nearby chair, oblivious to the nature of the conversation. Tye, a liquor distribution magnate, had agreed to cover Rakan's medical expenses, and now he was saying he would pay whatever it took to keep Rakan in the United States.

"Why not bring one of the sisters over?" Tye suggested. "Maybe we could get a family to adopt him."

Ronan looked at Tye, then at Rakan.

"God," Ronan said, sighing, conflicted again.

* * *

Spaulding Rehabilitation Hospital has big plans, plans to build a $100 million facility at the Charlestown Navy Yard. In early December, the hospital held a dinner for donors, and someone had the idea of inviting Rakan.

Rakan had other ideas. "No way, Jose," he said, crossing his arms, and using one of the stock phrases he has picked up from hospital staff.

The idea of attending a glitzy gala at the Boston University Club, 33 floors above the city, held exactly no appeal for Rakan. But Aomar Nait-Talb, a Moroccan native on the Mass. General housekeeping staff who had become a regular visitor and male authority figure in Rakan's life, persuaded Rakan that he owed it to the people who had taken care of him.

Tate, Simpson, Alyssa McCarthy, a speech therapist, Anne Dodwell, the program director at the pediatric unit, and Nait-Talb accompanied Rakan to the dinner. Tedy Bruschi, the Patriots linebacker who had been treated at Spaulding after suffering a stroke, was the featured speaker, and came over to the table to meet Rakan.

"Hey, buddy," Bruschi said, bending down.

Rakan smiled, but said nothing.

A publicist came over and told Bruschi the plan for the evening. Toward the end of a video that would show images of Rakan's rehabilitation, the linebacker was to pick Rakan up out of his wheelchair and carry him on stage to the strains of the song "He Ain't Heavy, He's My Brother." The publicist and Bruschi walked away.

Tate's mouth hung open. "Is anyone going to ask Rakan if that's OK?" she asked.

Nait-Talb did, in Arabic. It wasn't.

At the end of dinner, a video was played, and Bruschi was shown making tackles during a game. Rakan recognized him as one of the helmeted men whose posters hang in the therapy room. He warmed to the idea of going up on stage. But it would be on his terms, not theirs. At the appointed time, when Bruschi came over to get him, Rakan pulled himself out of his wheelchair and insisted on walking up to the stage, assisted on either side by Tate and Bruschi.

The dining room erupted in cheers.

* * *

On Dec. 14, the day that Rakan had believed he would touch down on Iraqi soil, his roommate and pal, Will Parr, was discharged from the hospital.

The nurses came in and told Rakan he had to move across the hall, to a new room.

It was all too much. He refused to empty his bladder, and resisted attempts to do it for him. He wouldn't shower. He wouldn't eat. He became listless at therapy sessions.

Tate walked into Rakan's room and told him if he didn't tend to his bladder, he could develop kidney problems.

Rakan shrugged. "I don't care," he said.

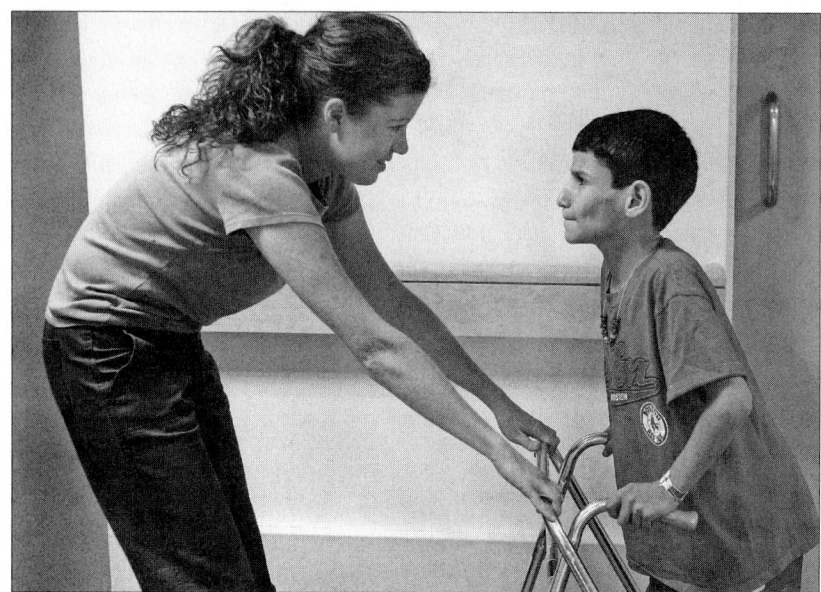

Physical therapist Alison Tate encouraged a determined Rakan to walk. Their last weeks together had been stormy, but Rakan knew that without her pushing him, he would not have been able to walk again. (Photograph courtesy of Michele McDonald/*The Boston Globe*)

"Well, I care," Tate told him, folding her arms across her chest. "If you don't do this, you could die."

Rakan folded his arms back at her.

"I don't care," he repeated.

Rakan's rebellion convinced Ronan that to keep him in the United States, against his will, would be a disaster.

"You know something," Ronan said one evening after work, "We've done the best we can ... What Alison has done, getting him to walk, is a freakin' miracle. He has all these visitors, he gets all these gifts. But you know what? Ninety percent of the time, this kid is by himself. Alone. All alone."

Even as Rakan grew moodier, he grew stronger. By mid-January, Ronan was back on the horn to Gerber, making the elaborate plans to bring Rakan home. In a rare retreat, Gerber had deferred to Ronan on the wisdom of returning Rakan to Iraq.

On Jan. 23, Rakan walked into Dr. Patrick Brennan's office to make the most important telephone call in his life. If he was nervous, he hid it well. As Ronan punched in the 16-digit phone number to Iraq, Rakan burped six times, in rapid succession. It was one of the skills Rakan had perfected during his convalescence—the ability to burp, on cue.

"I'm coming home," he told his brother-in-law and guardian, Nathir Bashir Ali. "Saturday."

Bashir Ali asked how he felt.

"Fine," Rakan replied.

His brother-in-law asked for more specifics about his health, but Rakan was purposely vague. He had a surprise for his family. After hanging up, he seemed pleased with himself.

"I told them nothing," he said, smiling, rubbing his hands together.

The day before he was to go home, Rakan sat on his bed, absent-mindedly playing a video game. He was asked what he would miss most about Boston and he replied that he wanted to grow up to become a fighter pilot, so he could come back and destroy Boston.

But, he was asked, if he did that, what would happen to Alison Tate?

He didn't want to hurt Alison, he said.

What about Amy Simpson?

He didn't want to hurt Amy, he said.

What about Himmet and Hesna Taskomur, the Turkish couple that visited him and treated him like a son, and Dr. Ronan, and Renee Wilson, the nurse who introduced him to the joys of Fruit Loops?

Rakan sighed.

"OK, OK," he said.

When he grew up, he said, he would become a commercial pilot instead.

* * *

When the day came, Hesna Taskomur tried to hide her tears but didn't do a very good job of it. Rakan, in what amounted to a victory lap, had just walked down the long corridor on his crutches, pausing to high-five other kids and to receive hugs from nurses and therapists.

Just before the door, he got to Tate. Their last month together had been stormy, but Rakan knew that without her pushing him, he would not have reached this point. He tried to give Tate a tough guy look, but it quickly melted.

He smiled and he hugged her and she rested her forehead on his.

49. At Homecoming, a Gift Elicits Wonder

MARCH 1, 2006

By Kevin Cullen

A half-hour before the C-17 jet was to touch down in Iraq, the Mississippi Air National Guard crew strapped on body armor and then moved to help Rakan Hassan, the boy they were flying home, put on his.

The vest and helmet weren't just ludicrously big for the wiry 12-year-old; they were a mystery to him.

"What's this?" Rakan asked.

"This is to keep you safe," crewman Bobby Evans told him. "You need to put it on."

"Why?" Rakan asked. "Why?"

Despite his own story—wounded by U.S. soldiers in an accidental shooting that left his parents dead—Rakan seemed the only one on board who saw no reason to fear a night landing in his native land.

Until that point, Rakan's long return journey had been remarkably relaxed. From Boston, where he'd been hospitalized, to Andrews Air Force Base in Maryland to Ramstein Air Base in Germany, and now into Iraqi airspace, the atmosphere was convivial. But that all changed as the lights inside the C-17 dimmed and the huge plane began a sudden, steep descent.

The jolting dips in altitude, meant to evade hostile fire, elicited shrieks of delight from Rakan, who greeted each ear-popping drop like a kid on a roller coaster. In just a matter of seconds, the huge jet was on the ground, landing with a bump.

"Iraq!" Rakan said, rolling the r, half his face covered by the three-sizes-too-big helmet.

He had come home.

But to what?

When he left Boston on the first leg of his journey home on Jan. 25, Rakan was wearing a Red Sox wool hat. By the time he boarded the C-17 jet at Andrews 12 hours later, he had ditched it for a cap with Spider-Man on it.

"Too many people talking," he sighed, tired of the attention lavished on him by citizens of Red Sox nation, from maintenance men at Logan International Airport to Air Force personnel at Andrews. Despite the best efforts of his physician, Dr. Laurence Ronan, to convince Rakan of the virtues of America's pastime, Rakan had maintained a yawning disinterest in baseball.

Five months earlier, when Rakan was airlifted from Iraq for treatment at Boston's Massachusetts General Hospital, he had to be carried aboard, his legs apparently paralyzed by the bullet that had clipped his spine. Silent and serious, he was plainly in awe of the aircraft and his entourage.

Now, as his litter was slotted into the metal racks that transform the jet into a flying hospital ward, he was chewing gum, his thumbs flailing away at a Game Boy. He weighed 58 pounds, almost 10 more than when he left Iraq. He had grown 2 inches. His wheelchair was packed away. All he needed was his crutches, and sometimes he didn't need them.

Rakan was allowed to take three duffel bags back home. One was full of his medical supplies. Another held toys, mostly gifts for his siblings and cousins.

A third bag, which Rakan also helped pack, was marked "essentials," and was supposed to carry clothing and medicine. When Ronan unzipped the bag, a box of Lucky Charms peeked out.

"Hey," Ronan said, straightening up, pointing down at the cereal. "What's with these?"

Rakan craned his neck out and looked down at the duffel bag. He shrugged and smiled.

"They're magically delicious," Rakan said, offering the cereal's advertising slogan as his excuse.

During the 20 weeks his Boston medical team had worked to get him walking again, bits and pieces of American culture had seeped in.

Ronan, his own Red Sox cap firmly in place, stood to the side, eyeing his charge. After months of ambivalence, Ronan was at peace with his decision to return Rakan to Iraq. If some were unsure of the ethics of returning a 12-year-old boy to a war zone, Ronan was certain that it would be wrong to deny Rakan's fervent wish to be reunited with his brother and sisters in Iraq.

"He seems more reflective the last few days," Ronan said, raising his voice over the thunder of the engines.

Beyond Rakan's obvious excitement at going home, Ronan sensed some anxiety. "Sometimes he acts 12 going on 20, and sometimes he acts 12 going on 6."

Realizing that people were talking about him, Rakan put his Game Boy down and stuck his tongue out.

He said he was hungry for a snack, but wouldn't open the Lucky Charms or the box of Fruit Loops he had also packed. He was saving them for his baby brother, Muhammed.

On a cot in a C-17, a playful Rakan flew from Ramstein Air Base in Germany to his home in Iraq while Dr. Laurence Ronan wryly wondered how he'd endure the long ride. (Photograph courtesy of Michele McDonald/The Boston Globe)

After an eight-hour flight to Germany, there was a required 24-hour layover. Rakan was taken to Landstuhl Regional Medical Center, a U.S. military hospital which treats U.S. soldiers wounded in Iraq, and where Ronan had first met and taken custody of Rakan in September.

Rakan had sometimes fought with his caregivers in Boston—most of them women—often refusing their requests that he use a catheter to urinate. But when Major Edwin Jeske, a nurse at Landstuhl, told him to empty his bladder by pressing his abdomen, Rakan went to a urinal and did as he was told.

For all the emphasis on getting Rakan up and walking, the most immediate and lasting threat to his health would be urinary tract infections. His newfound ability to manually trigger his bladder reflex reduces his risk of infection, and should dramatically improve his quality of life.

Inside a coffee shop at the hospital, Ronan bought Rakan a chicken sandwich. After a few bites, Rakan's attention was drawn to a big-screen TV in one corner. Tuned to the Armed Forces Network, the TV was showing cartoons, and Rakan used his crutches to amble over, taking a seat directly in front of the screen. Moments later, the cartoon was interrupted by a video feed from Washington, where President Bush was holding a press conference. When Bush's image came on screen, Rakan turned back and made a face.

Back in his room, Rakan played with a remote control toy Humvee that one of the soldiers brought in for him, and spoke with Ronan, who was slumped in a chair next to the boy's bed.

"He just told me he'd never come back to Boston," Ronan said. "Not even to visit."

Rakan stopped playing with the Humvee. He looked up at Ronan. He understood what the doctor had said, and he didn't dispute it. Neither did he smile. Or explain why he was so adamant on this point.

For all the kindness and generosity shown to Rakan by Americans, there was in him a reservoir of bitterness over what had happened to him and his family. He was thankful for the help he had gotten from his doctors and therapists, and often said so. But there were also harder feelings that, in part because of language barriers, his caregivers couldn't get at, and which Rakan guarded with vague answers or no answers at all.

Part of his heart was off-limits. No one quite knew what Rakan really felt.

The next morning, Rakan said he was done with beds and litters and stretchers. For the five-hour flight to Mosul, he would sit in a jump seat, like everybody else.

Nap Bryan, who used to fly fighter jets for the Air Force and now flies commercial jets for American Airlines, piloted the C-17 for the Mississippi Air National Guard. Shortly after takeoff, Bryan turned the controls over to his co-pilot and ambled over to Rakan.

"You wanna ride up front, with me?" Bryan asked, in a soft drawl.

Moments later, Rakan was in the cockpit, sitting in a chair behind Bryan, looking down from 6 miles high. The tips of the Alps peeked through the clouds. Bryan and Rakan talked to each other over headphones.

"What's Alps?" Rakan asked.

Rakan reluctantly returned to his seat for landing. After the plane had touched down in Mosul, Rakan's wheelchair was unpacked, as it would be the fastest way to get him from the tarmac into the hospital, a few hundred yards away. As the rear flap on the C-17 lowered, Ronan stood in back of the wheelchair, gripping its handles. Two crewmen, Evans and Mike Hall, took their positions, one in front, the other behind Ronan and Rakan. Other crew members surrounded the boy: if there was sniper fire, or shrapnel from a mortar, they would take the hit.

As Ronan pushed the wheelchair into the dull, eerie light at the bottom of the ramp, Colonel James Polo, commander of the 47th Combat Support

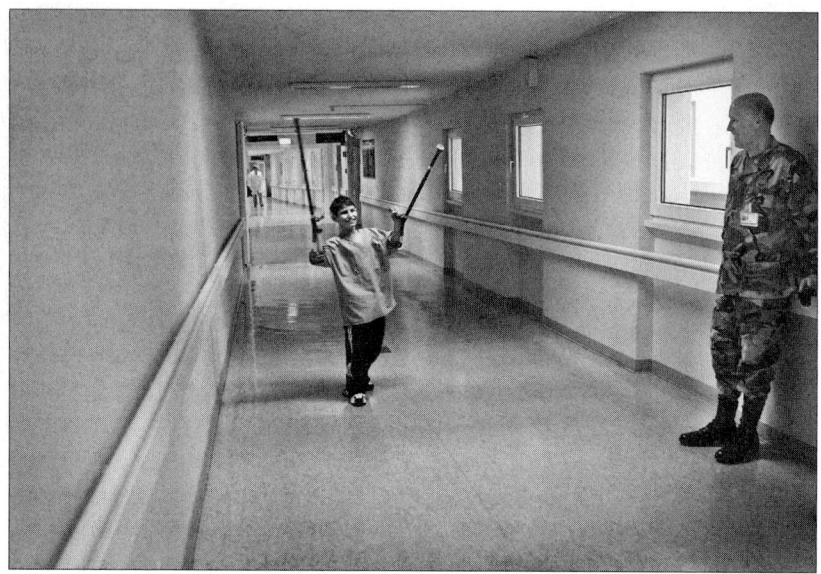

Colonel W. Bryan Gamble watched with delight in late January as Rakan walked without crutches down the hallway of the Landstuhl Regional Medical Center in Germany, a military hospital which treats U.S. soldiers wounded in Iraq. Five months earlier, Rakan had arrived at Landstuhl on his way to Boston, unable to walk on his atrophied legs. (Photograph courtesy of Michele McDonald/*The Boston Globe*)

Hospital, emerged from the darkness. Polo, a child psychiatrist, knelt on the tarmac and pushed his face within inches of Rakan's.

"You're safe," Polo told him. "And you're home."

Polo did not tell Rakan that, about an hour before the plane touched down, two mortar shells had exploded on the tarmac, tearing holes just yards from where Rakan's wheelchair rested.

Inside the hospital, Nathir Bashir Ali, 50, who is married to Rakan's 25-year-old sister, Intisar, waited patiently with his other wife, Sabah, and their 17-month-old daughter, Kadega. Bashir Ali bent down to embrace Rakan. Sabah did the same.

In Bashir Ali's presence, the silly, sometimes mischievous Rakan disappeared, replaced by a boy who in an instant seemed older, deferential, mature.

After the formal greetings, Rakan told his brother-in-law he had something to show him.

Rakan climbed out of his wheelchair and walked across the room on his crutches. Then he turned around and walked back, banging the crutches together over his head, triumphantly.

A dignified, soft-spoken man, Bashir Ali kept his hands folded in front. But his eyes widened, in disbelief, as he watched Rakan walk.

"This is a miracle," he said, bowing his head. "There is no other word for this. This is a miracle."

He turned to Ronan, and repeatedly placed his right hand over his heart, a sign of thanks.

His wife Sabah stepped back. She shook her head, side to side, slowly, as if amazed, and allowed herself a smile.

Habeel Al Jovany, a translator who worked in the hospital and had kept Rakan company during the 45 days Rakan had spent there last summer, rubbed his eyes with clenched fists when Rakan got out of his wheelchair.

He rushed to Rakan, and hugged him tightly.

"You can walk!" he cried.

"Yes," Rakan replied, laughing.

"He was crooked, like a pretzel," Al Jovany said, sitting on the floor to demonstrate what Rakan had looked like just six months ago.

Rakan was led to a bed to spend the night in the hospital's open ward. The scene there seemed almost a tableau of the conflict—its combatants, its bystanders, and its grievous price.

Less than 15 feet away, to the left of Rakan's bed, lay a wounded teenager who U.S. soldiers said was an insurgent. He was hidden behind a curtain so that Rakan couldn't see him. An armed guard sat discreetly to the side. Two other suspected insurgents, much older, and also shielded behind curtains, were in beds nearby.

Directly across from Rakan's bed was Samah Arajy, a 12-year-old girl who had been wounded in a crossfire between U.S. troops and insurgents. She sat up and smiled sweetly at Rakan, who nodded almost imperceptibly at her. Next to the little girl was a sheik who had been wounded by gunfire. Told of Rakan's circumstances, the sheik pulled $100 from his wallet and handed it to his 21-year-old son, who walked over and gave it to Rakan.

Rakan smiled at the sheik and nodded in respect. Of the dozen patients in the ward, only a couple were U.S. soldiers.

"About 80 percent of our patients are Iraqis," Polo explained. "There were some boys from Rakan's hometown, Tal Afar, playing soccer last week. They kicked a metal contraption that turned out to be a buried mine. Two of the kids were killed. Two others, cousins, were brought to us. One was 8. The other was 6. One boy lost his left arm. One boy lost his leg."

Jim Polo nodded, watching Rakan, the new eminence on the ward, receive visitors.

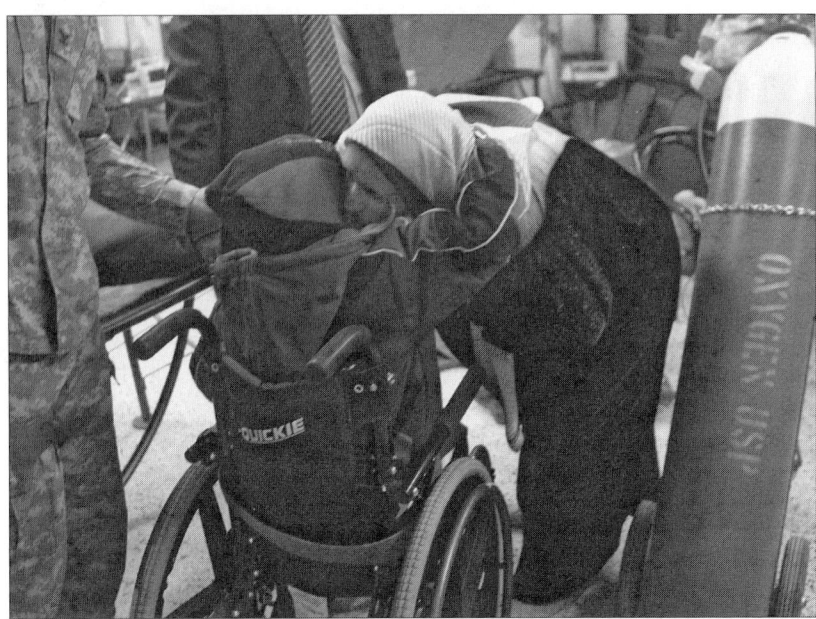

Rakan greeted his brother-in-law's first wife, Sabah, on arrival at the 47th Combat Support Hospital in Mosul. Rakan's 25-year-old sister is the second wife of Nathir Bashir Ali, who has taken in Rakan and his siblings. (Photograph courtesy of Michele McDonald/*The Boston Globe*)

"Rakan is one of many," Polo said. "He was the one in a hundred thousand who got what he needed medically."

Around midnight, Rakan fell asleep watching "Spider-Man" on a portable DVD player.

As dawn broke, Bashir Ali sat in a chair next to Rakan's bed, watching him sleep.

"I stayed up, all night," he said. "How can he walk? I met with the best doctors in Mosul. They said, 'Don't make yourself tired. There's nothing that can be done.' They said he would never walk again. And now . . ."

He stretched his right arm out, over the sleeping boy, as if to bless him.

"I will treat him as my son," he said, softly, almost to himself. "He is my son now."

In Iraqi society, Bashir Ali is a man of substance and responsibility. He is in charge of 100 men who provide security for the museums and antiquities in Mosul, Iraq's third largest city. He earns about $500 a month, nearly twice as much as a doctor, but the money has to go a long way: he has nine children with Sabah; he has two children with Intisar and a third on the way; he has also taken in Rakan's five unmarried siblings. He keeps two houses, a wife in each of them.

Rakan began the final trip home in the front seat of his brother-in-law Bashir Ali's Opel sedan. Bashir Ali is the guardian to Rakan and his siblings. Bashir Ali's 17-month-old daughter, Kadega, waved from the back seat. (Photograph courtesy of Michele McDonald/*The Boston Globe*)

Ronan and Polo spent hours explaining to Bashir Ali what Rakan's family has to do to keep him healthy. They had arranged for Rakan to see Iraqi doctors and therapists on a regular basis. Rakan needs to take eight medications, twice a day.

"I'd like to lose the wheelchair," Ronan said. "I need to get the family to minimize the chair, to make sure that he walks every day, that he takes his medicine every day. He has to wear his leg brace. He has to pee every four to six hours."

Ronan was impressed by Bashir Ali, by the questions he asked, and by the ones he didn't.

"He never once asked for money," said Ronan. "All he did was express gratefulness."

As Rakan packed up his things, Ronan went digging through one of Rakan's duffel bags, looking for the $400 that Himmet and Hesna Taskomur, a Turkish couple from Cambridge, had given Rakan when he left. Ronan wanted to give it to Bashir Ali, and panicked when he couldn't find it. Rakan calmed the doctor with a wave of his arm, and beckoned him close to explain.

Rakan had, the night before, given the money to his brother-in-law, thanking him for taking care of his brother and sisters.

"You did that?" Ronan asked him. "On your own?"

Rakan nodded.

Ronan walked away, chuckling.

On the way to Bashir Ali's car in the parking lot across from the hospital, they had to wait as a heavily armored Army vehicle called a Stryker passed. Rakan eyed it briefly—it was the kind of vehicle used by the soldiers who shot up Rakan's family, and in which he had been rushed to the hospital a year before.

Then, using his crutches, Rakan walked hurriedly, almost hopping, to the front passenger side of his uncle's Opel sedan. A bunch of plastic grapes hung from the rear-view mirror.

"I'll miss you," Ronan told him. "I'm glad I met you."

They embraced.

Rakan climbed into the car, the same model his father used to drive. He waved, then pressed his right palm against the window and left it there.

And then he was gone.

Lessons Learned

BY KEVIN CULLEN

In early September 2005 I bumped into Dr. Larry Ronan, a globe-trotting humanitarian who is a physician at Massachusetts General Hospital in Boston. He looked, as the Irish would say, knackered. He said he had not slept in several days, having flown to Germany to fetch an Iraqi boy who had been shot and apparently paralyzed by U.S. troops. The troops had panicked and shot up the car carrying the boy's family, killing his parents.

As Ronan explained what had happened to one boy, the youth's story seemed to reveal a glimpse of the war, of the inherent dangers facing U.S. troops in the middle of it, of the inevitable mistakes that happen, of the tragic impact those mistakes have on so many Iraqis, of the desire of ordinary Americans to make better what a war fought in their name has wrought, and of the clash of cultures.

Without giving it much thought, I asked Ronan if I could follow the kid's rehabilitation and write about it.

"I don't see why not," he replied.

Thus began an odyssey that was supposed to last, as Ronan put it, "eight weeks, tops," but which became five months of reporting, culminating with the return to Iraq with the boy, Rakan Hassan.

If there were lessons I took from the project that became "Rakan's War," the most important were the willingness to let the reporting process take you where it will, and that when writing, you shouldn't pretend you know more about your subject than you really do.

Originally, my editor, Mark Morrow, and I expected that the dramatic narrative would focus on whether Rakan would learn to walk again. But after a couple of months, it became obvious that the real story was whether he would go home again. Everybody wanted to keep Rakan in the United States.

There were plenty of people who wanted to adopt him. But Rakan wanted to go home, even though home was in the middle of a war zone. Ultimately, the Solomonesque decision about Rakan's fate fell to Dr. Ronan, who struggled mightily with it.

Language was obviously a challenge, not just for the reporting process but also for the writing process, because Rakan spoke in short, staccato sentences—not in long, elaborate thoughts. It was extremely difficult at first to get Rakan to explain what had happened to him and his family, and how he felt about that.

I also worried that I might retraumatize him by getting him to go too far, too soon. It seemed to me the only alternative was to spend as much time with Rakan as possible, to gain his trust, to learn his body language, his moods, his expressions, and to watch him alternatively blossom and withdraw.

Hardly a day went by that I didn't spend time with Rakan at the hospital, including most weekends, when he was really alone. After we realized he was especially lonely on weekends, I would take him out—for pizza, a Celtics game, his first visit to a seashore—and my two sons were his only peers for several months. It was striking that there was no language barrier between Rakan and my sons.

I was wary of using translated conversations, especially because Rakan's native language was Turkoman and his words were being translated from a combination of Turkish and Arabic. Nearly everything attributed to him in the series came from his rudimentary English.

But even as Rakan picked up enough English for meaningful conversations, one of the real difficulties for me, especially when writing, was in trying to truly convey what Rakan was feeling. He was shrewd, and he allowed all outsiders, including me, only so close. When it came to writing, I did not assume to know more about Rakan than I did.

There was some criticism of the series on those very grounds—that we didn't get inside Rakan's head. But you can only get inside someone's head if they let you.

In the writing and editing process, Mark Morrow and I were very conscious of not overreaching or overwriting. Mark is extremely skilled at policing my penchant for adjectives. We tried to be understated, because the facts surrounding the tragedy that turned Rakan's life upside down were compelling in themselves, just as his interactions with his caregivers, and his homecoming, were moving in their simplicity.

The response from readers was overwhelming, and there was a common theme in what they said: That, as presented, the series was powerful because it was understated—not some omniscient, purple-prose anti-war screed, but, as promised up front, simply a story about a boy.

Sometimes, simple is better.

Kevin Cullen has been a Globe *reporter since 1985 and is currently a* Globe *columnist. He has been the newspaper's law enforcement reporter and legal affairs correspondent and a reporter-at-large. He has also served on the* Globe*'s investigative unit, in the* Globe*'s Dublin and London bureau and as a European correspondent. Cullen was part of the* Globe*'s investigative team that broke open the story of sexual abuse in the Catholic Church, an achievement for which the* Globe *was awarded the 2003 Pulitzer Prize for Public Service. With other members of the team, Cullen is co-author of "Betrayal: The Crisis in the Catholic Church." He is also a co-author of a book on contemporary Anglo-Irish relations, "Britain and Ireland: Lives Entwined II." Cullen won the 1988 Livingston Award for local reporting and the 1994 Overseas Press Club of America's citation for excellence in interpretive reporting for his coverage of Northern Ireland. He was a 2003 Nieman Fellow at Harvard University.*

The Washington Post

■ Finalist

Anthony Shadid

ASNE, Individual Deadline News Reporting
Finalist, Pulitzer Prize, International Reporting

50. 'God Stop the Bombs!'

JULY 26, 2006

TIBNIN, LEBANON, July 25—The Israeli shells thundered into the charred hillside above the Tibnin General Hospital. There were two, then another, then two more, the uneven cadence of an attack on Tuesday. The walls shuddered and acrid smoke drifted through the building. Huddled inside were at least 1,350 Lebanese in hallways, rooms, stairwells, a lobby and a basement lit by a few candles, hiding with little water, less food and almost no hope of salvation from a war that provoked their flight and had returned to their doorstep.

"Oh Lord!" cried 60-year-old Saadeh Awadeh, leaping up from a tattered cushion against a wall. "God stop the bombs!"

Her screams made children cry, their tangled wails wrapped in suffocating heat. Her pleas, in vain, angered others.

"Shut up!" one man shouted from down the crowded ground-floor hallway barely lit by the sun.

The Tibnin hospital, eight miles from the Israeli border, a half-hour drive to the coastal city of Tyre in peace, is a Guernica-like tableau of suffering, desperation and anguish, the nexus of the country's unfolding humanitarian crisis in a hilly redoubt near an ancient fort almost unreachable by perilous roads. There are no doctors here. Water does not run. The electricity was cut on the war's first day.

Elderly women, fleeing two weeks of fighting since, have wrapped their swollen, bloodied and bruised feet in gauze. Five babies have been born premature since the fighting started. There is nowhere to bathe them. In another hallway, Abeer Faris cradled in her arms her 3-day-old infant, whom she carried on foot from the besieged city of Bint Jbeil nine hours after giving birth.

About 1,350 people who have fled the fighting in southern Lebanon are sheltered in the hospital in Tibnin, which is eight miles from the Israeli border. (Photograph courtesy of Michael Robinson-Chavez/The Washington Post)

"The country is grieving," said Hussein Qadouh, a 43-year-old who had left his home in Tibnin and sought shelter inside.

"There's death all over the place," said Mustafa Wehbe, a 45-year-old, standing next to Qadouh.

Lebanese along the border started fleeing to Tibnin on the war's first day. It was a bigger town than most, known as a picnic spot, perched over tobacco farms, rows of pines and the gracefully aged, rocky hills of southern Lebanon. The first stone of its fort was laid in 1850 B.C., and the town was long ago a resting place for caravans. The hospital was renovated, a seemingly safe place from bombing. So they came—a few at first, then hundreds and dozens more Tuesday, from fighting growing more intense by the day. And here they wait, in a narrative of war's suffering, tragedies more personal than political.

Entering the lobby was like opening an oven door, and anger, fear and abandonment poured forth. People crowded for space along the tile floors and underneath an entrance that bore the hospital's name in metalworked, gold lettering. The walls were adorned with faded red-and-white Lebanese flags.

"Get us out of here!" one person pleaded.

"Help us!" another cried.

"Have you brought any food?" someone else shouted.

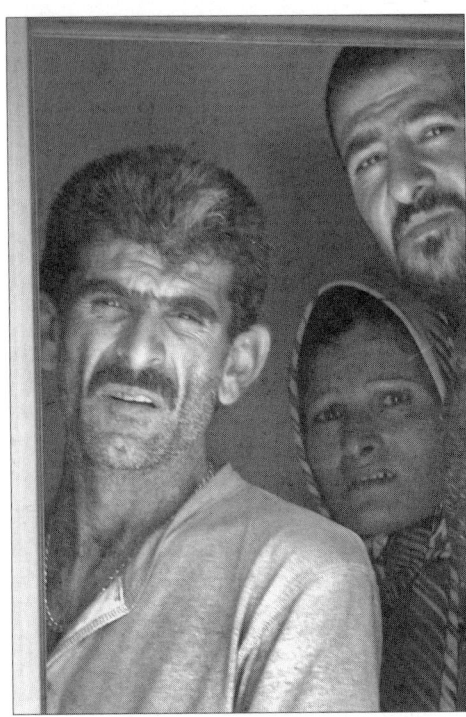

Israeli airstrikes on the town of 4,000 reverberate through the hospital, which has no doctors or running water. (Photograph courtesy of Michael Robinson-Chavez/The Washington Post)

There are no shops open in Tibnin, once a town of 4,000. Families said they were surviving on one meal a day; estimates of the sick ran from 40 to more, mostly children. The hospital administration has largely fled; so have the doctors. Hardly any aid can reach the town on winding, remote roads where Israeli forces have repeatedly struck civilian cars. The hospital's lifeline is the Lebanese Red Cross, which lost two ambulances Sunday night when Israeli rockets pierced their roofs. On most days, sometimes in several trips, the ambulances bring 300 to 500 packets of flat bread, 10 pieces in each, and maybe 100 cans of tuna.

"It's one drop of water in the ocean," said Qassem Shaalan, a Red Cross worker who was wounded in Sunday's attack.

"It's not 1 percent of what they need," he added. "It's one in 1,000."

Wehbe, in soiled clothes, his moustache heavy, arrived at the hospital Tuesday morning, with 50 others from his village of Ainata. They were some of the last still there after bombing had gone on three days, day and night.

"They were destroying the houses over our heads," he said. "Fine, let soldier fight soldier, but we're civilians."

They took their chances, walking six miles through the morning. Shelling punctuated their exodus, along roads littered with the shuttered artifacts of everyday life: the La Ciel salon, Maatouk Café, the Mansour restaurant and the Mehdi schools.

"And they're still coming from all over the place," Wehbe said, pointing to a family that had just arrived from Bint Jbeil, where fighting raged Tuesday between Hezbollah fighters and Israeli troops trying to occupy the town.

He listed the other towns emptying into Tibnin: Aitaroun, Maroun al-Ras and Yaroun. Family after family listed dead and wounded relatives. Time and again, they pleaded for help in getting the bodies excavated from rubble that had entombed them in their villages. The Red Cross has focused on saving the living; other than ragtag civil defense units, there is no government left.

"How can we get in? How can we get their bodies?" asked Awadeh. "God show me."

She had arrived a week ago from Aitaroun, after her brother, Moussa, his wife, Jamila, and their five children—Ali, Abeer, Hassan, Mariam and Mohammed, ages 5 to 15—were killed in an airstrike on their village. They left the corpses behind. She sat with her sister, Haniyeh, who had trekked with her and others from the village about 10 miles.

Haniyeh pointed to her bandaged feet, still swollen and bruised from the walk.

"It's more wretched here than there," she said glumly, sitting on a mattress against the wall.

"We just don't know what's going on," her sister said.

The hospital is a two-story building of concrete, part of it unfinished. The rooms have a sickly glow, barely lit by the sun. The fortunate have occupied rooms; others sleep on mattresses in the hallways, their few belongings stuffed in plastic bags. Weak children sit silent with their mothers. Tempers have frayed, the combustible emotions created by too many people in too little space. They grew worse Tuesday as the shells landed near the fort. An hour before, blasts had ignited fires on the hillside below.

More found room in the darkened basement, where a few candles cast ghostly silhouettes of the displaced against the wall.

"Every day, the numbers keep rising," said Fatimeh Assem, a 13-year-old wandering the halls.

A ride out of Tibnin costs $100, far more than most of the families here have. Even with the money, drivers are reluctant to take roads punctuated with buildings flattened by blasts and cars either incinerated or abandoned, some still flying white flags. At times, rubble spills into the roads. Tracks are cleared by vehicles passing under the iconography of Hezbollah, which draws on the southern Lebanese for much of its support. "The resistance will remain, remain, remain," one sign read. At several spots along the way, fires have charred the terraced hills, along with their pine and olive trees. At bends in the road, signs on the walls of buildings, perched on top of cars and scrawled on concrete walls read "Toward Tyre," directing travelers to relative safety.

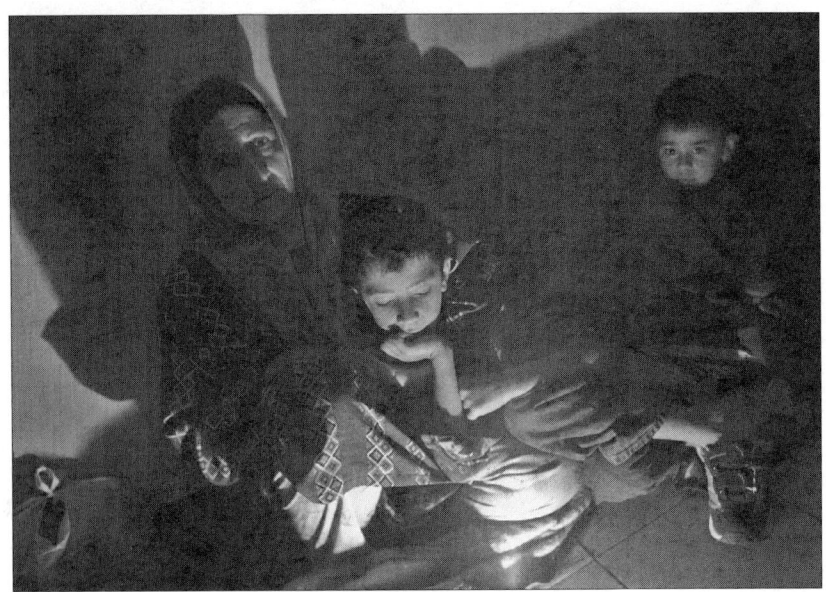

With no electricity in the hospital, people use a few candles for light day and night. Some people walked dozens of miles to the shelter. (Photograph courtesy of Michael Robinson-Chavez/*The Washington Post*)

"What can we do?" asked Sabah Hashem, a 50-year-old woman, gathered with her family of 16 in a room at the hospital where dentists work. "There's no medicine, there are no supplies. If we try to take people to another hospital, they'll hit the ambulance on the road."

Her niece, 4-year-old Zeinab Hashem, played with a blond doll, on a blanket. The girl's brother slept in a dental chair. Clothes were draped over the equipment. On a sterilizer, a Koran was turned open, black prayer beads laying atop a page.

"Is there no way you can get us out of here?" Hashem asked. "God be with you if you can find us a way."

Her sister Fatima rushed toward her. "Can you get the foreigners to come get us? What about the United Nations?"

Another woman, 70-year-old Fahima Abbas, added her voice.

"If the United Nations would just give us a truce for four or five hours, we could get the people out of here and to Beirut."

Southern Lebanon, already the country's poorest region, has suffered the war's greatest toll. In the hospital, the desperation was woven with a sense of abandonment, directed at virtually everyone except Hezbollah.

"What's the Lebanese government providing us?" asked Hassan Hamza, a 19-year-old from Tibnin, here for 13 days.

Others joined the conversation.

"The government only loves the Americans," said his friend, Assem.

"It only loves money and the Americans," Hamza said.

Hoda Fawwaz, a 50-year-old from Tibnin, approached the group. She carried a small, blue radio, its batteries still working.

"It's the resistance that loves the people," she said. "It's the only one that protects the children and the young."

Down the hall, Faris carried her 3-day-old son, Khattar, and an empty bottle with a blue cap. She gave birth to him at 10 p.m. Saturday in Bint Jbeil. By 7 the next morning, she, her husband, Mohammed, her sons Aissa and Mustafa and her daughter, Israa, were walking to Tibnin. They arrived by noon, stopping along the way when bombing was especially fierce.

Mohammed said they brought nothing but the clothes they were wearing. As he talked, Israa slept on his shoulder.

He pleaded for help: He had relatives in Beirut, he could take care of himself there. He needed just one thing: a ride.

"We have to leave today," he said, his thick, black hair streaked with gray. "We can't stay here any longer."

Lessons Learned

BY ANTHONY SHADID

Most journalists would probably agree that logistics often prove the most difficult challenge to reporting in times of conflict. There are variously questions of access, time and the actual risks in getting to the story.

The scene at the hospital in the southern Lebanese town of Tibnin, halfway through the war in summer 2006 between Israel and Hezbollah, was remarkable in tangling itself in all those challenges. It was tough to get to the hospital. Once there, time was short. During that brief window, it was crucial to narrow in on people's stories, identifying as quickly as possible the story's structure.

High up in the piece, I described Tibnin as "a Guernica-like tableau of suffering, desperation and anguish." The image struck me minutes within walking into the hospital. But I knew that if the story were to convey somehow the depth of people's emotions that day, I'd have to find the details and narratives that would bring the image to life.

Once there, I chose a hallway and limited myself to that one stretch of the hospital. At times, it was like directing traffic. The scene was chaotic and angry. Fights were breaking out. Some people were resentful of journalists, viewing them as no better than voyeurs. Others were desperate simply to have their stories heard.

I didn't just want quotes. I wanted to hear those stories. And I knew I had maybe 10 or 15 minutes to listen to what each family had gone through. I often try to remind myself that stories like this have to coalesce even during the reporting, essentially a constraint of time. Tibnin proved that lesson. When I felt like I had one family's narrative—perhaps just enough for a couple of paragraphs—I had to break away and turn my attention elsewhere. Every question had to count, eliciting answers that would, I hoped, fit like pieces of a puzzle.

I usually try to divide each page of my notebook. On the top, I write details that strike me, quotes that I overhear, bits of scene, ambient sounds and possible themes to develop. The bottom of the page is reserved for direct quotes. Time and again during that conflict, I found myself drawing most heavily on the top portion of my notes. There were women who had wrapped "swollen, bloodied and bruised feet in gauze." There was a Koran resting on a sterilizer, "black prayer beads laying atop a page." Those kinds of details often served as the connective tissue between narratives, the hints of a broader drama.

Even in the busiest days of the war, I took time to sketch an outline. This practice is not for everyone. But I've found it almost impossible to bring narrative to a spot story without it. A good outline often lets you focus on the writing, since the structure is already there.

In writing "'God Stop the Bombs!'" I wanted first and foremost to convey the urgency of the scene. It was indeed a Guernica-like image, and the writing had to convey that. Short sentences were essential, and I tried to alternate longer description and background with brief, declarative phrases. I didn't feel the need to qualify or hedge, particularly in writing about the vagaries of conflict and the trauma people are forced to endure. It was easier to call it like it was. In hindsight, it felt more honest, real and representative of what I saw.

Even in a spot story, particularly from a place readers know hardly anything about, a few sentences of background help—the town's population, its history, the scene there, its reputation. One simple question I like to ask is what the town is famous for. It sounds a little banal, but it's remarkable how often the answer adds a compelling detail. Another, perhaps obvious lesson: Names and ages are always essential. In their own way, they restore a bit of humanity to victims who often go nameless in times of conflict.

The piece on Tibnin might not be the best example, but to me, it's the most compelling. In spot writing you must find a way to weave very detailed scenes with the larger context and background. I sometimes think of a story swaying back and forth between the two. The pivots themselves often serve as transitions, and they can ensure that a narrative doesn't lose its pace.

The last lesson I took away from the Tibnin piece was how essential actual narrative can be. A narrative can play out over two paragraphs or 10, so space is rarely a legitimate excuse. Stories can be brief, yet still driven by detail, or they can stretch for an entire article. But in the end, those kinds of stories are what really matter.

Anthony Shadid is the Middle East correspondent for The Washington Post. *Since September 11, 2001, he has reported from Egypt, Syria, Israel, Palestine and Iraq. Shadid won the Pulitzer Prize for international reporting in 2004 for his dispatches from Iraq. That year he also received the ASNE award for deadline writing and the Overseas Press Club's Hal Boyle Award for best newspaper or wire service reporting from abroad. Shadid also won the 2003 George Polk Award for foreign reporting for a series of dispatches from the Middle East while at* The Boston Globe. *In 1997 Shadid was awarded a citation by the Overseas Press Club for his work on "Islam's Challenge." The four-part series, published by the AP in December 1996, formed the basis of his book "Legacy Of the Prophet: Despots, Democrats and the New Politics Of Islam." His second book, "Night Draws Near: Iraq's People in the Shadow Of America's War," was published September 2005. Shadid's coverage of the conflict in Lebanon also made him a finalist for the 2007 Pulitzer Prize in international reporting.*

Narrative Strategies

BY THOMAS FRENCH

War—viewed from the other side of the planet and from our own backyard—haunts this year's collection of writings by ASNE winners and finalists. Many of the writers whose work is honored in this volume show us what happens when human beings are plunged into battle, and what happens once the battle is left behind.

These stories, different in so many ways, are united in their exploration of this theme. Again and again, they demonstrate narrative's ability to usher the reader inside other lives, other worlds. These stories take us—among other places—to the front lines in Iraq, inside a beleaguered Lebanese hospital, and into a suburban Florida home where the children wait for the safe return of their mother, who is thousands of miles away on a tour of duty for the Air Force.

Using dialogue, scene and carefully chosen detail, the stories transport us to places most of us will never experience on our own. In Iraq, we see the sweat dripping from a medic's face after he has worked to save a wounded Marine. In southern Lebanon, we feel the shuddering of a hospital's walls, shaken by Israeli shells, and we smell the smoke wafting through the corridors. In Florida, we hear the singsong murmurs of children praying for their mother.

The writers' ability to put us inside these moments is achievement enough. Even more impressive is that they somehow find ways to take us inside the internal landscapes of the people who are living through these moments. They show us what their subjects are thinking and feeling, the contradictions that drive them, the depth and complexity of their fear and dread and love. Describing events of global importance, these gifted journalists render not just experience, but intimacy.

C. J. Chivers, *The New York Times* reporter who followed the medic in Iraq, doesn't just show his subject staring at his hands, still bloody from his attempts to save a critically wounded member of his platoon. Chivers goes much further, letting us overhear the medic's rambling, emotional outpouring after his patient is evacuated by helicopter. We hear the medic describing how he had been roommates with the Marine, how he fought to keep his friend breathing, how he wished there was something more he could have done. We hear him asking for water to wash the blood off his wedding band and confessing his desire for vengeance on the sniper who shot his friend.

> 'I would like to say that I am a good man,' he said. 'But seeing this now . . . I want to hurt people. You know what I mean?'

At one point he turns to Chivers and asks a personal question.

> 'Do you pray?' he asked. 'Do that. I'd appreciate it.'

Many of us might have been tempted to leave out this exchange, since it requires Chivers to place himself inside the scene. The effect, however, is anything but indulgent. While keeping the focus entirely on the medic, Chivers helps us recognize how desperately his subject needs someone to bear witness to what he's just experienced. In that instant, Chivers becomes the reader's surrogate, enabling us to connect with the medic and acknowledge his anger and grief. It's a startling, highly personal moment, not just for the reporter and his subject, but for us.

Remember, Chivers reported and wrote this story—with all its different levels—on deadline.

Other pieces in this collection tackle the subject of the Iraq War from completely different perspectives. My friend and colleague Anne Hull, of *The Washington Post,* has written a handful of stories describing the conflict's effect here at home. Hull, a veteran reporter with a finely tuned ability for chronicling other people's lives, turns her attention to her own family in a piece about a visit with her brother and his two young daughters, who live outside Tampa. Her sister-in-law—the brother's wife and the mother of the girls—is a master sergeant in the Air Force and is serving in northern Iraq.

Hull describes her visit like this:

> We spend the week eating Cocoa Pebbles and watching 'The Incredibles.' We hold dance parties in a bedroom where the stuffed animals are giving way to dreamy teen idol posters. We go to the mall and to the dentist. One night while I make dinner, the girls ride bikes outside in the waning winter dusk. It is a relief to be away from Washington, where politicians in marble hallways proclaim righteousness though they have never carried a canteen. Here in this linoleum kitchen, there is just a crayon calendar on the refrigerator marking the days until Mama comes home.

Many journalists avoid first person, worrying that they might lapse into sentimentality. Often this fear is well-founded. Other times it becomes a convenient excuse for us to hide behind, a way of pretending that we are fundamentally different from our subjects and are somehow removed from the daily ebb and flow.

In her account, Hull avoids both traps. She is never self-conscious or self-absorbed. As in the rest of her work, the writing is lean, honest, meticulously observed. Hull clearly admires her brother and her sister-in-law, but writes about herself with self-deprecation. The entire piece is all the more moving for its understatement.

> The girls sit at the kitchen table to write letters to their mother. Chrislyn picks up a pencil and stares out the window. A dreamer and sensitive soul, like her father when he was a boy. She looks down at her blank paper and begins. *Dear Mom: If you read this carefully, you might actually hear my voice.*

One of the most striking things about this piece is how quietly it reads on the page. This same quiet finds its way into many of the other award-winning stories in this volume. It's there in Chivers' piece, as he watches the medic with the blood-stained hands.

Another writer—David Finkel, also of *The Washington Post*—once told me that we need stories where the volume is turned low. I agree. As journalists, we already know what to do when a bomb explodes in a market, on a crowded bus, beside a school. The question becomes, what do we make of the silence that follows, when the bodies are carried away and the cries of the bereaved have finally died down? How do we chronicle the years of quiet moments that led to the blast?

These stories point the way.

Thomas French is a Writing Fellow at The Poynter Institute and a Pulitzer Prize-winning reporter at the St. Petersburg *(Fla.)* Times.

Part 7

Community Service Photojournalism

WINNER
Suzanne Kreiter
Community Service Photojournalism

The Boston Globe

"I have the greatest job in the world," Suzanne Kreiter says in a video produced for ASNE's 2007 convention. "I get paid to go on walkabouts in search of the unheralded everyday—and not so everyday—people who make up the city of Boston."

In "The City Seen" column, Kreiter captures slices of urban life, sharing with readers moments that make us smile, laugh and think.

Kreiter joined the photography staff of *The Boston Globe* in 1985. During her decades as a photojournalist she has traveled around the world, covering such subjects as the Nicaraguan civil war and the deforestation of the Amazon rain forest.

In 1992 Kreiter was awarded the Robert F. Kennedy Journalism Award for Outstanding Coverage of the Problems of the Disadvantaged for her photo essay illustrating the disparate lives of two groups of mentally disabled adults, one living in a group home and the other living in a large institution.

In 1996 Kreiter began *The Boston Globe*'s first photo column, a two-year project for which she documented the daily experiences of the Boston Police.

Kreiter was recognized as the 2005 Boston Press Photographers Association Photographer of the Year, becoming the only woman in the competition's history to win that honor twice.

She and her writer husband, Mitchell Zuckoff, have also been recognized with the ASNE Distinguished Writing Award for Nondeadline Writing (in 2000) and numerous other honors for their six-part series, "Choosing Naia," which documented a family's decision to continue a pregnancy after they learned their unborn child had Down syndrome.

Kreiter started her career at the *Concord Monitor* in Concord, N.H. She has seen many changes over the years but says "all this worry about the Internet and new media and the future of newspapers doesn't worry me at all.

"In a time when video cameras are overtaking our newsrooms, it would be a mistake to overlook the pure and simple power of the still image . . . In still photography, the eye has nowhere to go, the viewer is captive to what the photographer wants to say."

Kreiter's images in "The City Seen" speak volumes.

"I became a journalist because I love stories," Kreiter said. "I love to tell stories through my photography."

—Julie Moos, co-editor, "Best Newspaper Writing"

At the William J. Devine Golf Course at Franklin Park every Tuesday morning, the Elderly/Disabled Housing Program of the Boston Housing Authority brings senior citizens out for golfing. On a summer morning when the temperature was heading into the 90s, (from left) Euripedes Gonzalez, 71, Simone Whitter, 69, program director Alfred Davis, 61, and Leevonia Townes, 53, loosened up before hitting the putting green. They may not be Tiger Woods, but "they all feel like regular golfers when they come out here," said Davis.

51. About "The City Seen"

Meet Julia Sweeney, a regular fixture on a Brighton park bench who loves to share colorful stories of her late husband. Hear an immigrant family's first impressions of their journey from Honduras to America as they do their laundry in an East Boston laundromat. Glimpse into the lives of teenage girls—"Townies"—who live and play in the tough housing projects of Charlestown. These are among the more than 50 images captured by *Boston Globe* photojournalist Suzanne Kreiter in her column, "The City Seen."

These images are not traditional feature photos. They are not assigned or accidental. You have to be looking for them. The subjects of "The City Seen" are people who are not typically featured in the pages of daily newspapers. Their images, reflected in "The City Seen," show a city that is at once familiar and completely new.

For generations, East Boston has been a first stop for new immigrants. Today it has a growing Latin American population and a lively mix of established and newly arrived residents. Ten-year-old Javier Padilla, for instance, recently moved with his family from Honduras. On a recent Friday morning, after getting inoculations required to attend the Patrick Kennedy Elementary School, he and his younger brother, Omar, helped their mother do laundry at a laundromat on Bennington Street.

These are the people, places and scenes that give the city its heart and mind. Over the course of a year, Kreiter created a patchwork quilt of moments that reveal a little bit of Boston's soul. These moments give readers a chance to smile, commiserate, be inspired and ultimately understand their community a little better.

When the far-flung reaches of the globe are accessible with the click of a mouse, "The City Seen" brings our neighbors into the nooks and crannies, around the corner and up the block into the lives of *The Boston Globe* and Boston.com readers every Monday morning.

—Adapted from *The Boston Globe* ASNE contest entry

A conversation with
Suzanne Kreiter

This edited e-mail interview was conducted by Poynter's Visual Journalism Group Leader and Diversity Program Director Kenny Irby with The Boston Globe's *Suzanne Kreiter, winner of ASNE's Community Service Photojournalism Award.*

KENNY IRBY: Photographic columns aren't common. What is their value?

SUZANNE KREITER: Photo columns are a perfect marriage of image and words. The photo column can give readers a traditional feature story that they can 'ingest' in a few minutes when the words are amplified by the right image. When the photojournalist has control over the words *and* image, they can give you a bigger bang for the buck.

How long have you done this kind of work?

I've been a photojournalist with *The Boston Globe* for 22 years.

How did "The City Seen" photo column originate?

My boss, Paula Nelson, assistant managing editor/photography, came up with the idea for "The City Seen." She had originally designed it for the whole staff to contribute to. But as I started shooting the first ones, she decided it was a good idea to allow a certain sensibility (my particular shooting and journalistic style) to carry the column each week. I had a previous photo column that ran for two-and-a-half years in the 1990s called "On the Beat." It chronicled the daily travails of the Boston Police on the job.

Where and how did you gather information and identify your sources to make such intimate connections?

Every imaginable way. Sometimes, I would get an idea for a column and I'd call a government or social agency. Often, based on what they said, I might be steered in a totally different direction. For example, I'd been looking for a group of community gardeners. On my 20th call to the Boston Housing Authority, a woman mentioned that they had organized a group of disabled seniors to go on golf outings, and would I find that interesting? Yes.

Sometimes, when I'm out driving around I just find something interesting and decide to investigate. I've always been intrigued by the bait and

On warm summer days, the sidewalks of the Mishawum Park Apartments fill with portable tables, chairs, potted plants and flags as residents move their living rooms outside. From left, Bridget Roy, 13, Jordan Paquette, 15, and Meaghan Scanlan, 12, played cards on the sidewalk on Dunstable Street. "We're such losers," said Jordan. "We're 15 years old and playing Go Fish." The girls attend the summertime Mission Safe program at St. Catherine of Siena Church.

tackle shop in the middle of a tough, urban neighborhood of Boston, so I just walked inside one day.

In the end, everyone has a story to tell.

I read the Calendar section of the newspaper to see what people are up to. An NPR piece on a college chess team inspired me to search out a local chess club and see what they're all about. An ad on the radio about a costume shop going out of business led to a column. An old woman sitting on a park bench had a lifetime of stories to tell our readers.

How did the community focus come about?

As the column continued each week, it became clear that I was presenting pieces of a quilt. Separately, they are one thing, one small story in a moment. But when put all together, a larger story is told. A community is not about the people who hold the keys to the city, but about regular people in their everyday lives. "The City Seen" became a safe place to tell the stories of people who don't normally appear in the newspaper.

If it takes a village to raise a child, the neighborhood library is an essential stop along the way. On a January morning, first-grader Alonzo Robinson of the Emily A. Fifield Elementary School browsed through the stacks at the Codman Square Branch of the Boston Public Library. His first-grade class comes regularly to the library. Principal Craig Lankhorst says the 10-minute walk to the local public library serves a dual purpose: literacy and exercise.

Who did you include in the editing process?

My boss, Paula. She has rejected a few of the photo columns. And she has steered me to segments of society I wouldn't normally gravitate to.

How do you go about gaining access and building relationships with the people you document?

When I explain to people what the purpose of "City Seen" is, they almost always say yes to being a part of the gallery. I have used "spirit guides" in a few instances to introduce me to people who might not speak English, or might be wary of the media.

Tell me about the editing and selection process.

I'll shoot hundreds of images, sometimes over the course of one or two or three visits with a subject. I'll scan in anywhere from one to 10 images on a particular column. Then, Paula weighs in. We sometimes disagree. So we enter into a period of negotiation and we see who feels the most strongly

At a charity event held by the Massachusetts Melanoma Foundation at Neiman Marcus, attendees were encouraged to bring their dogs. Dale Roberts, left, of the Back Bay, and her toy poodle, Red, sat with Christel Whittier of Boston and Barbara Goldberg of the South End, who held her poodle, Coco Chanel, at a showing of the Neiman Marcus fall 2006 collections. At the end of the show, dogs and owners were invited to stroll the runway. Deb Girard, executive director of the Massachusetts Melanoma Foundation, says the "Bark Bash" doubled the group's net from last year.

At the Boylston Chess Club, 7-year-old Miguel Reid Sandoval reacts to a chess move against his opponent under a poster of chess champion Gary Kasparov. On Wednesday afternoons, Satea Husari, an international chess master, teaches strategy to children in grades K through 8. The Boylston Chess Club was founded in 1919 on Boylston Street in Boston. There are an average of 100 members.

When Boston firefighters risk their lives to protect people and property, a fire dog is often there, if for no other reason than to lend support. When the alarm sounds at Ladder 15 on Boylston Street, Colonel McSniff stands at attention and then jumps into his seat inside Engine 33. On this December afternoon, the 6-year-old yellow Labrador retriever napped on the way back from a false alarm—not much action for him or his owner, Lt. Bob Moriarty, left, and firefighter Chris Wright, who recently returned from a second tour with the Marines in Iraq.

Her bold print dress blowing in the breeze, her leg propped up next to her, 79-year-old Julia Sweeney is a commanding presence on a bench adjacent to the Artesani Playground along the Charles River. She and her late husband have been coming to this spot to cool off for "35 or 45 years, I've lost count." Her husband, Robert F. Sweeney, died in 1999, but when asked how long she was married, she counts the years since he has died in her total, so she says she's been married 51 years. Sweeney has a daughter, eight grandchildren and one great grandchild.

At Dreams Wedding studio on the edge of Chinatown, wedding images are created well before a couple says "I do." Yvonne Wong, a financial reporting specialist from Quincy, and her fiance, Kevin Chow, a software developer from Waltham, came to the studio on Lincoln Street shortly after their engagement to have the first of their official wedding photos done. After nearly two hours of preparing the bride's hair and makeup, the couple and the photographer, Danny Poon, headed to the Public Garden for their photo session. The Chinese character on the wall behind them means "double happiness."

about the photo they are backing. In the end, there's always another column next week, so most of the time it's not worth arguing about.

What role did your picture editor play?

Photojournalists are lucky when they have a good picture editor working with them. A good picture editor, like Paula, can help the photographer when they can't see the forest for the trees.

How did you interact with the online staff?

For a time they were supplying audio for each column, but like any modern-day multimedia journalist, I've started collecting and editing the audio portion myself.

What are your thoughts about online storytelling and presentation?

If it weren't for our online presentation, it would be a lot harder to visualize "The City Seen" as a collection of images. Boston.com provides a great platform for my photo column.

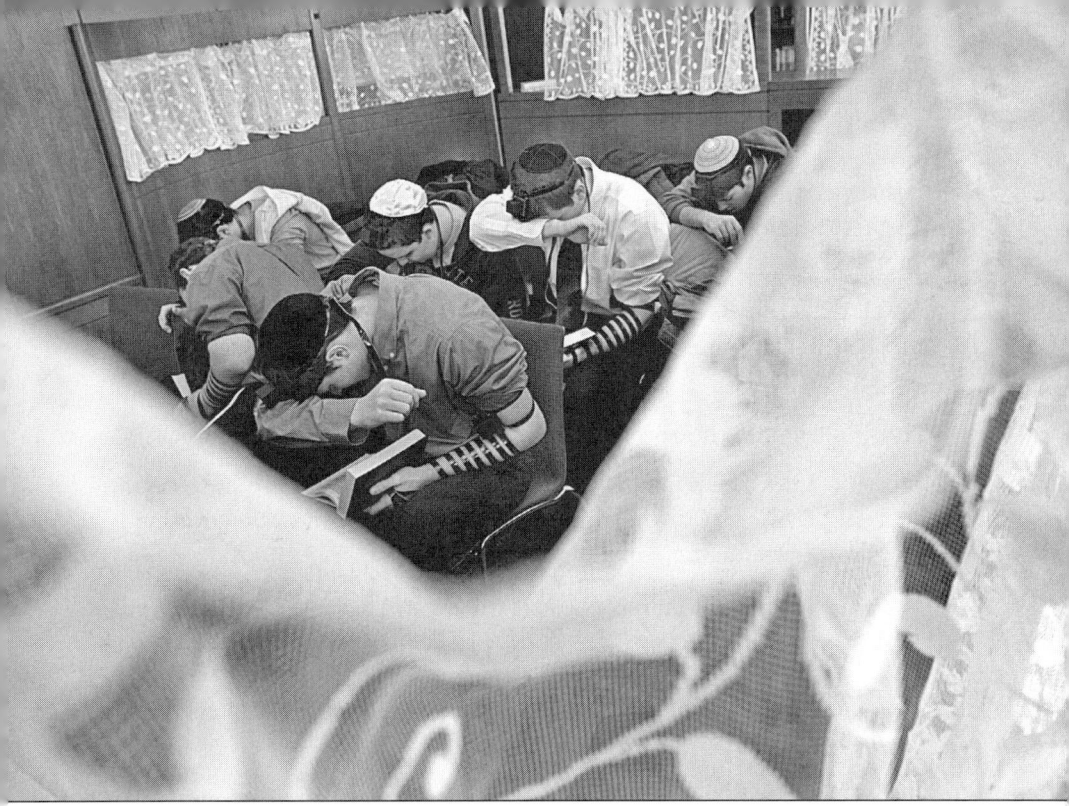

Observant Jews hold prayer minyans every day throughout the world. In the Orthodox faith, prayers such as these at Boston University cannot proceed past a certain point unless there are 10 men over the age of 13. A curtain separates male and female worshippers. Traditional Jewish men wear leather strapping around their arms and head, securing small boxes called tefillin. The boxes contain passages from the Torah. One box is worn on the bicep, facing the heart; the other is worn on the front of the head.

Are the goals different for online presentation compared with those for print?

Yes, the online presentation strives to create a way to see all the images, not just one at a time as in the print edition.

How much time did you put into the coverage?

On average, one-and-a-half to two full days of my work week goes into it. Often more.

What were some of the challenges that you faced? How did you overcome them?

The relentless nature of a weekly column can be very stressful. (My column runs even when I'm on vacation.) There are days when I simply need to sit and make phone calls for hours, or scan the Web for ideas. The photo assignment desk was terrific in understanding this important aspect of producing the photo column.

I believe strongly that ideas are the currency of the newsroom. What is your reaction to this statement?

Yes, I agree. I feel very wealthy because I can keep coming up with ideas for the column. I think that's one of the reasons "The City Seen" became my column.

How challenging is it to produce a powerful single image on a regular basis?

It can be hard. The photo column image has to tell the *entire* story in *one* shot. It's a different way of thinking and shooting than when covering a news story, or a multiple-image picture story.

What are the more memorable lessons you learned during this assignment?

If I find something to be interesting, there's a good chance others will too.

How different was this particular assignment from the kinds of stories you have covered during your career?

In the end, I think I gravitated to similar themes of interesting/unusual people, how a society cares for those who can't care for themselves, and respect for differences.

What advice can you offer other photographers about being a visual reporter?

Stories are everywhere—you just always have to have your eyes and ears open (even when you're not working). Be nosey.

Tell me about your most unforgettable five photographs in the course of this past year. Why are they important, and what were the circumstances of the coverage?

The first is the firehouse dog, "Colonel McSniff," falling asleep inside the fire engine on the way back from a false alarm. I got so much response to this photo—it really seemed to make people happy. The Charlestown girls playing cards seemed to capture teens doing what they do best. The boy crossing the street with the stuffed tiger on his head, because of the sheer luck of finding him. Julia Sweeney, the old woman on the bench, because she had a thousand stories to tell and most of them could be read in her face. The homeless men and women standing in line for lunch on the tony streets of Beacon Hill, because some things will never change, and this photo looks like it could have been made in 1930 or 2007.

Would you like to add anything?

While the move to multimedia reporting has opened up some terrific new forms of storytelling, including video cameras in the newspaper newsroom, it would be a mistake to overlook the sheer power of the still photographic image. Freezing the right moment in time, whether in print or on a computer screen, forces the reader to focus on what the photojournalist finds most important about a story. When the eye has nowhere else to go, the message can't help but be delivered.

To view other images from "The City Seen" navigate to http://www.boston.com/news/globe/city_region/city_seen.

The Sacramento Bee

Finalist

Renée C. Byer
ASNE, Community Service Photojournalism
Winner, Pulitzer Prize, Feature Photography

52. About "A Mother's Journey"

Cancer kills more than 500,000 Americans every year, yet the media rarely give us an intimate view inside a home, a doctor's office or a cemetery where cancer is taking its toll. Through her photographs, Renée C. Byer tells the story of one family's struggle with cancer, showing the power, fortitude and determination of a mother and her terminally ill son as the disease takes over their lives.

This yearlong documentary project began when Byer met Cyndie French while covering a Race for the Cure. This saga of a single mom and her son Derek Madsen's fight with neuroblastoma, a rare childhood cancer, is no ordinary medical story. Published in a four-part series, Byer's images often take us places we don't comfortably go.

Byer gained the trust needed to be allowed to witness the cancer's emotional and financial impact and the complex relationship between a mother and son as they battle the boy's illness. Her photos show Derek in gleeful exultation as a worried Cyndie races his wheelchair through the hospital to distract him as he awaits a medical procedure. They also show 10-year-old Derek's meltdown as he refuses treatment.

Online, the series included 72 photos and audio of Cyndie explaining why she opened up their lives to journalists. The response was overwhelming, with more than 700 readers posting comments, calling or e-mailing. The series quickly became the most viewed, read and e-mailed package in the history of Sacbee.com.

One reader said, "The series could not have hit me deeper.... Thanks to Ms. French for trying to help others understand the pain and sacrifices involved when a loved one is stricken with a fatal illness."

Readers donated more than $40,000 to help Cyndie and Derek, and Cyndie has since started the nonprofit "Derek's Wish" to help other struggling families pay rent and buy groceries while their children are undergoing cancer treatment.

—Adapted from *The Sacramento Bee* ASNE contest entry

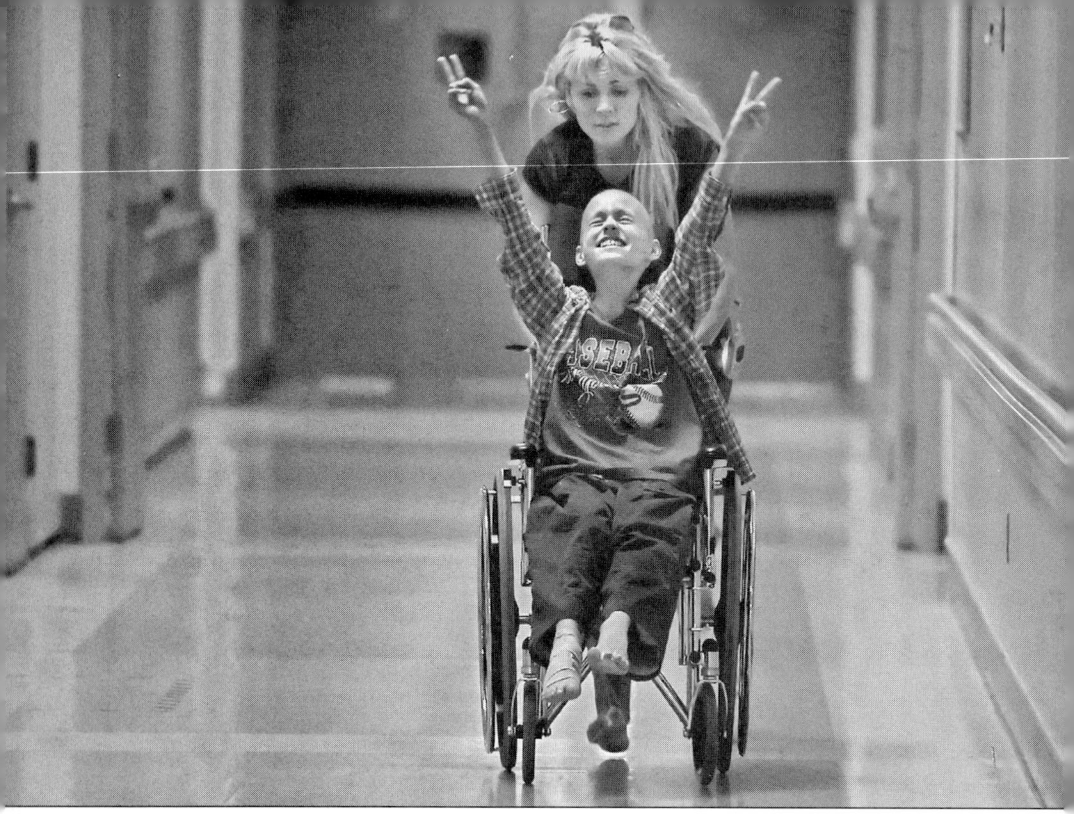

Racing barefooted, Cyndie French pushes her son Derek Madsen, 10, up and down hallways in the UC Davis Medical Center, distracting him during the dreaded wait before his bone marrow extraction. Doctors want to determine whether he is eligible for a blood stem cell transplant, his best hope for beating neuroblastoma, a rare childhood cancer.

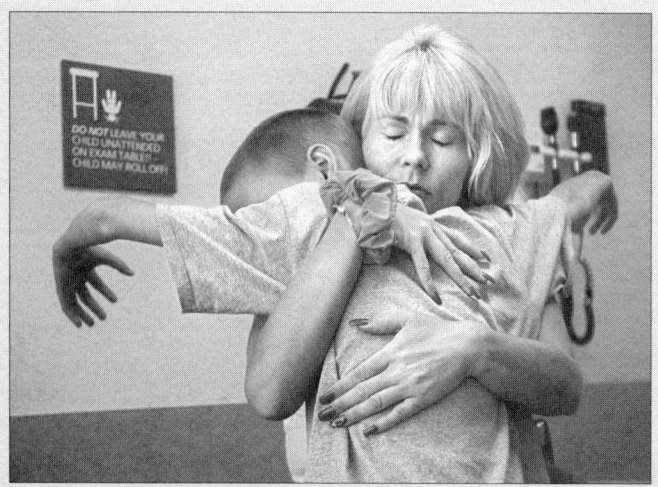

Cyndie embraces her son Derek after learning he needs surgery to remove a cancerous tumor in his abdomen.

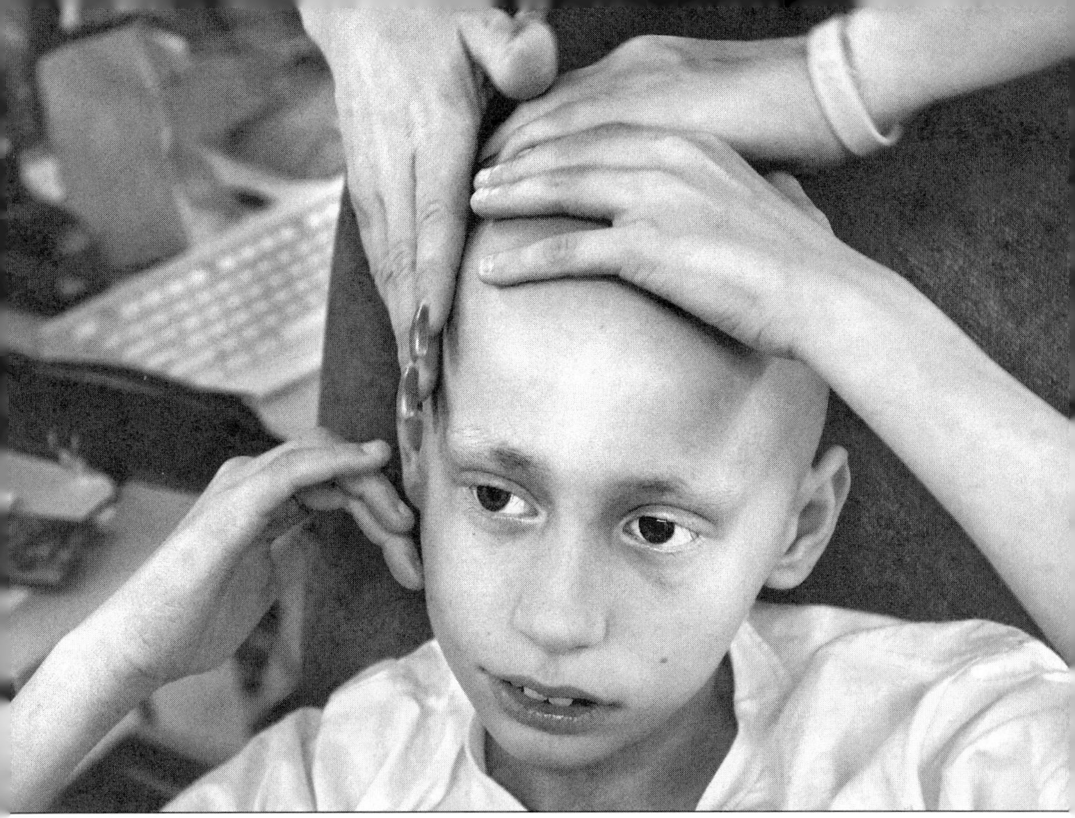

Derek gets a soothing massage from his mother, Cyndie, at her Sacramento nail and tanning salon. The boy is battling a rare childhood cancer that has invaded his bones and organs. "I'm going to do whatever it takes to make him happy, to see him smile," Cyndie says.

Derek taunts his mother playfully as Cyndie tries to coax him down from a wall outside the UC Davis Medical Center in Sacramento. They are there to admit Derek for cancer surgery the following day. Derek dreads hospitals and Cyndie has a hard time getting him to enter.

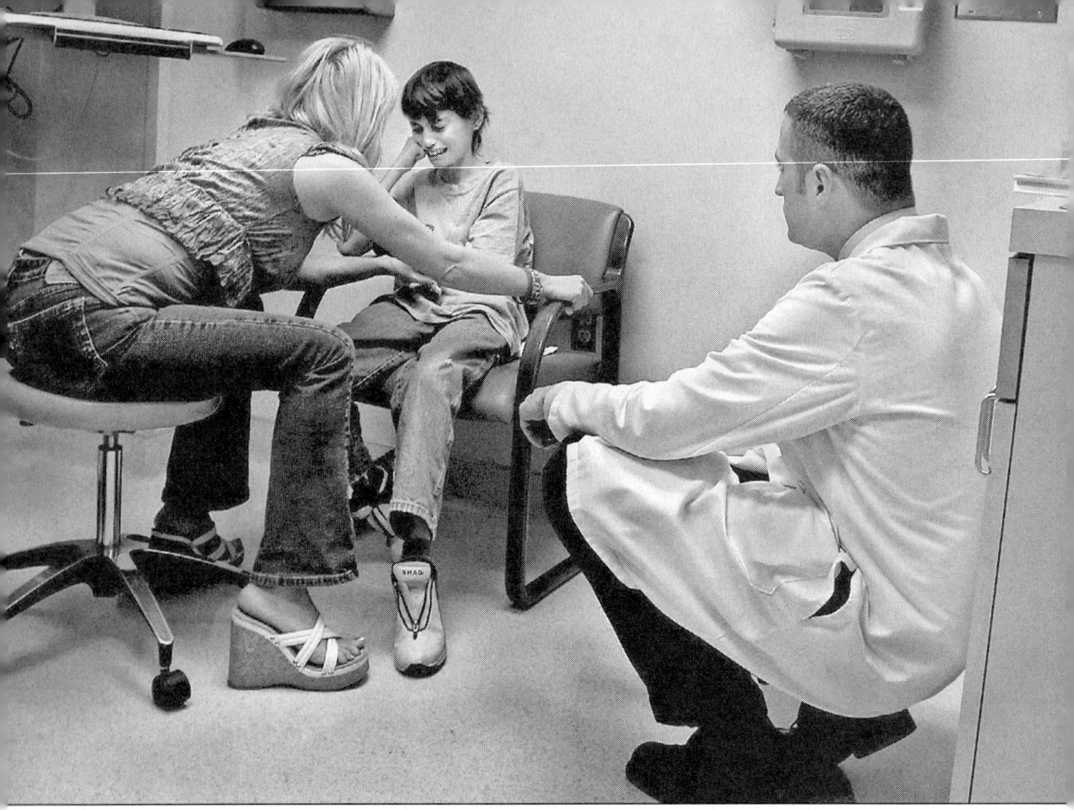

Derek is tearful as Cyndie tries to reason with him. She and Dr. William Hall argue that Derek should have a series of radiation treatments. "Derek, you might not make it if you don't do this," Cyndie tells him. Derek fires back: "I don't care! . . . Take me home. . . . I'm done, Mom! Are you listening to me? I'm done!"

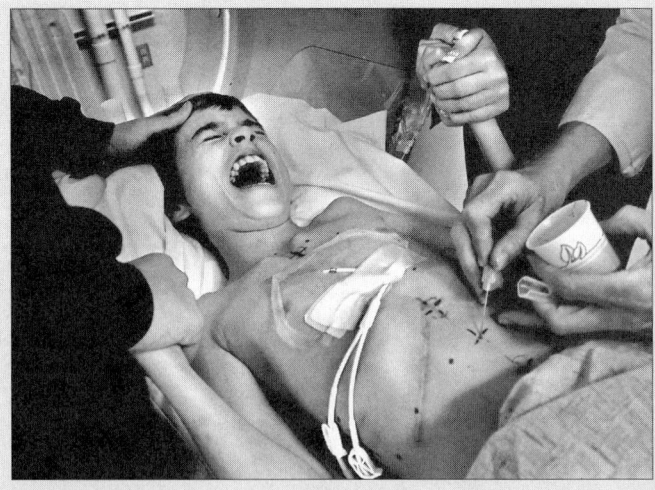

Derek is comforted by his brother Micah Moffe, 17, left, and mom, Cyndie, right, as he gets a tattoo in preparation for radiation therapy for cancer during an orientation in radiation at UC Davis Medical Center. Micah often accompanies Derek to treatments even though his schoolwork suffers.

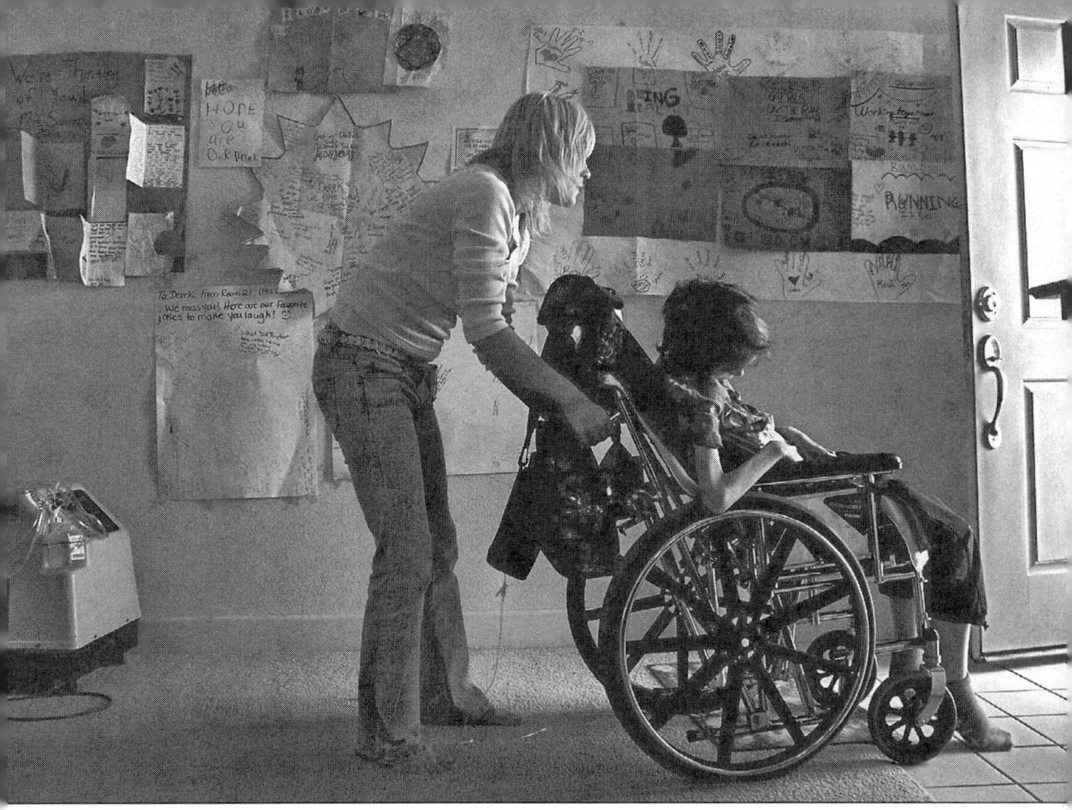

In an effort to get Derek outside, Cyndie wheels him through the front door, passing by artwork and cards given to her son by classmates at Bridgeway Island Elementary School. It was his last trip outside.

Cyndie fights her emotions as she prepares to flush out Derek's catheter with saline solution before hospice nurse Sue Kirkpatrick, left, administers a sedative that will give the 11-year-old a peaceful death. "I know in my heart I've done everything I can," Cyndie says.

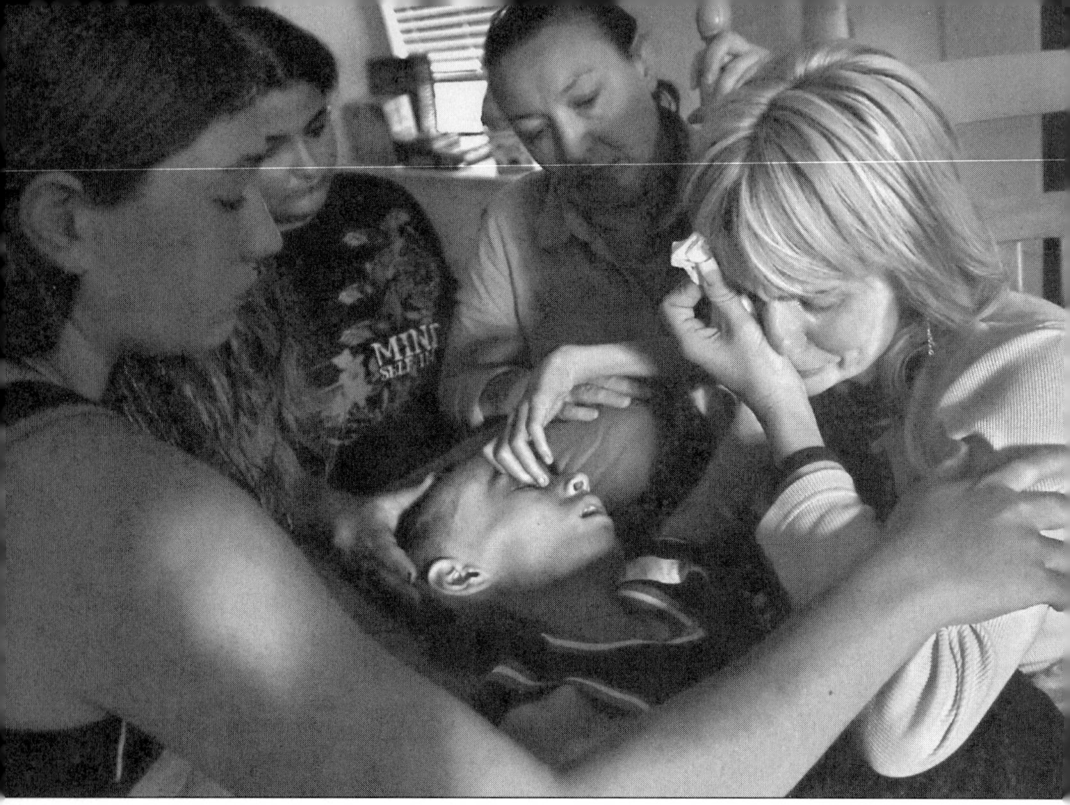

Cyndie tearfully rocks her dying son, Derek, 11, as the song "Because We Believe" plays. From left, family friends Ashley Berger, Amy Morgan and Kelly Whysong offer comfort as Cyndie tells Derek, "It's OK, baby. I love you, little man. I love you, brave boy. I love you. I love you."

Cyndie leads Derek's casket to burial with assistance from her sons Anthony Moffe, foreground, Micah Moffe, opposite him, and Vincent Morris, who is not visible, as well as several friends. "I will forever carry your memory in my heart and remind others to give of their time, energy and support to other families like ours," Cyndie says at the funeral.

Lessons Learned

BY RENÉE C. BYER

I met Cyndie French in May 2005 at a Race for the Cure. I was there on a daily assignment, having awakened at 5 a.m. to cover it. I had covered a similar event in Seattle and was aware that the survivor celebration that follows these races can yield emotional photographs. So after the race I remained for nine more hours in hopes of making a compelling image.

It was a blistering hot day. I was exhausted when I focused my lens on Cyndie in a sea of thousands of people. She was there volunteering, giving back for the second year in a row with her daughter Brianna, 5. I was immediately inspired by this mom, who was out helping others even though she was struggling herself with the terminal illness of her 10-year-old son, Derek, who was diagnosed with neuroblastoma, a rare childhood cancer. Thus began my yearlong journey documenting this family's story for *The Sacramento Bee,* where I continued to shoot daily assignments as well.

Derek was not a happy boy when I met him. In fact, he was upset and angry, as most pre-adolescent boys would be after almost five months of cancer treatments. Readers would later write commending us for showing his experiences in a realistic light. I didn't think I would be able to break through his anger and get him to accept me. But with a lot of patience and time I gained his trust and love. His mom would say that Derek could see through my eyes how much I cared.

"A Mother's Journey" was an extremely difficult story to tell because my instincts were to try to help this family. But I knew that as a journalist I had to let things unfold and that the most important thing was not to interrupt their daily life. There were many pictures I missed because the situations were so sensitive and emotional that I felt the click of my shutter would add to their pain—so I spent endless hours taking no pictures at all.

Many times I would get a feeling of pain as if I were being punched in the stomach. At times, I was overwhelmed with compassion for the family. But I knew how important it was to step back and make photographs, although doing so would take all my strength emotionally. I just hoped that in the end the photographs would convey the importance of the many issues I was documenting. Through patience, honesty and sensitivity I gained access to this story. When people let you into their lives it's a gift, and you have to honor and respect their space. Sometimes that means not making photos.

Getting inside hospitals and doctors' offices was especially challenging. Every day I had to work double time to get the access I needed. I was always justifying my presence with PR people, doctors, nurses, lab technicians and hospice workers. The person who cleared everything one day wasn't there the next. Appointments would be changed, often at the last minute. And even after I did gain access and trust, there were always a handful of medical professionals judging me as I shot every frame.

I had worked on long-term stories before, so I knew what to expect and how to proceed. What I learned was not to sweat the small stuff, because this family was going through tenfold what I was as I followed their journey, and it was very important to step back and tell their story.

The biggest challenge for anyone covering an intimate subject like this is to maintain your journalistic integrity. On a compassionate level, you want to step in and help. But as a journalist, you know it is important for people to make their own decisions. I didn't want to disrupt this family's patterns. I was honest with them about how I wished I could help them financially but could not cross that line. They understood.

The series had a significant online presence, including 72 photographs accompanied by audio of Cyndie explaining why she had opened up their lives to journalists.

Cyndie really appreciates the photos I made. She recently told me she feels sorry for all the other families who didn't have someone like me to document their journey. "I can't imagine not having these moments," she said.

Renée C. Byer's "A Mother's Journey" won the 2007 Pulitzer Prize for feature photography and the World Understanding Award at Pictures of the Year International 2007 (http://www.poyi.org). Byer has been a staff photographer at The Sacramento Bee *since 2003 and has been an award-winning photographer, designer and picture editor for more than 20 years. She has received honors from the National Press Photographers Association, Pictures of the Year International, Society of News Design, Associated Press and the Best of the West photo and design contest. Her series of photographs on biotechnology, "Seeds Of Doubt," won the Harry Chapin Media Award for World Hunger in Photojournalism in 2005.*

The Philadelphia Inquirer

Finalist

April Saul
Community Service Photojournalism

53. About "Kids, Guns and a Deadly Toll"

In Philadelphia, children are being lost to violence in staggering numbers. *Philadelphia Inquirer* photojournalist April Saul vowed these young people would not be forgotten. By chronicling their lives and what their deaths meant to the people around them, she could challenge the city to do something about the problem. She could keep the victims alive a little longer. She could bear witness by producing a column about each child killed by guns in the Philadelphia area.

Hers was a personal crusade. She ran to crime scenes no matter the hour. She met in a secret location with a frightened mother whose son was murdered while the family was in the city's witness relocation program. She visited neighborhoods so attuned to danger that mourners, hearing what they thought was gunfire, suddenly abandoned a street vigil and fled.

Angry, distraught families did not give their trust easily. Yet in response to her steadfastness and her passion, they opened their doors to Saul and her camera. And the images are wrenching.

Saul's photographs chronicle the arguments, insults and accidents that are killing children aged 17 and under. Her work dispels stereotypes. The tough teen who died in a drug house, for example, "was always on time for school," she wrote, "made good grades and delighted his teachers."

Her work brought attention to the issue. The Pennsylvania legislature held a special session to address new gun laws, and State Sen. Vincent Hughes read Saul's essays, day after day. Community groups and schools invited her to speak. A consortium of anti-violence groups gave her its Hero of Peace Award.

Through Saul's stories and photographs, people desperate for change found consolation and community.

—Adapted from *The Philadelphia Inquirer* ASNE contest entry

Markita Howard, 9, lets tears flow at a memorial for Kyle Brown, his brother Derrick and their neighbor Terrell Anderson.

On the 1900 block of Mountain Street in South Philadelphia, where they have spray-painted Darnell "Mook" Winn's name on abandoned houses, Mook's brother Dawoyne Winn (left), 16, and friends Quadree Walker, 14, and Vincent Pratt, 15, show their tattoos in his honor.

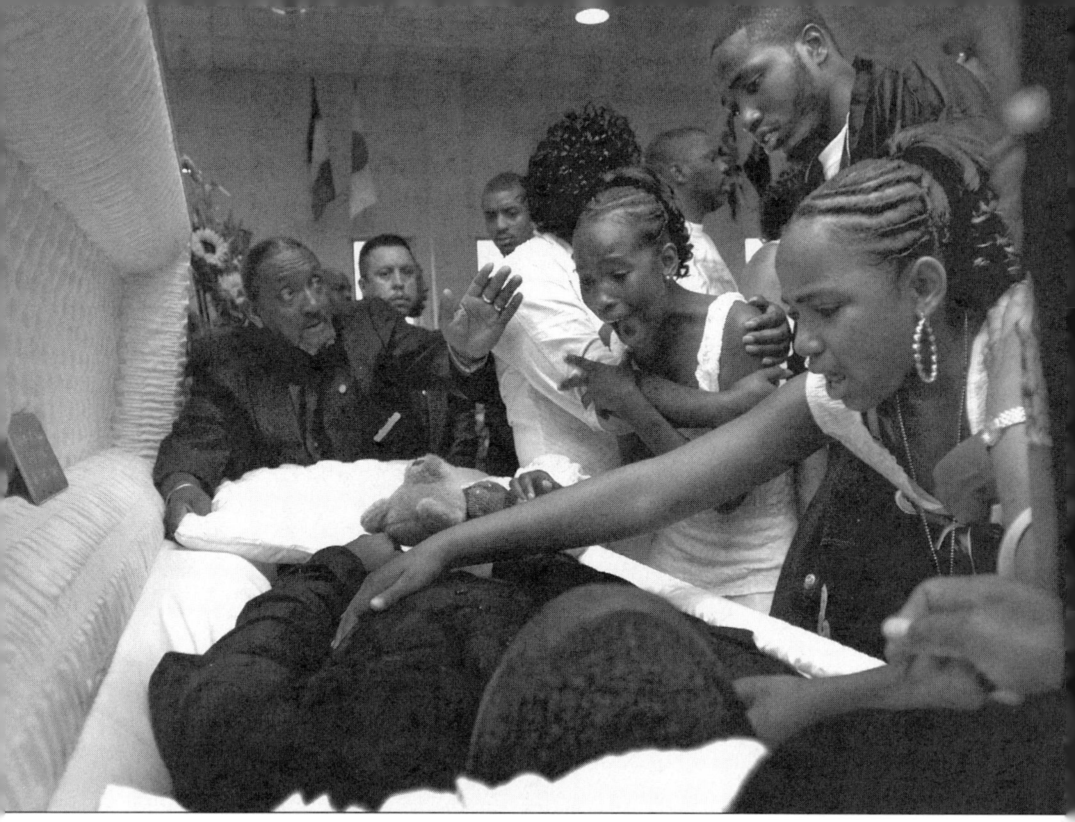

Standing alongside Jarrett Gore's casket, his siblings—from left, Dominique Coleman, James Patterson and Nancy Coleman—grieve at his funeral. Gore, 15, was shot during a playground altercation at 16th and Erie. His father was slain nearby in 1991.

At the south Philadelphia home of slain teen Terrell Anderson, his girlfriend, Dominique Rollins (left), cries as her sister Tanisha, 20, holds her 6-month-old daughter, Saniya.

At a candlelight vigil for Anthony Williams, his aunt, Kim Hartsfield-Stokes, holds her daughter Latroyah McLaughlin, 15. To the right of them is Shakira Autry, 14, Williams' half-sister.

Jy'mire Ryant, 11, wore clothes that matched his older brother Tariq Blue Jr.'s at Tariq's funeral. The 14-year-old eighth-grader was shot to death.

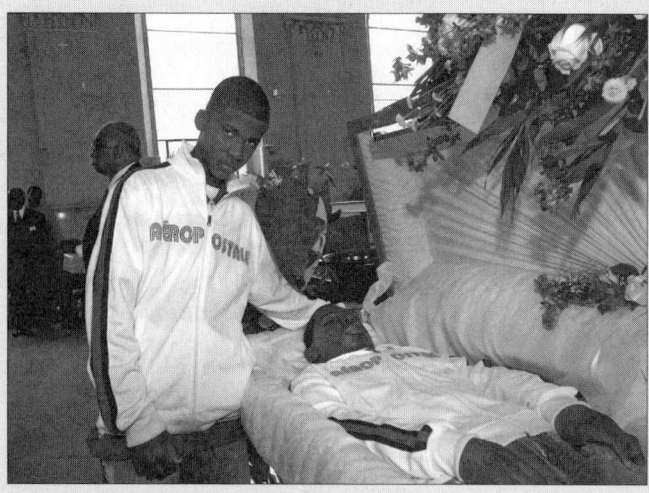

At the funeral for Damien Floyd, Tysheen Choice clings to Chantta Carter as they grieve for their friend. The 17-year-old was killed after confronting an acquaintance, friends say.

Johnny Strong, Shadeed Burke's father, and 2-month-old Nazir Morgan at the home on the 1100 block of Kenwood Street in Camden where Shadeed was shot and killed. Nazir was believed to be Shadeed's son, but DNA testing has since proved otherwise. Shadeed's parents say they will treat the child as their grandson anyway.

David Walter, whose .45-caliber pistol killed Talib Bailey-Hankerson, crying during the boy's funeral while sitting next to Lawanda Bailey (center), Talib's mother.

Kristen "Shortie" Mullin (left) cries in the arms of a friend at the vigil for Jarred Bullock outside the Northeast Philadelphia rowhouse where he died.

Lessons Learned

BY APRIL SAUL

I didn't choose to do this column; it chose me.

In the spring of 2005, little Nasir Hinton was caught in the crossfire in his own West Philadelphia home. The morning after the shooting, I watched the women who loved him sponge his blood off the front door, the soapy water turning a pale pink as they tried not to cry.

That fall, I followed Victoria Yancey, the Philadelphia School District's liaison to families whose children die or are seriously injured. In six days, four students were shot and killed—one in an argument over a video game.

By January 2006, with the death toll mounting, I had vowed to document in words and photographs the death of every child killed by a gun in the eight-county Philadelphia region that year.

We in the media are often too overwhelmed by the numbers to describe whom we're losing, and what those losses are like for friends and families. I began to believe that if gun violence were ever to be addressed, we had to see faces, not just numbers on charts and graphs.

I decided my columns would not try to distinguish between the "guilty" and the "innocent" or—as my colleagues worried—make delinquents out to be saints.

These victims were all children.

They all had mothers.

They didn't deserve to die in the streets of Philadelphia.

It's hard to write about kids you will never meet. I'd never see Yagouba smile, or hear Terrell laugh or listen to Darnell rap. I had to rely on what family and friends chose to tell me.

It wasn't until close to the end of the year, during a particularly violent week, that I realized I should have been asking this question: How many times had each child been shot—or shot at—before finally being killed?

My life revolved around homicide. I was a single parent myself and had dragged my own teenagers to murder scenes more than once. I was afraid to leave town for fear I'd miss a fallen child. Tears came to me unexpectedly, in supermarkets, or in rush-hour traffic.

I thought I knew something about violent crime because a close friend had been murdered. I realized I knew nothing about its daily presence after a car with tinted windows screeched up to a vigil for Kareek Adams in Frankford, and I stood there, stupidly, while everyone else ran for cover.

Because I had little space to write about each death, I often had to omit information that might have led to a better understanding of a child. After a reader wondered how Tariq Blue Jr., 14, could have afforded 60 pairs of blue jeans, I wished I had added that he made clothes money by standing in city traffic on hot days, selling bottled water.

The kids often surprised me, resisting any stereotypes I might have believed. The teen who looked to be the toughest—he died in the drug house where he allegedly lived and worked—was always on time for school, made good grades and delighted his teachers. If Vincent Thomas, 17, saw dealing as a safe way to support himself while pursuing an education, he was possibly the most naive of all.

Eventually, I began seeing the same faces at funerals. At Casha'e Rivers' service, I met Tomika Brunson, who told me the dead kindergartner had been her children's cousin. As was Raphael Glee, whose death I had covered a few weeks earlier. (Destiny Wright, infamously strangled in West Philadelphia two years earlier, was also related.)

Brunson's children, she said, were not taking this well; a son wept at her side as we spoke.

I will always be grateful for the generosity of the grieving families. Alisha Corley opened her door to me on the night her daughter Casha'e was killed, and we sat together as the little girl's picture flickered across the 10 o'clock news. Darnell DeLoatch's family allowed me to attend a private viewing of his body. Terrence Adams' mom, Debbie, invited me to pray with her.

More than once, a frustrated mourner yelled at me as I snapped pictures at a loved one's grave, then later apologized and assured me I had done the right thing.

Almost always, I was given a spot on the couch, a plate of fried chicken, and trust.

The first time I heard "We Shall Overcome" was more than 40 years ago. Three civil-rights workers had just been killed in Mississippi; my New Jersey community was hosting a group of Southern black teenagers who needed to get away until things cooled down. I was a spoiled suburban kid, but I'll never forget standing in a circle, holding hands with them, and singing that song.

The last time I heard it was at the burial of little Casha'e Rivers, just before her body was placed in the ground.

April Saul joined the staff of the Philadelphia Inquirer *in 1981, after spending the previous year at* The *(Baltimore)* Sun. *She specializes in documentary photojournalism and was the first recipient of the Nikon/ NPPA Documentary Sabbatical Grant for her work on Hmong refugees in 1985. Over the past 25 years, she has won numerous honors, including the Pulitzer Prize for Explanatory Journalism in 1997 for her work on a series about dying with dignity. She was a Pulitzer finalist in 1987 and 1984. She has also won the Robert F. Kennedy Journalism Award and the World Press Photo Budapest Award for Humanistic Photography.*

Suggested Readings

RECENT RESOURCES

Adam, G. Stuart, and Roy Peter Clark. "Journalism: The Democratic Craft." New York: Oxford University Press, 2005. Poynter authors Adam and Clark narrow the gap between the classroom and the profession with this collection of classic readings, writing instruction, study guides and exercises.

Baranick, Alana, Jim Sheeler and Stephen Miller. "Life on the Death Beat." Oak Park, Ill.: Marion Street Press, 2005. A handbook for obituary writers.

Boynton, Robert S. "The New New Journalism." New York: Vintage Books, 2005. Conversations with some of America's best nonfiction writers on their craft.

Clark, Roy Peter. "Writing Tools: 50 Essential Strategies For Every Writer." New York: Little, Brown, 2006. Easy-to-remember tips to sharpen your writing talents from Poynter's Roy Peter Clark.

Conrad, Mark. "The Business Of Sports: A Primer For Journalists." Mahwah, N.J.: L. Erlbaum, 2005. An exploration of sports business topics most relevant to journalists.

Goldstein, Norm, ed. "The Associated Press Stylebook and Briefing on Media Law." New York: Perseus Books Group, 2007. AP's rules on grammar, spelling, punctuation, capitalization, word usage and more.

Gutkind, Lee, and Annie Dillard. "In Fact." New York: W.W. Norton, 2005. A collection of creative nonfiction.

Harrigan, Jane, and Karen Brown Dunlap. "The Editorial Eye." 2nd edition. New York: Bedford/St. Martin's, 2003. This updated edition, co-authored by Poynter President Karen Brown Dunlap, deals with both the technical and management elements of professional editing.

Harrower, Tim. "Inside Reporting." Boston: McGraw-Hill, 2007. A well-illustrated introduction to the craft of journalism.

Hart, Jack. "A Writer's Coach: An Editor's Guide to Words That Work." New York: Pantheon Books, 2006. Practical advice and a step-by-step approach to the writing process.

Hennessy, Brendan. "Writing Feature Articles." Burlington, Mass.: Focal Press, 2006. An introduction to feature writing.

Hutchison, Earl R. "The Art Of Feature Writing." New York: Oxford University Press, 2007. Sensible advice for students about writing and freelancing.

Kramer, Mark, and Wendy Call, eds. "Telling True Stories." New York: Plume, 2007. The Nieman Foundation's nonfiction writers' guide.

Ludwig, Mark D. "Modern News Editing." Ames, Iowa: Blackwell, 2005. A handbook for media writers and editors.

McKane, Anna. "News Writing." Thousand Oaks, Calif.: SAGE Publications, 2006. McKane's book is designed for new and inexperienced writers.

McLellan, Michele, and Tim Porter. "News, Improved." Washington, D.C.: CQ Press, 2007. A report on how America's newsrooms are learning to change.

Plotnik, Arthur. "Spunk & Bite." New York: Random House Reference, 2005. A writer's guide to punchier, more engaging language and style.

Pumario, Jim. "Bad News and Good Judgment." Oak Park, Ill.: Marion Street Press, 2005. Useful tools for reporting sensitive issues in a small-town newspaper.

Reed, Robert, and Glenn Lewin. "Covering Business." Oak Park, Ill.: Marion Street Press, 2005. A guide to reporting on commerce and developing a business beat.

Roush, Chris. "Show Me the Money: Writing Business and Economic Stories For Mass Communication." Mahwah, N.J.: L. Erlbaum, 2004. Advice and examples on being a business journalist.

Scanlan, Christopher. "Reporting and Writing: Basics For the 21st Century." New York: Oxford University Press, 2000. Poynter faculty member Scanlan's practical guide to professional journalism skills.

Smith, Sarah Harrison. "The Fact Checker's Bible." New York: Anchor Books, 2004. A manual on how to get the facts right.

Stein, M.L. "The Newswriter's Handbook." Ames, Iowa: Blackwell, 2006. An introduction to journalism.

Titchener, Campbell B. "Reviewing the Arts." Mahwah, N.J.: L. Erlbaum, 2005. Helpful suggestions on how to produce all types of art reviews.

Weingarten, Marc. "The Gang That Wouldn't Write Straight: Wolfe, Thompson, Didion, Capote, and the New Journalism Revolution." New York: Three Rivers Press, 2006. Reprint edition. A look at the origins and rise of New Journalism.

Woods, Keith, Arlene Notoro Morgan and Alice Irene Pifer. "The Authentic Voice: The Best Reporting on Race and Ethnicity." New York: Columbia University Press, 2006. In addition to the book, a DVD and Web site offer comprehensive multimedia tools on the coverage of race and ethnicity. Co-authored by Poynter's dean of faculty, Keith Woods.

WRITING AND REPORTING ANTHOLOGIES

American Society of Magazine Editors. "The Best American Magazine Writing." New York: Columbia University Press, 2006. A wide-ranging collection of National Magazine Award winners.

Bowden, Mark, ed. "The Best American Crime Writing 2006." New York: Harper, 2006. An annual anthology of nonfiction crime stories originally published in magazines.

Cahill, Tim, ed. "The Best American Travel Writing 2006." Boston: Houghton Mifflin, 2006. This anthology includes well-written stories about travel.

Clark, Roy Peter, and Christopher Scanlan, eds. "America's Best Newspaper Writing." 2nd edition. New York: Bedford/St. Martin's, 2006. A collection of ASNE Distinguished Writing Award-winning stories and classic news reports from Poynter faculty Clark and Scanlan.

Flippin, Royce, ed. "Best American Political Writing 2006." New York: Thunder's Mouth Press, 2006. This fifth volume in a series focuses on magazine writing.

Garlock, David, ed. "Pulitzer Prize Feature Stories." Ames: Iowa State Press, 2003. Twenty-five Pulitzer Prize-winning feature stories published from 1979 to 2003.

Greene, Brian, ed. "The Best American Science and Nature Writing 2006." Boston: Houghton Mifflin, 2006. Some of the year's finest writing on a wide range of scientific topics.

Harrington, Walt. "The Beholder's Eye." New York: Grove Press, 2005. A collection of some of America's finest personal journalism.

Lewis, Michael, ed. "The Best American Sports Writing 2006." Boston: Houghton Mifflin, 2006. Examples of excellent sports writing.

Mills, Eleanor, et al., eds. "Journalistas: 100 Years Of the Best Writing and Reporting by Women Journalists." New York: Carroll & Graf, 2005. A collection of stories written by women during the 20th century.

Slater, Lauren, ed. "The Best American Essays 2006." Boston: Houghton Mifflin, 2006. This series has become a showcase for the country's finest writing.

Sloan, Wm. David, and Laird B. Anderson. "Pulitzer Prize Editorials: America's Best Writing, 1917–2003." 3rd edition. Ames: Iowa State Press, 2003. Historical and recent Pulitzer Prize-winning editorials.

Staff of *The New York Times*. "Tales from the Times." New York: St. Martin's Griffin, 2004. A collection of human-interest stories from *The New York Times*.

CLASSICS

Blundell, William E. "The Art and Craft Of Feature Writing." New York: Plume, 1988. A step-by-step guide to reporting and editing.

Brande, Dorothea. "Becoming a Writer." Los Angeles: J.P. Tarcher; Boston: distributed by Putnam Publishing, 1981. Reprint of 1934 edition. Timeless writing advice.

Clark, Roy Peter, and Don Fry. "Coaching Writers." 2nd edition. New York: Bedford/St. Martin's, 2003. Guidelines on how to improve communication between editors and reporters, from Poynter's Clark and Fry.

Franklin, Jon. "Writing For Story." New York: Plume, 1994. Lessons about how to write dramatic nonfiction.

Harrington, Walt. "Intimate Journalism: The Art and Craft Of Reporting Everyday Life." Thousand Oaks, Calif.: Sage, 1997. Award-winning articles are used to describe the process of combining traditional feature writing with in-depth reporting.

Mencher, Melvin. "Melvin Mencher's News Reporting and Writing." 10th edition. Boston: McGraw-Hill, 2006. A guide to writing well and reporting accurately.

Murray, Donald M. "Writing to Deadline: The Journalist At Work." Portsmouth, N.H.: Heinemann, 2000. Murray helps journalists understand the writing process.

Snyder, Louis L., and Richard B. Morris, eds. "A Treasury Of Great Reporting." New York: Simon & Schuster, 1962. Historical examples of great reporting and writing.

Stewart, James B. "Follow the Story: How to Write Successful Nonfiction." New York: Simon & Schuster, 1988. Stewart illustrates the techniques of compelling narrative writing.

Strunk, William, Jr., and E.B. White. "The Elements Of Style." Illustrated edition. New York: Penguin Press, 2005. A classic reference book on the rules of usage and the principles of composition.

Zinsser, William. "On Writing Well." New York: HarperCollins, 2006. The 30th anniversary edition of a respected writing guide.

This list of suggested readings was compiled by David Shedden, director of the Eugene Patterson Library at The Poynter Institute.